The Other Ancient Civilisations

The Other Ancient Civilisations

Decoding Archaeology's Less Celebrated Cultures

by Raven Todd DaSilva

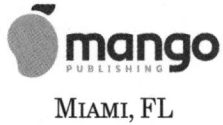

Miami, FL

Copyright © 2024, 2025 by Raven Todd DaSilva.
Published by Mango Publishing, a division of Mango Publishing Group, Inc.

Cover Design & Interior Illustrations: Rose Woollett
Cover Photos:
    Moche earflare frontal (Metropolitan Museum of Art, New York. The Michael C. Rockefeller Memorial Collection, Bequest of Nelson A. Rockefeller, 1979. 1979.206.513).
    "Flame-rimmed" cooking vessel (Kaen doki) (Metropolitan Museum of Art, New York. Mary Griggs Burke Collection, Gift of the Mary and Jackson Burke Foundation, 2015. 2015.300.258).
    Nebra Sky Disc (Frank Vincentz, CC BY-SA 4.0, Wikimedia).

Layout & Design: Megan Werner
Interior Photos: see page 347.

Mango is an active supporter of authors' rights to free speech and artistic expression in their books. The purpose of copyright is to encourage authors to produce exceptional works that enrich our culture and our open society.

Uploading or distributing photos, scans or any content from this book without prior permission is theft of the author's intellectual property. Please honor the author's work as you would your own. Thank you in advance for respecting our author's rights.

For permission requests, please contact the publisher at:
Mango Publishing Group
5966 South Dixie Highway, Suite 300
Miami, FL 33143
info@mango.bz

For special orders, quantity sales, course adoptions and corporate sales, please email the publisher at sales@mango.bz. For trade and wholesale sales, please contact Ingram Publisher Services at customer.service@ingramcontent.com or +1.800.509.4887.

The Other Ancient Civilisations: Decoding Archaeology's Less Celebrated Cultures

Library of Congress Cataloging-in-Publication number: 2023943736
ISBN: (hc) 978-1-68481-832-7 (pb) 978-1-68481-323-0 (e) 978-1-68481-325-4
BISAC category code: SOC003000, SOCIAL SCIENCE/Archaeology

*In memory of Gilbert Constantine Todd,
the greatest storyteller I will ever know*

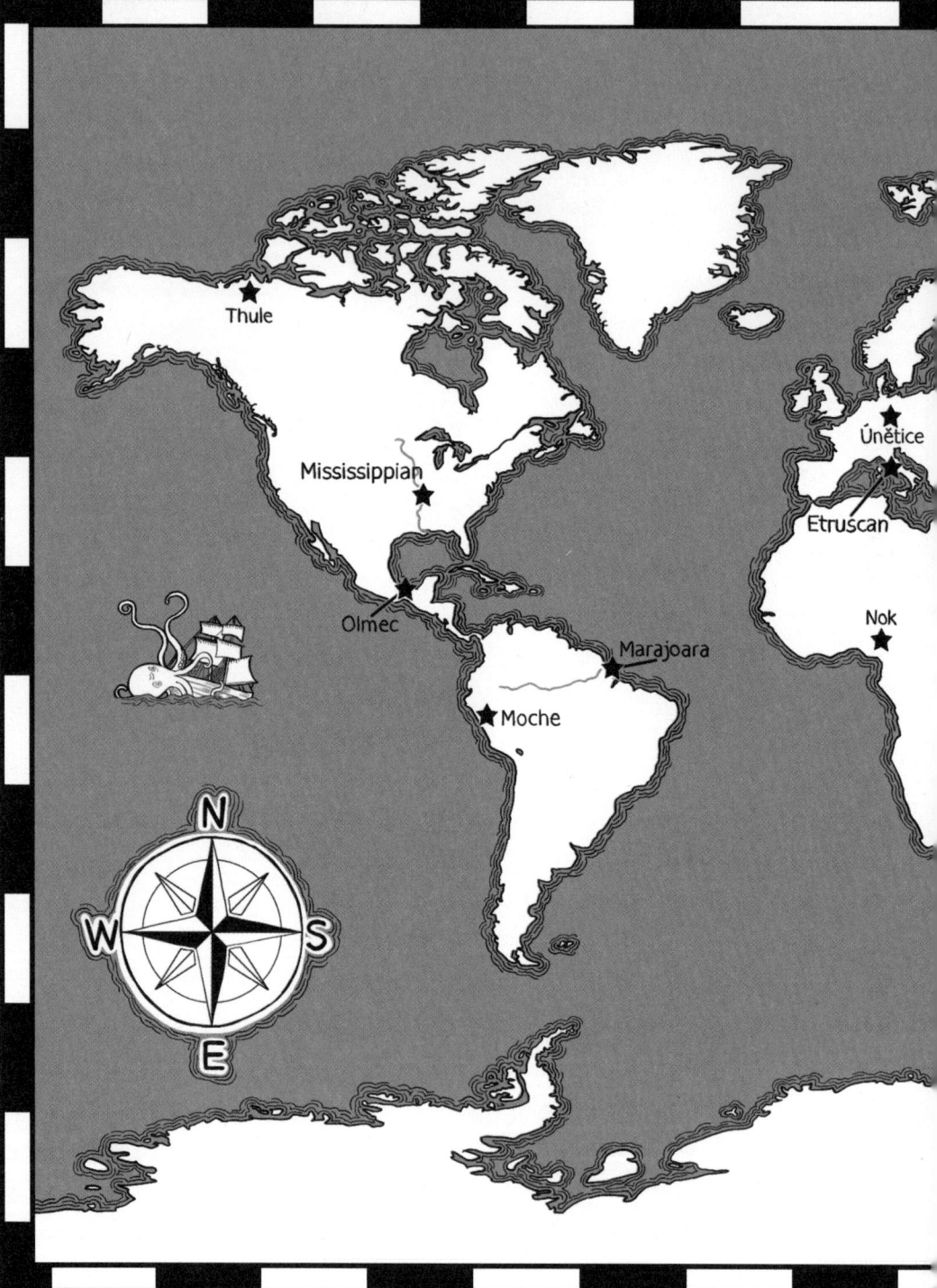

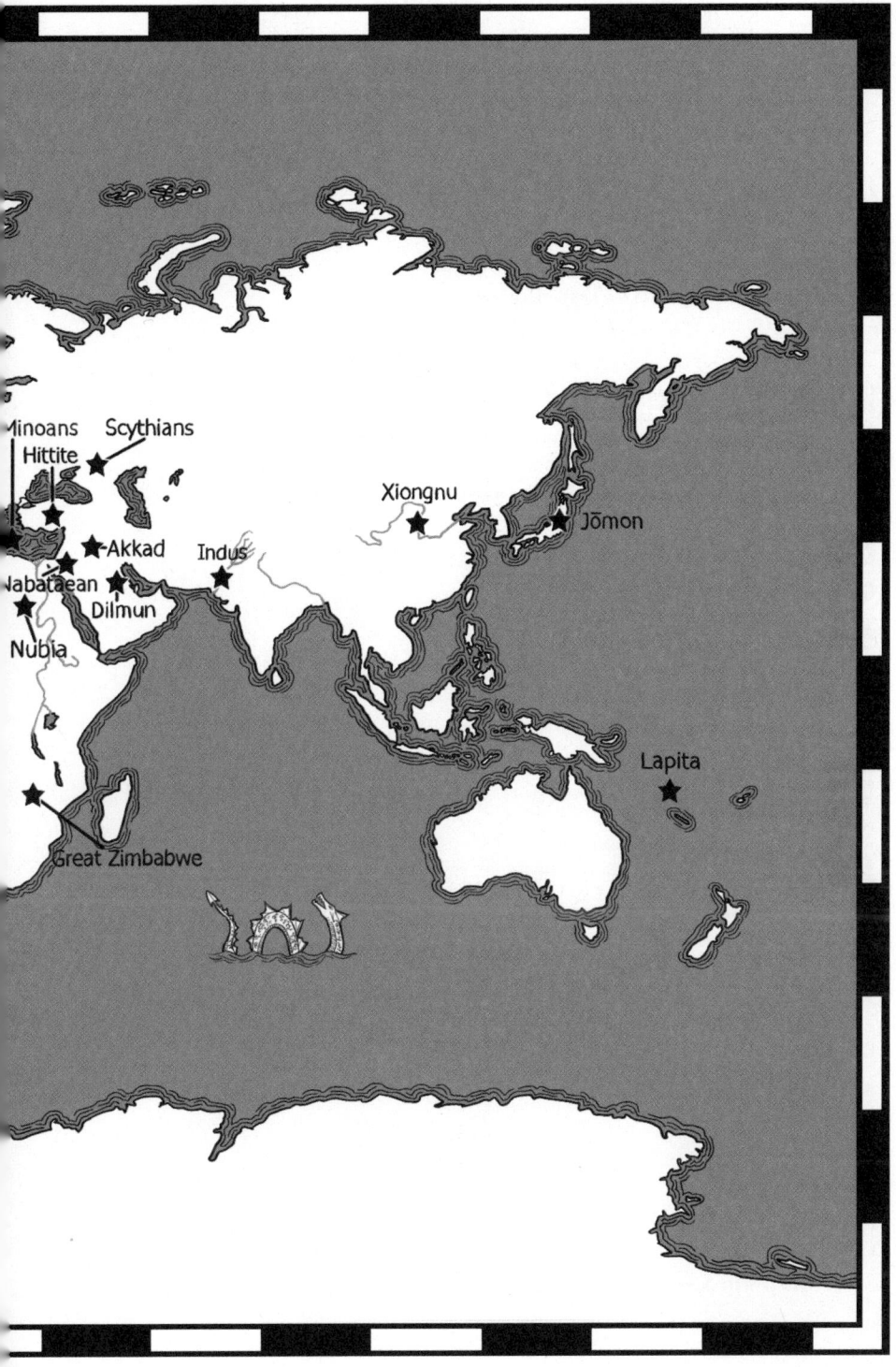

Contents

Introduction 10

Chapter One
Akkadians: The World's First Empire 21

Chapter Two
Dilmun: The Lost Trading Port of Arabia 33

Chapter Three
Etruscans: The Givers of the Toga to Rome 47

Chapter Four
Great Zimbabwe: A Stolen Past 59

Chapter Five
Hittites: The Charioteers of Anatolia 73

Chapter Six
Indus Valley: A Bronze Age Utopia? 89

Chapter Seven
Jōmon: The Oldest Pottery in the World 109

Chapter Eight
Lapita: Seaborne Explorers of Oceania 123

Chapter Nine
Marajoara: Monumental Mounds at the Mouth of the Amazon ... 137

Chapter Ten
Minoans: The Home of the Minotaur 151

Chapter Eleven
Mississippian: North America's First City 169

Chapter Twelve
Moche: 50 Shades of Sex Pots 183

Chapter Thirteen
Nabataeans: The Nomads Who Built a City 199

Chapter Fourteen
Nok: The Terracotta Heads in the Tin Mine 213

Chapter Fifteen
Nubians (Kingdom of Kush): More Pyramids Than Egypt & a Tale of Three Cities 225

Chapter Sixteen
Olmec: Land of Rubber and Colossal Stone Heads 239

Chapter Seventeen
Scythians: Mounted Warriors of the Steppes 255

Chapter Eighteen
Thule (Early Inuit): Whaling Ancestors of the Inuit 271

Chapter Nineteen
Únětice: Astronomical Bronzemasters of Central Europe ... 287

Chapter Twenty
Xiongnu: Nomadic Enemies of China 303

Acknowledgements 316
Bibliography 318
Endnotes 343
Photo Credits 347
About the Author 349

Introduction

"The lonely bipeds with the giant dreams."

—Diane Ackerman

The title of this book may be *The Other Ancient Civilisations*, but it is by no means meant to be an act of "othering." Rather, this book is a celebration. An invitation, if you will, to look beyond the popular ancient civilisations and cultures that dominate books, films, and television. That is not to say that the ancient Romans, Egyptians, Inca, and Maya are any less deserving of the spotlight they have received. It is more to say that for them to shine, others have been ignored or only briefly mentioned by mainstream media and education. Oftentimes, it is only small groups of archaeologists, historians, and scientists who have the privilege and opportunity to discover the hundreds of other groups of people the world over who lived hundreds and thousands of years ago.

This book then serves as a starting point for anyone wanting to venture through the mists of time to explore lesser-known ancient civilisations and cultures that have long been overlooked or marginalised. With each chapter, we will explore a new group of ancient peoples. We will traverse both continents and millennia. From the fertile river valleys of Mesopotamia, to the remote islands of the Pacific. From the frozen tundra of North America, to the windswept plains of Central Asia. Like today, each culture is as distinct as the next, but with similarities that I hope will remind us all that no one was ever isolated from the rest of the world. All cultures are enhanced through connection, sharing, borrowing, and transforming bits and pieces from their predecessors and contemporaries.

A large reason that so many groups of ancient peoples are less well-known and recognised publicly is that they are usually overshadowed by more powerful, longer-lasting groups that have left behind stunning collections of material culture, monumental cities, or robust written records. For lack of a better term, ancient civilisations and cultures like these are more popular because they are simply easier to access. But even with the ancient cultures that have left so much behind and had so much scholarly work devoted to them, there is still so much we don't know.

Archaeologists are left with fragments of stories written on parchment or clay, looted tombs, remnants of poor excavation techniques from early expeditions, and a skewed historical bias from the Antiquarian desire to look only for treasure. Preservation bias also affects what is found and known about ancient cultures. Organic materials like textiles, wooden structures, and food remains are the first to decompose if not in arid or frozen environments. Acidic soils eat away at bone and metal, farmers plough fields, and houses are built without knowing what might lie in the soil beneath. What we have determined as "important" and "worth saving" also shapes how we choose to understand history throughout time. It can be considered a small miracle that we have anything from the past that we can weave into a coherent story.

Much of the archaeological record that remains is composed of monumental buildings and complexes for the dead—usually for the elite, a population that is remembered and studied much more than everyday people. What is left to tell the story of women and other marginalised groups is even less. In many ways, the study of the past is like trying to complete a puzzle that only has a portion of its pieces and no reference picture. These pieces usually also fit together in multiple ways, so we can never truly confirm that a connected portion has no other interpretation.

Imagine then, how few puzzle pieces we have for ancient cultures that didn't produce writing, live in an environment well-suited for preservation, or use the ever-enduring pottery that shapes so much of what we know about the past. This makes reconstructing their past and communicating it to the public even harder. There are no documents with pertinent quotes, or grand frescoes on walls to display in museums. While some of the ancient groups discussed in this book had writing and rich visual culture, they are still not as popularly known as the powerhouses that bring droves of visitors to museums around the world.

No matter how much physical evidence we have for an ancient culture or civilisation, we will never fully understand the people who lived before us. We will never know their hopes, dreams, or fears, their quarrels, their music, or how they danced. Their reasoning for their actions or architectural and artistic choices will always be a matter of speculation. But because humans are storytellers by nature, we are desperate to use the physical remains of what is left behind to construct a narrative to help us understand them and bring us closer to our past.

These narratives are generic and lump the many into one—especially when they are about the everyday people who lived in these early societies. Thousands of people lived lives just as rich as yours and mine, but we will never get to know them on an individual level. As Garth Bawden stated so eloquently: "It is always easier to interpret the archaeological record of domestic life in terms of the taste represented than of the families that performed them."[1] The humans involved in these tasks often become a singular entity, an anonymous conglomerate to represent the masses. These everyday stories are just as culturally important as those of great battles and powerful rulers, but they are often taken as a given and therefore not celebrated or highlighted enough, even though these are the puzzle pieces that most of us can relate to.

Even though we'll never be able to get a full picture of the past, these glimpses still provide us with the motivation to keep searching with the hope of finding one more piece of the puzzle. Archaeologists and historians, though, must be careful with how they craft these stories of the past. People use them to create connections to history, whether it be with everyday objects still used for the same purpose, or philosophical thought from a thousand years ago. Often this is done for good: to gain a connection to one's heritage or to feel a connection to something larger than oneself. Other times, these stories are used to vilify outsiders or the unknown. Just like how some ancient cultures become more popular than others, biassed aspects of the past are highlighted to push a narrative or preference that suits our current worldview that differs so much from what theirs would have been. The entire picture is not always presented to the public. More nuanced, or negative features of these popular groups are frequently swept under the rug to push one image instead of one that is more balanced, accurate, and human. Just like our societies and communities, there is bad amongst the good, and good amongst the bad.

Many people like to group some of the cultures and civilisations in this book together and call them "lost." The term *lost civilisation* belittles and is disparaging to the people who created and thrived in these communities.[2] Many times, these "civilisations" were never lost. These past peoples were known for millennia by their descendants. Often, Western people attempting to expand their territories by entering foreign lands were discovering ruins that the locals had always known about. These newcomers then separated the living communities from their past in order to mistreat them by claiming they were in no way related to the "complex societies" that lived before them. One must only look at the rich ancestral ties and culture of living indigenous populations to see that this couldn't be further from the truth. Calling a civilisation "lost" ensures its separation from modern societies and allows its remains to be sold to the highest bidder and shipped around the world, creating and embedding a narrative of marvel and mystery.

The purpose of this book is therefore twofold: to introduce you to these lesser-known ancient civilisations and cultures, and to highlight as much of the magic in the mundane and everyday as possible. Together, we will explore the complexities of their societies, cultures, and legacies, highlighting what makes each culture unique and worth celebrating. By looking at archaeological remains, texts, and scientific investigations, you, the reader, are invited to embark on a journey across continents and epochs, from the rainforests of Mesoamerica to the steppes of Central Asia and beyond. Read them in the order in which they are presented or choose your own adventure as we zigzag around the globe.

This book does not solely discuss "civilisations" as we define them today. The word *civilisation* is problematic and often misunderstood. What we define as "civilised" or not is often the result of looking through our biassed lens based on the values of the period in which we are living. All too often, the word was used to set up a distinction between societies around the world, creating a harmful environment where "civilised" societies are seen as superior to "non-civilised" ones.

The word *civilisation* was first used in France in the 1700s, and by the middle of the century, it came to mean "the process of being civilised."[3] In the broadest sense, it was used morally to denote a contrast between "superior moral and intellectual" urban societies that conformed to Eurocentric ideals, and more "barbaric" ones that did not have a hierarchy system, agriculture, literature, art and science, or a division of labour. The word quickly spread throughout Europe, replacing *civility* in English, and it soon became synonymous with the word *culture*—though their distinctions were often noted and argued by multiple nineteenth-century authors, with civilisation denoting materialistic concerns and culture focussing on the spiritual. By the nineteenth century, civilisation had become plural and had come to mean "the characteristics common to the collective life of a period of a group."[4] It no longer denoted a specific level of cultural achievement. Rather, the term could now be used to refer to distinct groups around the world from various periods.

Even from the earliest definitions, many ancient societies could be called civilisations but were often ignored in the early development of this term. "Civilisation" and other associated terms were used to differentiate societies that historians deemed culturally superior and those that they saw as inferior. Until recently, what constituted "civilisation" was defined by white male scholars with European ancestry and came to define Western society as a whole. Because of this prejudice, complex societies from other parts of the world were seen as "lacking" for one reason or another. For example, Africa has produced many great and powerful kingdoms. They created masterful pieces of art, had complex and hierarchical societies, and developed vast trade networks throughout the continent and beyond. Yet, when European colonists arrived, the people thriving within the lifeways they had created for themselves were deemed lesser to the point of not even being considered human for centuries to come. Even into the twentieth century, impressive societies like the Inca Empire of Peru were not considered to be "civilisations" because they did not use the wheel or possess a written language.

Luckily, today's archaeologists, anthropologists, and historians are a more diverse group. But even though great progress is being made to deconstruct these outdated definitions of civilisation and the classification of societies based on Western ideals, much more work needs to be done. Communities and societies are too complex to fit within a binary of "civilised" and "uncivilised." The sprawling cities hidden below the canopy of the Amazon Rainforest and the vast interaction networks among Neolithic societies in Southwest Asia that have come to light in recent years are proof that we cannot simply fit human history into a set of standard definitions.

Another term that will often come up in this book is *archaeological culture*. Without getting too deep into what defines a culture and the heavy theory and debate that has followed this term throughout the decades, an archaeological culture consists of a collection of a variety of materials or artefacts, buildings, and monuments associated with one another that occupy a specific period of time and geographical area.[5] It is a constructed term, created to assist archaeologists in making sense of what is pulled out of the ground and help identify possible groups and societies who would have associated with one another or defined themselves as belonging together as a people.

The assumption that is made with archaeological cultures is that they reflect a wider group of people. It allows archaeologists to interpret and discuss their finds as a group of people and cultural practices rather than a collection of inanimate objects with no meaning. It also allows us to link other forms of evidence and try to determine why cultures change over time. For example, if one type of pottery suddenly replaces another dominant type, it can be interpreted as a completely new group migrating to the area. If the dominant pottery undergoes a change such as adopting a particular decoration from a neighbouring group, then we can determine that these two groups were in contact with each other and probably shared ideas, possibly even material goods. Simply put, an archaeological culture is a classifying device that expresses culture through physical artefacts instead of people.[6] And since archaeology is the only means by which we can learn about the majority of ancient groups, frameworks like this are needed to help solve the puzzle of the past.

An archaeological culture gives a group of ordinary objects life. Since we don't know the names of the groups of peoples who belonged to these assemblages, archaeological cultures are usually named after the places where the first evidence of their existence was discovered. For example, the Nok culture was first discovered in a tin mine located in the village of Nok in Nigeria. The Únětice culture got its name from a cemetery that was found in the village of Únětice in Czechia. Other times, archaeological cultures can be named after a type of artefact that is diagnostic of that culture, such as the Corded Ware and Bell Beaker cultures. Both have a distinctive form of pottery that sets them apart from other cultures that existed contemporaneously.

Archaeological cultures are often just shadows of the actual groups of people who lived in the past. Interpretations of inanimate things usually have no resemblance whatsoever to the rich and complicated lives being lived by the people using them. A culture is also not solely defined by one set of fixed types or decorations. A culture can discard certain traits that no longer suit it or pick up new ones that meet a new need from an evolving population. It is this very ability to change and adapt that makes cultures so long-lasting and resilient in an ever-changing world.[7]

The same can be said for time periods that have been constructed to add structure to history. Some of these periods encompass hundreds, if not thousands, of years. Multiple generations are lumped together to define a period in such generic terms that much of the nuance and subtle change that defines brief moments in these periods are lost. Because so much is missing from the archaeological record, we must rely on these larger time periods. But it is so important to remember that much of the human experience that we look for in history is often lumped into generic characteristics to help us cope with the vastness of time. Think about how much has happened in your own lifetime. So much change can occur over a few decades; imagine then how much we are missing over centuries.

Some of the ancient cultures discussed in this book have complicated pasts. The trails of the nomads belonging to the Xiongnu and the Scythians are difficult to trace. Their transient lifestyles mean that historians must often rely on the writings of their contemporaries—usually their enemies—to gather information about them and try and fill the gaps in the archaeological record as best they can.

Countless ancient cultures and civilisations have been overshadowed by the passage of time and by the majority of attention being placed on familiar narratives such as the towering pyramids of Egypt, and the majestic temples of Greece. This book is an attempt to begin illuminating these lesser-known peoples and shed light on parts of the world often overlooked for having a complex ancient past. It is an attempt to uncover a personal story from each chapter to help bring them to life.

Throughout this exploration of these lesser-known ancient civilisations and archaeological cultures, we will encounter societies that thrived in harmony with their natural surroundings, such as the Indus Valley in the Indian subcontinent, whose urban centres flourished along the banks of great rivers. We will uncover the Olmec of Mesoamerica, whose colossal stone heads stand as silent sentinels of a bygone era, and visit the bustling ports of Dilmun in Arabia. We will hunt whales with the Thule Inuit of the Arctic, harpoons poised at the ready, and marvel at the artistic ingenuity of the Moche of South America. If we're lucky, we'll even get to race horses through the steppes of Central Asia with the Xiongu, and sail to distant shores with the Lapita.

While on this journey, the lives of everyday people will be highlighted whenever possible. Questions regarding the rise of these societies, their challenges, successes, connections, and their eventual decline will be tackled in hopes of uncovering as much of the story as we can with the puzzle pieces that remain. The groups discussed each deserve their own book to do them justice, and there are many available that I deeply encourage you all to read. There is only so much I could include in a volume of this nature, and what I have written is just the tip of the iceberg of what there is to know about each group. My advice is to use this book as a starting point, a reference to the beginning of your journey into the far corners of the ancient world. Though you may have heard of some of these groups before, I hope that you learn something new in each chapter and come away with a better understanding of the richness and diversity of the human experience.

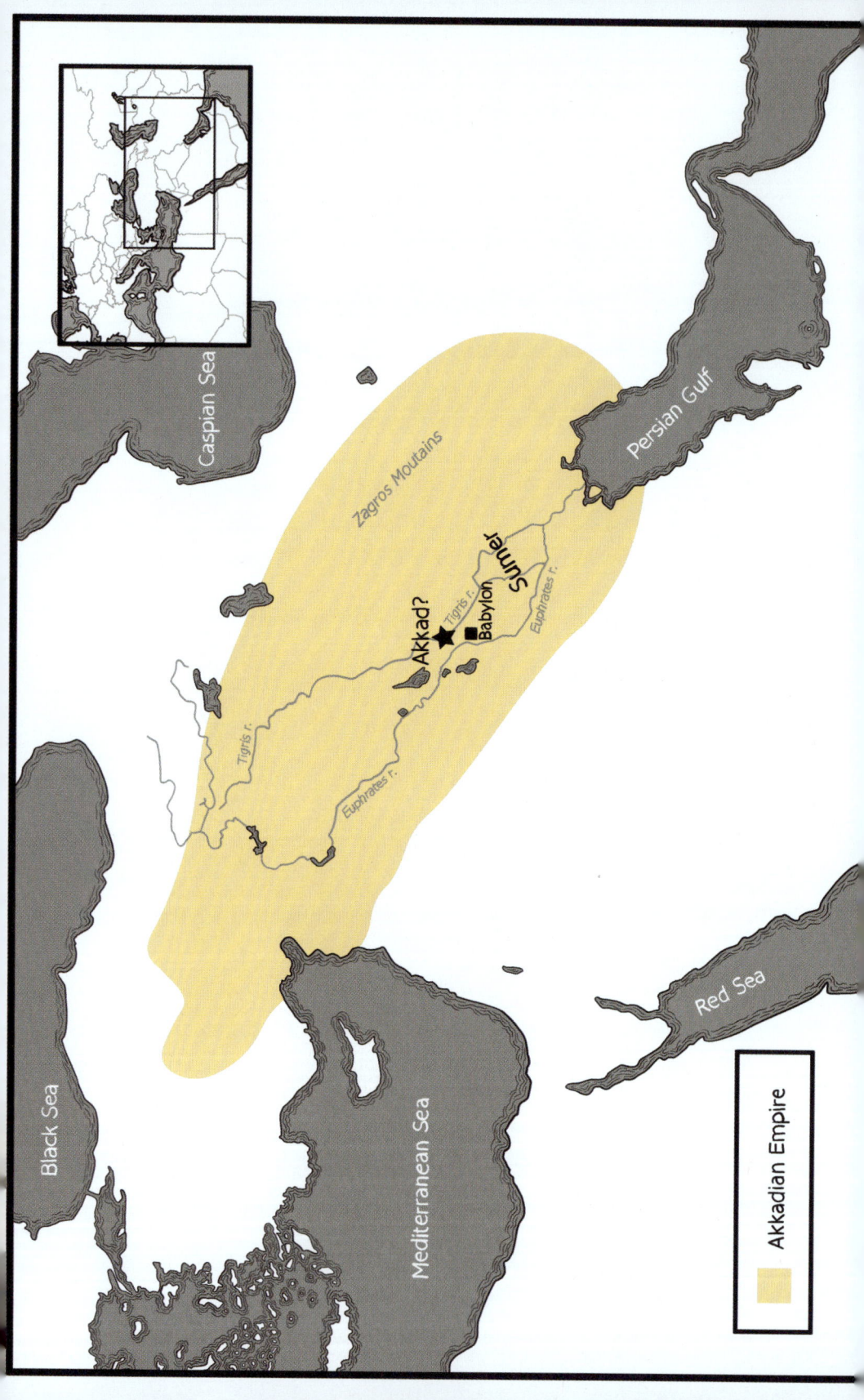

Chapter One

Akkadians
The World's First Empire.

The rumble of the carts and the braying of donkeys in the streets awoke Enheduanna. Though she had already been in Ur for many years, the sounds of this city still felt foreign. There was no rest for the countless merchants outside the temple which she now called home, selling their wares and embarking on great expeditions across the sea. Her father, the former King of the Universe, had sent her here to become the high priestess of the god Nanna, a position she understood to be more than a simply religious one. In many ways, Enheduanna identified with this city filled with outsiders, as she was one herself; married to a foreign god to help unify the religions of this land newly conquered by her father and her homeland in the north. But there was a new tension in the city. The new king of Ur, Lugal-Ane, was demanding to confirm his position of power over the city, independent of her nephew's ruling of the empire. It was a dynasty Enheduanna had dedicated her life to solidifying through her work at the temple. As the consort of the god of the city, her denial to legitimise his reign meant she was being stripped of her title and exiled from what had become her home.

Regardless of the dangers awaiting her in the coming days, there was work to be done in honour of the ruler of the gods. Enheduanna dressed and left her chambers to undertake the first rituals of the day. The air was heavy with incense as she navigated her way through the darkness of the temple complex. The moon was still out, Enheduanna's powerful husband greeting her before his descent and lighting the way to the great ziggurat. Once she and the other priests and priestesses completed their duties, Enheduanna watched as her now-satisfied husband gave way to the rise of Utu, ushering in a new day across the four corners of the world.

The last of her duties completed before she embarked on her exile to Ĝirsu, Enheduanna went back to her chambers to aid her ladies in waiting in collecting her belongings. She took extra care to personally attend to her writing tablets and stylus reeds. Picking up her latest work, Enheduanna read over the previous day's writing. She was impressed with her prose. The tablet was the beginning of the story she was currently experiencing: the rebellion of Lugal-Ane and her exile. It was a holy song dedicated to the goddess Inanna to help protect the dynasty her father created. A call for the judgement and destruction of Ur and its new usurper. This she took care in packing to not damage what had already been written. While this was not her first hymn, Enheduanna felt it would be her most important, and the best way to ensure her safe return to her temple and ethereal husband.

A New Idea of Kingship

Before they came to be known as one of the most influential powers of the ancient Near East, the Akkadians were simply one of the many tribes that populated Upper Mesopotamia in the third millennium BCE. These tribes would have lived amongst each other, alongside the Sumerians who dominated the region for many years. That is, until an Akkadian by the name of Sargon rose to prominence in the twenty-third century BCE. He transformed his people from a tribe to the rulers of the first ever empire that, at its greatest, extended throughout all of Mesopotamia to the Persian Gulf and stretched to southcentral present-day Türkiye, the Mediterranean Sea, and Elam in Iran.[1] The Akkadian kingdom became an empire that was considered a turning point in history to future Mesopotamian kings. Generations of Assyrian and Babylonian rulers who came after studied inscriptions of the Semitic Akkadian kings after their demise. Literature was written about them, and the site of their ruined capital, Akkad (Agade), was excavated in an attempt to claim their legacy as their own.[2]

Sargon appears to have been the son of a gardener and former cupbearer who rose to (and possibly usurped) power in the city of Kish. He then set out on a mission to defeat Lugalzagesi, the king of Uruk, around 2292 BCE. Through this defeat and subsequent battles with fifty other governors, Sargon unified southern Mesopotamia into a single state for the first time. This laid the foundations for his kingdom and dynasty to dominate a vast area of the Near East for over a hundred years.

Sargon gave himself the title "King of Kish," meaning King of the Universe, and established his capital city in Akkad. This city and region of the same title is where the name of the kingdom and their famous language that spread throughout all of Mesopotamia for centuries after gets its name. The city of Akkad is still undiscovered, but it was most likely located near where the Tigris and Diyala rivers converge. Some scholars believe it could also be located underneath modern Baghdad in Iraq.[3] The unknown location of this ancient capital city makes the study of the Akkadians, their daily life, culture, and societal organisation difficult.

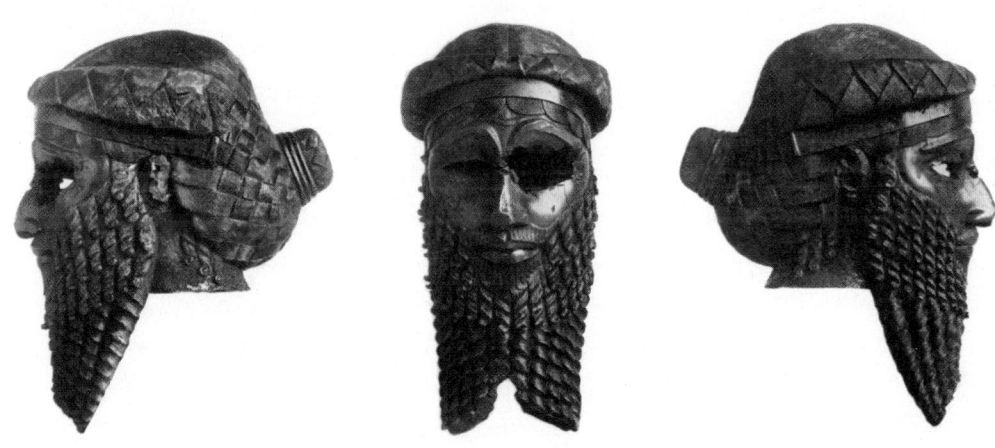

Bronze head of an Akkadian king, most likely representing Sargon or Naram-Sin.

Because the Akkadian tribe was already established in the area and thriving alongside the Sumerians and other local cultures, the rise of the Akkadian dynasty didn't leave much evidence of a significant demographic or economic change.[4] That means we can imagine that the people who inhabited the areas under Akkadian control probably went about life as they always had, prospering off of their highly organised agricultural system, worshipping their gods, living in walled cities, and sending their male children to the first public schools in history. Of course, not every newly defeated city-state and region was happy with their new overlords, and revolts against the Akkadians were a near constant throughout their century of dominance and rule.

By Might and Militia

The Akkadians owe much of their success and domination to their military might. Evidence from written sources at the time claim that Sargon had 5,400 men eating in his presence every day, which could possibly refer to a standing army.[5] This group of soldiers was one of the first professional military forces in history. The composite bow was already common and in use during Sargon's time, allowing armies to take down their enemies from farther distances, but his improvements to the Akkadian military allowed this weapon to be used to its full potential. By creating compact rows of archers, showers of arrows could rain upon the approaching donkey-drawn chariots that often led the first attack. This led to the widespread use of the composite bow throughout Mesopotamia.

The armies of Sargon and his successors (his grandson Naram-Sin in particular) were the first to campaign consistently throughout their dynasty and reached corners of the world as far away as the Indus Valley, Arabia, Egypt, and Cyprus. Much of this military action would have been to secure access to trade routes in order to guarantee the supply of precious materials such as wood, hard stones, and silver. Sargon claims that ships from Dilmun in Arabia, Magan (Oman), and Meluhha (Indus Valley) had all moored at the quay of Akkad.[6] This would have inserted the Akkadians into a rich trading network that would have provided everything needed for their empire.

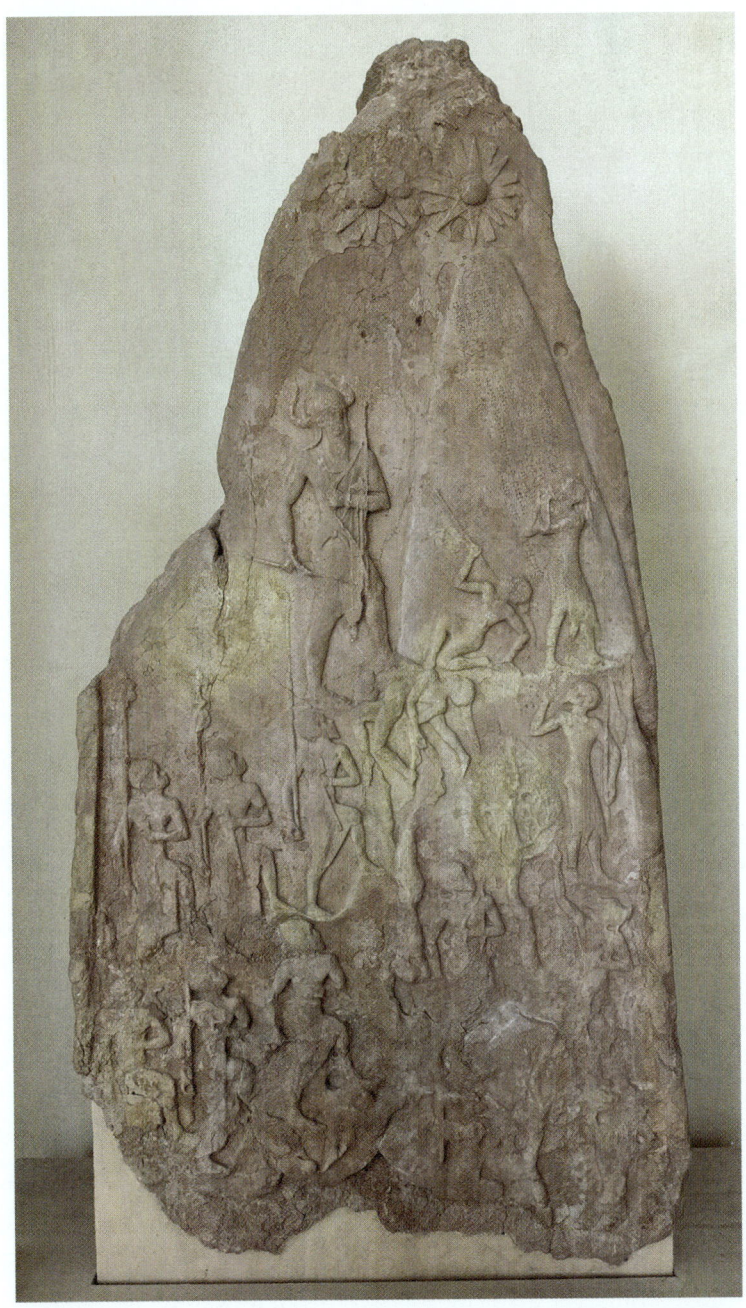

The Victory Stele of Naram-Sin. This stele dates to c. 2254–2218 BCE and depicts King Naram-Sin leading the Akkadian army to victory over the Lullubi, a group of Bronze Age tribes originating from the Zagros Mountains.

Out with the Old, in with the Centralised

As the Akkadians took control over more territory, the system of city-states that had defined Babylonia had to be reconfigured to work together under one central ruler and ruling city. With Sargon claiming power over a vast area of land, a new system of government had to be developed. Former Sumerian city-states were integrated into a larger entity that encompassed political, economic, and ideological ways of life. Original rulers remained in their positions but now acted as governors who focussed on administration, reporting to one central ruler for support and approval. The Akkadians then focussed their attention on instituting policies that encouraged the centralisation of all other goings-on.

One of the major changes that occurred under this process of centralisation was the widespread adoption of the Akkadian language, born from the Sumerian cuneiform script. While Sumerian had been the most widespread language for over a millennium, it was geographically isolated. Akkadian, on the other hand, was a Semitic language, meaning it belonged to the same linguistic group as languages spoken throughout the Near East and Arabia. As a result, it was much easier for these new territories to assimilate and integrate within the empire.[7] Akkadian became so widespread and vital to Mesopotamian society that it was the official native language of future Mesopotamian empires throughout the Bronze Age and was used until the eighth century BCE. Sumerian professors even created the oldest known "dictionaries" to aid in the widespread adoption and understanding of Akkadian.

In addition to a unified language, the Akkadians also developed a new system of taxation where a portion of the income from each region was sent to Akkad or used to support the local state bureaucracy. This system of government became the standard throughout Mesopotamia. Administration was also centralised through the introduction of an annual dating system used throughout the empire. Each year was named after a major event, either from the year prior or earlier in the year. The years were usually given names referring to military campaigns, building projects, donations to temples, or appointments of high priests and priestesses. This naming system was used in Babylonia until around 1500 BCE and gives us invaluable insight into what the rulers themselves found important to their rule.[8] The Akkadians also implemented royal units of measurement, which standardised the previous system where each city-state or guild had their own measurement system.

Religion and the First Named Author

Alongside the administrative changes, the Akkadians changed how kingship was viewed and established their power through religion. The style in which Akkadian kings wrote about their wars and military expeditions became more focussed on their heroic feats rather than a conflict between city-gods as they had previously been viewed. Monuments created during Akkadian rule were transformed from depicting a ruler worshipping a god to focussing on celebrating the king's achievements. The inscriptions from the kings on these monuments put themselves at the centre of the action. Akkadian kings made themselves the initiators of military conflicts by depicting themselves as strong, unchallenged rulers, similar to how Mesopotamian heroes of myth such as Gilgamesh were described. This caused ideological and religious problems for the Sumerian cities in southern Mesopotamia, who viewed this self-representation as impious,[9] although the criticism didn't seem to affect the Akkadians. Around 2230 BCE, Naram-Sin, who brought the Akkadian Empire to its height of power by defeating a coalition of rebellious kings known as the "Great Revolt" and conquering lands to bring the empire to its greatest extent, took on the title "King of the Four Corners, King of the Universe." He even went as far as deifying himself, giving himself the title "God of Akkad," which he claimed was a request from the citizens of the city.[10]

While some acts by the Akkadians were seen as going against the religious norm, they by no means disrespected the Mesopotamian pantheon. In fact, the Akkadian dynasty used religion to try and unite the north and south by connecting the cult system of Mesopotamia to the royal family. Sargon appointed his daughter Enheduanna as the high priestess of the moon god Nanna, and she became the god's wife in the city of Ur. It has been debated whether Sargon was the first one to have done this, but nevertheless, it was a political move to gain control over the clergy.[11] This was a vital move for the Akkadian rulers, as temples served both a religious and administrative function. This appointment of Enheduanna as high priestess set a precedent for future kings to cement their right to rule.

Enheduanna was more than a political pawn. She understood her roles, both as the daughter of the founder of the Akkadian Empire and high priestess, and wrote multiple religious documents. The "Sumerian Temple Hymns" are believed to have been written by her. These hymns describe the kingdom of Akkad as a unified north and south, indivisible and strong. Writings like this that religiously sanctioned Akkadian rule made it easier for the multiple cultures living under it to integrate, connect, and develop a collective identity.[12] Clay tablets of Enheduanna's hymns have been found in thirty-five cities around Babylonia, showing just how widespread her influence was. Another composition that she is thought to have written whilst in exile after the rebellion of Lugal-Ane against Naram-Sin is "The Exaltation of Inanna." This hymn is semi-autobiographical and discusses the rebellion and her exile. She then calls to the goddess Inanna to intervene and destroy Lugal-Ane and protect her family dynasty. These compositions credited to being written by Enheduanna make her the first identifiable author in the world.

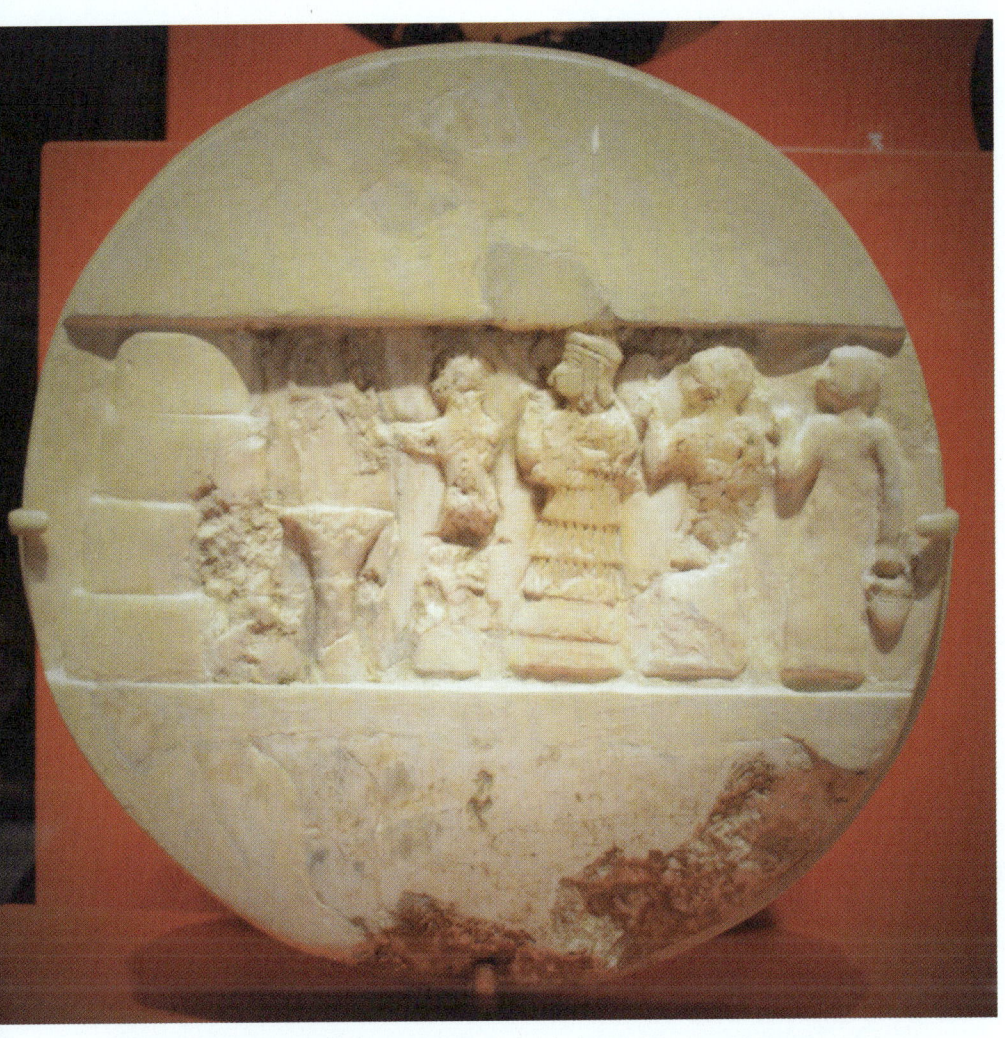

The Disk of Enheduanna is the only surviving artefact that contains both Enheduanna's name and her image engraved upon it. The object was found during excavations at the city of Ur, with one side containing a cuneiform inscription identifying her as the wife of the god Nanna and as Sargon's daughter. A copy of this script was found on a tablet dating to centuries after her death. From this copy we know that Enheduanna dedicated this disk to a temple to commemorate the construction of a hallowed dais. The opposite side depicts a ritual taking place, with Enheduanna at the centre wearing a tiered garment and a headdress.

Dust to Dust

The Akkadian Empire reached its greatest extent under Sargon's grandson, Naram-Sin (c. 2254–2218 BCE). After his death, Akkadian power began to quickly disintegrate and the empire ceased to exist after the reign of his son, Shar-Kali-Sharri (c. 2217–2193 BCE). The near-constant revolts against their rule and the efforts required to suppress them would have created a lot of internal pressure. This could very well have been the main source and trigger of their demise. While ambitious, Akkadian kings didn't have the resources or organisational capabilities to maintain their control.[13] This left them open to an array of external and natural threats, and soon after Shar-Kali-Sharri came to power, both of those threats would arrive on their doorstep.

The developing political instability within the Akkadian Empire attracted the attention of outside forces and was coupled with what appears to have been a devastating drought. Scientists have taken sediment cores from the bottom of the Gulf near Oman, as well as soil samples from a major Akkadian city, Tell Leilan, that both show evidence for the worst dry spell of the past 10,000 years occurring just as the city was being abandoned.[14] The soil samples show fine, windblown dust and very little sign of earthworm presence or rainfall. This drought lasted three hundred years and was devastating to the Akkadians in northern Mesopotamia, who relied on irrigation for their agriculture.

With their crops withering, the Akkadians lost their main source of economic wealth and livelihood. They would have had to migrate south to survive. Archaeologists have found evidence of a massive migration in southern Mesopotamia, which caused urban chaos as droves of people had no choice but to leave their homes.[15] Written documents from the royal court of the Third Dynasty of Ur, the dynasty that succeeded the Akkadians, tell us of an influx of people from the north and the construction of a wall to keep them at bay.[16] The south was not impervious to the drought though, and these immigrants would have put a huge strain on the already-suffering socio-political system. This resulted in a total collapse, with even the Third Dynasty of Ur collapsing around fifty years later.

The final blow for the Akkadian Empire was the invasion of the Gutians from the Zagros Mountains. Seeing the depletion of their wealth and resources and their string of weaker kings, the Gutians were able to take control of the region and claim that they were the heirs to the throne. The entire Near East transitioned back to a system of powerful independent city-states, but the kings of Akkad were never forgotten. Sargon and Naram-Sin became models for later rulers, and the cultural and political influences of the short-lived dynasty permeated through the rest of Mesopotamia's history.

Even though the Akkadian Empire didn't survive to see a second century in power, their rule and influence over the ancient Near East happened at a scale never before seen in history. Through their consistent military campaigns, the Akkadians were the first to incorporate multiple ethnicities, cultures, and societies into a single centralised state. They set the precedent for kingship and empire in the ancient world, and much like Latin after the fall of Rome, Akkadian became the language of diplomacy across the entirety of the Near East for over a thousand years.[17] Except with the Akkadians, they didn't require a millennium of rule and conquest to leave a legacy.

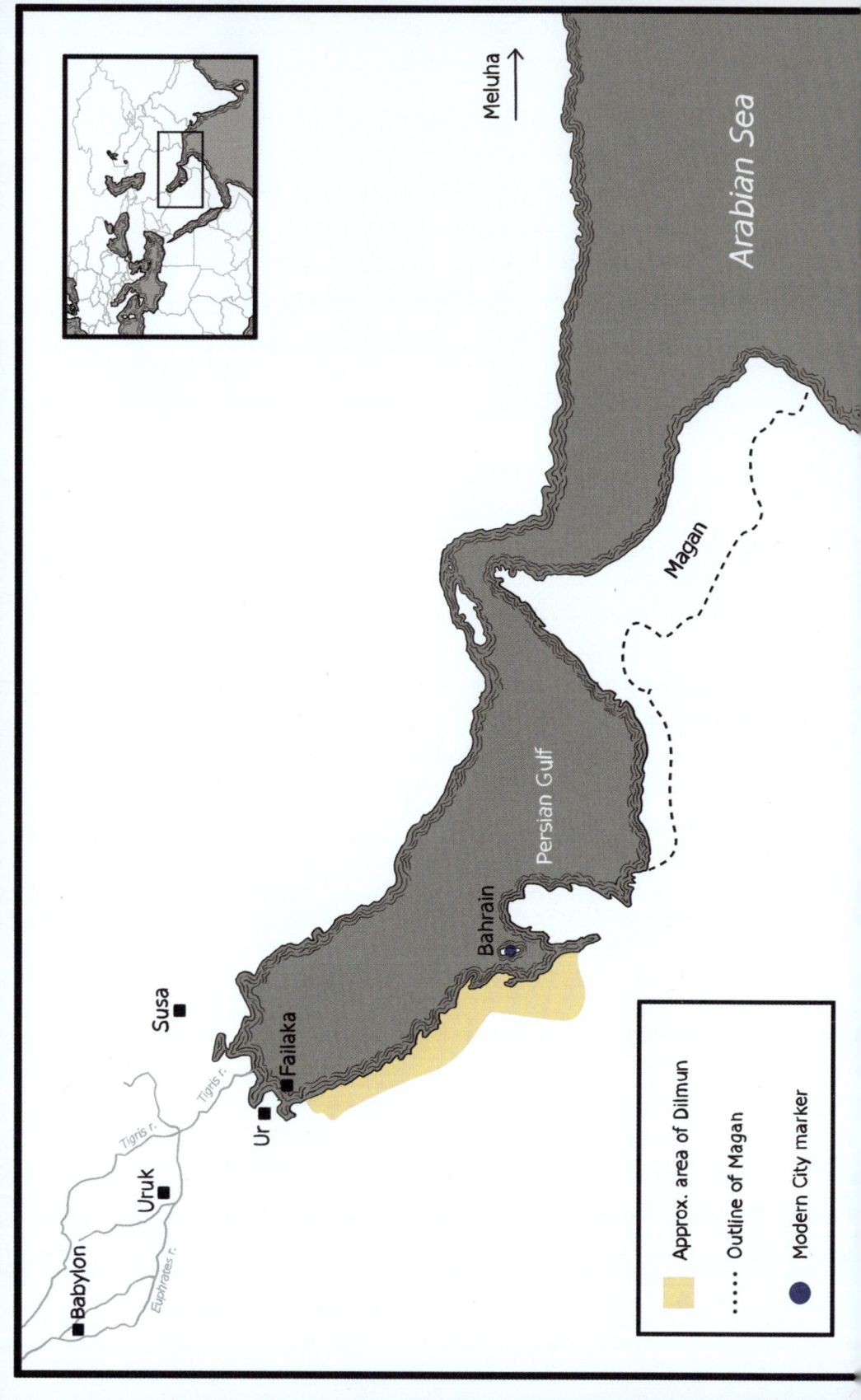

Chapter Two

Dilmun

The Lost Trading Port of Arabia

The smith was met with a wall of heat as he approached his furnace, an invisible barrier between him and the red glow of the stone crucible inside. The sun had been cruel today, and although the heat of midday had broken, his apprentice who was stoking the flames had received no respite from the warmth. Thankfully, the smith's apprentice understood the importance of today's work for the temple and never faltered in his position. The smith looked at him gratefully. His last apprentice would have abandoned him hours ago. Complaining of exhaustion, the smith's previous employ had regularly escaped to the harbour to watch the flurry of excitement as goods were loaded on and off ships, and the bustle of people from faraway places with their exotic cloaks and headpieces bartered their wares with each other.

The smith grabbed the heavy wooden tongs, their ends charred and blackened from years of service, soaked them in water to prevent them from burning in the flames, expertly pinched the lip of the crucible, and lifted it out of the furnace. His expert hands remained steady as he quickly brought the crucible towards the clay mould he had prepared earlier. The apprentice watched his master in awe. He had watched this dance of careful footing and expert handling hundreds of times before, but it amazed him every time.

With a flick of the smith's wrists, molten copper poured out of the crucible and into the small opening of the mould. The red-hot liquid quickly filled the cavity and overflowed onto the wet sand in which the mould was nestled. The smith straightened his arms and returned the crucible beside the cooling furnace.

Once the overflown copper faded from molten red to its natural colour, the smith motioned for his apprentice to remove the mould. Carefully removing the wire holding the two sides together, he began chipping away at it to free the newly cast sculpture, taking care to not damage the copper horn emerging from the clay. Once it was free, the smith grabbed the piece with his wooden tongs and dunked it in a bucket of water. Finally cool enough to touch, the smith examined their work. Picking up this new piece and its other half that was made earlier that day, the smith held them together and raised his arms towards the horizon.

The late afternoon sun shone through the hollow eyes of the bull. Its intricate horns faintly glistened in the light, hinting at the shine these pieces would exude after their edges were joined and smoothed, and their surface polished. The smith was satisfied with the outcome of these casts and sent his apprentice home for the day. The rest could be finished tomorrow.

Loved, then Lost

Even though the name Dilmun appears on some of the earliest written documents in the world dating to the fourth millennium BCE, the civilisation disappeared from memory for almost two and a half millennia. It was, in the most literal sense, a lost civilisation. Yet for over two thousand years before it was lost to history, it was a household name; a trading emporium considered to be a sacred place by the Sumerians, where gods and heroes lavished in their immortality.[1]

Throughout its existence, Dilmun was internationally known as a major trading port in the trading network that connected the ancient Near East, Arabia, and the Indian subcontinent. Stops like Dilmun were generally small kingdoms located on the coast and functioned as a marketplace, a rest area, and a source of supplies for restocking on longer journeys in the early second millennium BCE.[2] Dilmun was able to set itself apart from regular port stops and become a legitimate trading power in the Persian Gulf. For trading vessels travelling between Mesopotamia, Magan (modern-day Oman), and Meluhha (the Mesopotamian word for the Indus Valley civilisation), Dilmun was the only easily accessible source of fresh water. Ships would offload at Dilmun, creating a profitable opportunity for trade and exchange between merchants, and Dilmun would collect its share of transit income.

By the end of the Ur III period in Mesopotamia, c. 2000 BCE, Dilmun had become a trading monopoly, a middle point for Mesopotamia in the north, and Magan and Meluhha in the southeast to meet, trade, and partake in cultural interaction. Even though it remained a prominent trading centre past its decline until c. 800 BCE, Dilmun remained lost to history for thousands of years. Unlike other ancient cultures that were mentioned in classical and biblical texts, or in epic poetry, Dilmun seems to have been forgotten beneath the sands of its once bustling shores. Because of this, the location of this once-powerful trading emporium has been difficult for archaeologists to find.

Searching for Dilmun

The rediscovery of Dilmun began in 1861 with a cuneiform inscription from Khorsabad. The inscription describes the Akkadian King Sargon's military campaign against a rebel king of Babylon. Sargon then continues to mention all other foreign lands he "brought under sway...as far as the Border of Dilmun."[3] Dilmun is mentioned multiple times alongside the names of other unknown lands, and like them, it was dismissed for many years due to its obscurity. But unlike many of these other unknown lands, Sargon gave directions to Dilmun. He states that Uperi, the king of Dilmun, resides "thirty double-hours away, in the midst of the sea of the rising sun."[4] Cryptic though it may be, this provided archaeologists with enough of a starting point to determine the geographical area of Dilmun, and led them to the island of Bahrain.

Only in recent decades have researchers been able to piece together archaeological, historic, literary, and economic evidence to pinpoint the most probable location for Dilmun. Ancient texts dating from the third and second millennium BCE speak of the copper, timber, pearls, and dates all brought by boat to Mesopotamia from Dilmun. They also state that Dilmun was located in the middle of the sea, and "at the mouth of the great rivers," associating it with Magan and Meluhha, but placing it closer to Mesopotamia.[5] Another text from the Neo-Assyrian king Assurbanipal says it was in the "midst of the lower sea," the Assyrian term for island.[6] By taking these descriptions, archaeologists pinpointed Bahrain as the most likely candidate for the location of Dilmun. Bahrain is an island "in the middle of the sea" known for its freshwater springs, and until recently, was renowned for its dates and pearls. Although the exact extent of the area that belonged to Dilmun has been the subject of debate and fluctuation, the core of this trading civilisation is now agreed to constitute Bahrain and the Eastern Province of Saudi Arabia, with evidence of it extending to the island of Failaka in Kuwait.

A Clean and Pure Land

While Dilmun was a real place that facilitated trade with Mesopotamia and the known worlds of the southeast, the Sumerians also believed it to be a sacred land. According to the Mesopotamians, this far-off land was a paradise of sweet water and lush gardens inhabited by immortal beings and the setting for mythical events.[7] A Sumerian creation myth describes Dilmun as a pure, clean, and holy place where the god Enki impregnated the goddess Ninhursag.

The land of Dilmun also appears in the Epic of Gilgamesh, the oldest epic poem to have survived. Gilgamesh, the king of Uruk, travelled to Dilmun on his quest for immortality. There, he met Ziusudra, the survivor of the great flood who was given immortality by the gods and sent to Dilmun to live out eternity in paradise. Others may know him by his

Babylonian name, Utnapishtim. The poem declares that Enki created Dilmun's freshwater springs. The Sumerians also believed the earth floated atop two oceans, a freshwater ocean beneath a salty one. Their belief in two oceans further aids in the probability that Bahrain, with its freshwater springs under the saltwater sea, is the original location of Dilmun. To add further fuel to the fire, *Bahrain* in Arabic translates to "two seas."[8] These fantastical attributions to Dilmun have led some to think that the descriptions of Dilmun were the inspiration for the Garden of Eden.[9]

The Pearls in Planned Cities

In addition to its strong literary legacy, Dilmun was also a force to be reckoned with in the real world. The kingdom of Dilmun rose to prominence c. 2050–2000 BCE, trading in copper from Magan and other sources, as well as in the export of their local commodities, dates and freshwater pearls. Bahrain's underwater springs provided the optimal environment for these valuable pearls to grow with its natural mixing zone of fresh and saltwater. Pearl divers would also bring watertight bags made from goat skin to collect fresh water from these springs, which provided another trading commodity for merchants spending weeks at sea.

As Dilmun grew to a major trading port with extensive contacts between Mesopotamia, Magan, and Meluhha, it would have required a sophisticated level of administration to coordinate the collection and shipment of the raw materials and other specialised goods passing through their harbours. The first evidence of this rise in administration is the appearance of stamp seals. These seals are a defining object of Dilmun's culture, both economically and artistically. The presence of these seals shows their response to their new status in the international trading world, but the iconography also attests to their international contacts and economic success as they appear to be strongly influenced by the Indus Valley.[10] Dilmun also adopted a standard weights and measures system that corresponded exactly with the Indus Valley civilisation, further evidence of the close socio-economic relationship between the two, and the influence of this culture on Dilmun.[11]

This development of political and social organisation began around 2050 BCE, with Dilmun coming to its full power around 1850 BCE. This allowed for the rise of wealthy merchants, a ruling elite class, and the emergence of specialised crafts such as pottery, stamp seals, and metalwork. Written evidence for this new ruling class can be seen in the Mari texts. These three letters, dating to the eighteenth century BCE, were exchanged between the Assyrian king Shamshi-Adad and his son Jasmag Addu and mention a present that was sent from them to the king of Dilmun.[12] The Mari texts are the only evidence we have for a centralised, ruling authority. No palaces have been distinctly identified, and overall, Dilmun society does not seem to have been as separated into social hierarchies as other surrounding civilisations and cultures were at the time.

The increasing complexity in both social and economic life was due to the interaction and exchange happening as a result of Dilmun's regular visitors from the north and the east. There is little evidence for us to imagine what Dilmun looked like in the first half of the third millennium BCE before trading and contact with outside territories were made, but it seems like the population was made up of small subsistence farming and fishing villages set up along the coast. Once contact with Magan was made and trading became an integral part of Dilmun society at the end of the millennium, town life emerged.

A prime example of Dilmun's new urban life is the site of Qala'at al-Bahrain, which is believed to have been its capital city. Archaeologists have uncovered a fully urban site surrounded by fortification walls that, when found, stood eight feet high with a walkway on top of it that was protected by another four-foot-high wall for marching sentries. This settlement also contains warehouses and planned streets that intersect at right angles and run parallel to each other. City planning appears at other Dilmun sites such as at Saar. We also see the emergence of temples that acted as religious sanctuaries while also possibly serving as administrative and commercial centres, as well as the establishment of a colony on Failaka, an island in modern-day Kuwait.

The people of Dilmun lived in towns that were built on a grid pattern, just like many cities are today. At both Qala'at al-Bahrain and Saar, two main roads intersected to form a main intersection, with the rest of the roads shooting off from them. Houses were made from stone, and the overall standardisation hints at some sort of central regulation and authority. Although some were renovated over time as families grew and relationships changed, most houses were rectangular buildings with small, covered rooms, and had an L-shaped outside area that was probably roofed with palm leaves and used for cooking and storing water and other goods.

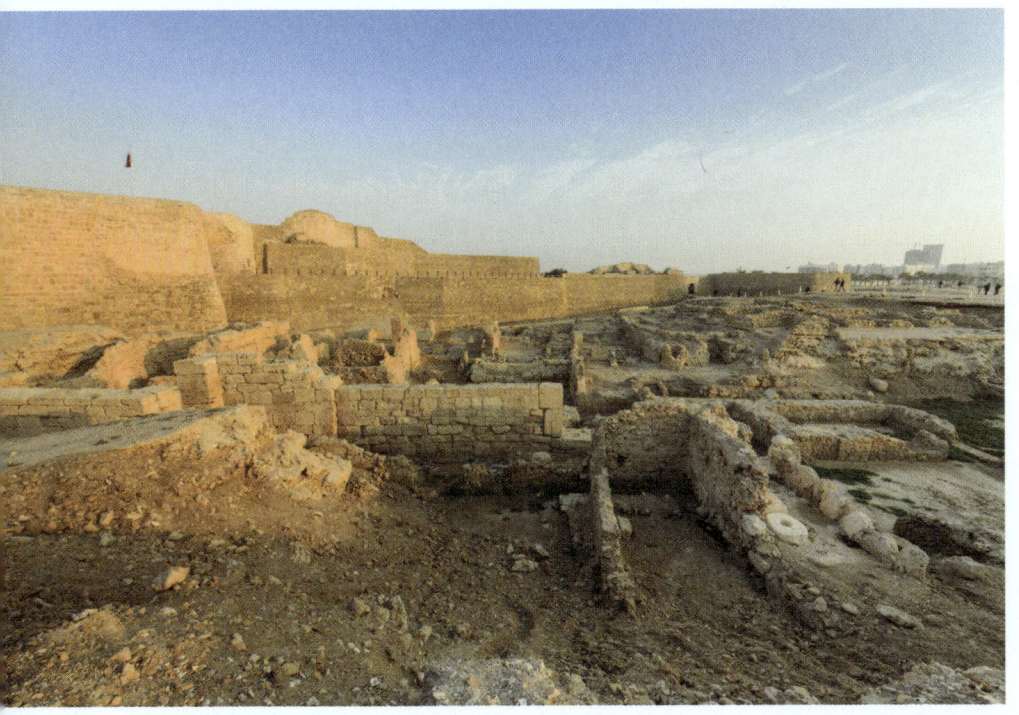

Site of Qala'at al-Bahrain.

Complex, but Illiterate?

While not all complex societies need to develop a writing system,[13] Dilmun's contact with literate and highly administratively organised cultures such as Mesopotamia and the Indus Valley would suggest that they too had a record-keeping system in order to trade with them. Commercial trade appears to have been the reason for the development of a recording system in Mesopotamia, which would then hint to the same need evolving at Dilmun. But if Dilmun did develop their own writing system, or adopted one from a neighbour, no evidence has yet been found. Seeing as Dilmun used the standardised weights and measures system from the Indus Valley, they may have also borrowed their script, or even combined influences from their trading partners and adopted Mesopotamian cuneiform.[14]

It is likely that Dilmun did have some sort of record-keeping system, as archaeologists have found many seals and seal impressions that were used in trade to seal packages and perform other administrative tasks. This means it's probable that they wrote on organic materials that have since decomposed and left no trace in the archaeological record.

The Melting Pot Beyond the Mounds

Along with the development of planned cities as Dilmun rose to prominence, a new style of burial and cemetery emerged. Cemeteries were built outside settlement areas and were densely populated with burial mounds built out of local stone. These mounds contained burial chambers that varied in style, from above-ground rooms, to those cut into the bedrock, or a central burial connected to others within the mound. Some contained a shaft entrance, and others were entire complexes. These chambers were large enough to lay one to two people inside, possibly members of a nuclear family, in the foetal position. The largest and most lavish of these mounds were found at the A'ali Royal Cemetery. The largest mounds measure over twelve metres high with a diameter of over twenty-five metres, and some contain a double burial chamber, one atop the other. These elite tombs were encircled by stone walls to signify their status, though in general, Dilmun appears to not have been a stratified society.[15]

People interred in these mounds were often buried in a variety of customs inspired by their trading partners, with varying grave goods such as ceramic vessels, jewellery, metal objects, and food offerings. More exotic goods that would have likely belonged to those of a higher status such as an ivory box and figurine fragments, ivory "wands," and cups made from ostrich eggs were also found in these mounds.[16]

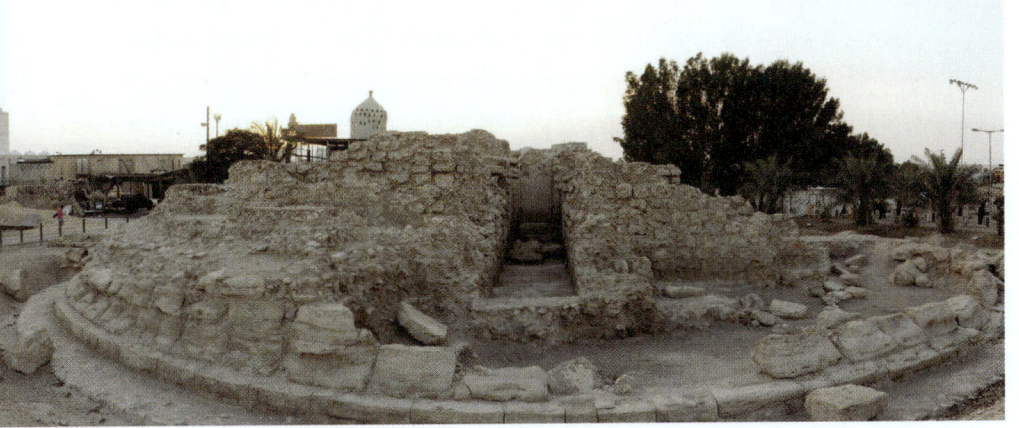

Excavated royal burial mound at the site of A'ali.

While the goods found inside the mounds are all quite similar in style, the various burial practices within the mounds tell a story of people from a more diverse area. With many cultures, burial practices tend to develop over time, with certain features changing across the culture from one preferred style to another. In Dilmun, different burial practices were used at the same time as others. This range of practices tells us that a diverse population lived in the Dilmun area, and with their position in international trade, this should come as no surprise. People from neighbouring areas or tribes in Arabia, as well as merchants from far-off lands, could have settled in Dilmun, bringing with them their culture and practices. But the similarity of the grave goods within these different burial practices indicates that by the end of the second millennium BCE, these groups formed a distinct, cultural unit that defined Dilmun's character, one that appreciated and took inspiration from their trading partners but set them distinctly apart.[17]

Another example of Dilmun's inspired but distinctive style is the copper bull's head that was discovered in the temple at Barbar, not far from the port of Qala'at al-Bahrain. The copper head was found in the second construction phase of the temple where two wall foundations intersected, along with pierced strips of copper sheeting and 118 copper nails. The nails and perforations in the copper pieces indicate that they would have originally been attached to a wooden structure. The bull's head is open at the back, suggesting that it would have been mounted onto an object, which many scholars think could have been a musical instrument, such as a lyre.[18] Examples of bull-headed lyres were found in the royal cemetery of Ur, and have also been depicted on stamps from Dilmun. Alongside this, the Barbar temple has elements of Sumerian architecture and several religions at Dilmun were known to have worshipped some Sumerian deities. These elements demonstrate the Mesopotamian influence on Dilmun religion and culture, but in keeping with true Dilmun character, the bull's head is not a complete imitation. The Dilmun iteration has a unique horn shape, hollow eyes, and a flattened muzzle. Therefore, while some traditions and practices were inspired by Mesopotamia, the piece was most likely cast to reflect local tastes.[19]

Of course, the influence didn't just bleed one way, as Mesopotamia's contact with Dilmun can be seen not just in their literature as mentioned above, but also in copper items used for religious purposes. Dilmun traded and travelled with a distinctly styled boat that, when arriving in Mesopotamia, sparked the imagination of those watching from the shores. Because of this, boat models and copper bowls in the unique shape of Dilmun boats were created and used for various religious purposes and dedicated to multiple deities.[20]

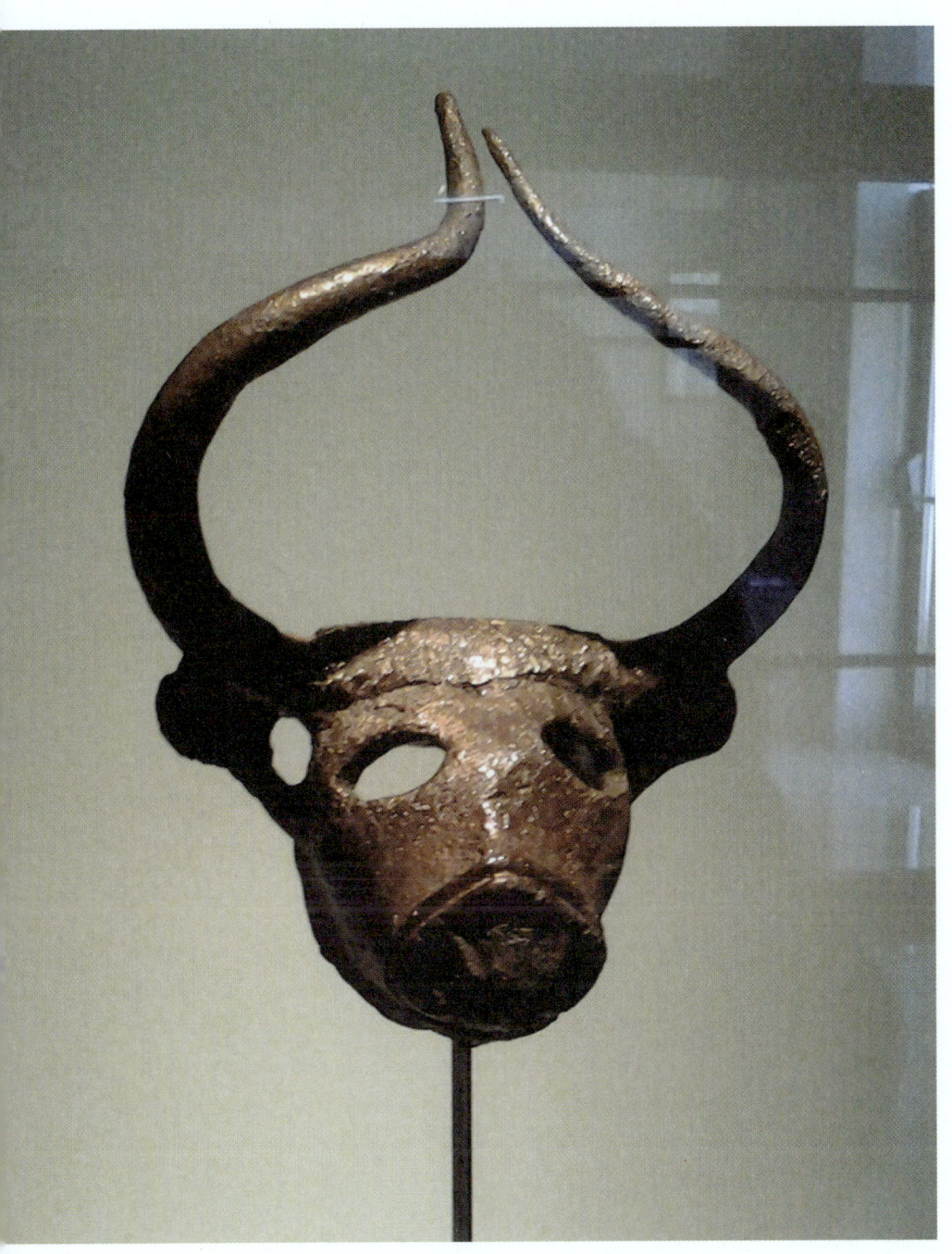
Copper bull's head found in the temple at Barbar.

The Return to Sand and Myth

Dilmun's geographical position allowed it to prosper and become a major link in the trade routes connecting Mesopotamia and the Indian subcontinent. This allowed Dilmun to reach markets and lands as far away as Syria, Anatolia, Iran, and even Central Asia. This prosperity continued throughout the beginning of the second millennium BCE, until sometime during the eighteenth century BCE when their prosperity began to decline and continued to do so for three centuries. The Barbar temple was abandoned, cities shrank, urban planning was abandoned, and trade began to slow. It seems that this slow decline was due to external political and economic factors.[21]

The Indus Valley civilisation began its decline as early as 1900 BCE, with their ports falling into disuse, and King Hammurabi in Mesopotamia gained control over Ur, preventing goods from being imported from the gulf and shifting the trading focus north to Anatolia. There was no longer any use for Dilmun, the middleman. By 1500 BCE, Dilmun came under foreign rule, first by the Mesopotamian Sealand Dynasty, then the Babylonian Kassite dynasty. Further sources claim Assyrian control over Dilmun until the first millennium BCE, with the Neo-Babylonians taking their place until the collapse of Babylon in 538 BCE.

While Dilmun lost its independence for many centuries, it remained a well-known area before it was forgotten. It became known as Tylos or Tilmun during the Hellenistic period, when it continued to play its role in pearling and maritime trade but without its past economic influence. With this change of name and decreased importance, the memory of the great Dilmun survived mostly in Mesopotamian legends as the centuries progressed. The bustling Bronze Age city then lay in wait under the sands until the nineteenth century to prove its legend was in fact a reality.

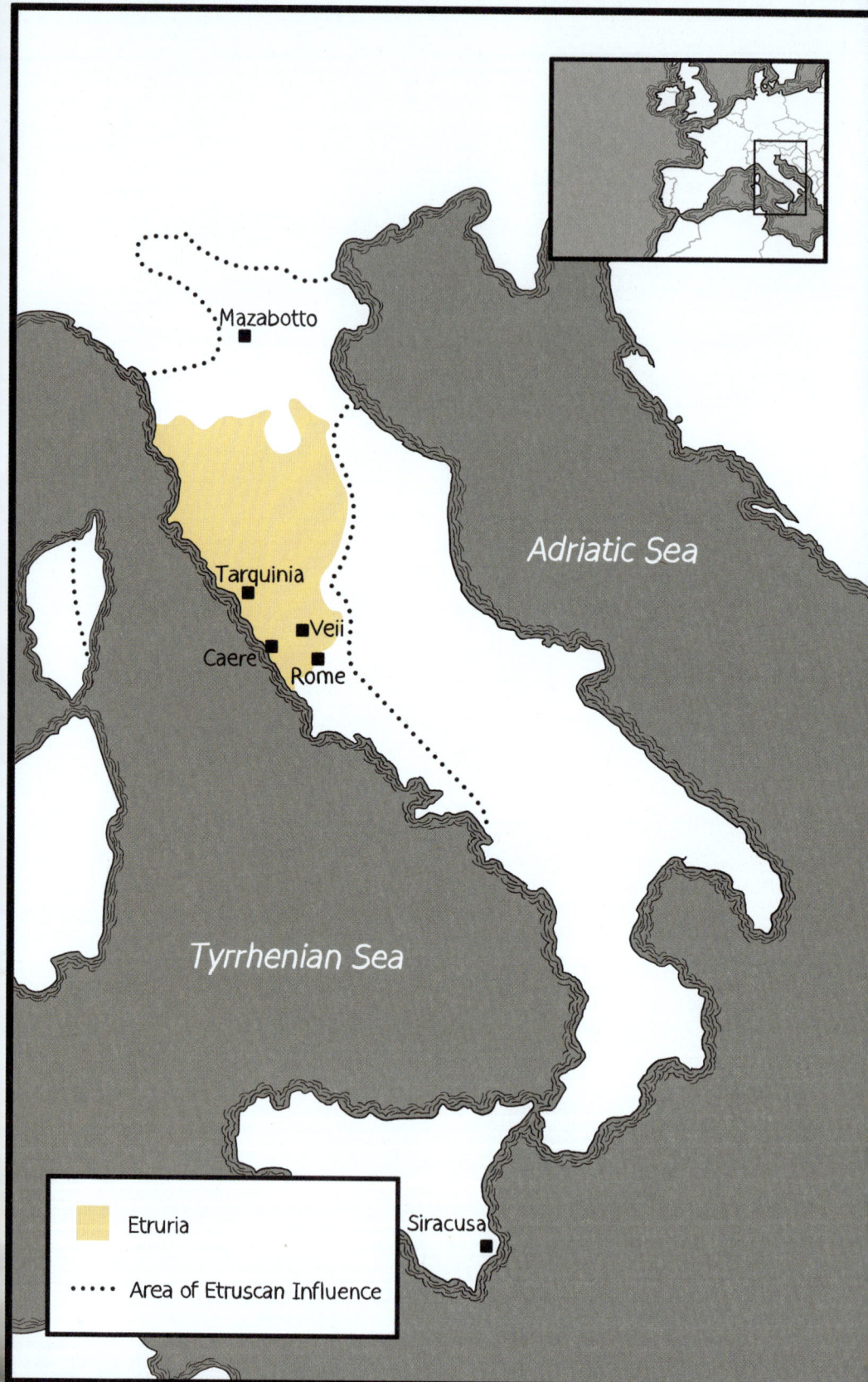

Chapter Three

Etruscans

The Givers of the Toga to Rome

The priestly haruspex felt the rush of warm blood flooding over his hands as he glided his knife around the sheep's throat. The sheep let out a defiant bleat before falling limp before him. With a quick prayer and a glance to the sky, the priest went to work, rolling the sheep onto its side and beginning the dissection. After having removed the entrails, the priest undertook the careful removal of the sheep's liver, placing it next to him on the wooden table, upon which was a bronze model of the organ he had just removed—his guide for predicting the future and discerning the will of the gods.

Gingerly, the priest poured over the liberated liver, inspecting each ridge, blemish, malformation, and colour change. He then compared his findings to his bronze guide, attributing each section to the homes of the gods in the heavens. The markings all hinted at deities whose favour his client was in, and who was displeased with his actions.

The man who had brought the sheep and requested the reading stood still while the priest worked away at the puzzle, sweating through his tunic. He sent another quick prayer to the gods in hopes of a positive prophecy for the battle that he and his legions were about to enter.

"The gods are in your favour," said the haruspex, "provided you are not too proud, you will be fruitful in battle."

The man sighed in relief. He knew the greatest challenge was still ahead, but with the heavens on his side he now had the confidence needed to rally his troops and lead them into combat.

A Question of Origins

The Etruscans called themselves Rasenna. From around 900 BCE to 400 BCE, they were the most powerful and influential people in Italy. They inhabited the land of Etruria, a stretch of hills and plains that makes up modern central Italy between the Tiber and the Arno rivers. The Etruscans were known across the Mediterranean and had an enormous cultural impact on ancient Rome. Yet, for the better part of recent history their origins have been hotly debated.

Some ancient Greek writers claimed that the Etruscans came from Lydia, a kingdom once located in modern-day western Türkiye. They were also linked to the Pelasgians, a group of people already extinct in the ancient world who the ancient Greeks believed inhabited Greece before them. However, there was one ancient writer, Dionysuis of Halicarnassus in the first century BCE, who dismissed these theories, claiming that the Etruscans were indigenous to the land on which they resided. The Etruscan culture, religion, and language were so unique compared to those surrounding it, not because of foreign invasion or settlement, but because of its deep-rooted regional development over a long period of time.

Some archaeological evidence can be interpreted in favour of both origin hypotheses. Objects found in Etruscan burials dating to the end of the eighth century BCE possess some eastern Mediterranean influence in their design and imagery, with some of the raw materials used to make them coming from as far away as Egypt and Sub-Saharan Africa. This influence is most likely due to their contacts and trading around the Mediterranean rather than through ancestral practice. With their land being rich in mineral resources, Etruria attracted the attention of the outside world. This open trade allowed the Etruscans to acquire luxury goods from the eastern Mediterranean for their tombs that gave way to an influence in this foreign style.[1]

Based on excavations at major Etruscan cities, there appears to have been a cultural continuity from the Late Bronze Age (c. thirteenth to eleventh centuries BCE) to the time when historians begin talking about the Etruscans.[2] There is no evidence of an incoming population, or any upheaval or conflict that would mark an end to the Villanovan culture that preceded the Etruscans in Italy. This means that the Etruscan civilisation was built off of their Villanovan ancestors who had inhabited the region for at least two hundred years prior. This natural progression doesn't completely discount the eastern origins claimed by ancient authors. DNA analysis has shown that the ancestors of the Etruscans arrived in Italy during the Neolithic period, but they shared ancestors with the Near East 7,600 years ago.[3]

Cementing a Civilisation

By the seventh century BCE, the Etruscan culture had become more defined, and the people were well-known around the Mediterranean and farther inland in Europe. The major urban centres that had Villanovan roots, such as Veii, Tarquinia, and Caere began to develop and expand. Commercial expansion through the trade of their unique glossy-black bucchero pottery, wine, oil, and precious minerals around various locations, such as southern France, Spain, Carthage, Campania, and the Greek colonies in Sicily, allowed the Etruscans to acquire resources and connections with the outside world. This gave the Etruscans access to new craftsmanship, materials, and technology such as the introduction of roof tiles and stone foundations to enable larger building projects and a reorganisation of urban spaces.[4] Their presence on the sea garnered attention similar to the seafaring Phoenicians as both groups were often called pirates in ancient sources.[5]

Such flourishing within settlements brought about significant changes in Etruscan society. Over the course of the seventh and sixth centuries BCE, fortifications were built at some settlements, road networks were improved, and underground water channels were used to improve agricultural production by draining marshland and irrigating drier areas. They began to expand beyond the confines of Etruria in all directions, eventually leading to the founding of the Tarquin dynasty in Rome by Lucius Tarquinius Priscus in the sixth century BCE. By 600 BCE, the Etruscans were the most prosperous people in the region, and their society was evolving to account for it.

Etruria's military became more sophisticated and social hierarchies also developed into cemented groups, creating new categories of wealthy merchants and landowners who liked to live well. A frieze that once decorated the walls of a sixth-century BCE building at Poggio Civitate, and multiple frescoes found in tombs depict diners on elaborate couches partaking in feasting and revelry. The pottery found indicates that wine was consumed at a grand scale, and the high amount of animal bones, including tusks of wild boars, shows just how lavish these feasts could be.[6] Feasts appeared to have been central in Etruscan life and death, as this banqueting imagery is a popular motif in their tombs.

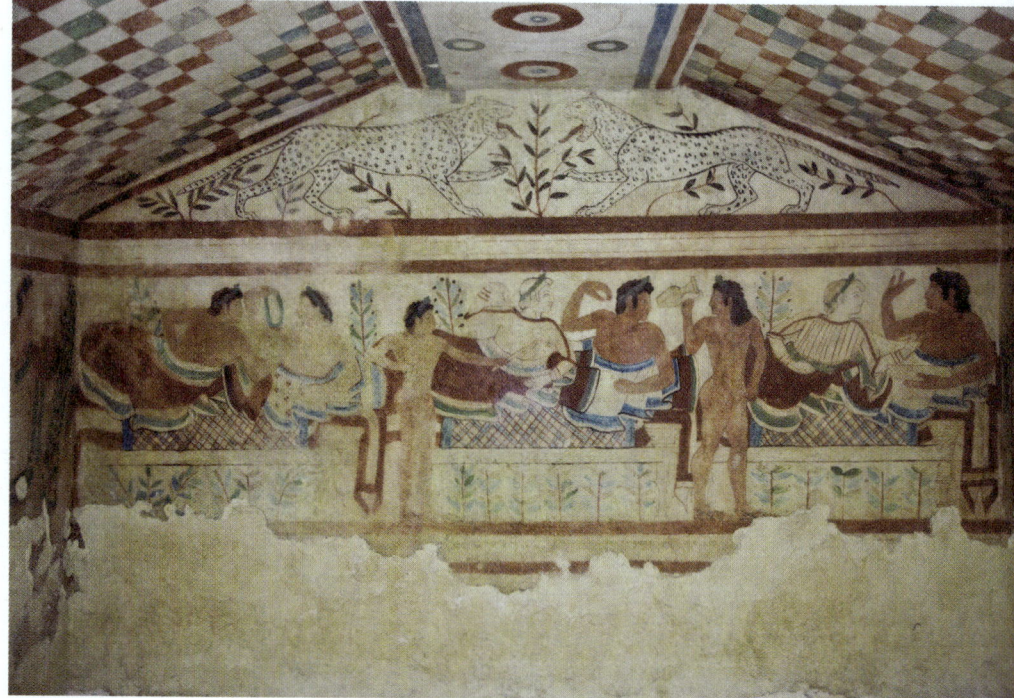

Fresco depicting a banquet scene from the Tomb of the Triclinium found in the Necropolis of Monterozzi near Tarquinia c. 470 BCE.

Little evidence of Etruscan domestic architecture survives, as much of it was built over by the Romans. The greatest amount of archaeological evidence that we have regarding their daily life comes from the elaborate tombs of wealthy citizens (believed to resemble parts of their homes), which only provide one view of history. Excavations at some cities, like Marzabotto, an Etruscan colony dating to the fifth century BCE located in the province of Emilia-Romagna, can help in recreating what life may have looked like for everyday people. The city was built along a grid pattern. Houses and streets were both neatly organised into city blocks, and many would have had access to drinking water and wells. We do know that houses of this period grew in size and sophistication, with tiled roofs, open courtyards with columns, and a series of rooms for both public and private use.

Familiar Letters, Unfamiliar Words

Though we have many inscriptions, dedications, bilingual Etruscan-Latin texts, and even a linen book that was preserved as wrappings on mummified human remains from Egypt, we cannot understand the Etruscan language. Etruscan did not share the inherited grammatical structures that most other European languages possess.[7] It is almost completely unique and not related to the Indo-European languages that geographically surrounded it. The only languages that can be seen as somewhat related to Etruscan are Raetic, which was spoken in Switzerland and parts of Austria, and Lemnian, a dialect only spoken on the island of Lemnos off the coast of Türkiye, which may have developed from Etruscan-speaking traders who settled there. While the majority of the inscriptions that survive in the archaeological record are funerary or dedications and mostly contain names, scholars are able to understand the Etruscan alphabet and have identified some words adopted into the Latin language.[8]

Etruscan used an alphabet derived from a mix of ancient Greek and Phoenician scripts. This then became the foundation for the Latin script, with twenty-one of the twenty-six letters of the Latin alphabet being of Etruscan origin. The alphabet itself is understandable, allowing us to discern that it was written right to left, but the words themselves are not as simple. Words can be read, and we know in general how the letters were pronounced, but much of the meaning comes from referring to other languages and the context of the writing itself.

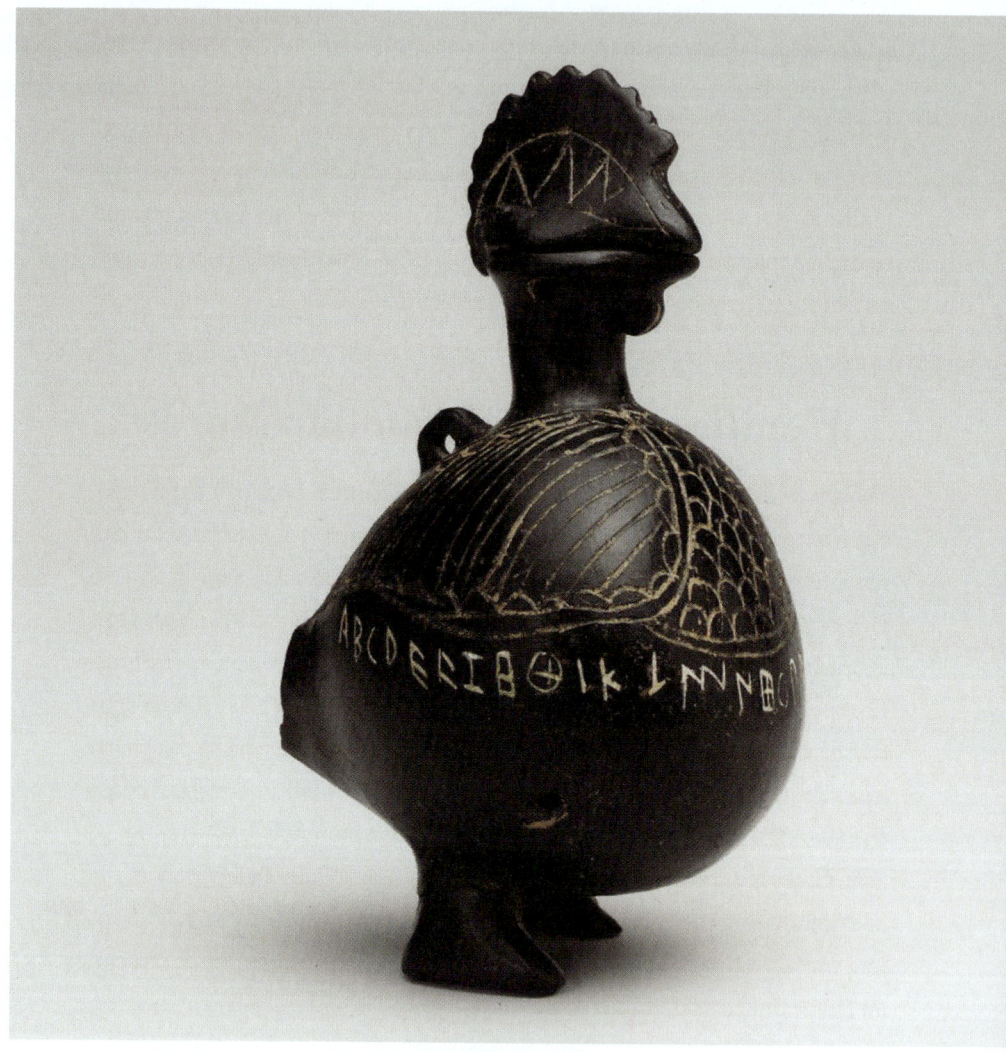

Bucchero vase in the shape of a cockerel inscribed with the twenty-six letters of the Etruscan alphabet. Bucchero was the distinctive type of Etruscan pottery and is known for its smooth, fine grey or black clay and shiny polished surface.

A Religion Revealed

According to Etruscan tradition, one day, a peasant was ploughing a field near Tarquinia when a child named Tages appeared, possessing the face of an old man. Everyone in Etruria came to witness this revelation as the child taught them the secrets of haruspicy, an important form of divination done by examining the entrails of animals, and possibly also about the nature of the underworld, before disappearing. A deep hole containing the burial of a child who may have been epileptic close to the major temple of Tarquinia dating to the ninth century BCE might add some real-life plausibility to this mythical story.[9] The Etruscans seemed to enjoy their prophetic figures, as a nymph named Vegoia is also said to have revealed the secrets of thunderbolts and property laws.

The Etruscans were renowned in antiquity for their religious devotion and skill in haruspicy. The priests who carried out this divination even held an important position in Roman religious life. Their accuracy was famous, and it was even said that it was an Etruscan priest named Spurinna who told Julius Caesar to "beware the Ides of March."[10] One of the key artefacts revolving around Etruscan religion that survives is the Piacenza Liver. This bronze model of a sheep's liver includes strange bumps, is divided into forty sections and inscribed with the names of twenty-eight deities. Representing the heavens, each section corresponded to the celestial homes of the various gods. Similar examples have been found at Babylonian and Hittite sites, and it would have been used as a guide for reading a real liver, its blemishes, colourations, and malformations all discerning which gods were angry or in a favourable mood, and what the future held.

We know quite a few of the Etruscan deities. Many of them were subject to the influence of the Olympian gods of the surrounding Greek colonies, but their exact roles and functions are not as clear as their neighbours.[11] Nine different gods threw thunderbolts that required interpretation, including the chief god Tinia, and some deities even had both a male and female version. Overall, there appears to have been an overarching theme of fatalism in Etruscan religion.[12] The daily life of the Etruscans was at the whim of the gods, their futures already set. Regardless, the Etruscans were still devoted and generous to their deities. Communal worship took place in urban centres, with objects such as shields, trumpets, and even full dining sets being intentionally destroyed and given to the gods in hopes of receiving a gift in return.

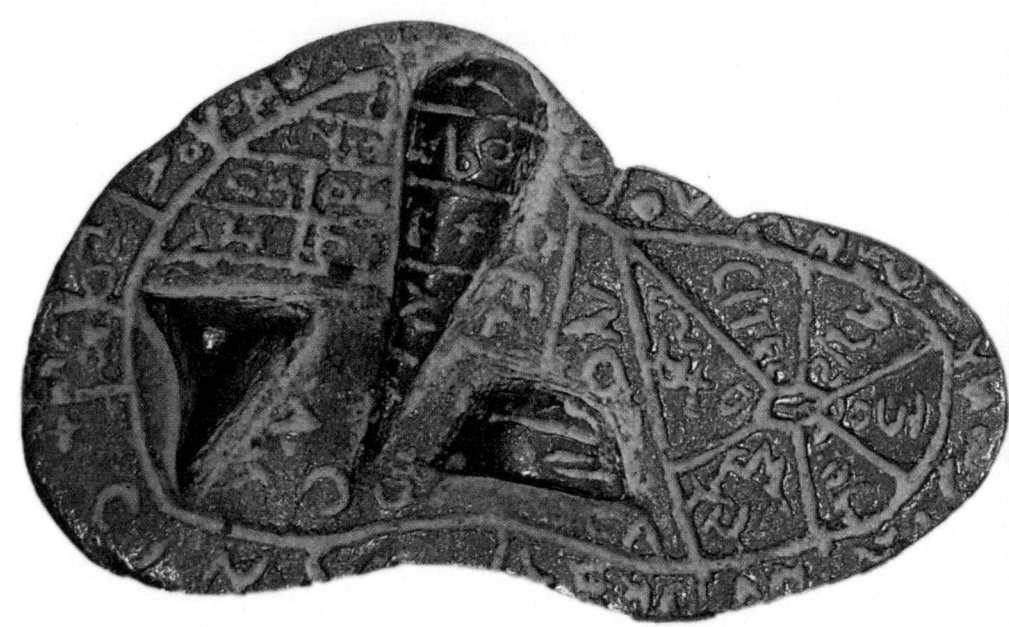

Etruscan Haruspex known as the Liver of Piacenza.

Glimpses of Life in Tombs

Much of what we know about Etruscan life and society comes from their final resting places. Early Etruscan, or Villanovan, hut urns depicting oval buildings with square doorways and roof beams, and rows of birds adorning the top ridge seem to be representations of real houses.[13] As the Etruscans expanded both in size and wealth, so did their tombs. With the rise of an elite class, burials became more elaborate from the seventh century BCE onwards, with elite tumuli concealing imposing architecture that is often thought to resemble Etruscan settlements.

Burials became large, single-family chamber tombs that lined well-planned streets, and their grave goods reflected a society of wealth and connection. Imported red and black figure pottery from Greece was abundant, and anthropomorphic urns often with articulated arms, wigs, and even jewellery have been found seated on a chair in front of banqueting tables. These wealthy tombs used the Etruscan tradition of feasting to flaunt their control over natural and agricultural resources.[14] Extremely rich banqueting services were buried with the dead, along with large terracotta containers that would have been filled with wine, olive oil, and other liquid and solid produce. Other rich grave goods also included items made from precious metals such as brooches, military equipment including chariots and shields, bronze mirrors, and amazingly detailed filigree on gold jewellery and diadems.

One of the largest aspects of Etruscan burials that give archaeologists and historians the most insight into their lives are the elaborately fantastic wall paintings inside. Much of the tomb painting is architectural, but other scenes include ordinary and fantastic animals, plants, and human activity. Both men and women are memorialised on these walls, partaking in various activities such as weaving, banqueting, and even in battle. At times reality appears blurred, with humans and gods dining together at banquet tables, and Charun, the Etruscan god of the underworld, escorting the deceased into the afterlife. The Etruscans took caring for their dead seriously. Construction of these elaborate tombs and detailed sarcophagi would have come at great expense, and the familial celebrations of feasting and dangerous games that inspired the gladiatorial games of ancient Rome, all add up to a community that cared deeply about their ancestors.

Leaving a Mark on an Empire

As with all rising cultures, the tides always turn, and powers begin to shift. By 509 BCE, the Roman Republic began with the expulsions of the last Etruscan king, Lucius Tarquinius Superbus. After this, the fifth century BCE saw the Etruscans losing more and more of its hold on the Mediterranean. They were defeated by the Syracusan navy at the Battle of Cumae in 474 BCE, which resulted in the loss of access to important trade routes, affecting the number of Greek imports at some sites and threatening the wealth the Etruscans had enjoyed for centuries. Enticed by the mineral, agricultural, and maritime resources of the Etruscans, Rome began to expand into Etruria, embarking on a campaign of conquering its cities and laying waste on the land. Veii was conquered and destroyed in 396 BCE, and by around 250 BCE the entirety of Etruscan territory was essentially under Roman control.

Despite this new Roman domination, wealthy Etruscans still maintained social and economic independence.[15] Rome simply created cities in Etruscan territory that were privy to Roman law, and Latin became the official language. Centuries after the Roman incursion, Etruscan was still spoken. Bilingual texts were created, and there was never any official decree forbidding the language from being spoken. But the increase in Latin-speaking settlers, and the ever-growing power of Rome meant that by the mid-first century BCE, Etruscan was barely used. The Roman emperor Claudius, who reigned from 41–54 CE, was one of the last recorded Etruscan speakers as his first wife was from an Etruscan family. He also wrote a history of the Etruscans as well as an Etruscan dictionary.

While the Romans conquered Etruria, the Etruscan culture left quite the legacy on the new reigning power. Much of Roman religion was derived from Etruscan tradition, and their prophetical haruspices were highly regarded. The Romans also co-opted the war trumpet, the triumph, the toga, boxing, and their funeral games into their everyday society. Indeed, many of the iconic cultural pillars associated with ancient Rome today had their beginnings with the Etruscans.

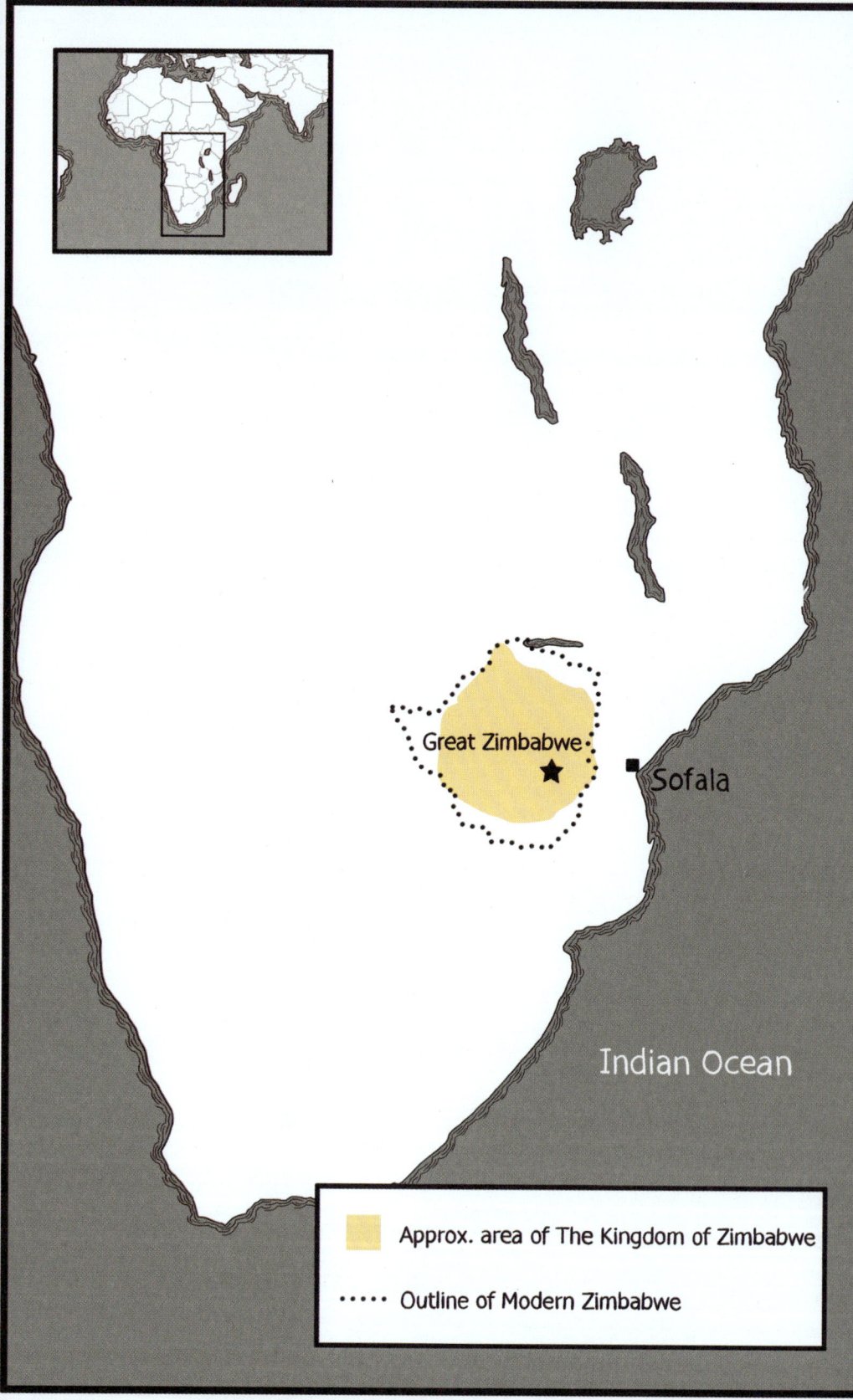

Chapter Four

Great Zimbabwe
A Stolen Past

The stew simmered over the crackling fire pit as the woman walked around the glowing centrepiece in her hut. Leaning over, she added chunks of fresh beef into the pot, seasoning it with salt. Her husband would be home from tending to the cattle soon, hungry after a long day's work. The scent of food filled the air as the woman tidied away her cooking utensils, replacing them in their rightful nooks before walking over to the bench and picking up her spindle to resume her other duties.

As she spun the thread she needed for her next weaving project, the woman could hear her children playing outside within the enclosure of their homestead. Her eldest son was growing so fast these days. Too fast. He would soon be out in the pastures with his father, learning to care for their large beasts and provide for his own family one day.

This vision of the future occupied her mind while she fell into the meditative rhythm of spinning. Lost in her thoughts, the faint sound of cattle approaching brought the woman back to reality. Her husband was home. She replaced her spindle on the bench, returning to the fire to check on their meal. Stirring the meat to ensure it was cooked through, the woman removed the pot from the flames and went to the entrance of the hut. Looking out, she smiled at the scene before her.

The sun was getting lower on the horizon and her children were running to greet their father, who had just entered the enclosure. The woman couldn't help but smile and thank her ancestors for this abundance. She quickly sent them a cautious prayer for her family, and asked them for their continued guidance in a future she knew would contain hardships, before joining her family outside to welcome her husband and ushering them in for dinner.

A Stolen Past

The story of Great Zimbabwe is a difficult one to tell. For three hundred years, Europeans believed it was created by foreigners. For them, the great walls of the settlement couldn't have been made by African people. The Portuguese, who were the first Europeans to arrive in southeastern Africa, wrote that these "great stone buildings" were created by biblical figures like King Solomon, the Queen of Sheba, or Prester John. Word quickly spread that the legendary city of Ophir and its golden riches had been found.

The Portuguese maintained these beliefs, from their first arrival in the sixteenth century, until quite recently. Karl Mauch, the first person to record and document the site in 1871, maintained this bias, even claiming that the stonework was too sophisticated to have been made by Africans. He found a wooden lintel that he identified as cedar wood, and declared it was brought there by the Phoenicians. This idea permeated all work done on the site by foreign teams. Archaeologists were even sent with the mission to prove that Great Zimbabwe wasn't built by its current inhabitants. From that moment, Great Zimbabwe and other Iron Age sites in the area were savagely looted. Gold and anything of value were stripped from the site, and structures were even torn apart in the hopes of finding more treasure. Anything that was considered of lesser value, such as pottery (the very thing modern archaeologists would deem most important), was thrown away and lost.

In 1891, James Theodore Bent, funded by the Royal Geographical Society and the British Association for the Advancement of Science, excavated at the site and declared that Great Zimbabwe must have been built by the Phoenicians or the Arabs. More specifically, it may have been Semitic traders who built these massive stone walls as fortifications to protect them from local tribes. To the European colonists, Great Zimbabwe was made by who they considered to be the great people of the ancient world, and centuries older than what it really was. Bent also destroyed large areas of stratigraphic evidence, erasing much of the history needed to learn more about the site and the people who lived there.

It wasn't until the early 1900s that proper, scientific archaeological investigations were undertaken at Great Zimbabwe by Egyptologist David Randall-MacIver. His study concluded that the ruins were African in origin and constructed by the ancestors of the Shona people. Further work done by J.F. Schofield in 1926 and Gertrude Caton-Thompson in 1929 reaffirmed this claim. In Caton-Thompson's report, she also added that Great Zimbabwe was of Bantu origin and dated to the mediaeval period.

Most European settlers in the British colony of Rhodesia (modern day Zimbabwe) refused this proposed version of history. In the 1960s, the ruling political party, the Rhodesian Front, even went as far as blocking books about Great Zimbabwe. Some archaeologists who refused to accept the narrative of the site's biblical origins were imprisoned and deported, and Africans who claimed their ancestral right to the site lost their jobs. It was not until recent decades, after Zimbabwe gained independence in 1980 and named itself after these great stone houses that defined its landscape and cultural history, that proper work in reclaiming its past could begin with fervour.

Reconstructing the history of Great Zimbabwe and the story of the people who lived there is difficult. With so much early destruction by European explorers and politicised archaeologists, an exorbitant amount of valuable information has been lost that can never be recovered. Most notably, information about the lives of the everyday people who lived there. Their practices and their daily activities are difficult to interpret without referring to the daily lives of the indigenous peoples who inhabit the surrounding areas today. We also have no written records of what was happening on the Zimbabwe plateau until sixteenth-century Portuguese accounts describe towns with monumental stone buildings. Because of this, any study on Great Zimbabwe now relies heavily on the reexamination of work done by these early investigators who removed so many of the finds and archaeological deposits that would prove invaluable to us today.

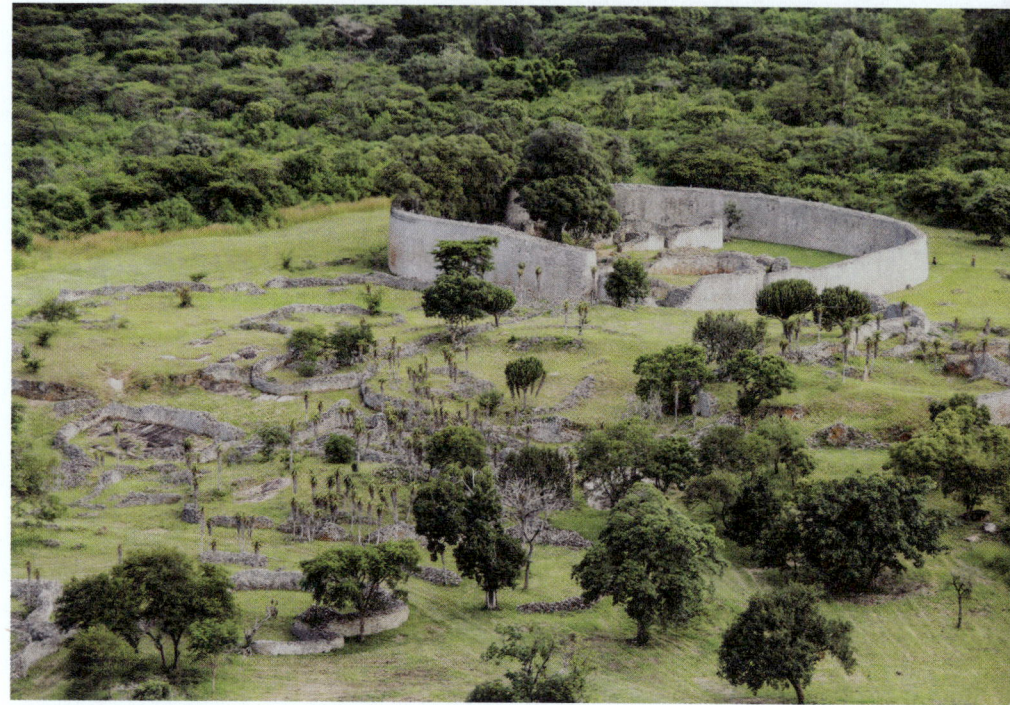

The ruins of Great Zimbabwe with the Great Enclosure at the back, surrounded by smaller stone-walled enclosures.

The Arrival of the Bantu

The city of Great Zimbabwe emerged in southern Zimbabwe from a local iron-producing agricultural community. These people have generally been attributed to the Bantu-speaking early Shona people, who migrated south in the middle of the first millennium CE into the Limpopo River Valley. These farmers grew crops, smelted iron for food preparation, had agriculture and jewellery, and settled into communities of farming villages, attaching much of their wealth to cattle and cattle ownership.[1] Within a few centuries, these communities were trading locally with each other for items such as pottery, copper and iron jewellery, cattle sharing, and salt. This tradition of exchange expanded in the mid-seventh century, when contact with the Indian Ocean coast began. These farmers then began to trade internationally. This contact with the outside world allowed these communities to increase their wealth and complexity, as well as their social stratification. Increased wealth meant more political power, and state-like formations throughout Zambezia, like that of Mapungubwe, began to appear.

The Mapungubwe state rose to prominence from 1100–1280 CE and thrived both locally and through international trade. The elites settled on the main hill of the site, the common people in the valley below. Hilltop settlements were much roomier than those in the valley, and the elite who lived and died there were buried with rich grave goods. The construction of their houses also differed, with chiefs living in *dhaka* (a clayey soil bound together with fine gravel) houses and commoners constructing their homes out of clay and wattle.[2] Mapungubwe enjoyed prosperity for almost two hundred years, trading and enjoying foreign imports such as glass beads from India and porcelain from China. In the second half of the twelfth century, Mapungubwe began to decline as an important trading centre, possibly due to droughts and shifting trading activities. Political power and centralisation then shifted three hundred kilometres north to Great Zimbabwe.

Great Houses of Stone

Rising to prominence around 1270 CE, Great Zimbabwe was the centre of a larger, powerful sector of allied ancestral groups. It was also the largest precolonial state in southern Zambezia and is home to the largest stone structures in Sub-Saharan Africa, their size second in the entire continent only to the Pyramids at Giza.[3] Because it is located along the shortest route between the rivers in the north that were panned for gold and other precious metals, and the Indian Ocean, Great Zimbabwe most likely controlled the mediaeval gold trade.[4]

Ivory, gold, and other precious trade items were taken to trading stations on the African coast, like Sofala. They were then loaded onto ships and taken up along the coast to other port cities on the continent before traders would use monsoon winds to reach destinations like southern Arabia, India, and possibly even China. After exchanging their goods for items like glass beads, textiles, and glazed ceramics, traders would ride the next monsoon winds home to spread their newly acquired treasures. Apart from this trade, Great Zimbabwe also gathered its wealth from cattle and local trade with other parts of Africa, trading things like tin ingots, iron bells, copper, and salt.

Great Zimbabwe must have developed a system for collecting taxes to garner the wealth needed to build the massive stone structures that the site is now so famous for.[5] The site of Great Zimbabwe itself is just one of over two hundred sites in southern Africa that are home to monumental stone buildings that were constructed without the use of mortar or any other binding material apart from gravity and human ingenuity. These structures are called *zimbabwe*, a word derived from the Karanga dialect of the Shona term *dzimba-dza-mabwe,* which translates to "houses of stone." It is also thought that the term could come from *dzimba-hwe,* which means "venerated houses" or "the chief's house."[6]

The stone buildings were constructed from granite quarried from the surrounding hills. Instead of being bonded together with mortar or another form of cement, the walls were abutted against one another to help with their stability. These massive stone walls are curved and often twice as high as they are wide, with added drains, doorways, and wooden lintels. Some walls are even decorated with chevron and other patterns and motifs which add to their sophistication and masterful construction.

Stone walls on a homestead signified elevated status in Great Zimbabwe. It was only the richest who lived in stone-walled homesteads and settlements, with regular people living in unwalled settlements or those made from *dhaka*. Apart from these walls, many of the houses that people lived in would have looked the same, though like today, the size of the house would have been based on the wealth of the owner. According to Shona tradition, homesteads consisted of many different living spaces: a kitchen, bedroom, dormitory for girls, dormitory for boys, and a visitor's house. On top of these, there were usually storage spaces like granaries. Despite their difference in size and wealth, these living spaces all conformed to a similar style. For example, cooking houses contained a central fireplace, a moulded bench, and a raised platform at the back of the house. Some also had built-in sockets or nooks for pots along the edges for storage.[7]

Where there is life, there is also garbage. Homestead middens (archaeological garbage dumps) have been found to contain ash, animal bones, spindle whorls, pottery, glass beads, and iron slag. One midden even had a key from a thumb piano called a *mbira* found in it.[8] With this material, archaeologists are able to get a better sense of how people lived in Great Zimbabwe. We now know there was music at some houses, metallurgy was practised, and, because many spindle whorls were found, weaving was important. People were spinning cotton and making their clothing at home. With so much activity taking place within the homestead, it must have been an important space where much of their daily work took place.

This emphasis on the home shouldn't overshadow what was happening outside of domestic spaces, though. Great Zimbabwe was a major trading centre, and some households kept one eye on the rest of the world. A hoard was found in the residence of someone who was possibly a trader, located in an area of the city called the Renders Ruin. It contained luxurious imported items such as a glazed Persian pot with Arabic script on it, a lamp holder, wire, tens of thousands of glass beads, a jade teapot, fragments of Chinese celadon pottery, copper finger rings, a bronze hawk bell, and even an iron spoon—a utensil not used by the Shona.[9] It's clear from this wide collection of items coming from various areas along the coast of the Indian Ocean that the people of Great Zimbabwe were collecting status symbols, and that they had power over trade and exchange in the larger area of Zimbabwe. While this power is hard to imagine today, the walls that signified it are not.

The Walls of the City

The site of Great Zimbabwe covers an area of 1,779 acres and consists of three major walled structures: the Hill Complex with the Eastern and Western Enclosures, the Great Enclosure, and the Valley Ruins. When looking at the overall layout of the site, it doesn't appear to have been designed around a central plan like many other ancient (or even modern) capital cities around the world. Instead, the site grew, shrank, and shifted with its changing population and status. Archaeologists have estimated that Great Zimbabwe could have had an urban population of around 18,000–20,000 people at its peak, but new research hints to a more conservative number of 10,000.[10] The ruling elite of Great Zimbabwe preferred to live on the hill, with the commoners dwelling below. This resulted in their isolation from the rest of the community until the stone structures in the lower valley were constructed in later centuries due to population growth.

The Hill Complex is the oldest part of the site, with evidence that farmers and hunters may have settled there as early as the fifth century.[11] The walls of the Western Enclosure, some reaching eight metres high and five metres wide, were the earliest to be built by the first rulers of Great Zimbabwe. Archaeologists have found gold, soapstone bowls, and bronze spearheads inside the enclosure, which have been interpreted to be symbols of kingship.[12]

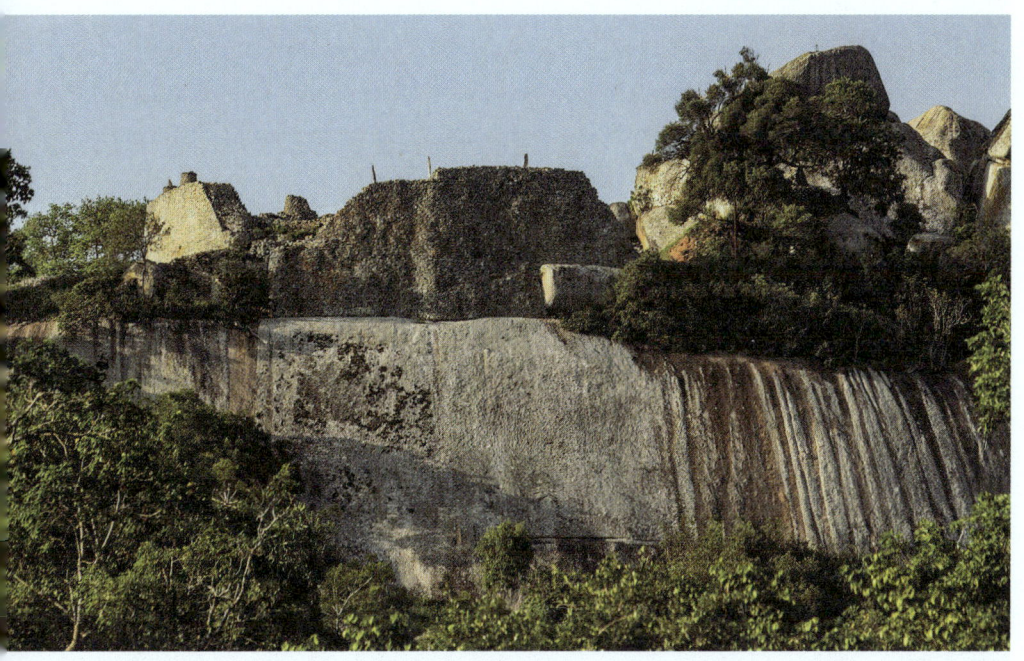

The Hill Complex of Great Zimbabwe.

Below the Hill Complex is the Great Enclosure, the largest stone-built structure in southern Africa. This huge enclosure was built at the height of Great Zimbabwe's power. The walls reach up to eleven metres high, measure over 250 metres around, and consist of over one million stones. An inner wall was constructed next to the outer wall to create a narrow passageway, and the enclosure also houses a nine-metre-tall conical tower measuring over five metres in diameter at the base. The function of the Great Enclosure is still not known. It has been thought to have housed the wives of the ruler or as an initiation school for adolescents to learn ethical and moral behaviour in order to become eligible for marriage. Recent studies on the walls of Great Zimbabwe, however, suggest that it was where the rulers resided after moving from the Hill Complex.

The power of the city then shifted towards the stone-walled Valley Enclosures in the early sixteenth century. This was the last place to become abandoned in Great Zimbabwe. The archaeological finds at all three of these proposed royal residences mentioned above are similar.

This might mean that instead of moving to a new place designated for royal residence when power shifted from one person to the next, the new ruler presided over the state from their original home. When looking at modern-day Shona traditions, this image of a rotating royal residence becomes a lot clearer. For the Shona, succession follows a system of "houses." If the founder of the state has multiple sons, the power will alternate to all of these houses after the death of the ruler, beginning from the eldest son to the youngest. The new rulers do not move into the residence of their deceased predecessor and choose to rule from their own homestead. From this point of view, it would seem that these three major areas within Great Zimbabwe were, at times, residences of rulers during the two hundred years that the city was dominating the trade of African goods along the coast of the Indian Ocean.[13] It was also these homes of former kings that were often associated with religious activities.

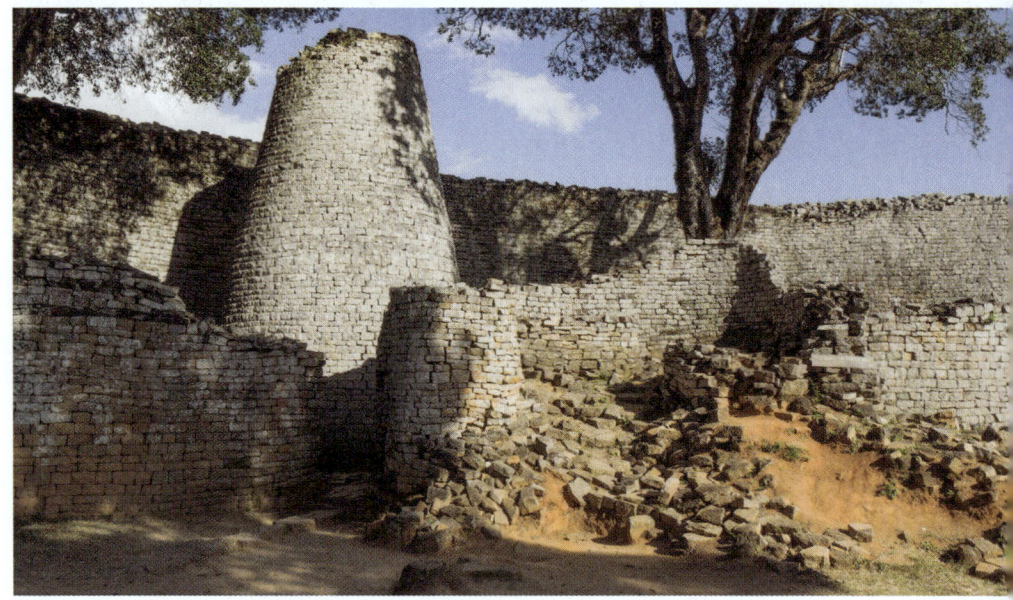

The Conical Tower inside the Great Enclosure.

On the Wings of Ancestors

The Eastern Enclosure located on the Hill Complex is thought to have been the ceremonial religious centre of Great Zimbabwe. While many rituals were practised at home,[14] ones pertaining to the greater state and the rulers were performed in a central area. Within the Eastern Enclosure, several green-grey coloured soapstone bird sculptures were unearthed. Each one is about thirty centimetres tall and shown perching on a pillar one metre in height. These birds are unlike any sculptures found in the area, and their original location within the enclosure is still unknown. What the birds represent has also been called into question over the years.

Continuing his mission to credit Great Zimbabwe to foreign builders, James Theodore Bent believed the birds represented the Assyrian goddess Astarte.[15] But the interpretation of these birds has much more meaning closer to home. In Shona symbolism some birds, like the bateleur eagle, are important messenger birds. They travel between the afterlife and Earth to pass on messages from ancestor spirits. For the Shona, spirits of former chiefs attend to national problems such as rain and epidemics, and because they are no longer earthbound by their physical bodies, they can fly like birds between the land of the living and the dead, communicating messages from God to the rulers.[16]

It is now generally accepted that these birds possibly represented the former rulers of Great Zimbabwe and their power. Each bird has a different pattern or markings, and none of them is identifiable as a local animal because of their unusual features, such as human-like limbs and toes. These birds continue to hold their importance for the modern country of Zimbabwe, with the national emblem being modelled after one of them. It appears on the national flag, the coat of arms, and the country's banknotes and coins.

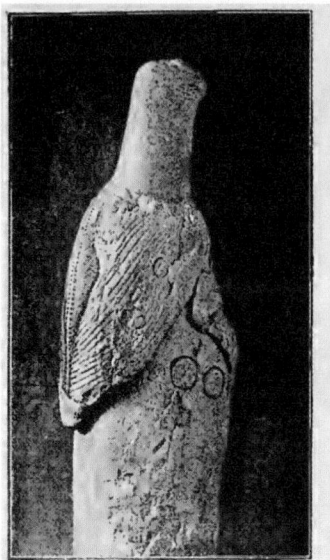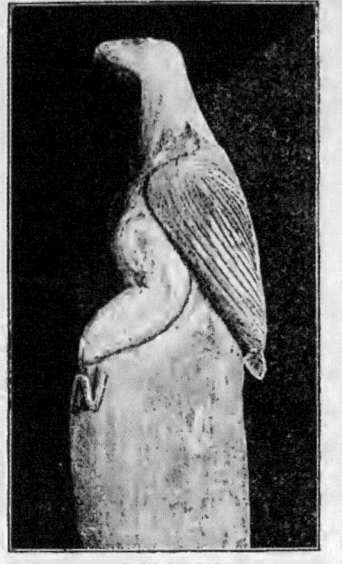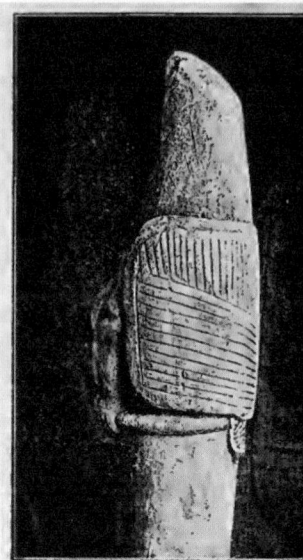

Soapstone birds of Great Zimbabwe.

Shifting Trade Winds

Great Zimbabwe emerged as a local agricultural community adept at making iron tools for everyday use. Through their accrued wealth of ownership of cattle, and strategic use of the commodifiable resources around them, they grew to become a major trading force along the mediaeval coast of the Indian Ocean. Once established, they rose to prominence in the late first millennium and continued to flourish until the fifteenth century, when other states began to gain more attention from the outside world.

The popularly accepted date for the collapse of Great Zimbabwe is around 1450, when populations began to abandon the site, moving to the Towra and Mutapa states as they rose to power and began taking over trading routes. However, new information has come out showing the coexistence of all three states for a while, with evidence that Great Zimbabwe continued to receive imports in the sixteenth and seventeenth centuries.[17] Other theories for its decline have been environmental degradation, overpopulation, or disputes regarding royal succession.[18]

Regardless of the reason, the decline in Great Zimbabwe's wealth and population did not mean the site was completely abandoned, as Karanga villages were still found in the area in the mid-nineteenth century. Great Zimbabwe lived on, but with another function—one that was not reflective of the centuries-old great walls that still towered over the farmers. The site may have been forgotten by outsiders once their trading moved elsewhere, but it was never lost to the Shona people. Even with the decades of suppression and attempts to use it for colonial gain, the walls of Great Zimbabwe and its descendants still stand, proud of their culture and heritage, their ancestors a mighty power that dominated the Indian Ocean.

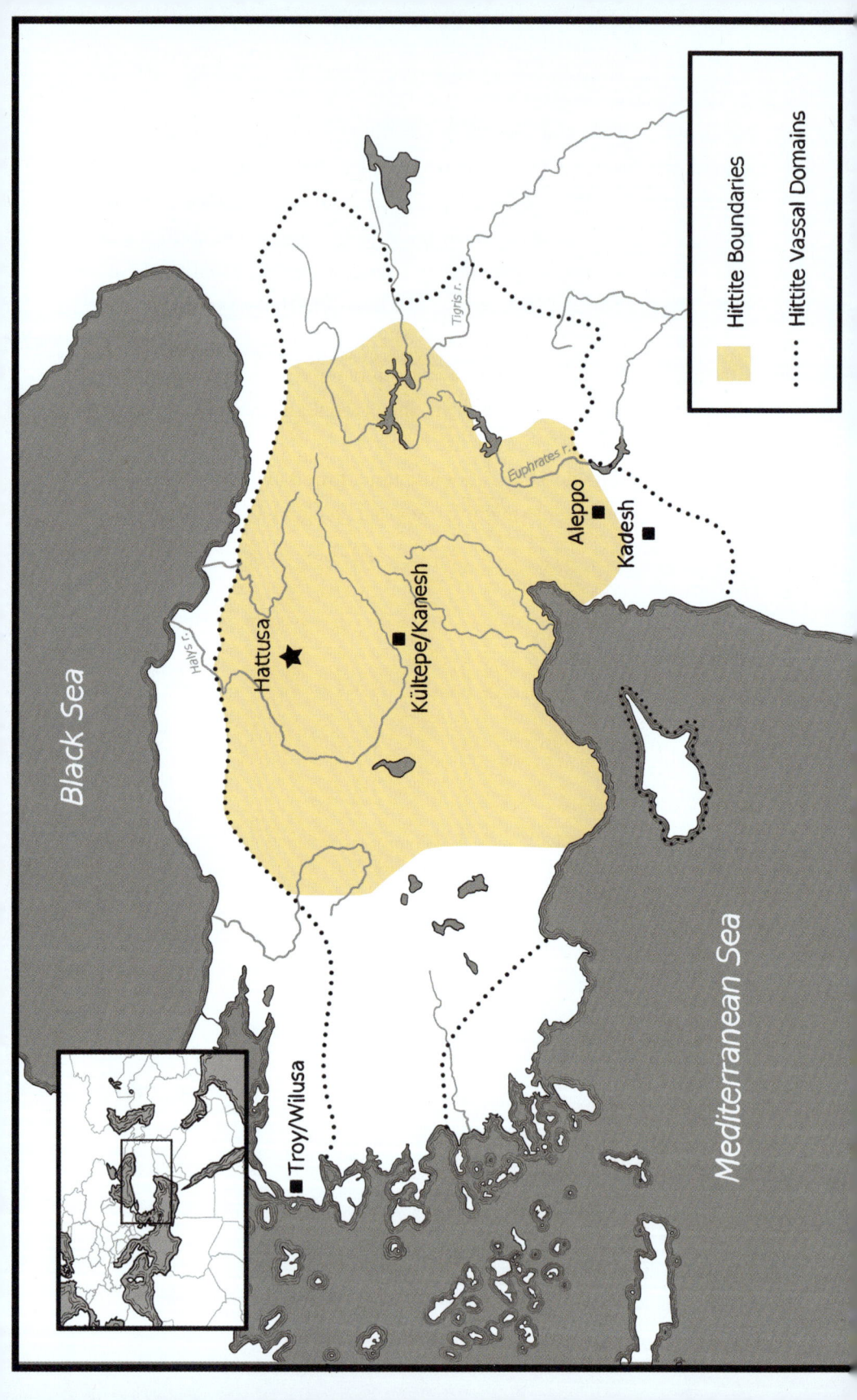

Chapter Five

Hittites

The Charioteers of Anatolia

The girl poked her head around the stable door, careful not to alert her father of her presence. Kikkuli didn't like to be disturbed when training a new horse, but she loved watching the master work. Kikkuli took the horse out of its box and led it out the other end of the building into the small, fenced paddock. The girl crept quietly through the stable to the other door to get a better view. She knew her mother would soon be wondering where she ran off to and she wanted to take advantage of this small sliver of freedom.

Crouching by the door, the girl watched as Kikkuli guided the horse through various drills of trotting and cantering around the paddock from the platform of his chariot. The horse was sure-footed and responded well to even the subtlest of her father's commands. From all her years watching her father train horses for the king's armies, she knew this one would help win many battles. Fighting the urge to sneak closer, the girl gaped at the flurry of hooves grabbing at the dirt and thundering in circles around the edge of the fence. In contrast to the girl's amazement, her father appeared unphased. He moved as one with the horse, his chariot a seamless extension of the animal. To the girl, he looked as though he was flying.

The girl could feel her legs starting to go numb in her cramped position. Trying to shift her weight, she lost her balance and toppled to the floor, knocking over the bucket that was next to the door.

Kikkuli slowed the horse down to a walk to see what the commotion was as the girl scrambled to her feet. The girl looked worriedly at her father, expecting him to be angry, but instead he was laughing, smiling at her curiosity. At that moment, the girl heard her mother calling for her from their house. Kikkuli reared the new horse and waved at his daughter. She giggled with joy as she watched the steed's front legs fly high in the air, then ran back home to answer her mother's call.

A Culture of Many

The Hittites were one of the greatest powers in the Near East during the second millennium BCE, rivalling both the Egyptians and the Assyrians, two powerhouses of the Bronze Age. Forming an empire at their capital city of Hattusa in Anatolia (modern-day Türkiye) around 1600 BCE, they soon went on to conquer areas across Asia Minor, Upper Mesopotamia, and the Levant less than three hundred years later. Despite their formidable power in the ancient world, no archaeological evidence of this civilisation and culture existed until the latter half of the nineteenth century. Before this, they existed only in brief mentions in the Hebrew Bible.

The origin of the Hittites remains a mystery to the archaeological world. Most scholars believe they were part of a larger Indo-European group from the steppes of Eurasia or north of the Black Sea, while others think that they originated in Anatolia. Regardless of how they arrived, it seems that centuries before the Hittites rose to power, they began to associate with and live alongside another lesser-known group indigenous to the region called the Hattians. It appears that the Hittites gained prominence and established a kingdom in the early seventeenth century BCE into which the Hattians were absorbed as they began to gradually adopt the Nesite or the Hittite strand of the Indo-European language family spoken by their new rulers.[1]

This absorption of other cultures became a defining trait of the Hittites. As they expanded their empire and brought more vassal states under their power, they became a mixed population made up of multiple Anatolian ethnicities, languages, and traditions, with other major influences probably coming from Mesopotamia and Syria. What gave the

Hittites their identity and set them apart was that they lived in a defined geographical region separated from their farther afield vassal states, the northern half of central Anatolia along the Kizil Irmak River. In fact, the Hittites did not refer to themselves as such. Our name for them comes from biblical references to several tribes living in southern Palestine, and a "Hittite nation," though the connection between them is unknown. The Hittites had no name for their people, referring to themselves solely as the people of the "Land of Hatti," a phrase used by the Assyrians and the ancient Egyptians who also referred to them as the kingdom of *Kheta*.[2]

A Dynasty of Kings and Chariots

Similar to how we classify ancient Egyptian chronology, the Hittite timeline is usually subdivided into an Old Kingdom (c. 1650–1500 BCE) and a New Kingdom (c. 1400–1200 BCE). A Middle Kingdom (c. 1500–1400 BCE) is also sometimes discussed, described to be like an Intermediate Period in ancient Egypt: a period of unrest and weakness in the empire. Labarna (?–1650 BCE) is regarded as the first ruler of the Hittite kingdom, and his military exploits set a precedent for all future warrior kings, where conquest and expansion of the empire were deemed compulsory. Labarna's successor, Hattusili I, moved the capital to Hattusa, which became the ceremonial and administrative centre of the empire.

Hattusili continued the tradition of military campaigns and territorial expansion, attacking cities that linked Anatolia with Syria and Mesopotamia. This was an important endeavour for the Hittites, as the establishment of vassal states all over Anatolia and northern Syria created a buffer zone between their main territory, protecting them from foreign threats and invasions.[3] These warrior kings therefore became the greatest military power in the Near East, powerful enough for Mursili (1620–1590 BCE), Hattusili I's grandson, to capture and destroy the cities of Aleppo and Babylon, bringing an end to the Babylonian dynasty.

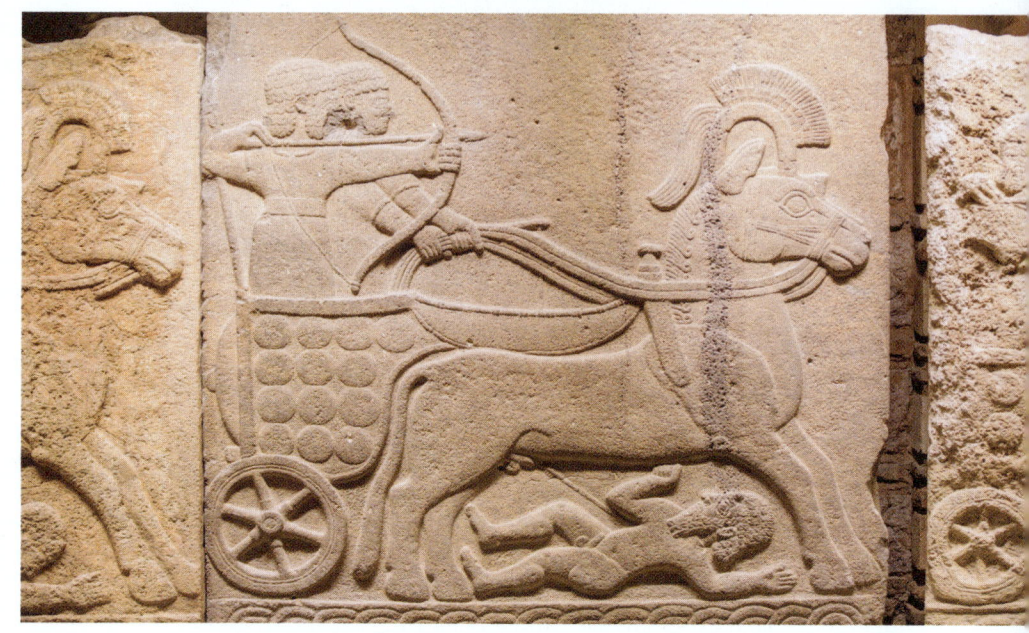

Hittite chariot.

One formidable aspect of Hittite warfare was their expert horsemen and charioteers. They took this form of battle extremely seriously, and the oldest known equestrian training manual was found at Hattusa. Written by a man named Kikkuli, this manual details a 214-day training program and covers diet, exercise regimes, drills, and more to ensure that chariot horses were in optimal health and performance for battle.[4] The chariots were constructed of wooden frames covered with animal hides, but they differed from the standard ancient chariots used by other civilisations such as the Egyptians and Mesopotamians. While standard chariots held two people (one driver and one fighter), Hittite chariots were modified by shifting the wheel axle from the back of the chariot to the front. This increased its stability and allowed for a third person on the chariot: the defender, whose job was to protect the other two with their shield so the driver could keep the chariot stable, and the fighter could focus on their attack. Those fighting on the chariot did so with spears and the composite bow, with quivers attached to the chariot box for easy access.

These constant military campaigns were a source of revenue for the Hittites because they collected tribute from vassal states and gained secure access to trade and supply routes. The sheer skill of their charioteers meant that they were formidable on land. While they generally stuck to what they knew, there is evidence of their engagement in naval battles. The first recorded sea battle took place in the mid-thirteenth century BCE between the Hittites and Cyprus, with the Hittites emerging victorious. Scholars believe that they used vassal or ally ships because of their inexperience with naval warfare.[5] The perks of military prowess don't come without their risks and consequences though. Campaigns are costly, and continuous fighting would have strained the Hittite economy. On top of this, the Hittites had an ongoing problem with a lack of manpower, meaning their homeland was left vulnerable and at risk of invasion for extended periods of time.

Finding the Balance Between Sacred and Secular

Since the majority of surviving Hittite texts are bureaucratic in nature and focus on royal endeavours, our understanding of everyday society and the daily habits of the people who lived in the empire are limited. The best resources we have to gain an understanding of everyday people lie in the archaeological record and their extensive law code.

Life in Hittite Anatolia was highly regulated, with everything and everyone working in the sole interest of the king and the welfare of the state.[6] Hittite society was agriculture-focussed, with farming and animal husbandry being the backbone of the economy. Villages were made up of households of extended families that supported themselves via livestock and farm plots. Streets were laid out as straight as possible and were covered with coarse gravel, while houses were made of wood-reinforced mudbrick built on top of stone foundations. Typical Hittite houses consisted of a lower level with at least two rooms and a courtyard that would have served as a front yard and a space for daily domestic activities.[7] A ladder would have been placed against the house within this courtyard to reach the upper story, and roofs were flat and made from mud and small branches, and supported by wooden beams. Houses were maintained and the mud mixture was replaced periodically to keep rain from entering through the cracks that formed over time. Rain seems to have been a concern for the Hittites as gutters were also created to carry rainwater away from the foundations.[8] Although they were careful with water entering their home, a major value of the Hittites was personal hygiene. It was of particular importance for those in the presence of the king, or who worked in the temples, and clay bathtubs have been found in houses that would have been used to help them stay clean.

Little is known about the daily life of Hittite people, but what we do know comes from their extensive law code. With over two hundred clauses that acted as guidelines and didn't focus on strict judgements or sentences, the Hittite law code, unlike others that were created around the same time, is entirely secular. Hittite law focussed greatly on family life and the protection of property. For example, marriages were arranged by the parents, and both parties maintained equal status if they were to get divorced. In the event of a separation, belongings were divided and the wife kept all but one child.[9] Of course, not everything was equal. In cases of adultery, the husband could punish his wife and her lover by sentencing them to death, though the death sentence was generally avoided due to the constant low population and need for manpower in Hittite territory.

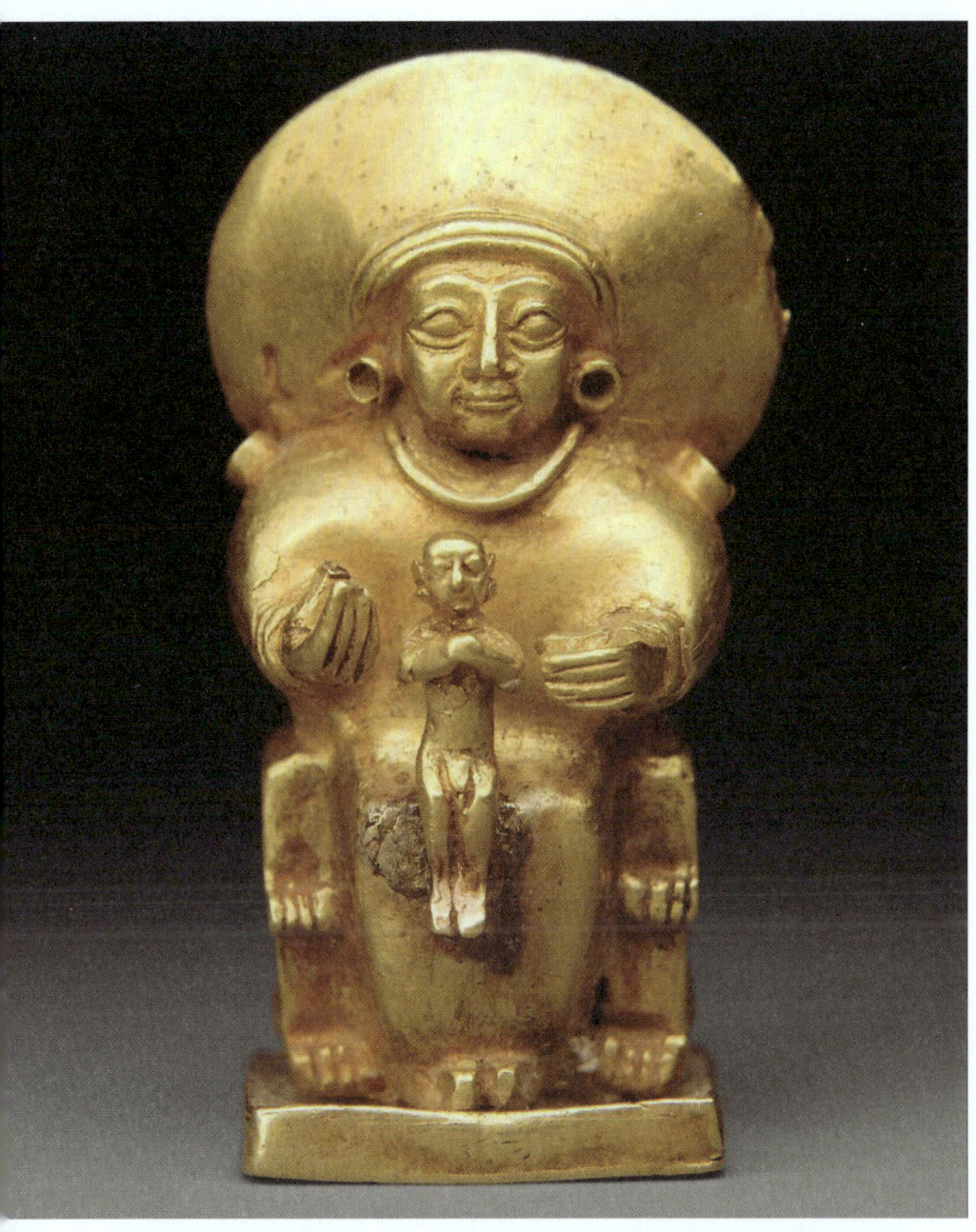

Small gold pendant of a seated goddess with a child. This tiny pendant was probably intended to be worn around the neck. Similar objects suggest that this was a portably representation of a Hittite goddess, possibly the sun goddess, Arinna.

While Hittite law was largely secular, religion was still an important part of society. The capital city of Hattusa was home to around thirty temples, the most important one being the Great Temple, home to the storm god and the sun goddess who ruled the Hittite pantheon. The storm gods were the most important to Hittite society as they brought rain and wind to fertilise their crops. The Hittites also adopted the practice of bringing back and worshipping deities from conquered territories to Hatti and referred to themselves as the "land of a thousand gods." This term symbolised their openness to accepting foreign gods into their pantheon, while also cementing their power onto these newly controlled states as they believed they were given divine permission from those divine beings to take the territories that worshipped them.[10] What's unique about the Hittites is that while they brought in foreign gods, they never combined or identified them with their own pantheon like the Romans often did, even if they were similar.

From the Battlefield to the United Nations

As the Hittites grew in power and territory, they began attracting the attention of other major Bronze Age powers, ancient Egypt in particular, as they became a threat along Egypt's borders. This led to increasing tensions between the two military forces that came to a head at the Battle of Kadesh (c. 1274 BCE) between Muwatalli II of the Hittite Empire and Ramesses II of Egypt. The battle itself took place along the Orontes River in Kadesh and is considered to be one of, if not the largest, chariot battles in history, consisting of over five thousand chariots.[11] The battle ended with both sides claiming victory, though evidence shows that the Hittites retained power over Kadesh and other surrounding areas. While accounts of the battle from both sides exist, Ramesses II was diligent in his retelling of events and recorded his version on the walls of five Egyptian temples, giving us one of the most detailed (although biassed) accounts of an ancient battle.

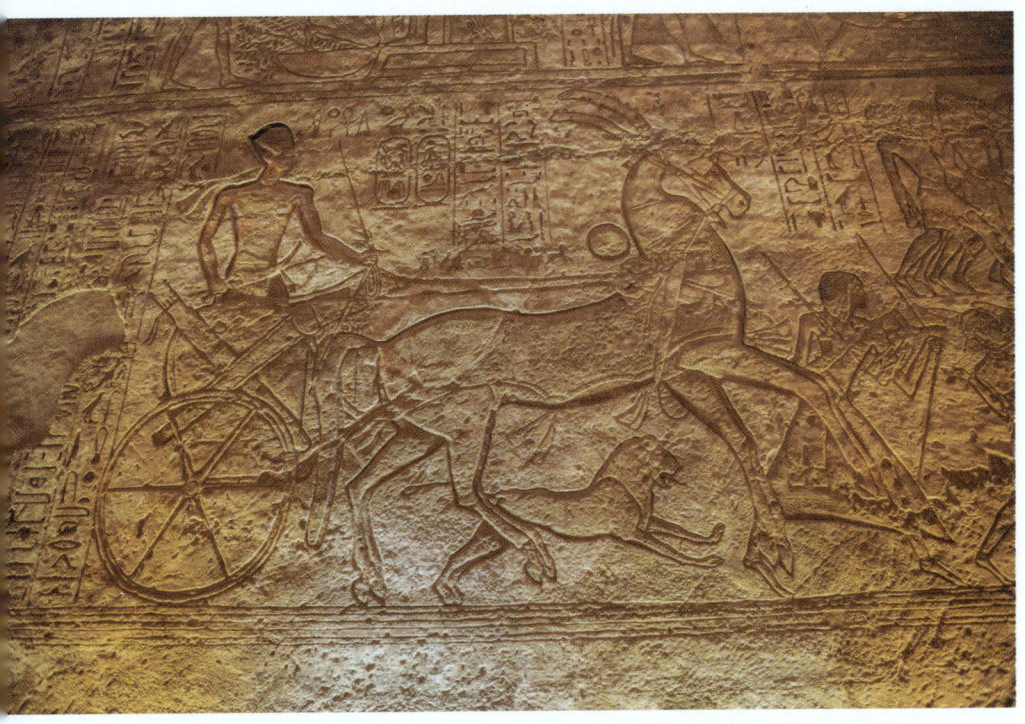

Relief carving of Ramesses II on a chariot during the Battle of Kadesh at Abu Simbel.

After the death of Muwatalli II, Hattusili III came to power, and fifteen years after the Battle of Kadesh, he set his sights on making peace with Egypt. Together, he and Ramesses II drew up the first international peace treaty in history. Both parties agreed on "eternal peace," vowing not to invade each other again, and created boundaries to prevent future disputes in Syria. The treaty also included stipulations that required both parties to return any fugitives. The Hittite version was originally written in Akkadian cuneiform and cast on a bronze tablet that has since been lost to history. But as luck would have it, a clay copy was discovered during excavations at Hattusa. The Egyptian version can be found inscribed on the walls of Karnak Temple and the Ramesseum in the surrounding areas of modern-day Luxor. This treaty has been deemed so important to human history, that a replica of the cuneiform version hangs near the entrance of the Security Council Chamber of the United Nations as a reminder of peace to all world leaders.

When Your Greatest Power Becomes Your Downfall

The Hittites gained their prominence through military conquest, but the continuous campaigning coupled with Hatti's constant shortage of manpower affected their ability to produce enough food to sustain the empire alongside maintaining an army, especially when any sort of military activity results in inevitable casualties.[12] This strain on human resources seems to have been coupled with increasing food shortages and unrest in the vassal states towards the end of the empire and during the reign of the last king of the Hittites, Suppiluliuma II (1207–1178 BCE). The fall of the Hittites also appears to correspond with a mass migration that swept through Anatolia, Syria, Palestine, the coast of Egypt, and the eastern Mediterranean in the early twelfth century BCE: the Sea Peoples.

Juniper tree-ring samples studied from central Türkiye indicate that a devastating drought hit Hittite territory from 1198–1196 BCE, which some scholars believe could have been the main reason for the collapse of the Hittite Empire.[13] While archaeologists have found grain silos at Hattusa, their capacity would have only been able to feed 20,000–30,000 people for a year, meaning they would have quickly run out of food.[14] This drought would have increased their dependence on grain from vassal states, causing these outlying territories to fall onto hard times of their own, breaking down the entire tributary system. For example, an increased tribute to Hatti was demanded from the vassal city of Emar in Syria, resulting in inflation and food shortages which left people no other choice but to sell their children to survive. The stele of Merneptah in Karnak, Egypt (c. 1213–1203 BCE) also mentions shipments of grain that were

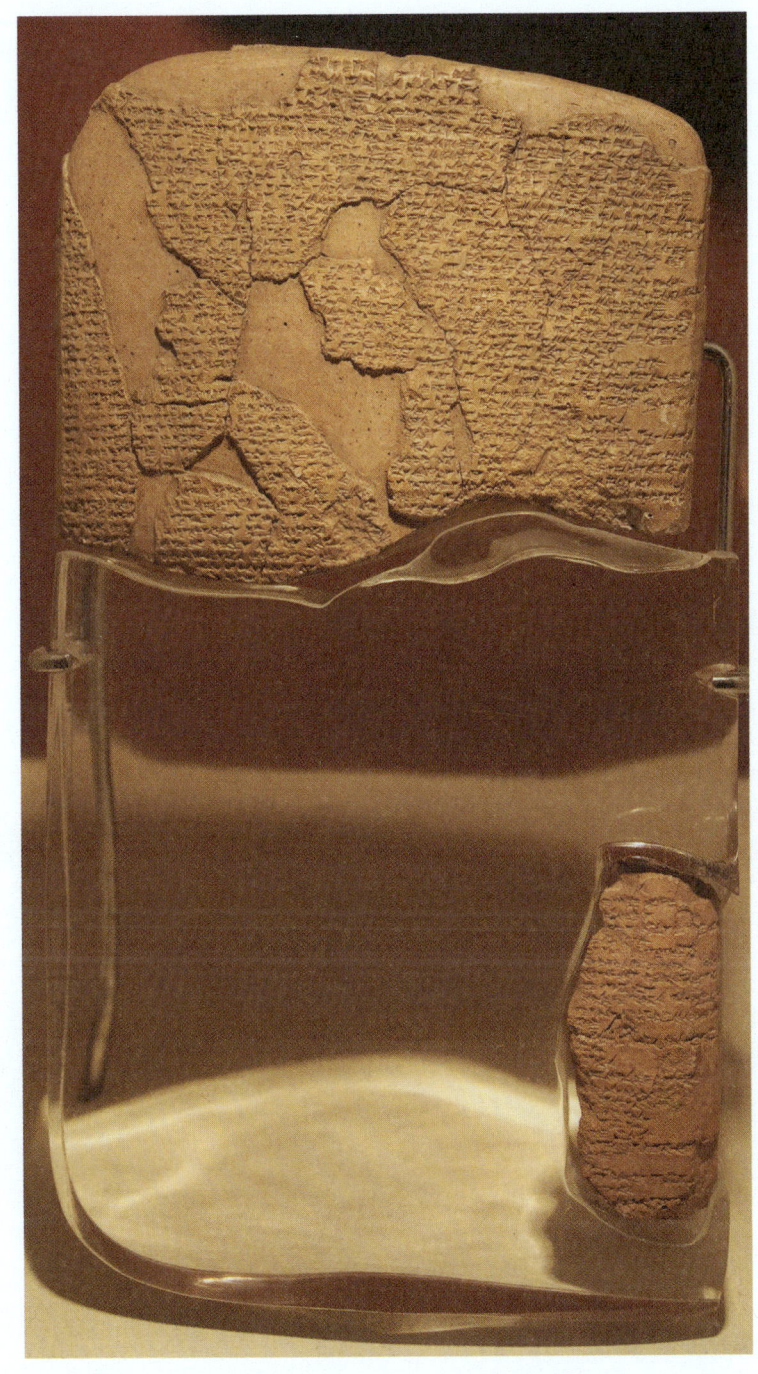

Hittite tablet of the Treaty of Kadesh.

sent to "keep alive the Land of Hatti," further alluding to the fact that the Hittites could no longer feed themselves and their vassal empire was collapsing.[15]

The Hittite Empire is thought to have fallen around 1180 BCE during the Bronze Age Collapse, a period of upheaval that saw the end of the Mycenaeans in Greece, and other Near Eastern kingdoms like Ugarit. According to ancient Egyptian texts, this period is thought to have been brought on in part, alongside climate change and internal strife, by the infamous Sea Peoples. The identity of the Sea Peoples is still unknown. Some theories believe they were Mycenaeans or Philistines, though it is likely that they were a mix of various groups who had no choice but to flee their homeland during the tumultuous end of the Bronze Age, bringing mass destruction and migration into increasingly fragile areas.

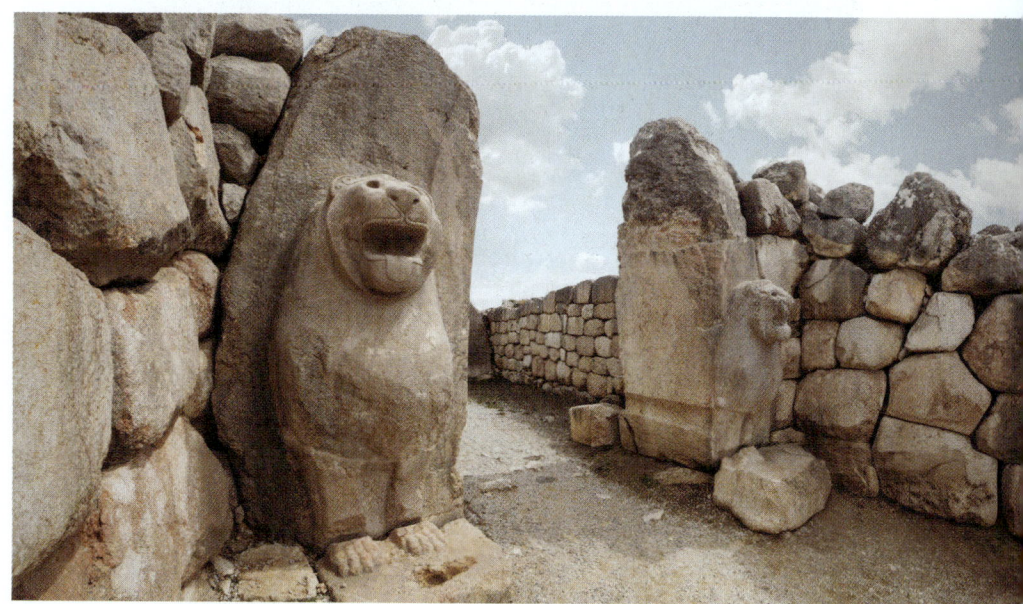

Lion's Gate at Hattusa.

Hattusa was abandoned at the end of the empire, and archaeological investigation shows later evidence of it being burned down. It seems that it was already evacuated prior to its destruction, as no remains of personal items, furniture, or major cultic items were uncovered during excavations of the city. The abandonment of the city appears to have been planned, with the royals choosing to pack up their belongings and leave, like many other urban sites in central Anatolia during this time.[16] After that, a small portion of the Luwian-speaking Hittite population (another Anatolian Indo-European language branch that became the dominant language during the New Kingdom) appears to have relocated to southeast Anatolia and northern Syria, where small Syrio-Hittite or Luwian-Aramaean kingdoms appeared. The Hittites themselves disappeared from history and lay waiting to be rediscovered until the nineteenth century.

Can the Hittites Prove the Trojan War Happened?

The infamous war between the Greeks and the Trojans that was immortalised in Homer's *Iliad* and *Odyssey* has captured imaginations for millennia. The search for the site of Troy culminated with Heinrich Schliemann undertaking the first large-scale excavations of the site of Hisarlik, located close to the Dardanelles/Hellespont, that would have held a large harbour during the Bronze Age in modern-day Türkiye. Most scholars now agree that Hisarlik can be identified as the remains of Homer's Troy. Since the Trojan War took place in Late Bronze Age Anatolia, Hittite texts may provide us with some clues to help determine if this fabled war actually took place.

In the 1920s, a Swiss scholar by the name of Emil Forrer claimed that he had discovered references to the Homeric Greeks in Hittite texts.[17] He proposed that the place name of Ahhiyawa was Hittite for the Greek name Achaiwia, which is the archaic form of Achaia (in Homer, the Greeks are called the Achaians). Today we call them the Mycenaean Greeks, and evidence points to them having close contact with western Anatolia at the end of the Late Bronze Age.

Another exciting piece of evidence hinting at Troy and a conflict with the Achaeans comes from the Tawagalawa Letter, a fragmentary Hittite text dating to the thirteenth century BCE. This letter was written by a Hittite king (thought to be Hattusili III, who ruled c. 1267–1237 BC) to the king of Ahhiyawa.[18] This letter mentions a former conflict between the Hittites and the Ahhiyawans over a territory called Wilusa, which is most likely the Hittite name for the Greek word *Ilios*, and what Homer called Troy.

Hittite texts state that Wilusa was subject to several attacks during the thirteenth century BCE. The reasons for these attacks are more likely to have been for more practical reasons instead of the Spartan king Menelaus seeking revenge and launching over a thousand ships to get his wife, Helen, back. The reason for an attack could have been due to a dispute over Greek merchant ships passing through the Hellespont. Troy may have tried to exert their power and control over this area by blocking ships from sailing through, or imposing tolls.[19] Regardless of the reasons for these attacks, now that we have documented evidence of conflicts between western Anatolia and the Mycenaeans, we can begin to understand the real events that could have inspired Greek poems and plays about Mycenaean kings and their exploits in Anatolia.

Archaeologically speaking, layer VIIa at Troy is the most likely candidate for evidence pointing to a Trojan war. This layer existed around the same time as the Hittites and was destroyed at the end of the thirteenth century BCE. Furthermore, the discovery of a seal with Luwian script at Troy provides another tie to the Hittites, and a possible connection to the site being identified as Wilusa. As this is the only known evidence of Bronze Age writing though, it must be taken with a grain of salt. The Luwian Seal is a small, transportable object, meaning that it could have been brought from anywhere and dropped on site. Until more substantial evidence is found, this one piece does not mean that Luwian was spoken by the people of Troy. Regardless, the Hittite connection and the archaeology behind the fantastical story of Troy only add to the imagination of what is yet to be discovered about the former rulers of Anatolia.

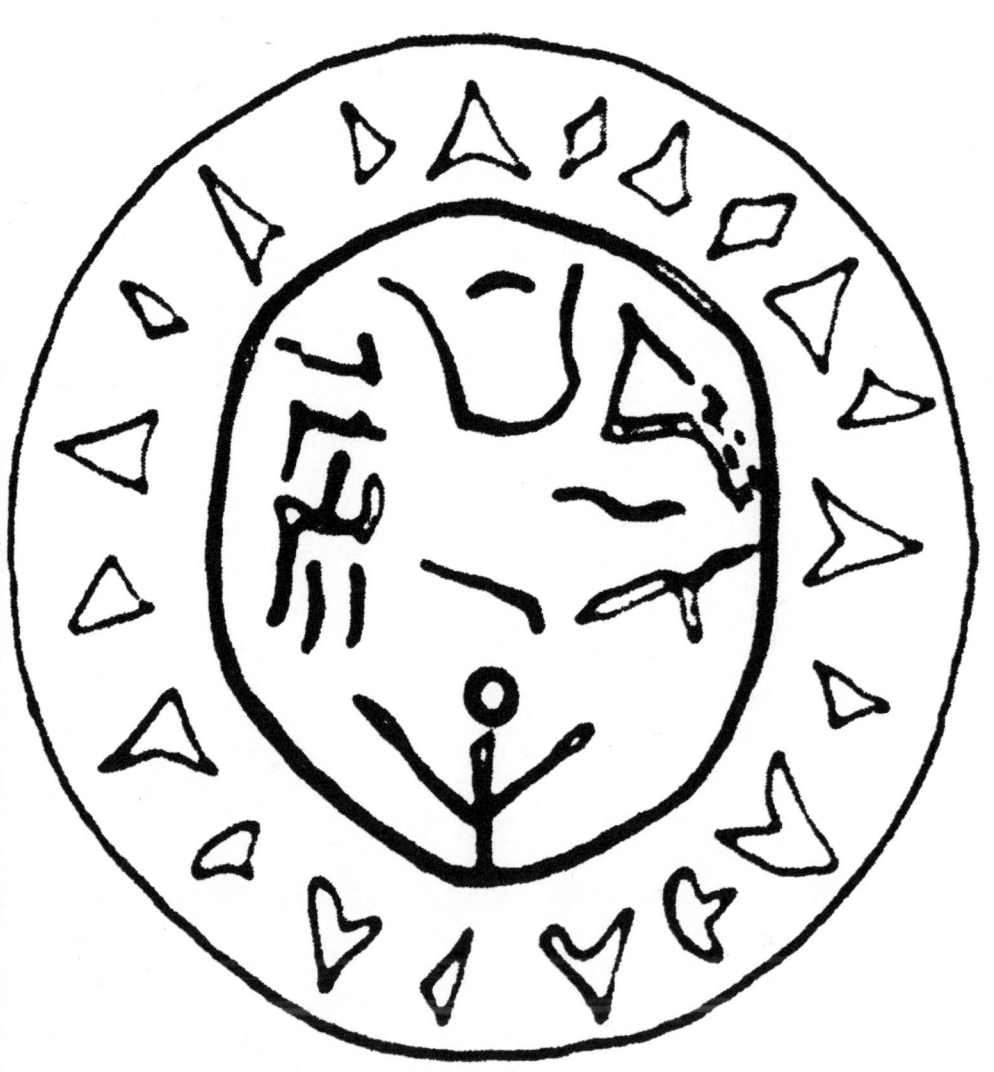

Drawing of the inscription on the Luwian Seal found at Troy.

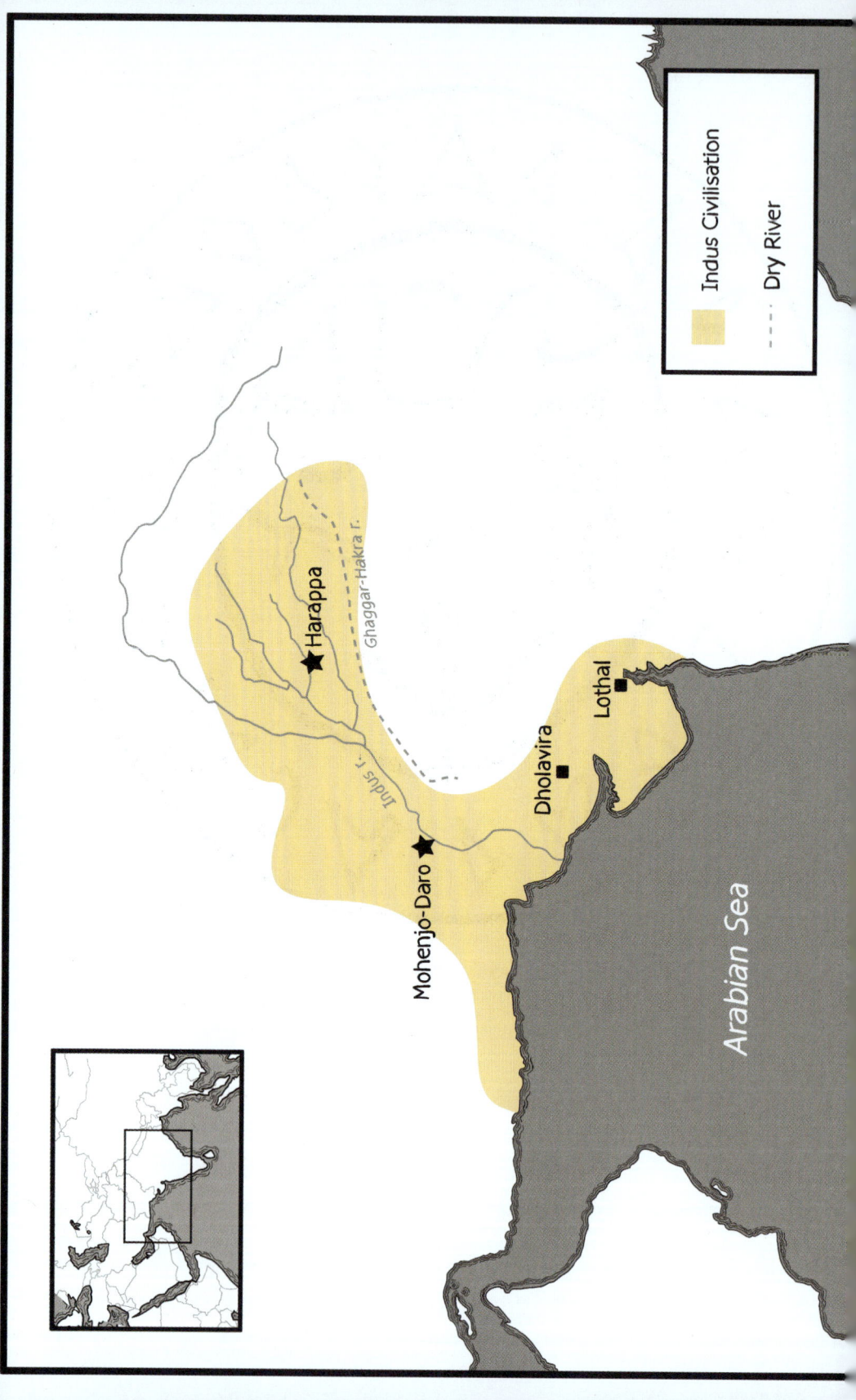

Chapter Six

Indus Valley
A Bronze Age Utopia?

"Come on...get out of there!" The man leaned his shoulder farther into the drain opening, angling his hooked rod to grab at the blockage. His legs were splayed out on the road for extra support, and he was thankful that his early start to the day meant that most of the city was still waking up. The fewer witnesses to his awkward stance and mumblings into sewers, the better.

After five years of maintaining the city's drains and sewers, the man was an expert on swiftly removing buildup, but this one was making him question his abilities. From the feel of it with his rod, someone had dumped wet clay into the drains instead of one of the many sump pots conveniently placed around the city. Some sticks had gotten lodged in there in the aftermath, making the problem even worse.

"Some people are so inconsiderate," he muttered to himself. The man removed his arm and stuck his head into the drain to get a better look, careful that his hair didn't touch the murky water below. The stench would stick to him for weeks, and his wife would make him sleep in the courtyard until it went away.

"Ah, there's the problem!" He repositioned his rod and with one sharp jerk, knocked the sticks and jolted the clay free. He scooped up his adversary and deposited it into the reed basket next to him. It was already filled to the brim with other waste he had collected from the public sump pots during his morning rounds.

Satisfied with a decent day's work, the man returned the brick that acted as the drain cover to its rightful place on the street. He then picked up his basket and hauled it onto his cart so it could join the others he had filled that morning. Climbing up onto the seat, he spurred on his ox and began the journey to the dump site outside the city walls, already dreaming of the shower waiting for him once he got home.

Ahead of Its Time, then Lost to Time

The Indus Valley, or Harappan (named aptly after one of the major cities) civilisation spanned an area more widespread than the territories of ancient Egypt and Mesopotamia combined with a population of perhaps one million people, numbers not seen again until the height of ancient Rome. It extended from northeast Afghanistan, down into Pakistan and India. Yet despite its size, its remains lay unnoticed, waiting to be discovered until the 1920s by Indian and British archaeologists. Since then, over a thousand settlements have been identified around the valley of the Indus River and the Ghaggar-Hakra River system, which has been identified as the possible defunct remains of the Sarasvati River mentioned in the Rig Veda.[1]

We first find written evidence of the Indus Valley civilisation from Mesopotamian texts around 2400 BCE under the name of Meluhha, describing it as a distant land to the east, where treasures such as gold, carnelian, and tin could be found.[2] Meluhha disappears from their texts by 1700 BCE, and subsequently fades into obscurity to the rest of the world. Neither Alexander the Great, who ventured into the Indian subcontinent in the fourth century BCE, nor Asoka Maurya, the emperor who ruled most of it in the following century, made any mention of this once vast and technologically advanced civilisation. Thus, beginning a trend that would continue for the next two millennia.

Since its discovery, we have finally come to understand the importance and influence of the Indus Valley civilisation. The people of the Indus and Ghaggar-Hakra Rivers were master urban planners, innovative geniuses, and skilled crafts workers and appear to have been part of a peaceful and egalitarian utopia. They sailed as far as the Persian Gulf to trade their finely crafted beads and plentiful resources with Magan in present-day Oman, Dilmun in Bahrain, and Mesopotamia. The Harappans also created a sewer and drainage system that included the earliest known indoor toilets. Although we've learned so much about this ancient civilisation in the last hundred years, many unanswered questions remain regarding the Bronze Age settlements of the Indus. Were they as peaceful as archaeologists once believed? Who was in charge of these large public works and international endeavours? And what ultimately led to their demise?

A Uniform Utopia?

While the Early Harappan Period, which saw the establishment of the first few settlements and towns, began around 4000 BCE, the Mature Period that marked the height of the Indus civilisation began in 2600 BCE. During this transition, many of the Early sites were abandoned or destroyed by fire and resettled, and major sites like the largest Indus city, Mohenjo-Daro, were built on virgin soil. The reason for such a dramatic change is unknown, but it's possible this was done to cut ties with a previous way of life or to ritually cleanse a site for a new beginning.[3] Regardless of the reason, this step would have required a large, collective investment in time, resources, and organisation.

The Mature Period is defined by an explosion of settlements and the emergence of major cities such as Mohenjo-Daro, Harappa, Dholavira, and Lothal. These cities were spread across the entire extent of the civilisation among smaller towns and farmsteads that would have all been interconnected. While much of the archaeological work and discourse has focussed on the two largest cities, Mohenjo-Daro and Harappa, they by no means define the Indus civilisation, especially as the majority of the population lived outside such cities and were farmers and pastoralists.[4] That being said, Harappa is the only major Indus site that was settled from the Early Period around 3500 BCE, through to the Late Period and the civilisation's decline around 1900–1700 BCE. This level of continuous habitation therefore provides archaeologists with vital information of the history of the Indus civilisation.

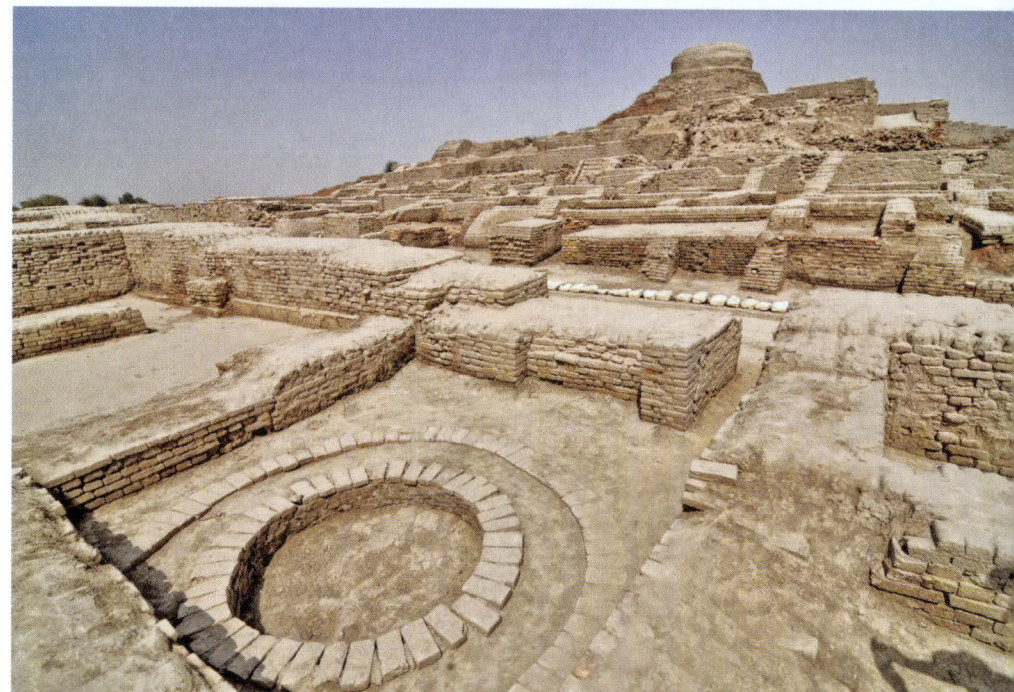

Mohenjo-Daro

With this explosion of settlements came the adoption of widespread uniformity and urban planning. Many sites, such as Mohenjo-Daro, Harappa, and Lothal, were built on platforms made from mudbrick and burnt brick intentionally laid out and constructed to build a settlement above the floodwaters. These platforms alone were feats of mass organisation and planning. It's been estimated that the platform at Mohenjo-Daro would have taken approximately 25,000 people working for over four years to complete it.[5] Streets within settlements were oriented to the cardinal points, though not everything was a perfect grid. While the main streets followed this pattern, the residential side streets were often crooked, and house walls were built at angles. These streets were probably dotted with trees, either for shade or religious purposes, and in some parts of the sites of Mohenjo-Daro and Kalibangan, brick platforms were built outside houses that may have acted as public benches, allowing people to meet, sit, and connect.[6]

Houses and public buildings also had elements of uniformity. At every site, bricks were created using the ratio of 1:2:4 for their dimensions. For example, bricks used for the construction of houses measure seven by fourteen by twenty-eight centimetres, and those made for constructing city walls measure ten by twenty by forty centimetres.[7] Rather than being a state-issued regulation, it appears that the development of this uniformity was probably the result of trial and error, with knowledge being passed down between generations and shared across communities.[8] Archaeologists have also uncovered four examples of graduated rules. These were likely used by craftsmen such as architects and carpenters for measuring lengths and were made of terracotta, shell, ivory, and copper.

This uniformity wasn't restricted solely to public architecture. The people of the Indus Valley civilisation participated in trade, both throughout their territory to share in their abundant natural resources as well as abroad, reaching other notable far away cultures like ancient Mesopotamia. For this trade, they devised a universal system of standardised stone weights that have been found at every Indus site. These stone cubes and truncated spheres were made with exceptional precision out of banded chert, agate, or coloured jaspers, and their system bears no resemblance to other ancient civilisations, even though they were in frequent contact with them. Most scholars believe these weights would have been used for exchanging goods in markets, but could also have been used for taxation because not enough have been found to indicate that everyone would have used weights for everyday transactions.[9] It's clear that the various groups of people comprising the Indus civilisation shared an affinity of uniformity. To achieve this, every site must have been in contact with the other, and open communication and sharing of ideas and values would have been the pillars of this society.

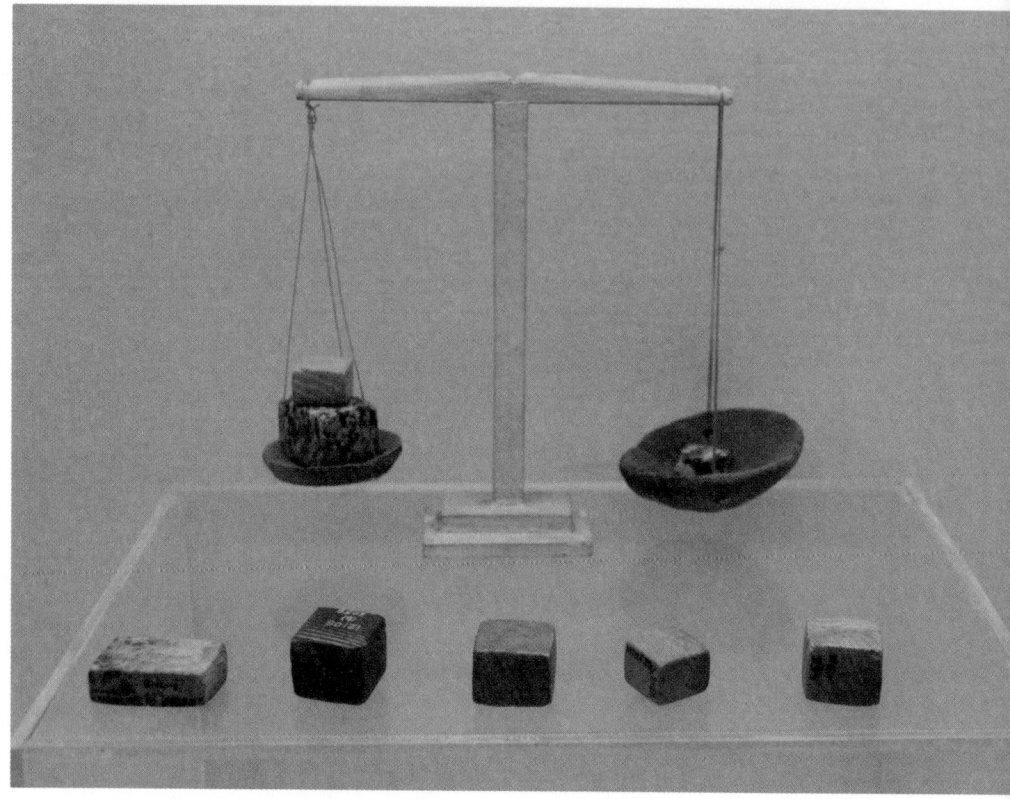

Examples of Indus weights. The weights are based on a complex system, but the base weight may have been based on a black and red seed known as the gunja, weighing on average 0.109 grams. The smallest known Indus weight is equal to eight of these gunja seeds, weighing 0.871 grams, with the largest coming in at the equivalent of 100,000 gunja seeds and weighing approximately 11.3 kilograms. This weight system is still used today by jewellers in present-day Pakistan and India.

Same, but Different

The people who inhabited Indus cities lived in multi-storied houses of various sizes that would have likely been decorated with colourful plaster and had windows with wooden shutters that were covered with wooden or stone lattice grilles to allow airflow. Houses acted as a private space away from busy city life, a necessity with populations reaching upwards of 40,000 at Mohenjo-Daro. Entrances to homes were located off back lanes, and life took place on the light and airy (and presumably quieter) second floor. Daily domestic activities such as food preparation, weaving, and storage most likely occurred in the open courtyard on the ground floor.

The people of the Indus Valley put the same amount of care and thought into their cities' public and monumental buildings as they did their homes. Most cities had a raised or walled-off area that most scholars call "citadels," although there is no evidence of them being used for defence. It's believed that the buildings in these "citadels" could have functioned as administrative or religious structures, but there is also evidence of residential buildings inside them.[10] The buildings within these walls varied in size, shape, and function for each city. Even though we don't know how Indus Valley society was governed, the separation of these public buildings either by building them on a hill or behind walls to restrict access could mean that some civic authority was recognised and were responsible for city planning. That being said, because there is no evidence of regulated uniformity in these "citadels," an authority institution that oversaw the entire area is questionable.[11]

Perhaps the most well-known public building in the Indus Valley is the Great Bath at Mohenjo-Daro. As the earliest known public water tank, it measures approximately twelve metres by seven metres and is 2.4 metres at its deepest point. The bath has two staircases that lead down into it, and the tank itself was made to be watertight by tightly fitting bricks together and covering the sides and possibly underfloor in a thick layer of bitumen. Because it's so unique and large, most researchers believe that the Great Bath was used for religious purposes of purification and renewal. The importance of water for the people of the Indus Valley went beyond this bath, though, and it permeated into their daily lives.

The World's First Toilets

Even though Indus cities were built upon platforms to protect them from the flooding of the rivers they were located near, their society was not one that feared water. Far from it, the Indus people held water in high regard, and strove to control it. They created water management and sanitation systems that were unheard of for their time, and not seen again until Roman times, two millennia later. Drains and sewage systems were built to help remove wastewater and other sewage from the city. They normally ran down the middle of the main streets, with smaller ones alongside houses on side lanes to catch wastewater that then flowed into these main sewer drains. The sides and bottoms of the sewers were built of carefully laid bricks set into clay mortar to prevent blockages and remove waste quickly and efficiently.

Most drains would have been covered in bricks similar to the rest of the street, and contained areas that had removable covers made out of a loose brick, flagstone or piece of wood for easy cleaning. Small heaps of sand have been found alongside drains at Mohenjo-Daro, showing they were regularly cleaned out to ensure a steady flow. Cesspits were strategically placed along the sewer systems to further help prevent blockages, and were especially useful in areas where multiple drains converged. In these pits, solids could settle to the bottom and be removed later, while liquids could flow freely out of the cities.[12] This widespread use of public sanitation, even in smaller towns and villages, exemplifies the importance of cleanliness and health in Indus society.

Cleanliness also played a large role in private domestic life. Houses had bathing and toilet facilities that wouldn't seem too different from today's. Bathing platforms in houses were usually located in a corner that connected to an outside wall and consisted of a two-metre square area

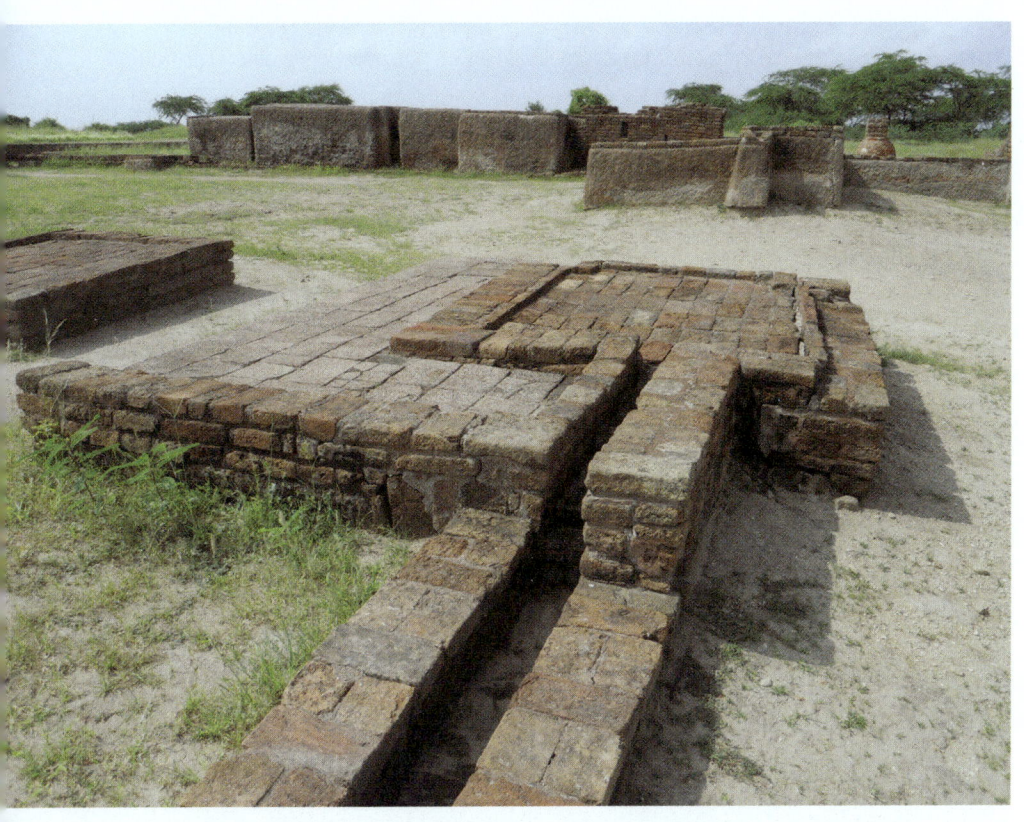

Remains of an Indus toilet and drainage system at the site of Lothal.

of specially laid bricks surrounded by a raised rim. These platforms usually sloped to one corner and connected to a drain that allowed wastewater to flow out into a soak pot or drain in the street. In many cases they also had a series of steps built into the back wall that would allow someone to climb up and pour buckets of water onto the person being cleaned.

The Indus Valley people also invented the first toilets. Made of baked brick or wood, some of these lavatories could even have seats, whereas others were simple holes in the floor, much like today. The toilets consisted of a vertical shaft that could be flushed by dumping water down it to flow into the city's drains or cesspits. Houses without direct access to the city's drains used a large jar or sump pot sunk into the floor that could seep out or drain liquids. These were cleaned out regularly, possibly by a workforce who would have been responsible for cleaning out the large sump pots that were placed around the city to collect household waste and seep out liquids into the sewers, as well as clearing drains.[13] Both the bathing platforms and toilets appear to have been part of everyday life for Indus settlements and were used by everyone. In fact, toilets were found in almost every house in Harappa.

To access the water needed for these activities, vertical shaft wells were constructed in public locations and in private houses. Over seven hundred wells were found in Mohenjo-Daro alone. The presence of private wells in the two largest cities of Mohenjo-Daro and Harappa, indicates that water cleanliness was an important issue in congested and increasingly polluted urban areas.[14] While these elaborate and advanced water management systems provided an efficient way to clear waste from the city and helped in protecting the population from disease, immense amounts of maintenance would have been needed to ensure they functioned properly.

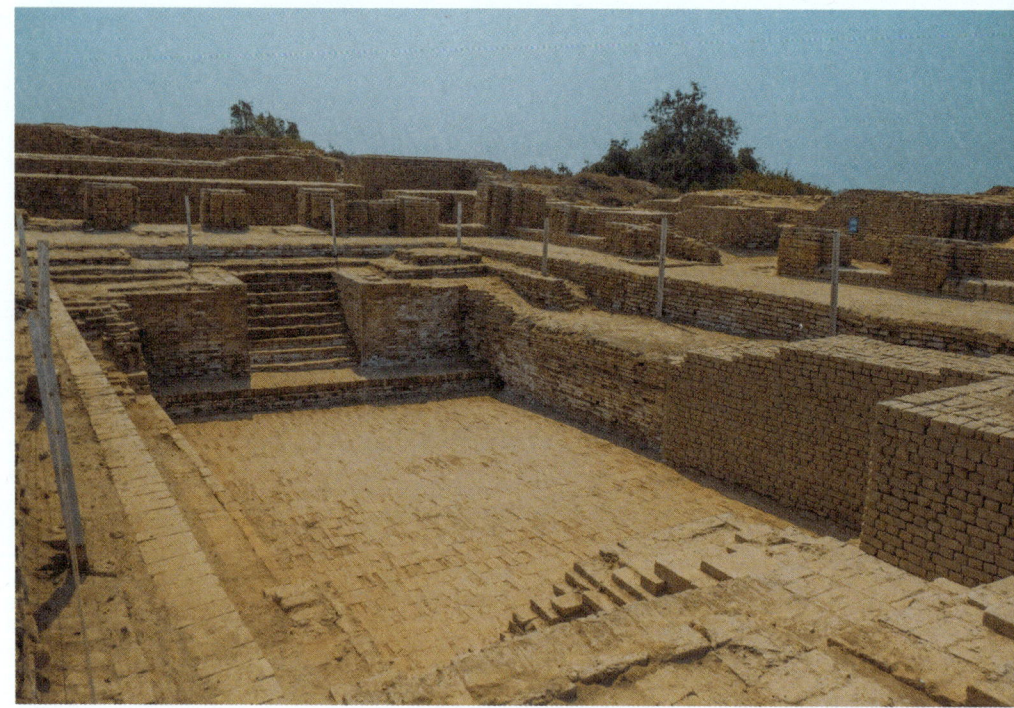

The Great Bath at Mohenjo-Daro.

Tens of thousands of people bathing and disposing of waste would have produced quite the smell that could have only been managed by a constant flow out of the city, and frequent cleaning by a specialised workforce. Evidence of the consequences of not maintaining these drains and sewers has been found at Harappa. In a later period of the city, sewage overflowed onto streets and into houses, forcing the city's inhabitants to raise the level of their doors and walls. Regardless of their shortcomings, the Indus sewers, baths, and toilets still proved beneficial to their society. Studies carried out on skeletal remains from Harappa found that the population was overall healthier than most other urban societies at the time.[15]

A Thirst for Adventure

On its own, the vast expanse of the Indus Valley civilisation covered a geographical area that provided every basic raw material needed for their society to thrive. Goods were circulated around settlements, cities and adjacent areas via road networks carried on wooden carts pulled by bulls, and by boat along the complex river systems. Craft objects produced in the large cities by artisans and specialists such as carved beads, seals, and jewellery would have been traded with pastoral communities for grain and produce to feed more urban areas. With all of this abundance surrounding them, it seems overseas travel to far-off lands would have been unnecessary, but the people of the Indus were active participants in international trade.

Mesopotamian texts from Akkadian King Sargon discuss ships from Meluhha, their term for the Indus people, docking at his capital of Akkad around 2300 BCE.[16] Other texts also state that Meluhha was the primary source for carnelian beads, which were highly prized and have been found in the royal cemetery of Ur. Some of the beads that have been found use the same techniques as those from the Indus Valley but are of different design. This might hint that Indus merchants were living in Ur at the time to sell their goods and create designs for the local population. While Mesopotamia benefitted from the acquisition of precious minerals from the Indus, it remains unclear what they were traded for. It has been suggested that the Indus people would have traded for popular Mesopotamian exports such as incense or wool, both of which would not have survived in the archaeological record.[17]

The Indus would have traded mostly within the Persian Gulf, with Magan and Dilmun, possibly swapping perishable goods such as pickled fruits and indigo dye for copper and shell. The evidence of such expansive international trade indicates that these boats can be considered quite a technological innovation, as Mesopotamian ships never ventured outside of the Gulf.[18]

Mysterious Symbols and Seals

The translation of the Indus script has eluded archaeologists and researchers since its discovery in the 1920s, and to date, over fifty different possible translations have been published. Over four thousand artefacts with these mysterious markings on them have been uncovered, primarily on stamp seals, pottery, and copper and bronze tablets. Around four hundred distinct signs of the Indus script have been identified that cannot be related to any other known script today. Unlike other ancient civilisations they were in contact with at the time, no long Indus inscriptions have been found to help identify the grammatical structure or other patterns in the script, and no bilingual texts have been found to aid with decipherment.

Their contact with Mesopotamia would have made them aware of writing systems used for taxation, trade and contracts, which has led scholars to believe that Indus texts used for trade and other official administration were most likely written on organic materials such as palm leaves. The most popular theory is that the Indus script is related to Dravidian languages that are spoken today in the Indian subcontinent. Another possibility is that it is related to the Austro-Asiatic language family that is spoken in India and across Southeast Asia. While linguists continue to try and crack the code, other scholars have suggested that due to the lack of long inscriptions found, the Indus signs aren't a script, but a series of religious symbols.[19]

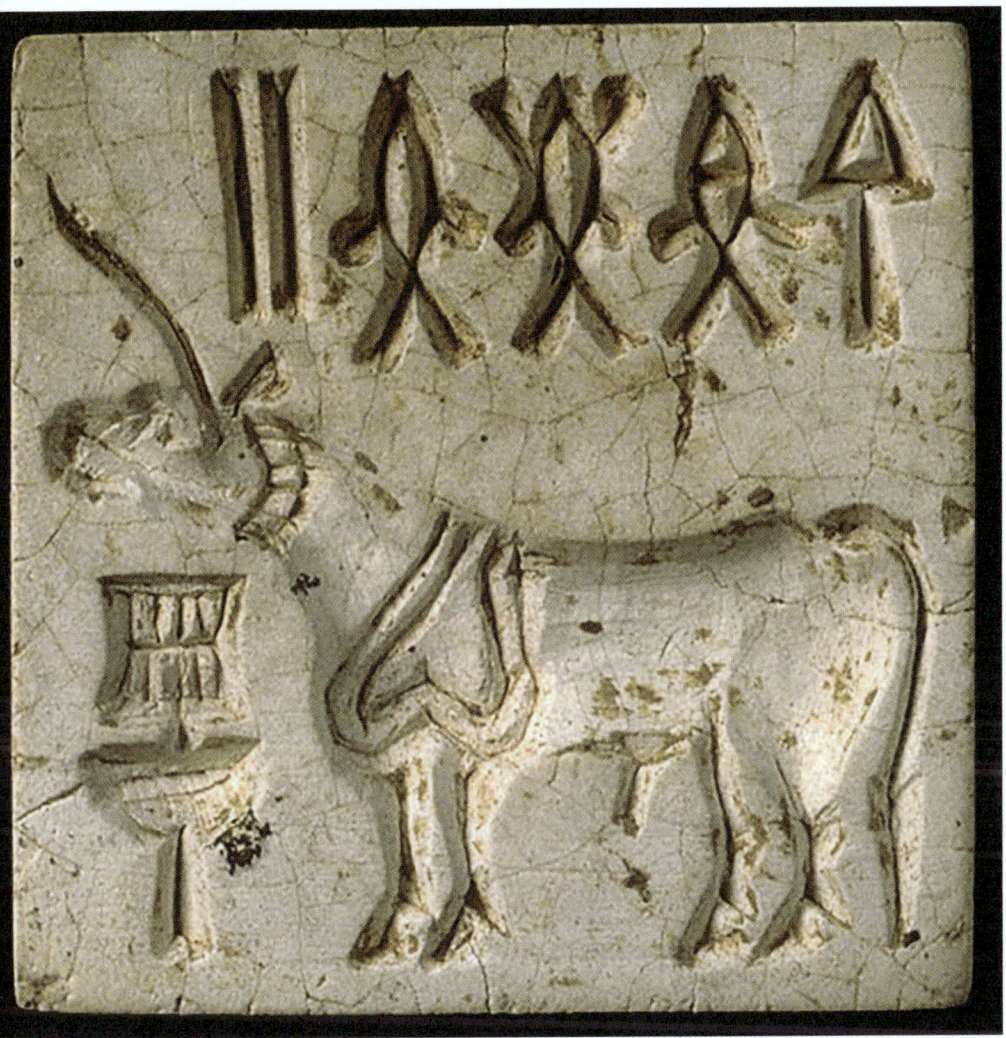

Example of a unicorn seal.

The famous seals carved out of steatite containing the majority of our evidence for the Indus script are also the subject of heavy discussion.

Few seal impressions have been found in the archaeological record, and many seals appear unworn. This has led scholars to suggest that they were instead used as identification tokens or badges of authority for travelling merchants. These objects were possibly totemic symbols with the animals on them representing a specific clan or city, or even used as identification tags for goods. Whatever their purpose, the seals have a nodule carved into the back with a hole running through it to allow for a string to pass through, meaning they could have been worn. The disappearance of these seals and evidence of writing on other materials by 1700 BCE shows that these items, and writing itself, were not essential to the general population and were probably only used by a specific group of people, likely those with some level of authority.[20]

Peaceful Priest Kings?

Like their writing system, the political and social organisation of Indus society is also highly debated. Because of the uniformity seen across Indus settlements, the initial interpretation after early excavations was that of a unified state governed by a central authority council, or a collection of regional councils or leaders.[21] Evidence for a central authority can be seen in the standardised weights and designs of their seals, the extensive trading networks, as well as in the organised planning of platforms on which the major cities were built.

This reality of how Indus society was organised is hard to determine, as there is no confirmable evidence of elite residences or palaces, royal burials, or luxury items that would indicate a ruling class. There is also a lack of administration and religious buildings that could provide insight into how Indus society functioned. Some of the larger houses at Mohenjo-Daro have been described as palaces, but some scholars have refuted this, calling them mansions at best.[22] Without these obvious buildings to help identify a ruling class, other possibilities of Indus society have been suggested.

Since the major Indus cities were located far away from each other, one possibility is that the entire region was controlled by a small group of elites made up of merchants, craftspeople, and priests. These large cities could also have been used as hubs for various regional polities or have functioned as smaller kingdoms due to the diversity of the sites, despite their overarching uniformity. The Indus Valley civilisation has no identifiable evidence for a standing army, so a possible ruling class of priest kings, who governed cities through the control of religion and trade, has become a popular suggestion, especially due to the large ritual significance they seem to have placed on water and ritual purification.[23]

Whether areas were independently governed or not, the amount of uniformity over such an expansive area means that there was likely an Indus culture that permeated throughout various communities thanks to a strong internal communication and distribution network. No matter how Indus society was governed or ruled, a great deal of organisation, planning, and execution would have been required at every settlement for the maintenance of their water management systems and busy trading networks.

Another traditional aspect of ancient civilisations, and even those that exist today, is warfare. This is surprisingly absent in the Indus Valley. Indus art rarely depicts violence, weapons are absent at most sites, and there is no archaeological evidence of violent destruction. The large walls surrounding cities appear to have been mostly for protection against flooding, though there is evidence of stronger fortifications at towns located on the west coast of the Indian subcontinent. These extra precautions are most likely because they were ports that held valuable goods for trading and required extra security.[24]

This physical absence of warfare and fortifications is a tactic that would have greatly benefitted the Indus. Because the different regions of the Indus civilisation were so diverse and valuable, and the population was low for an area that size, it would have been a great incentive for the Indus people to cooperate and reap the economic benefits of their resources. Of

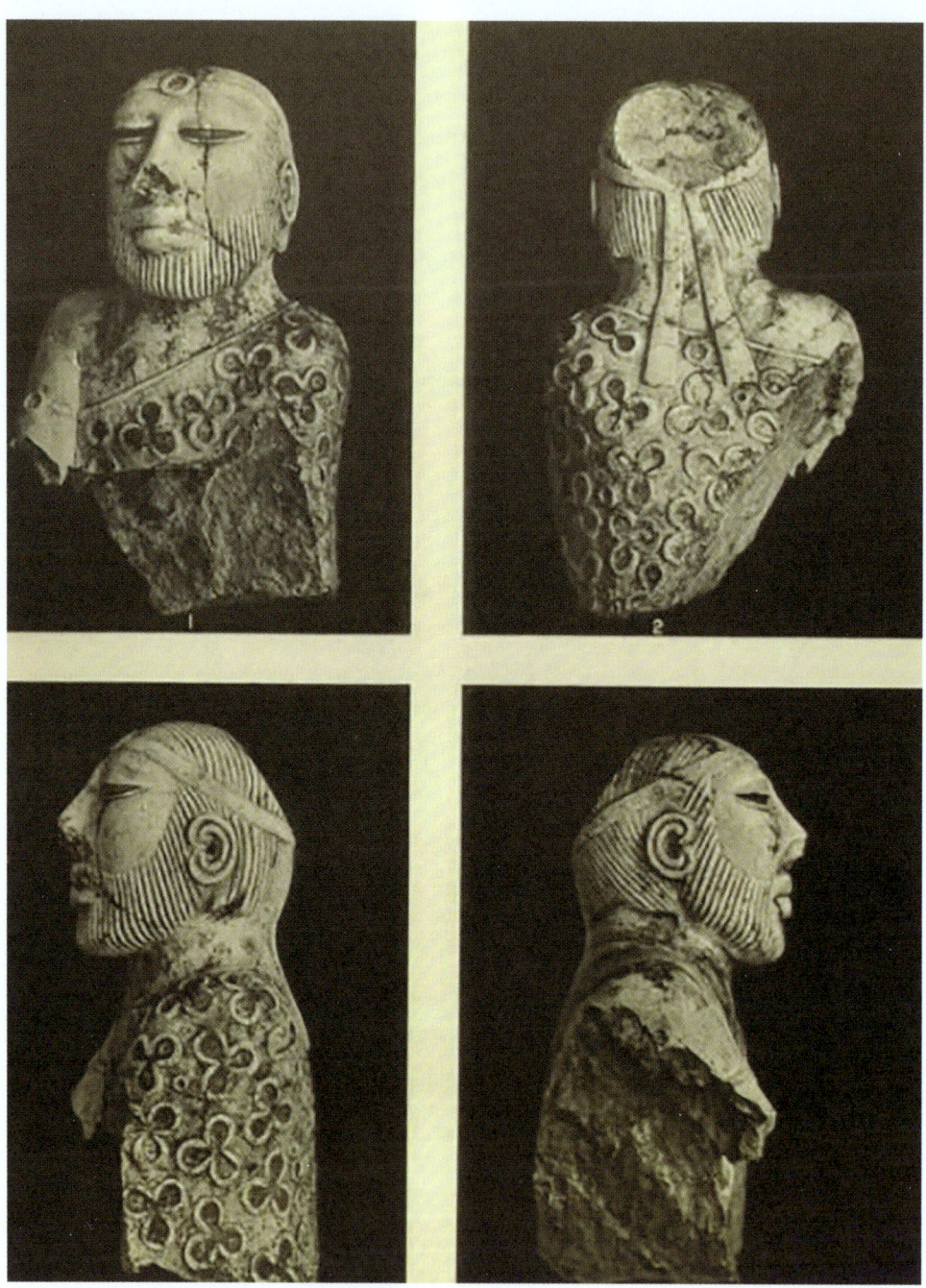

Small steatite statue famously dubbed the "Priest-King," though this title is highly speculative.

course, the absence of complex weapons used only for warfare instead of hunting and farming does not mean that the spears and axes found weren't used for violence, or that violence wasn't used as a method of social and political control.

Physical evidence of warfare in the archaeological record is difficult to find. Our knowledge of warfare in other ancient civilisations such as ancient Egypt and Mesopotamia comes from artistic portrayals and textual evidence. Seeing as no such evidence from the Indus has been found, there is no way to confirm or deny that fighting between different regions happened. Even though no Indus artistic depictions of warfare exist, studies on human remains at the sites of Harappa and Rakhigarhi have uncovered evidence of cranial injuries such as broken noses and blows to the head, with many people sustaining injuries more than once throughout their lifetime.[25] This violence was more prevalent after the Mature Period (post-1900 BCE). The Post-Urban Period in the Indus Valley was a period of dramatic social change from the peak of the Indus civilisation, which would have brought on a new level of stress that could explain this increased level of violence.

A Change of Course

The Mature Period of the Indus Valley civilisation came to an end around 1900 BCE. After this date, references to Meluhha in Mesopotamian texts disappear, and the Indus civilisation began to decline. The most probable explanation is likely a mix of both environmental and human factors. Dramatic shifts of the course of the Indus River over time would have flooded and destroyed some cities, while leaving others high and dry. Today, the Indus River is located farther east than it would have been in the third millennium BCE. The Sarasvati River also dried up in areas around the end of this millennium, which would have devastated the agropastoral communities that depended on its flow and left people with no other option but to abandon their homes.

Another possible reason for urban decay would be the poor health of those who inhabited large cities. Studies on human remains at Mohenjo-Daro dating to later periods of habitation show that many people would have suffered and died from diseases like malaria. The occurrence of this disease would have become an issue if drains were not properly maintained and began to flood, creating pools of stagnant water. Cholera is also suspected to have been present from the seepage of wastewater into drinking water.[26] If Mohenjo-Daro was the central control point of Indus society, as has been suggested, the poor health of the population there would have seriously disrupted communication and governance over the area.

The decline of the Indus Valley civilisation was gradual, most likely caused by environmental changes, a collapse in whatever leadership was ensuring the continuation of trading networks, internal communication and the continued maintenance of public works, and the increased prevalence of disease in urban areas. Cities and towns were abandoned, and rural settlements became more popular. The Indus civilisation as it was, ceased to exist, and when another dominant culture rose again in the Indian subcontinent, a new river, the Ganges, was at its forefront.

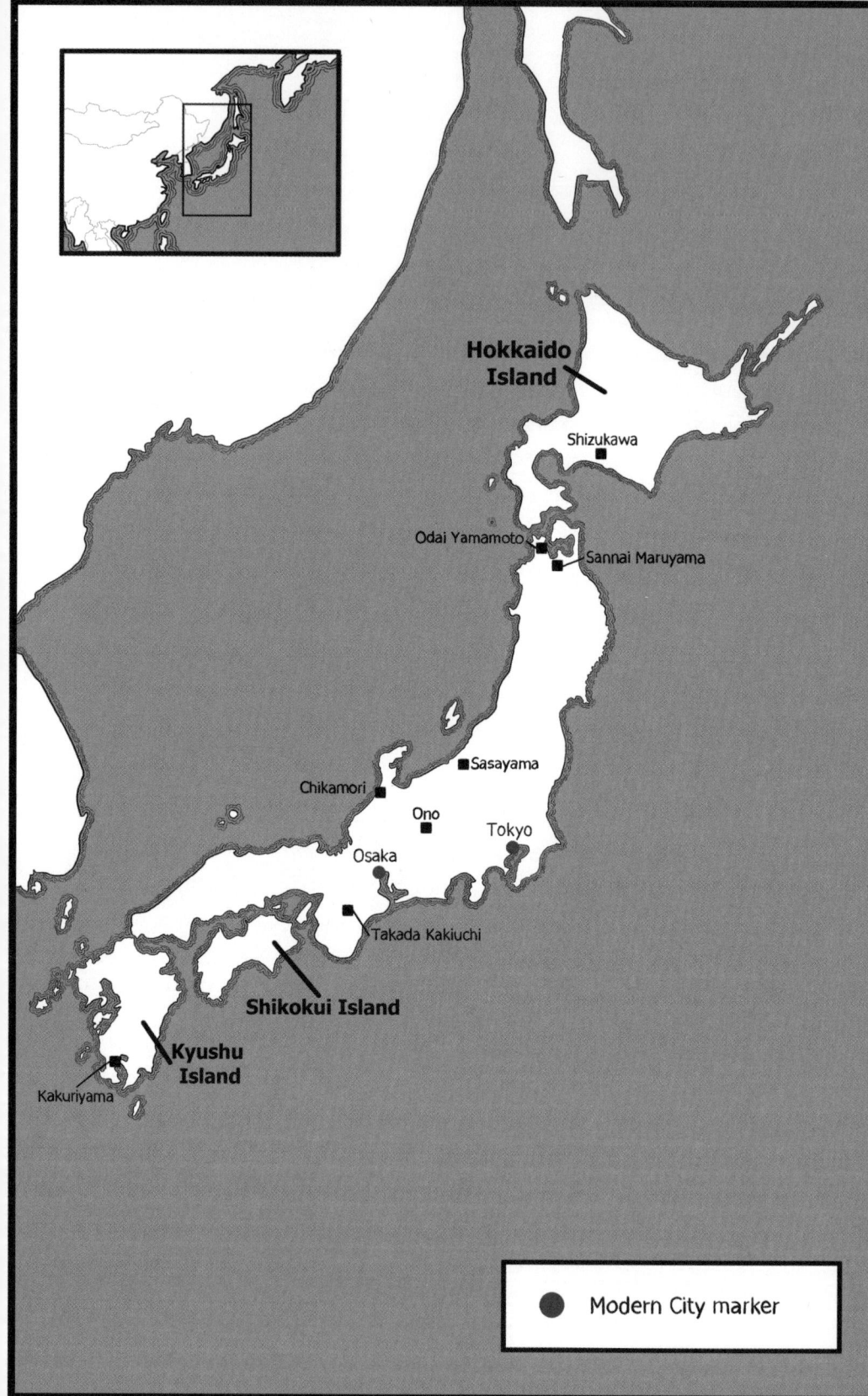

Chapter Seven

Jōmon

The Oldest Pottery in the World

The woman walked over to the woven tray sitting next to the hearth to check on the acorns she had taken out of their storage pit last night. Squatting down and giving them a quick feel with her hands, she determined they were dry enough and ready for the next step. The woman picked up the tray, careful not to let any acorns roll onto the ground and carried it over to the grinding stone at the entrance of her house. She always liked to prepare food in the fresh air and interact with the others in her settlement while they were going about their own daily tasks.

Dumping the first set of acorns into the worn-in depression of the large stone slab that she'd been using for years, the woman grabbed her grinding stone and began to crush the nuts, freeing them from their hard outer shells. Once all the seeds were out, she removed the shells from the slab and placed them in the refuse basket that sat next to her before beginning the laborious task of grinding the acorn meat into a mealy flour.

When it reached the consistency that she wanted, the woman scooped the flour into a clay pot and brought it back into the house. Sitting next to the hearth and the cooking pot nestled inside the ashes that had been simmering millet and other root vegetables for the last few hours, the woman poured some water into the acorn flour until it became a thick, sticky paste. She then grabbed small bits at a time and began rolling it between her hands to create dumplings, placing them in the cooking pot *as she went. The woman then added in the handful of clams that she had gone out and collected with the other women in her settlement earlier that morning, and finished everything off with a sprinkle of salt. The woman stirred everything together, leaned over and smiled as the aroma of the stew wafted into her nose. She couldn't wait for it to be ready to eat.*

Far and Wide, and Across Millennia

The Jōmon period of Japan spanned over 10,000 years. While many cultures and civilisations rise and transform or are taken over by others within a few thousand years, the Jōmon were able to maintain a relatively uninterrupted cultural tradition that lasted millennia longer—all without the invention of agriculture. For many years, the traditional view of the Jōmon period was that not much was happening on the Japanese archipelago while civilisations elsewhere rose and fell and built monumental architecture that still stands today.[1] On the contrary, the Jōmon people were far from stagnant hunter-gatherers.

The timespan of the Jōmon alone saw climatic shifts, natural disasters, and environmental changes that would have required multiple phases of adaptation and shifting in their ways of life. The environmental diversity of the Japanese archipelago also allowed for the development of cultural and social diversity.[2] This means that although the word *Jōmon* is all-encompassing for the time and space before the invention of agriculture and the emergence of other cultures, the Jōmon people should not be defined by a fixed set of cultural characteristics. There are, however, some overlapping traits that can be seen throughout the timeline and geography that were, regardless of space and time, distinctively Jōmon.

Because the Jōmon period lasted over 10,000 years and is so culturally diverse, historians and archaeologists have divided it into six sub periods:

Incipient: 13600–9200 BCE	Middle: 3500–2500 BCE
Initial: 9200–5300 BCE	Late: 2500–1200 BCE
Early: 5300–3500 BCE	Final: 1200–900 BCE

Sedentary Hunter-Gatherers?

Jōmon society was composed of sophisticated hunter-gatherer communities. A hunter-gatherer culture relies heavily on hunting, fishing, and foraging for vegetation such as wild fruits, vegetables, tubers, nuts, and seeds. Because these communities don't rely on agriculture, they are often mobile, sometimes travelling large distances to source the food they need to survive. Because of this, establishing long-term settlements and creating objects such as cooking pots that were difficult to carry and fragile can be seen as impractical. While many hunter-gatherers still exist today, the invention and spread of agriculture led to many people abandoning this lifestyle in favour of permanent settlements that supported larger populations. This in turn led to the development of "complex societies," meaning the emergence of division of labour and political hierarchy within communities, the creation of monumental architecture, and the advent of the leisure time required to develop specialised skills such as expert weaving, pottery, and jewellery or ornament making.

The Jōmon people did not live like typical hunter-gatherers, nor did they make the leap to agriculture. Rather, they appeared to have shared aspects from both ways of life. From the very beginning of the Jōmon period, sites have been excavated containing hearths made up of carefully placed stones intended for multiple uses. These show that the Jōmon people were adopting sedentism practices from the outset of their culture. This early development of sedentism first began when the climate became warmer in southwestern Japan, eventually progressing up the archipelago to the northeast.[3] The shift in climate changed the natural environment, and nut-bearing trees began to thrive in many areas around Japan. This new availability of nuts is believed to have allowed the Jōmon people to shift from purely hunting and gathering on the go, to storing food for future consumption. Gathering an abundance of food and storing it for multiple seasons meant that larger groups of people could be supported in one place without having to always pack up and find more.

With this transition into a more sedentary lifestyle, the Jōmon shifted from a hunter-gatherer tradition to more of what archaeologists call collectors. Collectors are closely associated with intensive subsistence strategies, meaning they became specialists in relying heavily on a small number of resources such as fish and marine mammals, acorns, and chestnuts.[4] On top of these staples, the Jōmon made sure to eat a wide variety of plants, planning food collecting strategies based on seasonal availability that allowed them to live in relatively permanent settlements. For example, fishing was done primarily in summer, plant food collection in the autumn, hunting on land was done in the winter, and shellfish were collected year-round, but primarily in the spring.

The abundance and variety of natural resources on the Japanese archipelago meant that the Jōmon made the most of what was available to them no matter where they were located. Archaeologists have identified around sixty different types of land animals, seventy different species of fish and sea creatures, and over fifty species of plants that were exploited during this period, showing the variety available to them.[5] Hoe-like tools made out of sandstone and shale have been found that could have been used for digging out roots, as well as an abundance of obsidian arrowheads for hunting, fishing nets, traps, hooks, and spears. These artefacts and more were all used to collect food for Jōmon settlements.

Storing food is typical of collector societies, and storage pits have been found at Jōmon sites from the Incipient Period, where large amounts of acorns have been found. The creation of storage pits indicates that the people living in these settlements were thinking and planning ahead to ensure their food supply was scheduled and maintained. Baskets and mats were also used to line storage pits, and even wet storage pits have been found at multiple sites. Wet storage was possibly used for removing the bitter tannic acid that is found in acorns, though it's more likely that this form of storing nuts prevented them from germinating over long periods of time and deterred insects.[6]

Such forward planning meant that if there were ever any natural disasters or famines, there would be enough food supply to sustain a settlement until their environment could recover and allow them to remain sedentary. While there is not much direct evidence for the storage of meat and fish, it's possible that the Jōmon also created methods to preserve these for future consumption as well. The presence of large shell refuse mounds has also led some researchers to believe that large quantities of shellfish were gathered and smoked or dried for storage, and possibly traded with inland settlements who had no direct access to the ocean.[7]

Cultivation Motivation

Typically, the adoption of agriculture prompts groups to become sedentary. In the case of the Jōmon, though, they stuck to their traditional ways of hunting and gathering, but there is a debate among scholars about whether they also practised cultivation—a step towards agriculture, but not a full transition into raising full fields of crops and domesticated animals. Most biologists believe that the forests in eastern Japan had more than enough wild vegetation to make cultivation more work than foraging, but there is evidence from some Jōmon sites manipulating resources within their natural environment and tending to plants. The change in lifestyle of the Jōmon from migratory to sedentary after the Incipient Phase created the need to establish a system to manage plant resources.[8] Plant remains excavated from lowland sites in Japan provide evidence for this management, especially with nut-bearing trees, as early as 5000 BCE. This form of cultivation could be seen as a form of wild gardening.

The current opinion among many archaeologists is that from the initial Jōmon period onwards, several plants were possibly cultivated. But this form of sustenance only made up a small portion of the Jōmon diet.[9] While this is a significant step from hunting and gathering, the limited occurrence of cultivation did not have a significant effect on the development of Jōmon society. What it did provide was more stability for food resources, exemplifying the careful food planning and management of the Jōmon.

Cultivated plants such as bottle gourds, yams, hemp, beans, burdock, and even some grains such as buckwheat, millet, rice, and barley have all been found at Jōmon sites. Cultivation over farming allowed the Jōmon people to make the most out of their natural environment. While agricultural societies are more vulnerable to natural disasters and environmental changes, this alternative version of sedentary life consisting of hunting, gathering, and the cultivation of wild food still allowed for the Jōmon to develop complex societies that contained many similar aspects to their farming contemporaries.[10]

Further evidence in favour of the Jōmon cultivating plants are the examples of lacquered wood, combs, baskets, hair ornaments, and even pottery that have been excavated over the years. The production of lacquered objects is a time-intensive process and requires many steps to make. Wild lacquer trees do not produce much sap, which suggests that they had to have been actively tended to.[11]

The Oldest Pottery in the World

The adoption of sedentism by the Jōmon provided them with the opportunity to begin creating pottery for food storage and cooking. In fact, Jōmon pottery is the oldest in the world. Based on radiocarbon dating, the oldest pottery from the Odai Yamamoto I site located in northern Japan dates to c. 14500 BCE. While pottery could very well have been invented by the Jōmon, it is also possible it was first created somewhere else on mainland Asia before being introduced to them through diffusion by people travelling on boats to interact and trade with those living on the archipelago.[12] Regardless, given the evidence, the Jōmon were creating pottery cooking vessels thousands of years before other cultures without the invention of agriculture, which typically coincides with this development.

Making cooking pots out of fired clay allowed the Jōmon to boil their food, a culinary skill unavailable to nomadic hunter-gatherers who normally do not carry such large, heavy pieces of pottery. With the addition of boiling, the possibilities for cooking and the foods they could prepare and consume greatly expanded. This new way of cooking and eating meant people could stay in one place for longer. Boiled food is easier to digest, and it allows the chef to unlock more flavours by combining multiple meats, grains, nuts, leaves, fruits, and vegetables into stews. Boiling also allowed previously inedible foods to become staples in the Jōmon diet. Acorns were heavily relied upon during the Jōmon period and need to be extensively boiled to remove their poisonous tannins before they can be used in cooking. Shellfish also began to be consumed in larger quantities by the Initial Period because boiling them in pots meant they could open their shells to get to the meat inside.[13]

Jōmon pottery ranges from crude, everyday pots to remarkably refined works of art that still served a utilitarian purpose. The pottery was made by hand and hardened in open fires instead of kilns. For almost the entire Jōmon period and throughout most of the Japanese archipelago, almost every vessel found has some form of design on it. Cord-marking was the most popular design on Jōmon pots, and it is this distinctive design that gave the Jōmon culture its name. "Cord-marked" translates to Japanese as *Jōmon*. This technique begins by twisting two strands of cord together into a single strand and then pressing it into the wet clay. Although quite a simple method, it can produce an unlimited number of designs by creating different types of twists or by adding extra strands. These strands could then be either impressed

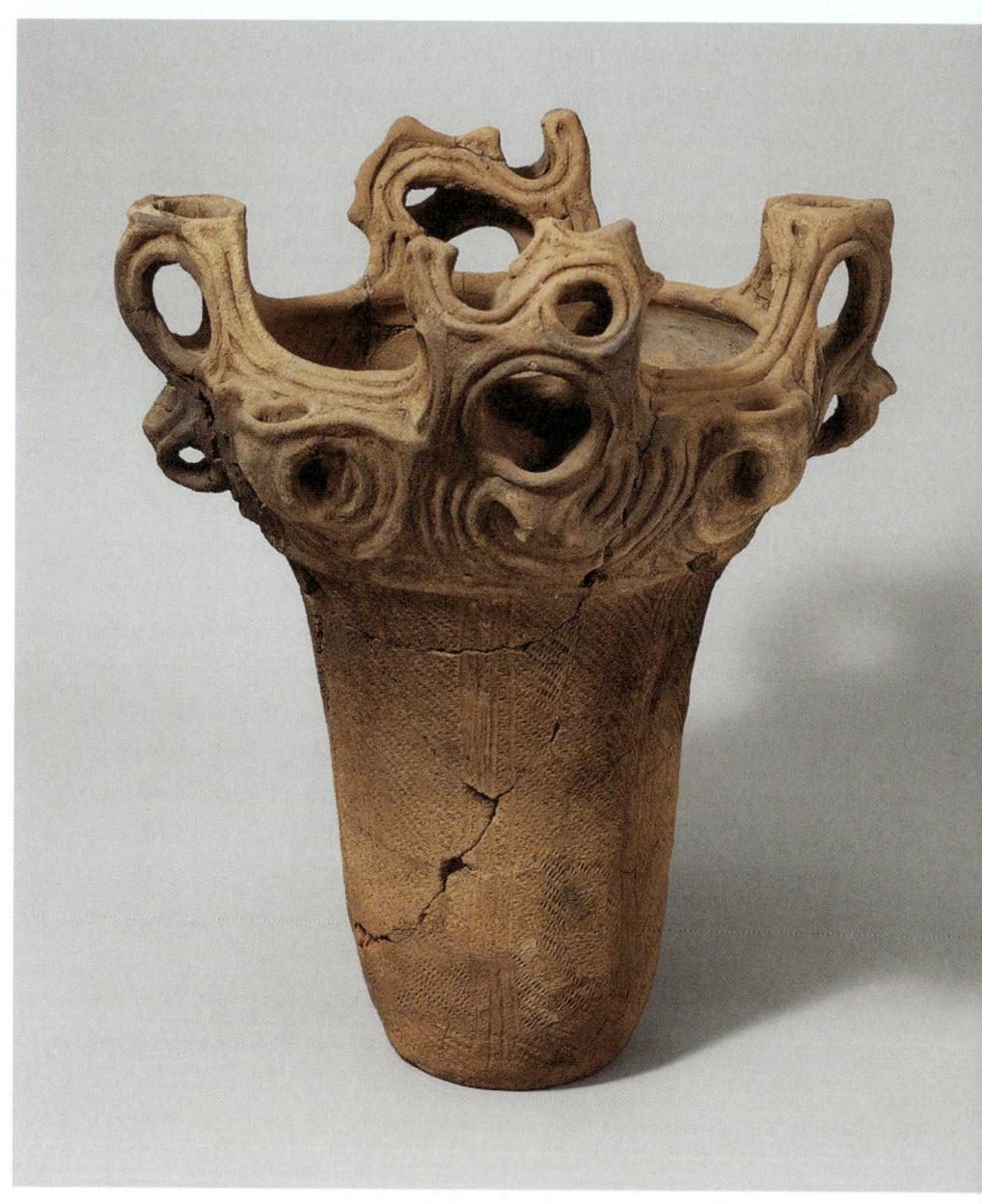

"Flame-Rimmed" cooking vessel. Pottery rims with this sort of design are known as the fire-flame or Ka'enshiki type because they resemble leaping flames. Most Jōmon pottery was plain and made for cooking, but this lavishly decorated piece was possibly used for special ceremonies.

onto the clay to create individual markings or rolled with the palm of one's hand over the surface. Other decorations also included nail and shell marks, grooves, and mat marks, as well as the application of extra shapes and strands of pottery to create intricate designs.

Pottery making was probably done independently by each family, with community members sharing ideas and techniques. This gave pots within communities and groups of settlements a common flair that has allowed archaeologists to group these pots and track cultural changes and developments over time. Researchers have also found evidence of cockroach and seed impressions on Jōmon pottery.[14] Cockroaches are house pests and invade habitations in search of food and shelter. This means that pottery was made in the homes of Jōmon people rather than in the open air.

Some Jōmon pots were elaborately decorated and extremely artistic in style with special motifs and symbolism. By the Middle Jōmon, there was a shift towards artistic expression over functionality, with the creation of heavily decorated pots with projections coming out of the rims resembling flames, waves, or rushing water. These are called flame pots today, and they were often decorated with narrative patterns that appear to have told stories that were important to the community and included symbolism that probably meant a great deal to the Jōmon, like curvy S shapes, and others that look like daggers or dragonfly eyes. These intricate pots were possibly used for ceremonies or other ritual activities, and the ability to create such pieces is another indicator that the Jōmon would have had the free time that only those who have access to a stable supply of food are afforded.[15] Coupled with other more specialty items such as slit stone earrings, pots possibly used as drums, and delicate shell bangles that have been found, the Jōmon people's methods of food storage and cultivation gave them the availability to create meaningful objects both for themselves and their community.

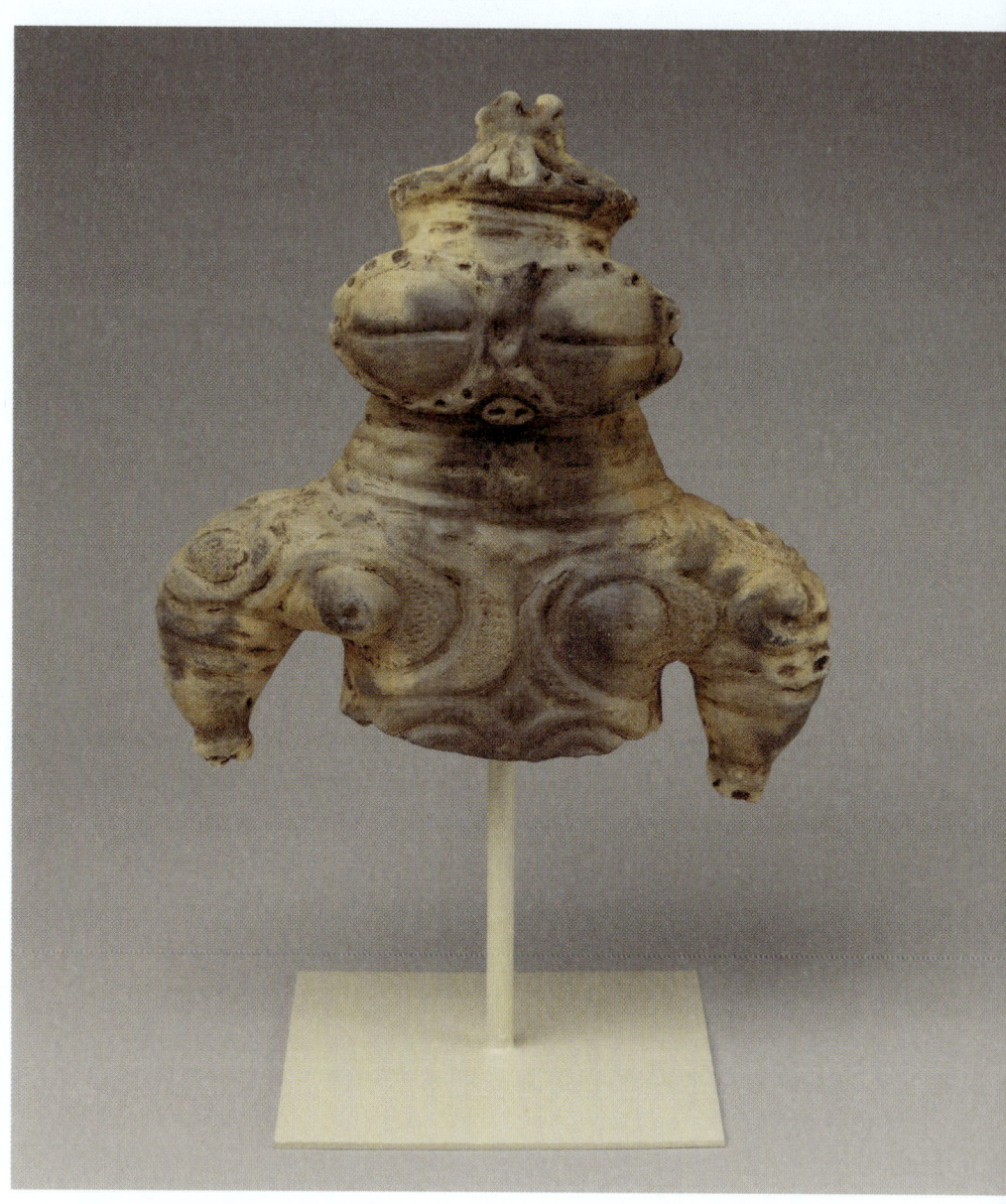

The Jōmon made anthropomorphic ceramic figures called Dogū. Most Dogū appear to be female, with small breasts and swollen abdomens. They were often painted red, but their purpose is unknown. Due to them almost never being found intact, their breaks may have been intentional and had a ritual or ceremonial function to let spirits out or prevent them from further use.

Life in Pits

The beginning of the Jōmon period saw a drastic change in how people lived on the Japanese archipelago, with the creation of the first settled villages. These settlements were circular or horseshoe-shaped, with storage pits, public buildings, and several circular or rectangular pit houses, each belonging to an individual family with floors sunk fifty to sixty centimetres into the ground, circled around a central open space. The rest of the house was raised up and supported by posts and there would have been beams, rafters, and thatched roofs. Apart from storage pits and hearths that were needed for daily domestic life, some Jōmon houses also had stone altars with standing stones and stone bars inside of them.[16] So while Jōmon houses were made for ordinary living, they may have also served other functions or held a deeper meaning for the people who resided inside. At some sites, much larger rectangular buildings were constructed. These have been interpreted as public buildings for community rituals or communal activities such as exchanging goods with other settlements.

Jōmon settlements appear to have been occupied for extended periods of time, and a few were very large and densely inhabited. Archaeologists have discovered that later houses were built overlapping earlier ones, which could indicate a communal tie to their ancestors.[17] Of course, not every site appears to have been permanent. Studies into Jōmon sites have uncovered various types of settlements. Some appear to be "base" settlements, which were very much a typical settlement for families and communities, whereas others have been called "satellite" settlements.[18] These "satellite" settlements contained specific tools that indicate those living there were relying heavily on one particular resource. These could have been used seasonally to gather the food needed for longer storage at "base" settlements.

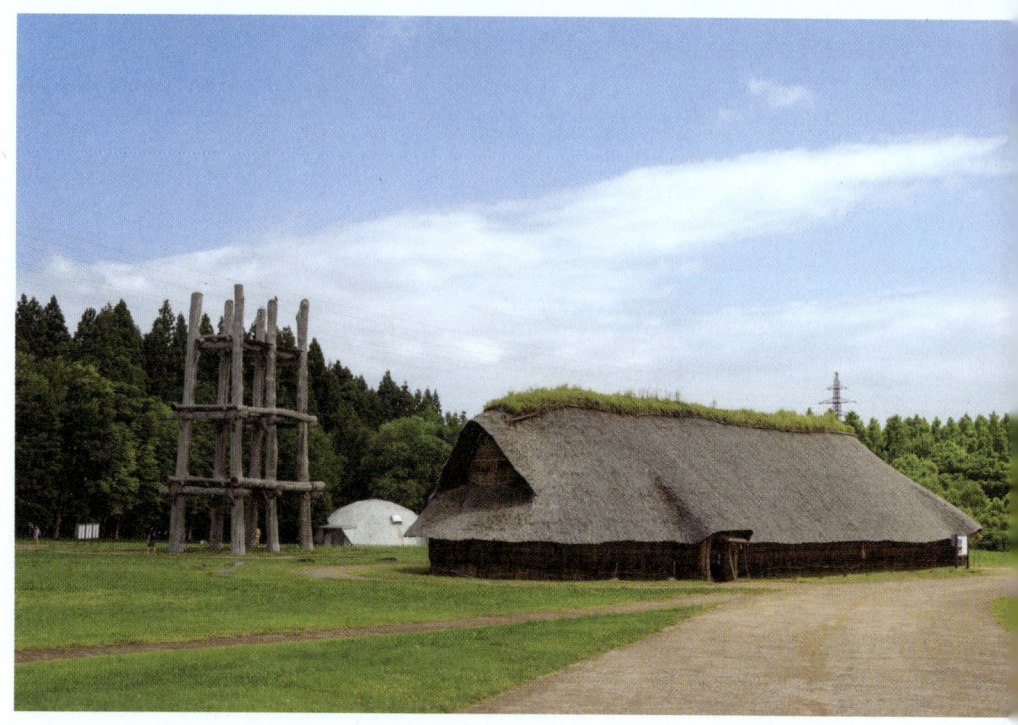

Reconstruction of a Jōmon period longhouse at Sannai-Maruyama.

Jōmon subsistence strategies were based on the seasonality and availability of each resource, meaning people would have been well organised and followed a strict schedule. Larger structures, such as one from the largest Jōmon site, Sannai-Maruyama in the Aomori Prefecture, appear to have worked as a calendar and helped with this scheduling.[19] The long side of the structure aligns with the summer solstice sunrise and the winter solstice sunset. This would have helped the Jōmon map out the seasons, and provided them with timing cues for food collection and community rituals and ceremonies.

It's clear that Jōmon society relied heavily on fitting in and creating systems to work within the environmental cycles around them. While the Jōmon still largely remained hunter-gatherers throughout their 10,000 years of existence, their sedentism meant that they could live in larger communities that more closely resembled tribes than the traditional mobile groups that were characteristic of non-agricultural communities. Until recently, archaeologists and scholars had believed that social complexity always leads to the emergence of elite people and hierarchy.[20] While there has been some evidence of luxury goods in some graves, it does not appear that the Jōmon people required or developed any distinct hierarchy or ruling class that set customs or exploited resources in their society. The vast diversity of resources along the archipelago and the high population density of the Jōmon could have made it difficult for a single group to do this. Instead, the Jōmon relied on the natural cycles of what their environment gave them, and organised their societies to allow for everyone (and everything) to thrive.

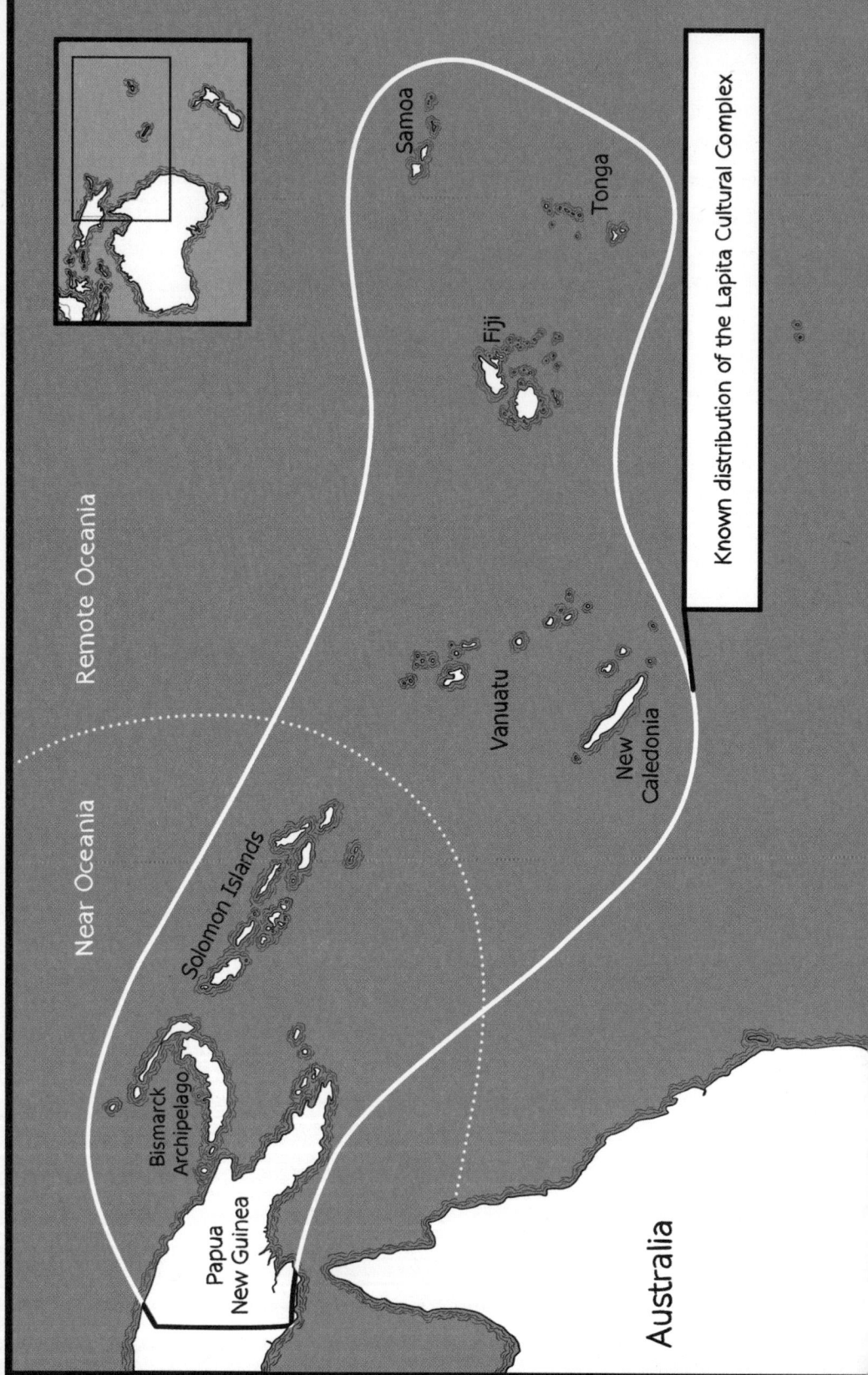

Chapter Eight

Lapita

Seaborne Explorers of Oceania

Morning broke over the horizon as the men and women pushed the army of canoes into the water. The weeks and days leading up to this moment had been filled with intense preparation. Canoes large enough to weather the unpredictable ocean waters had been hollowed from trees. Crops were gathered and prepared into food that would sustain them throughout their journey. Fresh water was stoppered in ceramic jugs and animal skins. Seeds were collected in woven baskets to ensure their survival after they made it to their destination. Shell ornaments were made, extra fish hooks fashioned, and intricately decorated ceramics fired to ensure the traditions of their ancestors were transferred to their new home.

The last few hours before sunrise saw a flurry of activity on the beach. Families were loading their boats with everything they had gathered, only to unload them and reconfigure their baggage when it didn't fit. The animals could sense that something big was happening. Dogs yelped and bounded back and forth along the sand, reflecting the nervous energy that hung in the air. The pigs prodded the grasses at the edge of the beach, wary of the waves.

Finally, with everything on board, those who had signed on for the journey into the unknown said their heartfelt goodbyes to their families and community. While many were excited and eager to get going before the weather rolled in, there was a great sadness to this moment. No one was ready to admit it, but this was the last time many in these two parties would *see each other. The distance was too far for regular visits, and families and friends would have to rely on trading envoys to hear updates from their loved ones. Their collective minds also pushed away the worry that some boats might never make it to the next shore.*

And with that, the canoes were pushed off towards the sunrise and into the ocean to the sound of cheers and well-wishes by those left behind. They waved until their arms felt like lead and then held each other as the boats became specks along the horizon and disappeared.

Archaeology on the Horizon

The Lapita were the first settlers on the islands of the Western Pacific. Little is known about them, but their most defining feature that has remained in the archaeological record is their intricately decorated red pottery. Lapita itself is a term that was given to encompass a group of people who created and used a culturally distinctive collection of artefacts, had a penchant for living on the coast, shared cultural values, and possibly a common language that appeared in the Bismarck Archipelago around 1600 BCE. As with many identified prehistoric cultures, Lapita is an archaeological construct, often referred to as an archaeological horizon, meaning it is a collection of recognisable artefacts and cultural traits found across a large geographical region over a long period of time.

In fact, the Lapita culture is the most widespread cultural horizon in Oceania. Their influence stretched from the Bismarck Archipelago to as far as Fiji, Tonga, and Samoa, a distance of some 3,500 kilometres with vast stretches of the Pacific Ocean between islands. The Lapita appear to have been expert seafarers and colonisers. It is even argued that they may have been responsible for the preliminary spread of Austronesian language speakers in the Pacific.[1] These early explorers were able to reach lands previously untouched by other humans and may also represent the initial diversification of the many cultures of Oceania.

They Came from the West

Archaeological evidence shows the Lapita appearing on the Bismarck Archipelago with a fully-fledged ceramic complex, and the knowledge of horticulture around 1600 BCE. Because they appeared as a fully-fledged culture, they must not have been indigenous to this area. The Bismarck Archipelago was simply the first stop, the beginning of a long tradition of exploration and colonisation. So where did the Lapita come from?

The ancestors of who would eventually make up the Lapita came from the far west, originating on the islands of Southeast Asia. Archaeologists have traced the development of their distinctive ceramic complex to similar Neolithic red slip pottery found in Taiwan, the Philippines, and as far away as the Sulawesi and Halmahera archipelagos—around three thousand kilometres from the Bismarck Archipelago. These sites also contain other artefacts such as stone adzes for wood cutting, shell tools and ornaments, and stone tools similar to those found in early Lapita sites. These early Austronesian peoples developed and spread over these islands beginning in Taiwan around 3000 BCE, making their way as far as Halmahera around 1600 BCE, around the same time that Lapita sites appeared on the Bismarcks.[2]

The initial reasoning for the push into this new area is unknown. It may have been due to population pressure, a need or want to search for new or more resources, or possibly to establish new trading contacts.[3] Regardless, the early Lapita soon found themselves on islands in Melanesia that had already been settled for over 30,000 years from previous migrations in the Pleistocene era. These established populations had already developed their own non-Austronesian languages and diverse cultures, and the early Lapita would have interacted with and been influenced by them. As with most interaction, the influence was by no means one-sided. After the arrival of the Lapita on the Bismarck and Solomon Islands, we see the appearance of domestic animals, a new style of pottery, and the introduction of agriculture. Early Lapita culture in the Bismarck Archipelago therefore developed through social, linguistic, and genetic interactions between these indigenous populations.

Evidence of Lapita migration and colonisation is not only identifiable in the archaeological record; it appears that their memory may also have been passed down through oral history in Oceanic cultures. Specialists of Oceanic folklore have identified a collection of myths and legends telling the story of an original "land people" invaded by "sea folk."[4] These myths could indeed be referring to the interactions and events on the shores of Melanesian islands over three thousand years ago.

The First Humans on Unknown Shores

Lapita sites cover an area of more than four thousand kilometres, stretching from the Bismarck Archipelago and Papua New Guinea, over the Solomons, Vanuatu, and New Caledonia, and all the way to Fiji and the islands of Tonga and Samoa. It's even possible that they may have landed on mainland Australia.[5] This expansion and dispersal of the Lapita culture happened in what could be considered an archaeological minute. After the earliest sites in the Bismarck Archipelago, around 3,500 years ago, the farthest sites in Tonga and Samoa date between 3,200 and 3,000 years ago. This can be interpreted as a literal explosion of culture throughout the Pacific spanning as little as three hundred years, or eight to ten human generations. This is a historical event completely unique to the Lapita and a testament to their tenacity and skill in navigating the Pacific Ocean.

The Lapita became the first humans to inhabit the islands of Vanuatu, New Caledonia, Fiji, Tonga, and Samoa. They colonised these islands successfully, bringing with them their ceramic traditions, their fully agricultural economy, and their language. It is thought that the Lapita peoples could have spoken a branch of the Proto-Central Pacific language family, as historical linguists have determined that the Fijian, Tongan, and Samoan languages all descended from a branch of this family.[6] This is no easy feat. The distance of water separating Fiji from Vanuatu and the

Solomon Islands is around nine hundred kilometres, a crossing that almost seems impossible for what would have been wooden canoes. Yet, there is archaeological evidence consisting of pottery and obsidian from faraway sites that proves the Lapita might have made this journey multiple times throughout their seafaring days.

Expeditions to colonise new islands were most likely undertaken by travelling in wooden canoes. No surviving examples of Lapita watercraft have yet been found, but their expansion patterns and their legacy have been extensively studied. Scholars have been trying to determine the reason for this widespread colonisation. There could be countless motivations for leaving one's homeland in search of somewhere new: wanderlust, warfare, exile, the need for more resources and raw materials, trade—the list goes on. Some have hypothesised that the Lapita had to search out new lands due to population demands.[7] With their preference for living on offshore islets and reef lagoons, higher population densities may have meant that new areas rich in marine resources were needed to maintain thriving communities.

Other reasons for colonisation could have been events such as natural disasters, or even a social change that prompted the need or want to explore the Pacific. A prominent individual may have risen to power and established a hierarchical or religious system that could have amassed a following and created a movement. Perhaps leaving one's community in the name of spreading their culture and beliefs would have made that person a revered ancestor to those who stayed behind. One theory based on looking at modern Austronesian-speaking cultures is that there could have been a birth-ordered ranking system in place, with the first-born sons inheriting the ancestral home.[8] This would have left the younger siblings with little choice other than to seek out new lands to establish a lineage of their own. We will most likely never know why the Lapita looked to the Pacific in earnest and undertook such perilous journeys, but we can say that it was probably a combination of both internal pressures and the pull of the unknown that led to their extensive expansion.

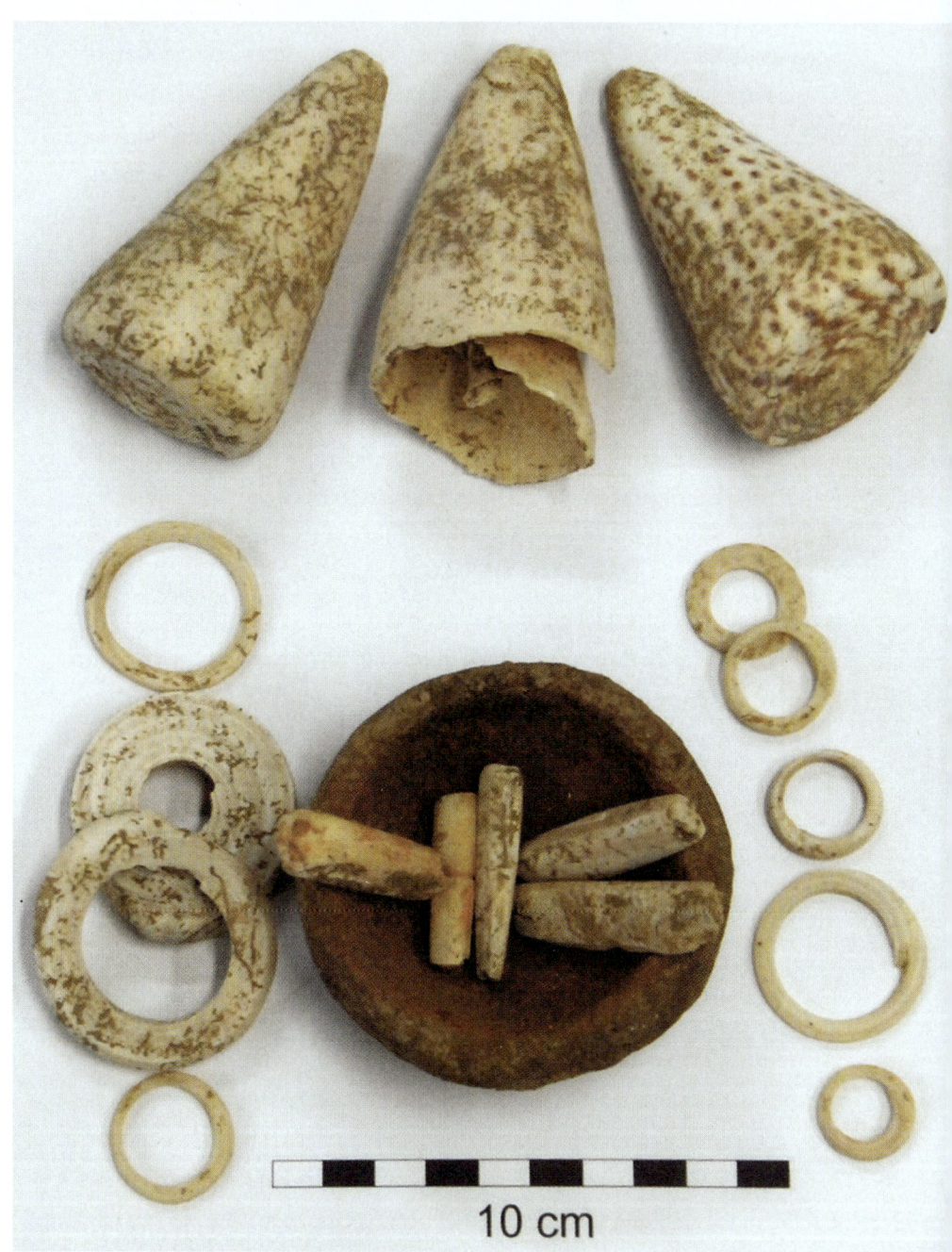

Shell jewellery from the Lapita site of Bourewa, Fiji.

Keeping in Touch

Lapita migration and colonisation were never a one-way street. There is strong archaeological evidence that Lapita communities, even dating to the earliest sites, were linked across the Pacific through a complex long-distance exchange network. Pottery and objects made from chert and obsidian can be geochemically sourced, and archaeologists have uncovered obsidian artefacts on islands hundreds of kilometres from where they were quarried. Some sites also had pottery imported from at least sixteen others.[9] Other objects such as adzes, oven stones, and rings, bracelets, beads, and pendants made of shells that were potentially highly valuable have also been found. Perishable items such as food, and objects made from organic materials like grasses and wood would have been traded between islands, but none have survived to tell their story.

This exchange between Lapita communities occurred both locally with islands in close proximity, as well as with destinations located considerable distances away. This continued long-distance trade and communication beyond the initial colonisation of a new settlement would have had to have been maintained at great difficulty and risk. Trips across the over-850-kilometre water gap from Vanuatu to Fiji would have required multi-day voyages.

Even with favourable winds, this would have pushed Lapita technology, and its people, to their limit. For the Lapita to undertake such a feat, it may indicate that social forces or ties had to be maintained.[10] It has been suggested that Lapita society was hierarchical, in which case there would have been a need to maintain control over these long distances and ongoing exchange to reinforce it. Trade and continued contact could have also helped these fledgling new colonies by bringing them the resources they needed for their community to thrive while they located local resources of their own. It seems that creature comforts from home still took precedence for some time, though. Even once local sources of certain items had been found, it appears that the imports from the western islands from whence the colonists came were still favoured. This again may have been to help maintain ties with their previous homeland.

Close exchange over vast expanses of water did not seem to last long, though. It seems that these long distances proved too much of an obstacle for maintaining regular contact once colonies were well-established, and eventually outweighed the need to maintain social ties. This resulted in the islands in Remote Oceania becoming isolated from their western neighbours, leading them to create their own localised and self-contained trade network that can be seen in the archaeological record. Eastern Lapita then developed in relative isolation from its predecessors, and their social systems and material culture began to evolve independently. Therefore, while in archaeological terms artefacts dating to the later centuries of the Lapita period in Remote Oceania can be attributed to the Lapita tradition, they display differences that did not evolve in Near Oceania.

Living Between Two Worlds

The Lapita enjoyed living in liminal spaces. Lapita sites are characteristically located on beaches, and they built their homes and villages on stilt houses along the coasts of main islands, over lagoons, and on smaller offshore coral islets that were always a short distance from shore. This sort of settlement pattern may have been for defence against the populations who had made it to the islands in Near Oceania thousands of years before, as well as to possibly avoid disease-carrying insects that could be found farther inland. This tactic could have also served the Lapita well when venturing to new lands. Staying close to the water meant they could defend themselves from unknown people or animals, as well as plan further missions to new lands while also being easily accessible by canoe. Well situated between land and sea, the Lapita were in a prime location to exploit both the rich marine resources of the lagoons and coral reefs, as well as practice horticulture by planting fruit, trees, and root crops on land.

Because most Lapita sites are located close to water, they are often in a poor state of preservation. Much of what they built has been eroded or redeposited, leaving archaeologists with only small clues as to how the Lapita lived. Some waterlogged evidence of carefully placed, human-worked planks and posts has come to light, showing that they lived in stilt villages built over water and sometimes on constructed piers or terraces.[11] Later on in Lapita culture, this housing pattern shifted closer to shore. Particularly in Remote Oceania at this time, they built their homes on beaches or slightly inland.

It is hard to say how these villages were organised, but size ranged from several to around 150 households. Reconstructing the stilt houses is also difficult, as all that remains are the bases of wooden posts, household refuse of shell and bone, seed and plant fragments, and burnt oven stones. Based on the artefacts discovered at these sites, it appears that many different activities took place inside. From prepping and cooking food, working shells to create rings, beads, or fish hooks, and even knapping obsidian flakes for woodworking and tattooing.[12] There may have been a "main house" within settlements used for rituals or ceremonies, as concentrations of decorated pottery were found in particular buildings. Wells, ovens built into the earth, and food storage pits were also dotted around sites.

While scholars do not yet have enough evidence to reconstruct a stilt house, they have been able to learn a great deal about how the Lapita sustained themselves. Because they were located between land and sea, the Lapita lived off of a mix of fish, shellfish, marine reptiles, and mammals, as well as whatever they could produce, gather, and hunt on land. Pig and dog bones are present at sites, proving that animals were being kept for food. The Lapita also cleared areas to create gardens.[13] Archaeological evidence shows they cultivated taro, banana, yam, and a wide variety of fruit and nut trees like coconut and Tahitian chestnut. The widespread presence of these remains speaks not only to the broad spectrum of food available to the Lapita, but also to the migration of many domesticated plants that originated in Southeast Asia or New Guinea.[14]

Intricate Faces Incised in Clay

While the Lapita had a rich material culture of adzes, shell objects, scrapers, fish hooks, and peelers, like many archaeological cultures, they're most famous for their pottery. The Lapita culture was first identified by its distinctive pottery, a hand-built, low-fired red earthenware ceramic fired without the use of kilns (most likely on open fires). Most of the ceramics are undecorated, but around 5 to 15 percent have been incised with a highly complex and stylised decorative system.[15] These designs were created with finely carved, toothed stamps that were likely made from wood or bamboo. After firing, these decorations were filled in with a white paste made from coral to make them stand out.

Lapita pottery decoration consists of simple design elements and motifs that can be built upon to create complex geometric designs. These consist of zigzags, labyrinths, and stylised faces, some even depicting earplugs. This ceramic tradition follows such rigorous artistic rules regarding placement and combinations that archaeologists have catalogued around 150 distinctive motifs that Lapita artists adhered to. These motifs have been thought to have come from Lapita basketry patterns, bark cloth decoration, and tattooing traditions.[16] And while the designs seemed to be quite homogenous over the large geographical area that the Lapita covered, differences between the east and west have been noted, most likely due to the large water gaps acting as a barrier for communication and contact.

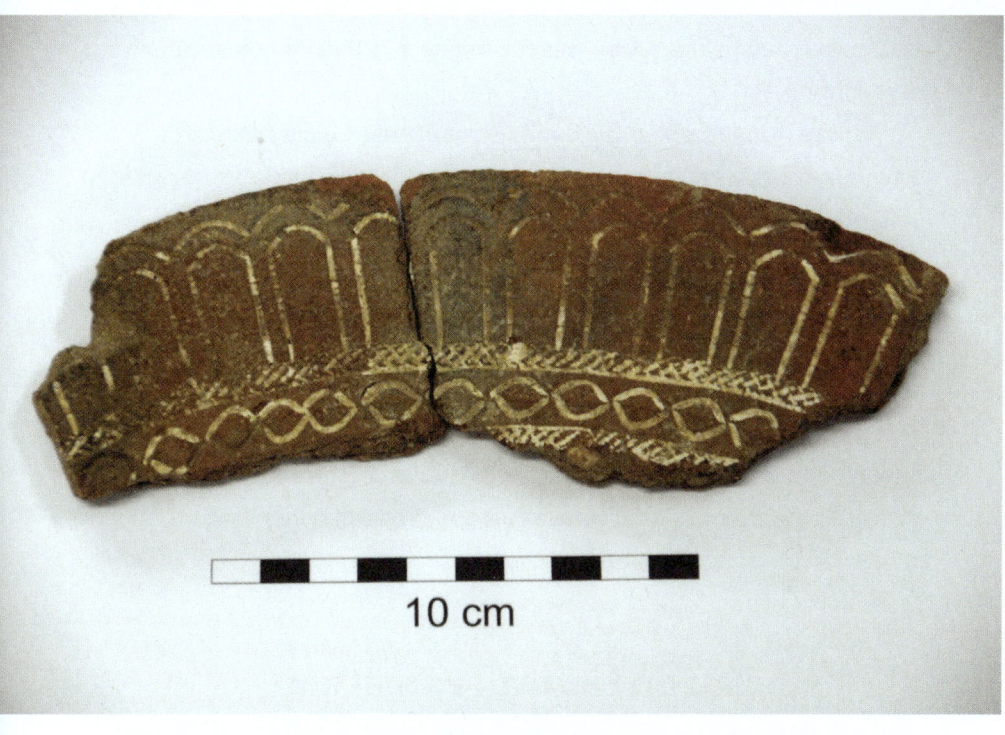

Example of dentate-stamped Lapita pottery filled with a white paste to make the design stand out.

Ceramics were not commonly used for cooking in Lapita communities. Burn marks from being placed in a fire to make food are not frequent due to their preference for steaming foods using an earth oven or roasting their meals over an open fire. While they did play a role in storing food and liquids, it appears that Lapita pottery held more significance than simple utilitarianism. Lapita ceramics were an important part of the complex exchange network that connected their isolated communities. Specific forms of Lapita pottery such as elaborately decorated cylinder stands and pedestalled bowls with human-like faces have been interpreted as representing household or lineage ancestors.[17] These could have been exchanged socially, or in more symbolic occasions such as marriage. Another possibility is that this decoration was used as a kind of "social glue" to keep together a quickly fragmenting society that was exponentially expanding.[18]

What's puzzling about the Lapita ceramic tradition, is that over time ceramics disappeared from the archaeological record. Unlike most parts of the world where societies only develop highly stylised pottery after they first master simple forms and gradually improve, Lapita pottery begins elaborately and gradually simplifies in form and decoration until it is completely plain. Eventually, after about a thousand years, the production of pottery on many islands inhabited by the Lapita disappears altogether or is transformed into something else. Because decorated pottery seemed to play such a vital role in ancestor remembrance, this evolution might indicate a significant social transformation that could be related to the similar decline in exchange and trade that took place.

Not an End, a Transition

The archaeologically defined Lapita culture begins to end with the retraction of their long-distance exchange networks and the creation of regionalised ones. By the beginning of the first millennium BCE, the Lapita had spread across the entire Southwest Pacific but seem to have run out of steam shortly after. Instead of looking outward, which they had done for hundreds of years, the Lapita started settling, interacting only with their closest neighbours. This led to the development of cultural differentiation in multiple locations.

Those living in Near Oceania increasingly interacted with the indigenous populations inhabiting the islands and began exchanging language, genetics, and cultural traditions. The ever-decreasing connections to Remote Oceania meant that these changes never made it to the more eastern islands, and they began their own evolution while adapting to their local environments. By around 500 BCE, these transformations became different enough that an archaeological "Lapita cultural complex" was no longer recognisable.

The end of the Lapita Culture was not an "end," as much as it was the new beginning for another culture. It has been argued the Lapita were the ancestors of modern Pacific Islander populations who speak Oceanic languages in Island Melanesia, Polynesia, and central-eastern Micronesia. Archaeologically speaking, there is a clear continuity in most Lapita sites that had later habitation. Work in Tonga and Samoa has revealed unbroken archaeological sequences that link later Polynesian cultures with their Lapita ancestors.[19] The Southeastern Pacific as we know it today, is therefore all thanks to a collection of wanderlustful oceanic explorers who dared to do the impossible.

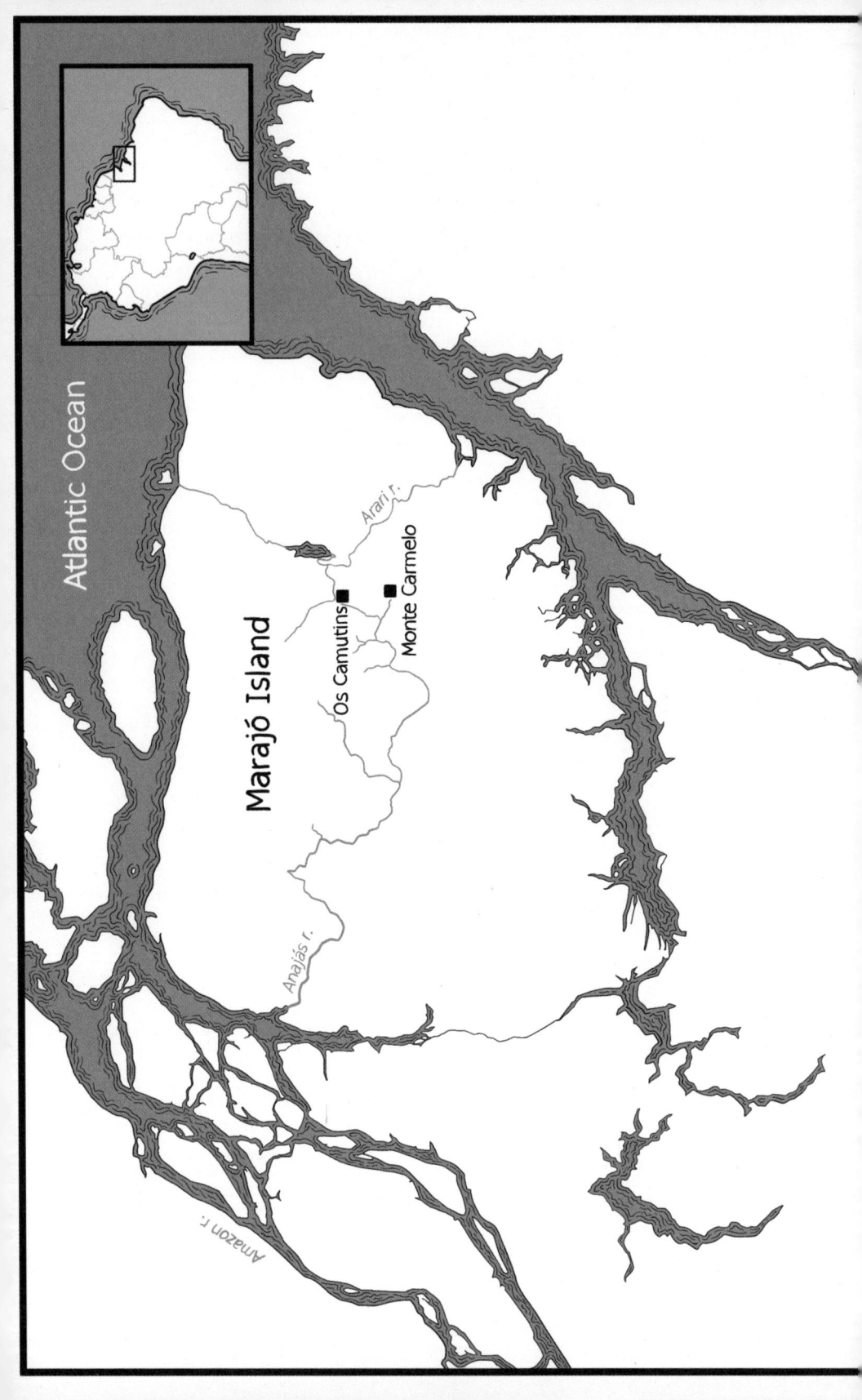

Chapter Nine

Marajoara

Monumental Mounds at the Mouth of the Amazon

"Your time has come," said the shaman as she picked up the bones the vultures had picked clean over the last few days. The bones belonged to the chief's mother, a respected elder who had helped her people through many hardships. The shaman took great care in placing each bone into a low-rimmed basket, cradling the head to ensure it wouldn't get damaged on her way back across the mound. She could feel the powerful essence of the dead woman still, as if she was still here.

The shaman picked up her basket and began making her way to the longhouse on the other side of the mound, where the deceased woman's family was waiting. Upon entering, she sat at one of the many hearths that trailed down its centre, in front of a richly decorated ceramic pot in the abstract shape of a woman. The dancing flames of the fire illuminated the swirling geometric lines covering the vessel, highlighting the moulded arms and shoulders, leaping across the incised face and bringing to life the now-glowing scorpion-shaped eyes. The shaman could feel the spirits' presence; they were ready.

The shaman lifted the tiny ceramic pot she kept strung around her neck over her head, uncorked the stopper, and poured the red powdered pigment out onto a ceramic palette. After mixing in some water, she took a brush and began to paint the bones. The shaman began chanting sacred incantations, the onlooking family of the deceased woman quickly joining in. The grief-laden *lamentations spilled out of the longhouse and over the mound into the winds and the rushing river below.*

After each bone was painted and dry, the shaman delicately placed them into the vessel, careful to arrange them just so. Covering the jar with a ceramic plate, she picked it up, and handed it to the dead woman's son with a nod before leading the procession to the final resting place of the dead, where he would inter his mother for eternity.

Defying the Odds at the Mouth of the Amazon

Marajó Island is one of many islands that sit at the mouth of the Amazon River in modern-day Brazil, dividing it up into multiple streams before it hits the Atlantic Ocean. Measuring around 40,000 square kilometres, roughly the size of the Netherlands, it is the world's largest island that was created by river deposits. The island is generally quite flat and lies low, close to the water. It is regularly inundated during the rainy season, completely flooding apart from its large man-made mounds that have drawn interest from foreign travellers since the 1800s. This was the home of the Marajoara.

For many decades, early archaeologists who investigated the mounds believed the presence of the Marajoara culture on Marajó Island was due to a migration of people from the Andes. Because of the tropical forest environment, the island was considered unfit to support the emergence and development of a complex culture with a large population. But Marajó Island, the northeastern side in particular, was a floodplain that proved early researchers wrong. Subsequent studies on South American ceramics show that the Marajoara culture was the result of a long-term tradition of people living and thriving in the tropical lowland of the lower Amazon. Sites with stone tools and rock art belonging to hunter-gatherers from around 10000 BCE have been found in parts of the Amazon basin. The earliest known ceramics in the Americas come from the lower Amazon River in Brazil and date to around

5000 BCE. There is also evidence of prehistoric people of the Amazon altering their environments for centuries to suit their needs and create a landscape that allowed them to thrive in a tropical rainforest.[1] The Marajoara culture was therefore never the exception or the result of an invasion. It was the peak of a long-standing Amazonian cultural tradition.

The Marajoara culture dates from around 350 to 1300 CE, though some radiocarbon dates from a site called Cacaol provide evidence of the culture's occupation on the island until 1675 CE.[2] Archaeological investigation has shown their habitation extending across the northeastern half of the island, over an area of around 20,000 square kilometres. The tropical savanna climate on Marajó Island is defined by two main seasons of extreme weather: a hot and rainy winter and a dry summer. While this is the climate for much of the Amazon, the rain on the island is more intense than in other areas. During this rainy season, much of the island is flooded by rising river waters. The rain can cause the rivers and lakes to rise up to four metres higher, making travelling the island in the winter only possible by boat or canoe.

These extremes of wet and dry are not ideal circumstances for agriculture, but the different conditions of each season allowed for a varied food supply of wild fruits, small seed crops, and palm trees. The Marajoara also relied on trees such as the açai and tucuma palms not just for food, but likely also to make everyday objects like baskets and canoes. They also hunted a great variety of animals such as capybaras, deer, armadillos, and various kinds of birds. Apart from plants, their largest source of food came from the great variety of fish that populated the rivers and lakes on the island. The Marajoara constructed efficient water management systems including channels, fishponds, and dams that allowed them to trap fish and even turtles that could be penned to provide eggs and meat when the flood waters receded. The ingenuity of the Marajoara, who took an unforgiving climate and used its resources to their advantage for sustenance, can be seen even further in the great mounds they built to defy the floods and create a complex society.

Living Above the Flood

To combat the yearly flooding of the Amazon, the Marajoara built hundreds of monumental earthen mounds on which to live and bury their dead. These mounds were circular, oval, or long and narrow in shape, and have been found on the lowest parts of the island often next to rivers, streams, and lakes where water is available all year. This allowed the Marajoara to take advantage of areas where fish migrated often while also providing them with easy means of transportation. These were areas where there was extensive flooding during the rainy season, meaning the mounds kept Marajoara settlements and cemeteries out of reach. The mounds range in size and height, some as low as three metres high while others measure more than twenty metres above the floodplain, with the majority of mounds measuring one to three hectares in size. Many mounds were built to rise a great deal above the floodplain, and even though worldwide sea levels are higher now, they still only come halfway up most of the mounds. This indicates that the mounds may also have had a defensive function to them, and could have been a marker of prestige and wealth.[3]

The Marajoara population did not solely live on mounds. Many non-mound sites have been discovered in recent excavations along rivers and ancient embankments, and it seems that they were more numerous than the mounds that have defined archaeological investigations on Marajó Island.[4] These sites lack many of the elaborate items and structures that have been found on the mounds and are generally much simpler in form and function. The differences in these two kinds of sites therefore indicate that the Marajoara lived in a stratified society, and your occupation and status determined whether you lived high above the floodplain or closer to it.

Some settlements were made up of multiple mounds of different shapes and sizes located close to one another, with non-mound sites in between that would have been related and connected in some way. Most sites like this consist of three to five mounds, but others are much larger. The site of Os Camutins on the Anajas River, for example, encompassed forty mounds of various sizes all located in an area of around ten kilometres. These mound groupings are believed to have represented groups of people descended from the same ancestors who would have controlled the fisheries and maintained contact with each other.[5] In each group, the largest mounds were located next to the best economic areas, and this is also where the most luxurious objects and living spaces have been uncovered.

Construction of such large settlement projects would have required planning and organisation amongst the community, including the existence of a labour force and some political or symbolic control of resources and people. These requirements further indicate that there was a social hierarchy among these collections of elevated and lower settlements. It's possible the Marajoara people were organised into chiefdoms across the island that would have traded, intermarried, and sometimes fought with one another.[6]

Large mounds were strategically located to control access to aquatic resources and were home to high-status houses, ceremonial spaces, craft areas for manufacturing items such as jewellery or stone tools, and cemeteries.[7] Once built, these settlements were occupied for long periods of time. Some mounds have as many as twenty house foundations built on top of one another, meaning settlements were inhabited for multiple generations, and the floors and hearths were maintained for decades, if not longer. The surface area on top of the mounds was small, and space was limited. Because of this, it appears the Marajoara preferred communal living over individual family dwellings.

Up to twenty large, multifamily longhouses made of wood and thatch with dirt floors that were kept clean and covered with a layer of white sand were built on top of each mound. Down the centre of these longhouses were a series of long, trough-shaped cooking hearths. Each one was large enough to hold three large pots that were probably meant to feed a nuclear family. Hearth groupings like this are common in many matrilocal societies, where the husband goes to live with the wife's community after marriage. It is therefore likely that each longhouse belonged to an extended family where the women were related by blood.[8]

The Dead Amongst the Living

All known Marajoara cemeteries were not separated from the communities that buried their dead there. Rather, they have all been found on mounds alongside longhouses and other domestic structures. The Marajoara buried their dead in large, richly decorated polychrome ceramic pots that have become an iconic identifying symbol of their culture. Urns were buried after being temporarily displayed and venerated by loved ones. Over time, the continued burial of these vessels created vertical layers of clustered urns, as generation after generation continued this tradition. This vertical layering, along with the excellent preservation of the urns, which were painted with water-soluble pigments, has led scholars to suggest that the urns could have been partially buried whilst on display, or that the cemeteries were covered by roofed shelters to protect the graves from rain and floodwaters. These shelters would have also provided a space for the descendants of the deceased to visit and make offerings to their ancestors.

Three main types of burial have been found on mounds dating to the Marajoara period: primary burials, secondary burials, and cremation. The oldest burials had the deceased placed in a seated position into large ceramic jars covered with an upside-down plate or bowl. Burial urns ranged from plain, unpainted urns to ones that were elaborately painted or excised based on the status of the person interred inside. These large jars measured up to one metre tall with walls up to three centimetres thick. Decorated urns were covered with multiple painted, modelled, and incised red and white decorations including scrolls, animals, strange creatures, and human faces looking out from every direction. These faces may have been to protect the deceased and magically ward off those who wished to disturb the remains.[9]

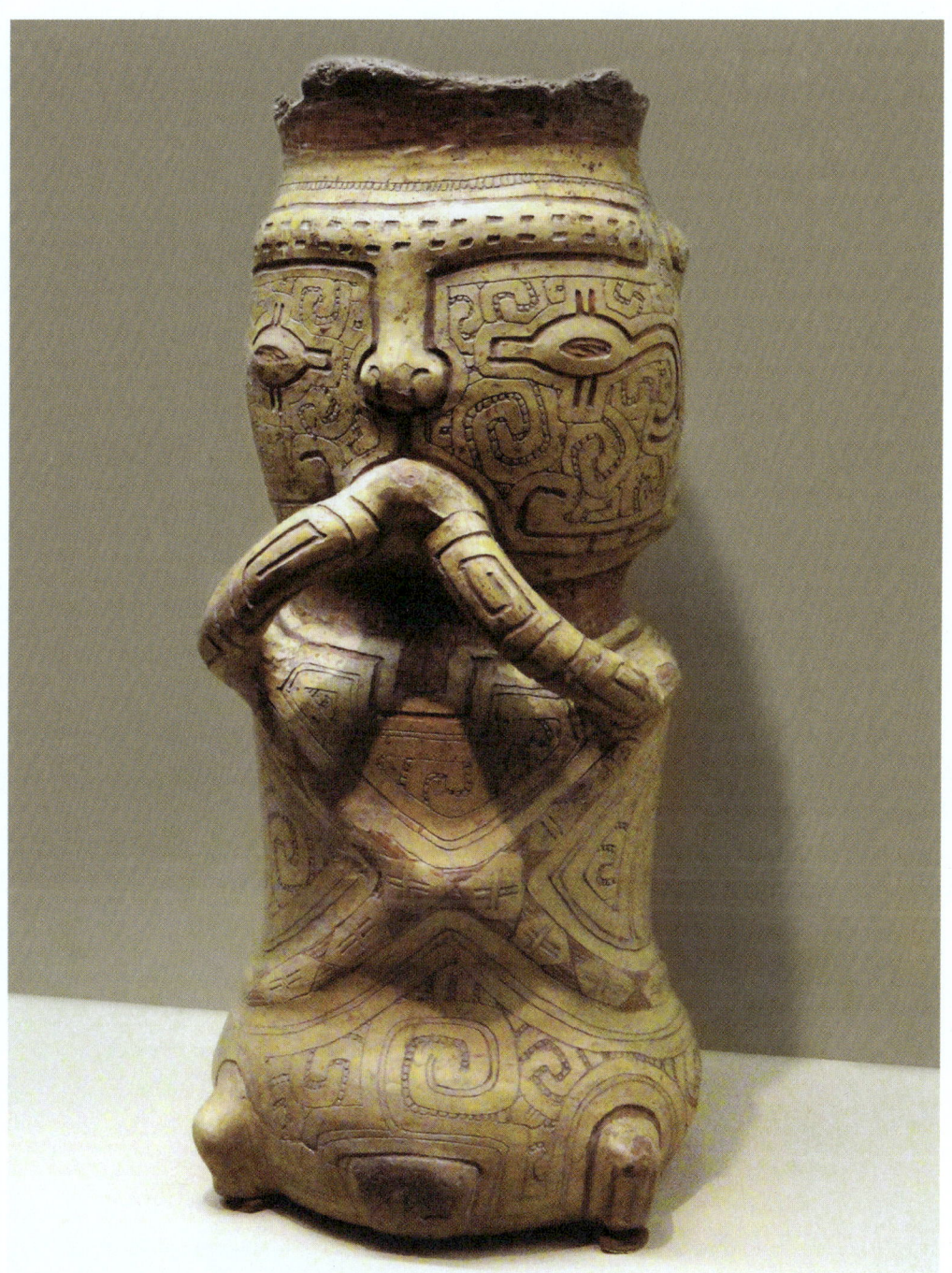

Example of a Marajoara burial urn depicting female anatomy.

Other visage decoration included large, modelled faces with heavy-lidded eyes, a short nose, and facial features defined with heavy lines and sometimes accompanied by a crouched body with a womb-like circle on the body with a face inside of it. This figure has been interpreted to be a sort of supernatural owl. Owls are known to swallow their prey whole and regurgitate the bones and the skin. The Marajoara may have believed that the owl transported the body of the deceased to the afterlife.[10] Funerary vessels would also have been decorated with familial symbols that identified their status, ancestors, and lineage.[11]

Marajoara burial practices changed and became more elaborate over time, eventually transitioning to secondary burials, with cremation displacing secondary burials in the later phases of Marajoara occupation. A secondary burial suggests the body is first placed somewhere to decay, flesh eventually separating from bone. Once this is complete, the bones are cleaned, sometimes coated in a red pigment, and then arranged in a pot. For these secondary burials, smaller jars were used as they no longer needed to fit in a whole person. Though smaller, these jars were no less elaborate. Some even took the shape of seated, possibly spiritual or shamanic female figures with rounded heads, eyes outlined in the shape of stylised scorpions or tadpoles, feet, and modelled arms and shoulders that sometimes took the shape of snakes or bird heads. This was the most popular method of burial for the mound-dwelling Marajoara, suggesting a belief that the soul or essence of a person was in their bones.[12]

Funerary urns contained more than just the bones of the deceased. Women were often found with ceramic pubic coverings called tangas (discussed below), stone beads, and small pots, while men were usually found with small stone tools. Organic objects and textiles may also have been included, but they have since decomposed and left no trace. The primarily female images on the urns suggest some form of ancestor worship within a ranked society that deified matrilineal ancestors. This, accompanied by the funerary practices and variety of imagery that has been found on these funerary urns, has led scholars to suggest that the

Marajoara believed in rebirth.[13] The sheltering of the bones within a female ancestor could serve as a womb for beginning a new life or receiving and delivering them to the next.

A Flurry of Lines and a Prevalence of Women

Marajoara ceramics are the earliest known group belonging to a widespread artistic tradition that originated in the lower Amazon called the Polychrome Horizon. They often painted their wares in a multitude of colours, but their most popular combination was black, brown, or red designs painted onto a white background. As with their funerary urns, elite and ceremonial Marajoara pottery was covered in intricate abstract and geometric designs such as scrolls, spirals, limbs with hands or feet, disembodied eyes, and heads of various shapes that filled every inch of the vessel. The Marajoara were also keen on representing the natural world, adding in human forms, bats, snakes, and even supernatural creatures such as one with two rectangular heads, large eyes, and a wide toothy mouth at either end of a slender body. This ornamentation would have held meaning for Marajoara communities and would have been connected to their cosmology, myths and legends, working as a visual code to complement their ceremonies and rituals, and to define and communicate their culture.[14]

Undecorated ceramics were used for daily domestic activities such as cooking, storage, fermentation, eating, and drinking. When looking at both the elaborate and everyday pottery, the technical ability of Marajoara potters shows highly skilled work that required a honing of the craft and specialisation within the community. Each chiefdom or group developed their own regional differences in style and pottery would have been produced locally with unique symbols or patterns according to their identity.

The majority of Marajoara art that depicts humans when the sex is clearly indicated, is female. Some of the most common ceramic figurines representing females are highly stylised and elaborately carved or decorated hollow pieces. Some have pellets inside to make them rattle, and they possess large heads and little or no arms. They are usually in a seated position with their knees spread open. While the sex of these figures is mostly female, their overall shape is phallic. These objects have been interpreted to represent sexuality and reproduction, and may have been used in shamanic rituals to possibly aid in fertility or protection during childbirth.[15] As they were only found in cemeteries, they most likely had some use during funerary rituals, and may have represented rebirth.

The most abundant ceramic objects found at Marajoara sites were triangular pieces that appear to be female pubic coverings called tangas. They were worn by attaching a belt made of cord through the pierced holes on top, and were custom made to fit the wearer. Like the rest of Marajoara pottery, some tangas were elaborately decorated. Painted ones may have been used for ceremonies such as marriages, puberty rituals, or other special occasions or rites of passage.[16] Plainer ones could have been used for daily wear, possibly by women who had completed these rites of passage and taken on new roles within their community.

Other well-documented pottery pieces that define Marajoara culture are small, pear-shaped containers with holes pierced through the rim that could have been hung around the neck. Some of these containers were used for holding ground red pigment that could have been used to paint pottery, bodies, or the bones of the deceased before their secondary burial. Other theories suggest they could have held tobacco or hallucinogenic drugs that would have been ingested via ceramic snuffers that have also been found at Marajoara sites.[17] After the tangas, the second most abundant ceramic items found are round stools consisting of a clay disc with a flaring base decorated with human faces. The faces could possibly represent ancestors meant to "support" their descendants, and reinforce their claims to precious resources or status.[18]

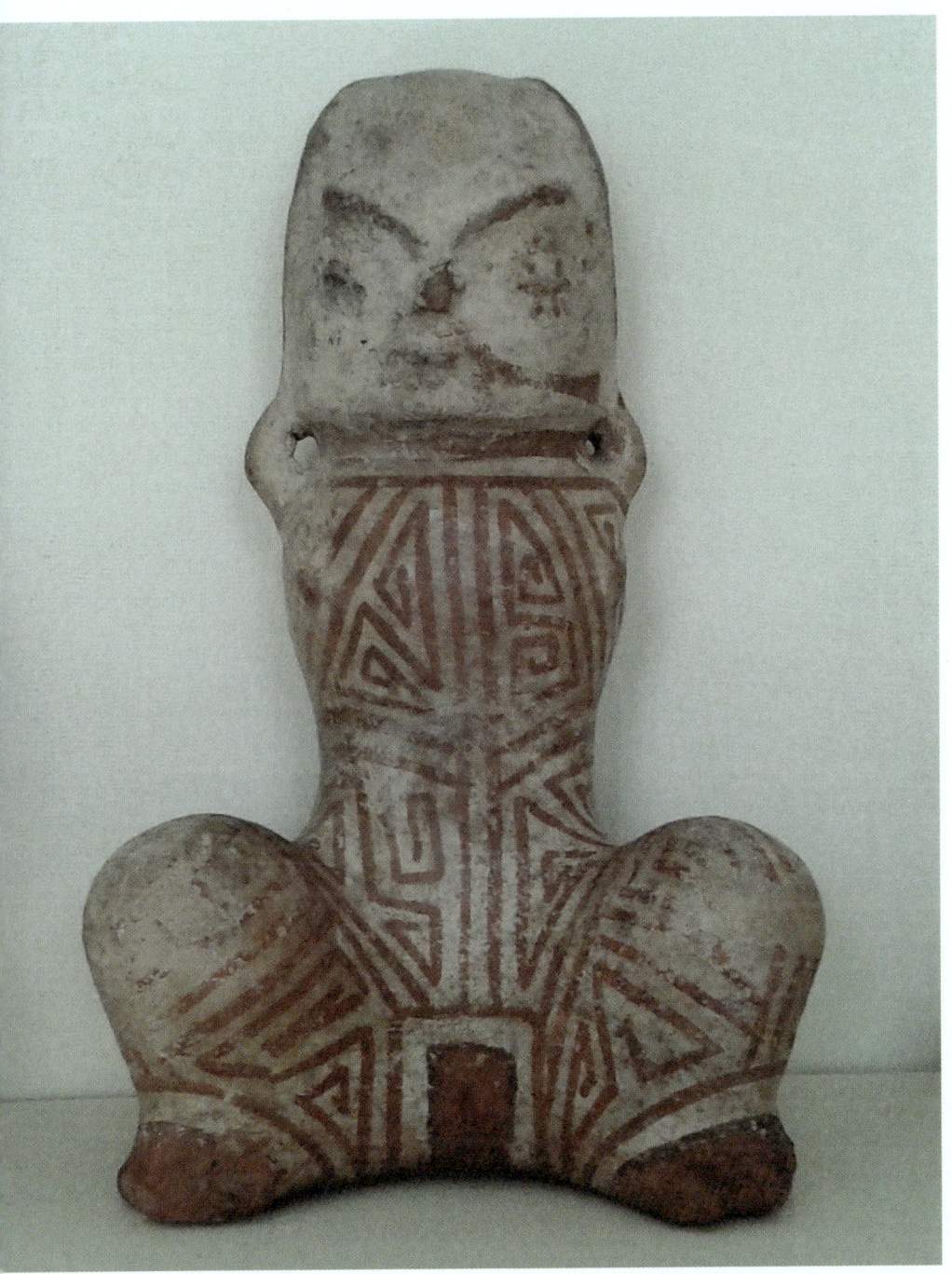
Phallic ceramic figure of a female.

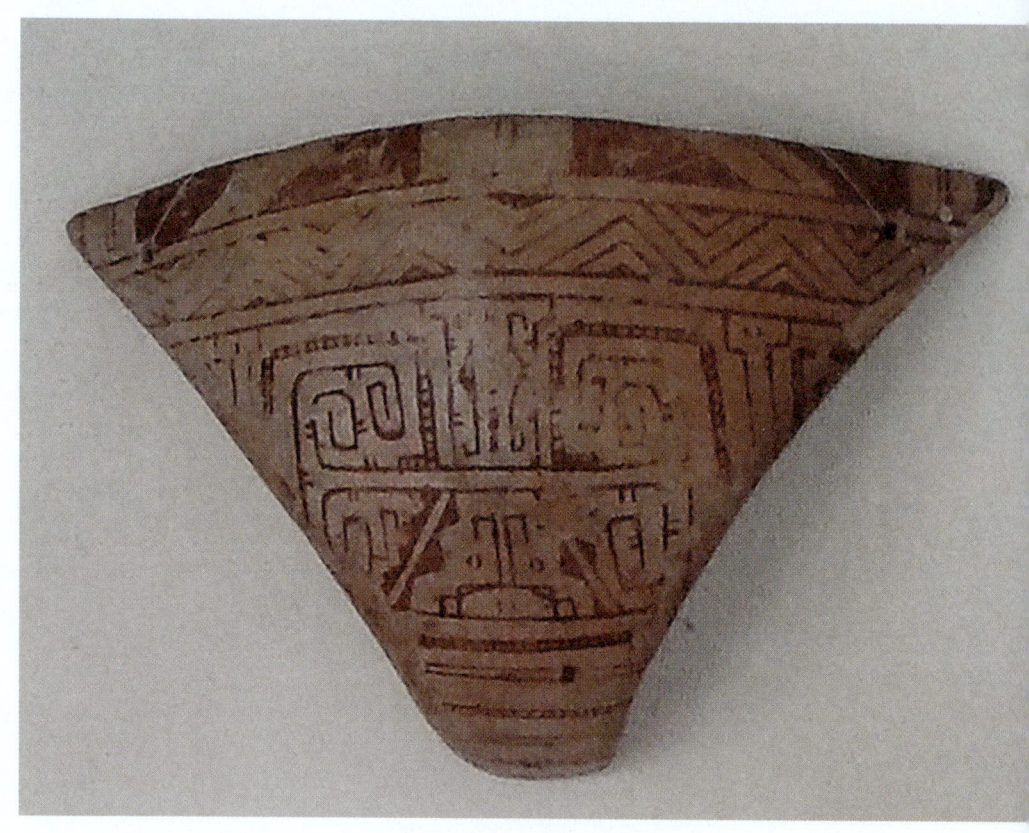

Example of a tanga.

Abandoning the Island

Marajó Island is thought to have been inhabited until shortly before European contact, and many scholars believe the Marajoara culture came to an end without any known reason around 1300 CE. While this can be attested to at some sites where buildings were no longer being repaired or built upon, recent radiocarbon dates have extended Marajoara habitation an extra three hundred years, putting them in direct contact with European colonists.[19] The first Europeans to make contact with Marajó Island were Dutch and French traders in the sixteenth century, and colonial documents discuss several indigenous nations known as the *Nheegnga bas* inhabiting the mounds on the savannas.

Based on the evidence available to us, these groups may have been the ethnohistorical equivalent of the Marajoara in their last phase of existence. If they were, Portuguese records claim that expeditions were launched to enslave and "pacify" the *Nheegnga bas*, but they resisted defeat by abandoning their settlements. A peace treaty was finally settled in 1659, and by the end of the eighteenth century, the remaining population on the island had been relocated throughout the lower Amazon. Regardless of whether the Marajoara were the *Nheegnga bas,* the presence of such a mound-dwelling society that developed a beautifully complex artform and belief system along an unlikely floodplain speaks to the ingenuity of pre-Columbian cultures, and the rich communities that thrived in South America before European contact.

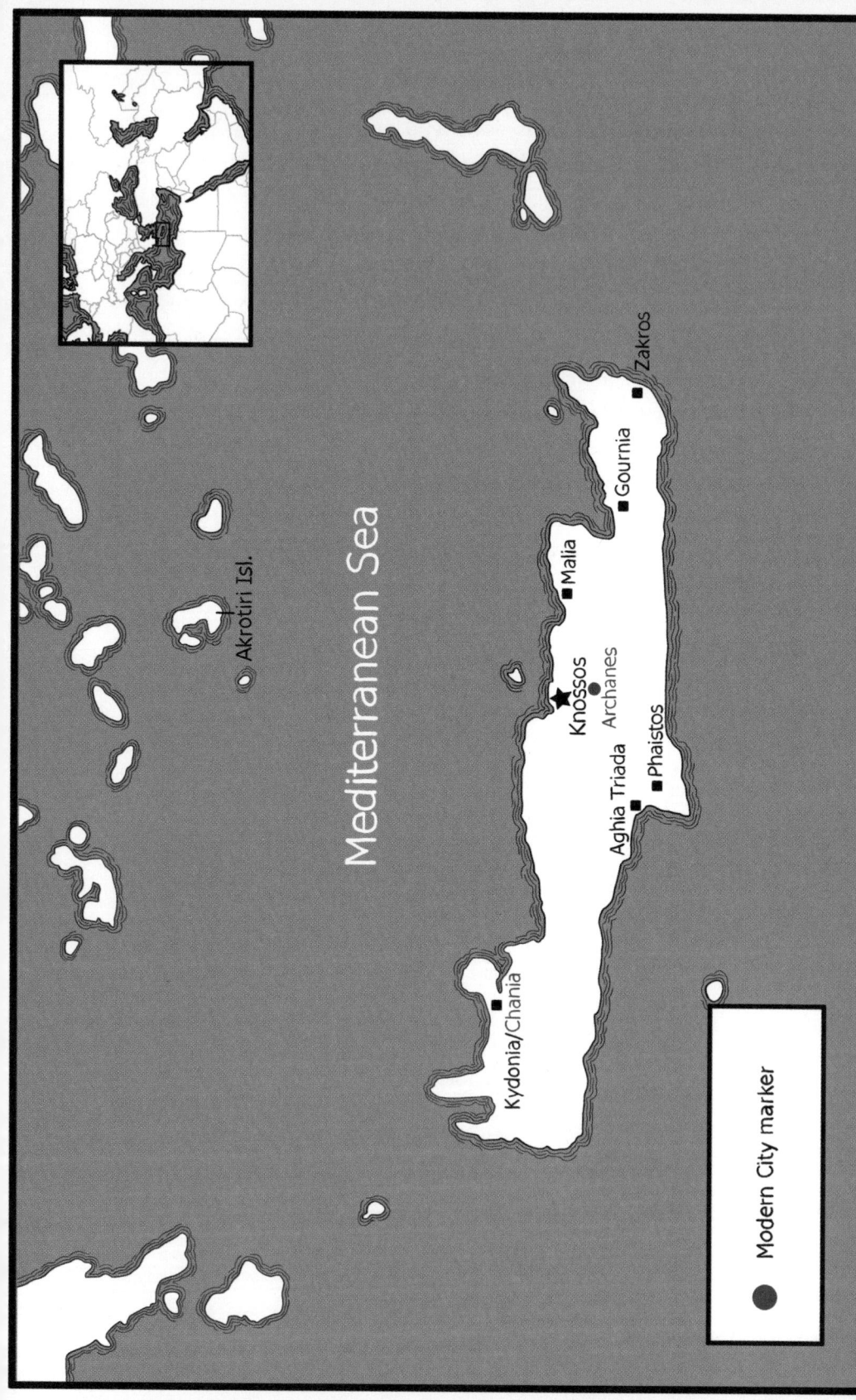

Chapter Ten

Minoans
The Home of the Minotaur

The crowd roared with awe and excitement as the bull was brought into the courtyard. The young man's palms were sweaty. He had been practising this leap for months, but when he laid eyes on the bull, the reality of what he was about to do in front of countless people finally set in. The bull tossed its head, swaying its pointed horns left and right in defiance, angry at being penned in the courtyard. The man looked over at his fellow acrobats, meeting their eyes as they gave him reassuring nods.

"It'll be fine," the acrobat next to him grabbed his shoulder in reassurance, "forget the audience and focus on the bull, just like we practised," she said.

The young man nodded, his eyes never leaving the bull as it paced around the courtyard. "I'm ready," he said.

The acrobats stepped forward into the courtyard as the crowd cheered and shouted words of encouragement. Some were even singing holy prayers. The cacophony of sound thrummed in the young man's ears. He closed his eyes, took a deep breath, then looked up at the bull now at the centre of the ring. The other two acrobats had taken their places at either end of the bull, moving with it to ensure they would always be where they were needed: one to grab its horns and the other to catch him on the other side.

"Now or never," the young man thought. He gave the signal to his team and began running towards the bull, adjusting his course as the bull tried to evade the other two. As he approached, the first acrobat grabbed the bull's horns and used their bodyweight to pull its head down as the young man leapt into the air, careening through the horns and landing his hands on the bull's back. In the same breath he used the momentum to push himself off the bull in a front flip, landing in front of the second acrobat.

It was all over in an instant. The crowd exploded into applause and the young man looked around the court, panting but never feeling more alive. His fellow acrobats came over and the three of them embraced excitedly as the bull wranglers took control of the beast.

"You did it!" they cheered. The young man could only smile and thank them before they turned to bow to the audience. He couldn't believe he pulled it off, and he couldn't wait to do it again.

An Island of Myth

We know very little about the Minoans. Most of what remains of this Bronze Age civilisation that once dominated Crete are the myths that have come down to us from both the ancient Greeks and the early archaeologists who tasked themselves with recreating the daily lives of the people who created complex, maze-like buildings, mysterious languages, finely detailed miniature art, and brightly coloured frescoes filled with fantastical scenes. As with most ancient cultures where no writing exists or the language has yet to be deciphered (many of which are in this book), we can only speculate and create educated guesses based on the archaeological record.

The Minoans get their name from the mythological King Minos. According to Greek myth, Minos was the king of Crete and the son of the Greek god Zeus and Europa, a princess from Tyre in Lebanon. This term was coined by Sir Arthur Evans, who began the first systematic excavations on Crete and believed he found the possible site of the palace of the legendary king, as well as the setting for the myth of Theseus and the Minotaur. We don't know what the Minoans called themselves or their island, but we do know that they had far-reaching contact throughout the Mediterranean and beyond. Minoan artefacts have been found throughout the Aegean Sea, the Greek mainland, and the Middle East. Their presence was even felt as far away as the Indus Valley, Sicily, Sardinia, and Spain, possibly through secondary trade.

Early Minoan society probably developed largely from the already-present Neolithic communities who most likely came from Anatolia and had inhabited Crete from around 7000 BCE, and possibly with another migration of newcomers from the east.[1] These Early Bronze Age peoples developed into more urbanised, stratified societies and thrived in the Mediterranean for thousands of years before power shifted and they became nothing but myth until the early twentieth century. The Minoan timeline has been pieced together over the years, and two different chronologies have been developed to help separate phases of development. One was created by Evans based on the pottery collected at the largest site on Crete, Knossos; another based on the development of the large, multi-room structures that have famously been called palaces. Both are used and generally accepted today, though the details and exact dates of each period are still disputed. While these periodisations help in our understanding of the archaeological record, the transition into each new phase would have been a gradual development. There are always moments of overlap, and more complexity than scholars can understand when restricted to archaeological investigations.

The Minoan Timeline

Evans Periods	Palatial Periods
Early Minoan: 3000 BCE–2000 BCE	Pre-Palatial: 3500–2000/1900 BCE
Middle Minoan: 2000 BCE–1600 BCE	Protopalatial: 2000/1900 BCE–1650 BCE
Late Minoan: 1600 BCE–1100 BCE	Neopalatial: 1650 BCE–1450 BCE
	Post-Palatian/Creto-Mycenaean: 1450 BCE–1100 BCE

As their Bronze Age technology developed and communities grew, local hierarchies took hold around Crete, creating larger hubs with ruling elites. The Minoans were expert shipbuilders, and quite early began expanding their outward look towards lands beyond Crete. Around 1900–1700 BCE, they began exporting pottery and stone vessels, and other commodities like olive oil, cloth, and skilled workers around the Aegean, Egypt, and the Near East. In return they imported precious materials such as alabaster, ivory, tin, and copper. This expansion of trade also came with an expansion of influence. Minoan frescoes have been found in a Canaanite palace at the site of Tel Kabri in Israel and Tel el-Dab'a in the Nile Delta of Egypt. Minoans also appear to have set up colonies on many of the Aegean and Cycladic islands, the largest and most well-known being Akrotiri located on the island of Santorini.

The Complexity of the Palace Complex

Starting around 1950 BCE, complex structures that have been dubbed palaces were built at Knossos, Phaistos, and Malia, along with a paved road network that connected these three communities. It is likely that Pre-Palatial buildings and meeting areas lie underneath these early palaces, but after 2000 BCE is when the large-scale building of local community and administrative centres began.[2] These first palaces were destroyed sometime around 1700 BCE, either by an earthquake or unknown invasion. Whatever the reason, the palaces were quickly rebuilt, with two more appearing at Zakros and Kydonia, and the road network was expanded to further connect the island. Similar, smaller structures have been found at other sites, and more are thought to be hidden beneath the modern towns of Chania and Archanes. Minoan culture became even stronger at this time, and the island of Crete began to flourish.

Minoan palace complexes were large, well-planned, and organised, and would have required resourcing large amounts of labour and materials. This means that people in the palace towns and the surrounding areas would have been involved in supporting their construction. By the end of the Protopalatial period, it seems that all palace sites had conformed to a similar plan. While each site may have been ruled or overseen by independent elites, there appears to have been some form of cultural, economic, and administrative unity throughout Crete.[3]

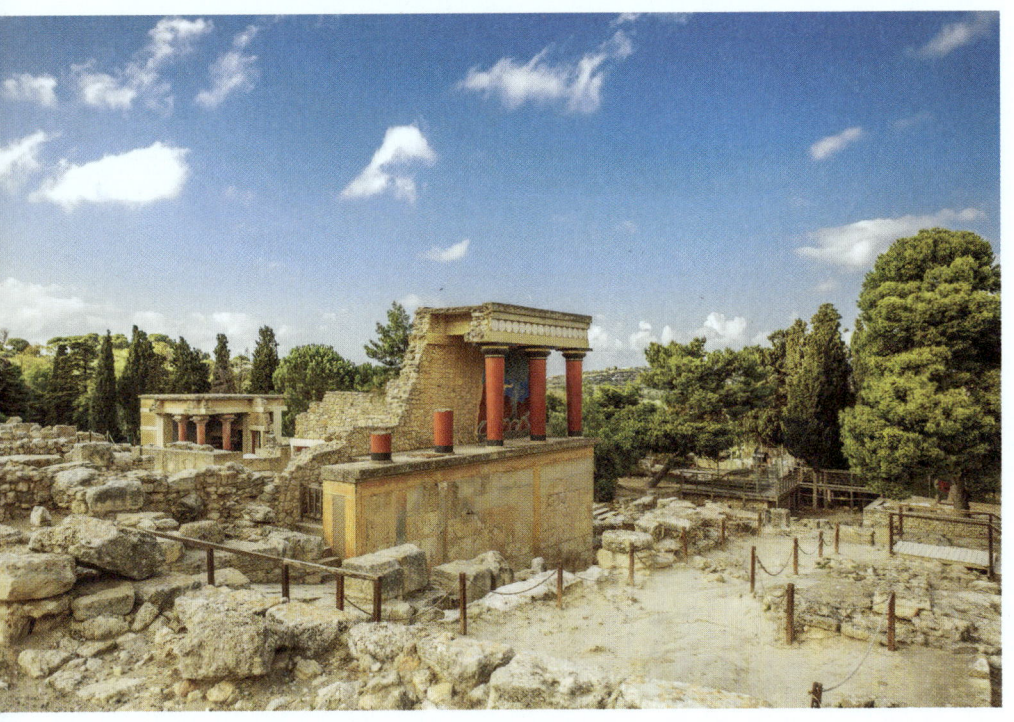

Partially reconstructed palace at Knossos.

The precise function of Minoan palaces is still unknown. Minoan rulers seem to have taken on the role of judge or high priest rather than king and there are no representations of powerful "rulers" in Minoan art. No wealthy tombs that could be considered as "royal" have been found until after the Neopalatial period. None of the palaces contain throne rooms either, except for the one at Knossos, which most likely dates to the period after the Minoans when the Mycenaeans spread to Crete. Knossos was the largest palace on Crete and was likely the ideological or cultural centre of the island.

Due to the number of storage rooms for agricultural goods and administrative records that have been found, the palaces themselves have been interpreted more as redistribution centres. Trade and exchange would have been organised within them, and all vital resources would have been controlled to ensure there was enough for the proper functioning of the cities and surrounding areas. Palaces have also been described as production centres for specialised crafts, and because Minoan communities lack temples within settlements, they have also been thought to be religious hubs or sacred buildings.[4] Because of the complexity of these structures, the term "palace" has been thought by scholars to be outdated, believing they functioned more as court compounds.

The Minoan palace has been described as being a city within a city.[5] Palaces could be up to three storeys high at points, contained elaborate staircases and were filled with colourful frescoes. They would have been a focal point in the urban landscape and were built to impress, with their outer facades made of gypsum so it would gleam in the sun. They were multifunctional buildings with a labyrinth of rooms arranged in four wings around a large rectangular central court, with a Western court that would have been more accessible to the public. Scholars believe the central courts were possibly used for ritualised communal gatherings,[6] while some Western courts had steps that would have enabled spectators to observe performances and processions.[7] Some of the most notable features of Minoan palaces were light wells that were cut into the ceilings to allow light and ventilation to pour through the building, and the monumental columns that were wider at the top than at the bottom. These columns were carved from wood rather than stone, painted a deep red or black, and rested on stone capitals.

There appears to have been little planning when the palaces were eventually expanded, creating a maze-like effect that can still be seen by visitors today. Remains of Minoan palaces possibly gave rise to the ancient Greek legend of Theseus and the Minotaur. Apart from multiple storage rooms, palaces were filled with workshops for craft production, possible state apartments for the royal family or ruling elite, and potential ritual spaces such as small crypts filled with pillars and lustral basins. These basins were sunken rooms entered by a series of steps that were possibly for some sort of purification or oil anointing rites, as "oil flasks" have been found in the basin at Knossos. Palaces seem to have been the centre of Minoan life, socially, politically, and religiously, and would have been bustling places filled with colour, fine objects, and people from all walks of life.

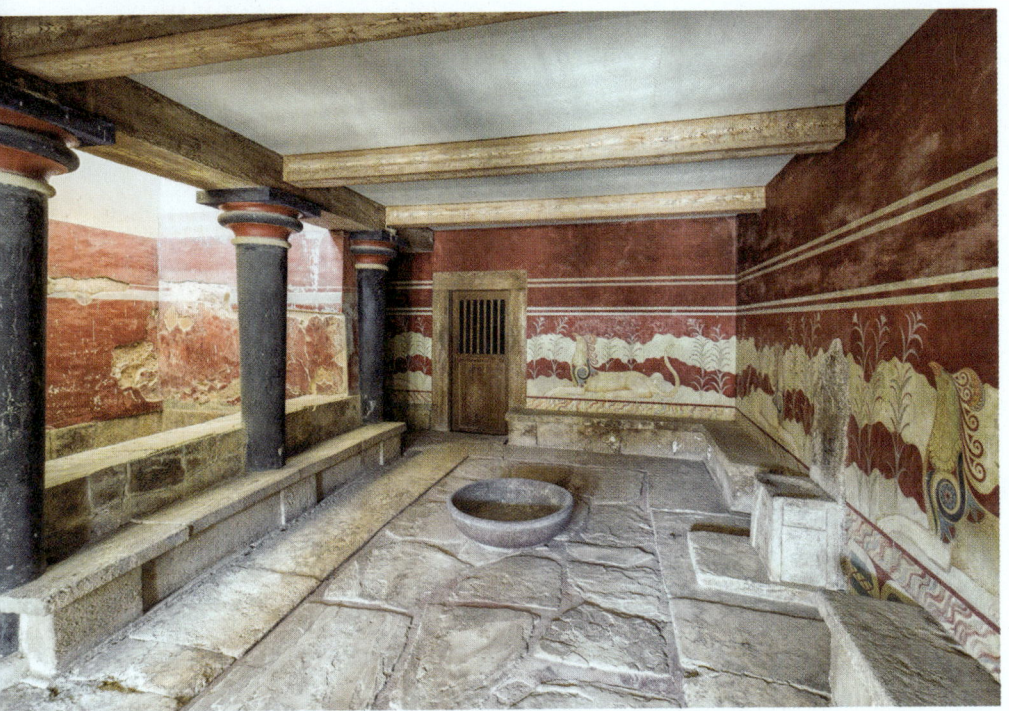

Throne room filled with frescoes at Knossos.

Living in Crete

Little is known about the lives of ordinary Minoans. Much of the research and excavations have been focussed on the palaces and other elite buildings, but that is slowly changing. Even outside larger palace settlements, most studies have looked at the large "Country Houses" or "Villas" that were possibly where the local governors lived. These structures would have acted similarly to palaces, storing food, conducting administrative activities, and possessing a cult or religious area.[8] One of the best visual examples we have that show us what regular people would have lived in is the Town Mosaic found in Knossos dating to around the seventeenth century BCE. The mosaic is made of faience and shows multi-storey houses with windows on the first floor and small flat roofs that may have been a cooler place to sleep on hot summer nights. Houses were also built with strength and flexibility in mind to withstand earthquakes.

The Minoans were skilled at water management. They built complex drainage and sewage systems that were so well made that the main water supply ducts at Knossos, Phaistos, Zakros, and Aghia Triada are still functional today. Sewer pipes were made of tapering clay tubes and sealed with cement. This allowed one to fit perfectly into the other, and the shape acted as a method of speeding up the water as it moved through the pipe so it didn't clog. Pipes brought water to every part of the palace where it was either purified by forcing it through a porous ceramic wall or filter made out of sand or charcoal, or used for baths or for flushing indoor toilets.

There is little evidence of war or settlement fortifications during the Neopalatial period, but this doesn't mean that Minoan settlements had no means of defending themselves. Some structures have been found along roads dating to the Bronze Age that could be interpreted as guard houses, though they seem to have been from an earlier period.[9] There are also defensive walls and a possible tower at the site of Gournia, and tombs have been found containing weapons such as swords and daggers. With their international trade, the Minoans were also expert shipbuilders, meaning they likely had a powerful navy. This would have ensured the maintenance of peaceful relationships with their trading partners.[10]

The Decipherment Dilemma

The Minoans developed multiple writing systems, and were the first people in the Aegean to develop them. The appearance of Minoan palaces and organised states that were focussed on trade and the redistribution of goods meant that writing was needed for recordkeeping and administration. The standardisation of writing throughout the island was possibly a way for the elite to legitimise their power in society.[11] As with most ancient cultures, literacy was used as a marker of status and control. Three writing systems on Crete were developed: a hieroglyphic script possibly based on the Hittite writing system, a syllabic script called Linear A that was developed on the island, and the script found on the infamous Phaistos disc which possibly originates from a foreign land.

Linear A and the hieroglyphic script have yet to be deciphered, and that is largely in part due to the limited number of examples that have been found. The hieroglyphic script was developed first, appearing on clay tablets around 2100 BCE. Linear A emerged around 1800 BCE and became the dominant language on Crete during the Neopalatial period, with the hieroglyphic script disappearing in the seventeenth century BCE. Both scripts are syllabic, each consisting of many signs that represent certain syllables, and it appears that Linear A may have developed from the hieroglyphic script. So far, scholars have identified about sixty Linear A syllabic symbols and about the same number of pictograms that are thought to represent words, objects, or ideas. These were inscribed on various objects like pottery, stone vases, and metal objects that were most likely for cultic or religious use. Mostly, Linear A is found on clay tablets that were used for administrative recordkeeping. It is also likely that it was used on materials like parchment or papyrus that have not survived in the archaeological record.

Linear A tablets have been found in palaces and "country houses" all over Crete, and although the script has not yet been deciphered, researchers have been able to decode their numbering system. If these texts are ever able to be understood completely, they would provide a rich insight into the movement of the goods coming in and out of the palaces, labour, and possibly even some personal details. The later Linear B script that appears on Crete seems to have been developed from Linear A but was adopted by the Mycenaeans for their early form of Greek. Linear B can be read, but as it was used for a different language, it does not help scholars in their quest to understand the language spoken by the Minoans.

A View from the Top

The Minoans appear to have had complex religious beliefs and practices. By looking at pottery, figurines, and engravings found on gold rings, it appears their deities were mostly female. These deities have been interpreted to represent mother goddesses, deities of animals and hunting, a goddess of snakes or of the earth, and even a protector of sailors. Some male deities do appear, like a Master of Animals, but the priesthood was almost entirely female, meaning women were possibly in charge of Minoan religious rites.[12]

There were also many symbols that seemed to have religious importance to the Minoans. Sacred trees and springs, and a double axe called a *labrys* that was pictured to be held by women and possibly used to sacrifice bulls (though all examples that have been found were too thin for practical use), all appear to have held significance.[13] There were also stone slabs with two upturned and pointed ends that have been called horns of consecration as they resemble bull's horns. These horns appear on many artistic objects such as frescoes, coffins, and rings. They were frequently mounted on altars, meaning they were probably an important religious symbol. Some scholars think that the horns were a symbol of the sun and related to the ancient Egyptian symbol of the horizon.[14]

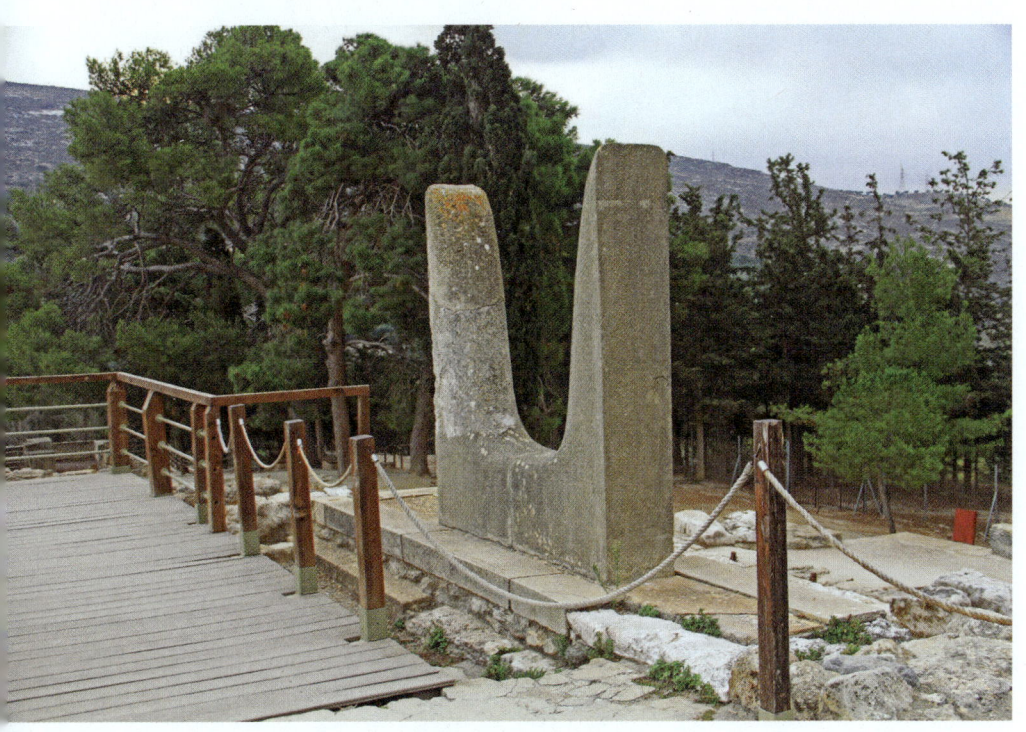

Horns of consecration.

There is no evidence of separate temples, so all religious activity within towns and cities likely took place in palaces and private residences. When the Minoans did want to host religious rites in a dedicated space, they did so at hilltop shrines or in the secrecy of caves. These shrines are known as peak sanctuaries and were open-air areas of worship. Archaeologists have found walls, movable sacrificial tables, benches, oil lamps, and libation vessels at these peaks, hinting that they would have been elaborately furnished when they were in use. Sites like this are where the Minoans came to worship their deities.

The presence of oil lamps hints at the possibility of nighttime rituals, and burnt ash and bones could be indicative of sacrifices and feasts that went until late in the evening. Many small clay figurines have been found depicting humans with their hands in a gesture of prayer, as well as animals. Individual body parts were moulded out of clay, and pebbles

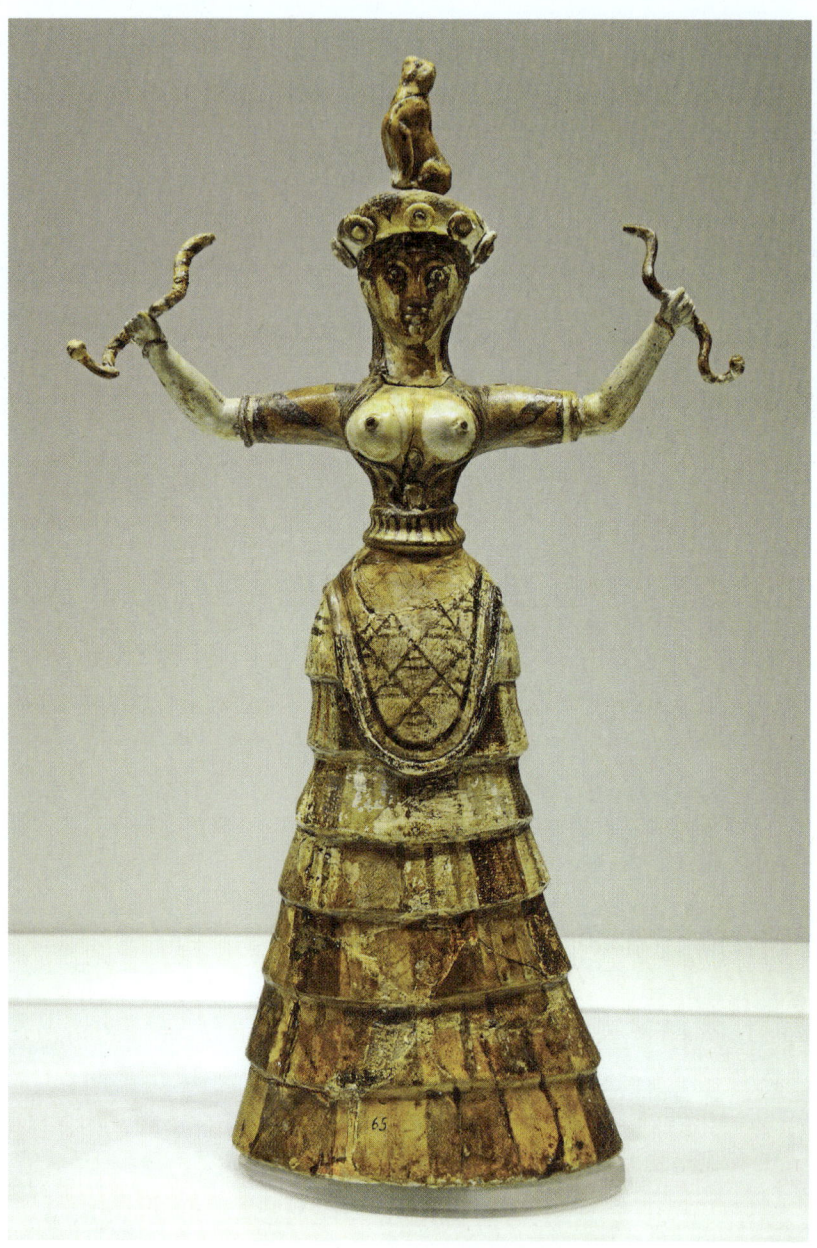

"Snake goddess" figurine found at the palace of Knossos. The reconstruction and interpretation of the snake goddess figurines has been heavily debated since their discovery in the early 1900s. While the true function of the "goddess" remains unclear, the exposed breasts hint at her being some kind of fertility figure.

were brought up from the valley below. These high peaks were possibly considered liminal zones by the Minoans, important points for contact with the divine.[15] The Minoans also seem to have developed a knowledge of astronomy comparable to ancient Egypt and Babylon, and some scholars have argued that these peak sanctuaries were also used as observatories.[16]

In complete contrast to the altitude and openness of the peak sanctuaries, the Minoans sometimes used cave entrances as spaces for cult activities such as animal sacrifices, dancing, and feasting. Unlike peak sanctuaries that were generally easy to reach from settlements, some caves were located quite far from living spaces. Visits to these sites would have required a pilgrimage that could have been part of the ritual process. The use of caves for ritual activities increased in the Neopalatial period, probably due to the earthquakes that shook the island at the end of the Protopalatial period, bringing more of a religious focus to the underworld.[17]

Walls Filled with Explosive Colour

Unlike other Bronze Age civilisations such as the ancient Egyptians or the Mesopotamians, the Minoans did not use their art to convey historical or political events. No rulers were shown in power, and there is no pictorial evidence for trade relations with foreign cultures. Instead, the Minoans covered the walls of their palaces and houses with bright and lively frescoes depicting their lifestyle from around 1700 BCE onwards. This unique art style, filled with naturalism and vivid impressions, was so well-known and popular that the technique spread as far as Egypt and Israel. Much of this style came from the method in which the Minoans created their frescoes. By painting on wet plaster, artists had to work quickly, giving the images a feeling of lifelike spontaneity. All frescoes found to date are just small fragments of what they once were. Most have been restored, though those completed in the

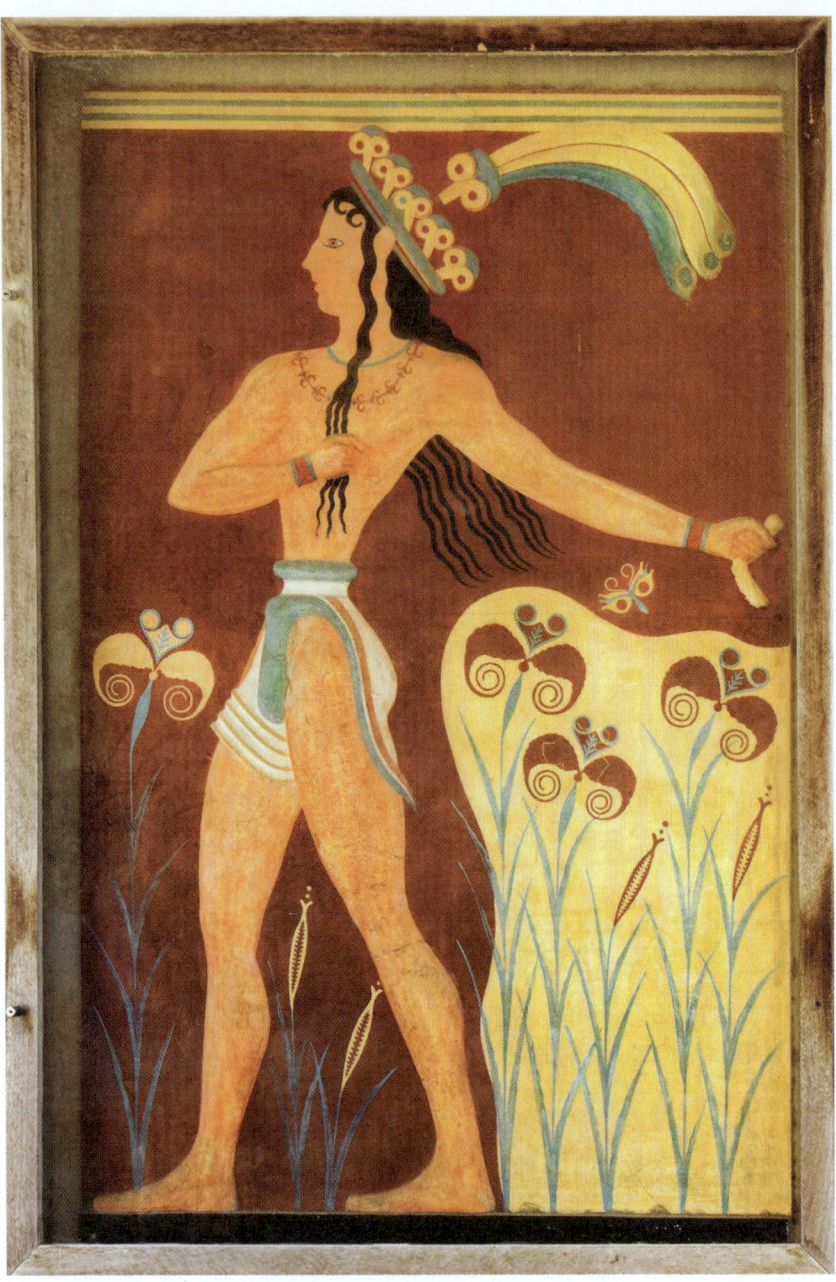

Fresco of the Prince of Lilies (also known as The Priest King Fresco). Only a few fragments of the original remain, so it has been heavily restored, with many artistic liberties taken. This current reconstruction has been heavily criticised and reinterpreted multiple times.

1900s were quite imaginatively done and are not accurate reconstructions of what they truly looked like in their original form.

Most of the frescoes depict scenes of palace life or images of nature. There are processions, court ceremonies, religious festivals, and animals in their natural habitats such as monkeys, birds, cats, and even flying fish and griffins. There were also scenes of human control over nature, like hunting, and sporting activities such as chariot driving, boxing, and the infamous bull leaping. Bull leaping has been suggested to have been both public entertainment and religious ceremony, with the beast representing a major deity. It was such a popular activity for the Minoans that it was depicted not just on walls, but also on gold signet rings and as tiny figurines, made of bronze and ivory. The feat would have taken place in front of a crowd of spectators, with young, athletic acrobats, possibly of both genders displaying their dominance over the animal world.[18]

The Minoans translated this fluid, vivid art form onto other pieces, such as their highly ornamented gold jewellery loved by both men and women, stone vases made of soft stone, and their pottery. Marine animals were of special importance on Minoan pottery and their pots were filled with decorations of shells, crabs, dolphins, and octopuses that sprawled over the entire surface. Even ordinary domestic ware was carefully decorated in multiple colours, showing just how much the Minoans loved beauty at every level of society. The prominence of women in Neopalatial art, depicting them as powerful figures in religion, administration, and business, and rarely in a domestic or child-rearing setting, is also striking in comparison to other Bronze Age civilisations, where those two traditions normally reigned supreme.[19] Minoan women therefore seem to have played an important role in society in the Neopalatial period, and could have had a greater degree of equality with men than other ancient Mediterranean cultures at the time.

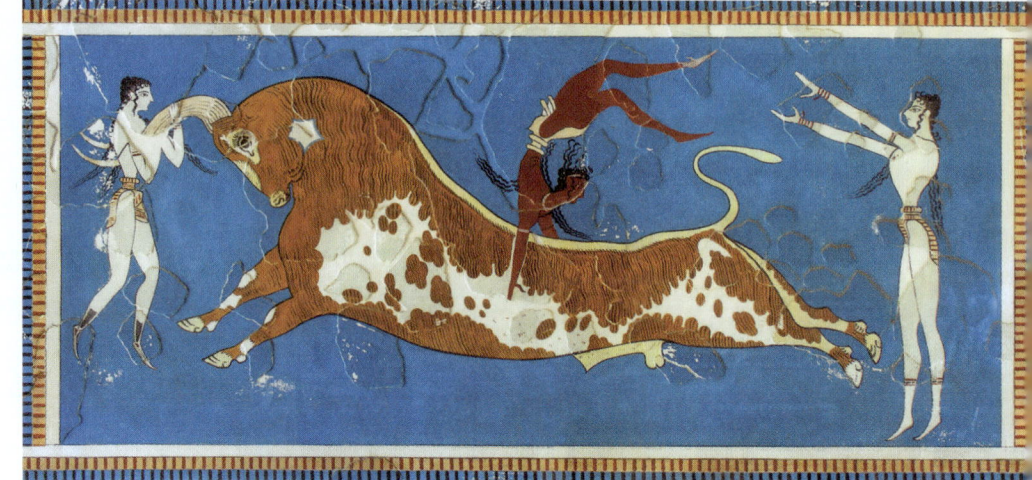

Bull-Leaping fresco found at Knossos.

Descending into Legend

The reasons for Minoan decline and disappearance from Crete are still debated today. For a long time, their demise was linked with the volcanic eruption on the island of Thera. Scholars believed that ash and flooding from a tsunami caused economic collapse. New analysis suggests that the eruption was actually much earlier and occurred during the Neopalatial period, having little effect on the island of Crete. Regardless of if it was affected by the eruption at Thera, by the middle of the fifteenth century BCE, most of Crete's palaces and villas were destroyed apart from Knossos. While the palace's living quarters were decimated, the building remained intact until 1375 BCE. Some believe that seismic activity dating to after the eruption in Thera could have devastated the coastal areas of Crete, leading to a decline in trade.[20] Another alternative is that a drought afflicted the island, leading to civil unrest and the weakening of Minoan society. It is possible, therefore, that a weakened Crete was invaded around 1450 BCE by the Mycenaeans who captured Knossos and ruled there after destroying the other palaces on the island to secure their reign.[21]

The Mycenaeans were more aggressive than the Minoans in their wants to expand their cultural influence around the Mediterranean, and they would have been in contact with them during the Late Bronze Age. While there is little evidence for conquest, by the second half of the fifteenth century BCE, Crete was largely composed of Mycenaean city-states, and the written language shifted from Linear A to Linear B. Over the next few hundred years, until the infamous Bronze Age Collapse during the twelfth century BCE, the Minoan culture slowly disappeared from Crete, eventually becoming the stuff of myth, and the home of the Minotaur.

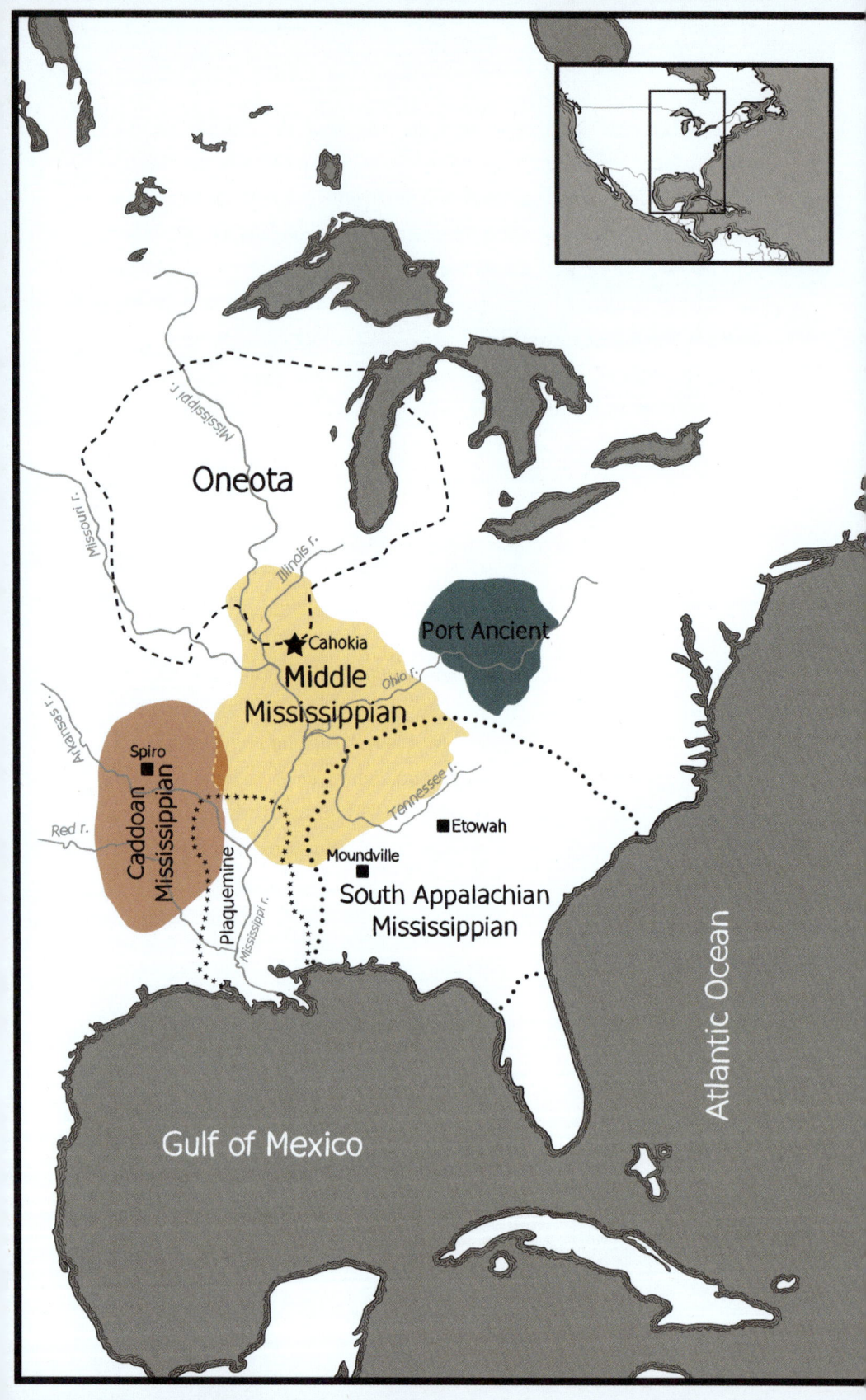

Chapter Eleven

Mississippian
North America's First City

The athlete looked up at the black earthen mound that rose behind him, and then at the crowd that had gathered around the plaza. The chief stood at its edge with the other elders, gazing upon the masses who had travelled great distances to be here for the festivities. For many, it was their first time in such a large place. The athlete had only been here once before, years ago as a child to witness the very game in which he was about to take part. He still remembered how small he felt when he first laid eyes upon the great mounds that were dotted throughout the city. He expected them to appear smaller this time around, now that he was older, but the behemoths still towered over him.

Turning to rejoin his team, the athlete straightened and prepared himself for the game. At the chief's signal, the athlete, his fellow teammates, and their opposition, shuffled into position at the end of the plaza. He could feel the tension rise as they all adjusted their grips on their throwing sticks.

The thrower emerged from the crowd carrying the discoidal stone, the object of the game, his fingers gripping its concave sides. Like the others, he too got into position by centring himself between the two teams.

The crowd quieted as they awaited the final signal for the game to start. The athlete eyed the stone with the careful precision of a hunter. The years that he had played this game with the other boys in his village growing up had all led to this moment.

The second signal was given, and the round seemed to be over as soon as it began. The crowd cheered as the thrower hurled the stone down the field. The athlete and his teammates sprang into action as both teams began their sprint down the plaza after the rolling stone. After only a few steps, spears began to fly through the air towards their target, each athlete doing their best to judge where the stone would land, hoping their spear would be the closest.

Never taking his eyes off the stone, the athlete coolly calculated the distance and threw his spear to where he believed the stone would fall. It was all he could do not to look away as he tracked his spear through the throng of others as they all cascaded to the ground. Too far. He had overshot his mark.

The athlete sighed with disappointment as the other team jumped and cheered when the scores had been tallied. But he couldn't help but smile. He loved the game, and it wasn't over yet; he knew his team could rally. The athlete collected his spear and sprinted back to the starting line to set up for the next round.

Born in the American Bottom

The Mississippian culture is not defined by one specific group of people. Rather, the term embraces a wide range of localised groups that flourished in what is now the Midwestern and Southeastern United States from approximately 800 CE. These groups are known as the Middle Mississippian, Fort Ancient, South Appalachian Mississippian, Plaquemine Mississippian, Cadoan Mississippian, and the Oneota. While each of these groups had their own unique traits, they shared aspects of an ethnic identity that went beyond their cultural, linguistic, and geographical differences.[1]

The origin of the Mississippian culture is still debated amongst scholars. There is a general consensus, however, that they were a continuation of the cultures (particularly the Hopewell) living in the floodplain of the Mississippi River at its confluence with the Missouri and Illinois Rivers in modern southern Illinois, known as the American Bottom, during the Late Woodland Stage (c. 500–1000 CE). What is debated is how fast this change happened. Some archaeologists believe that it was a gradual evolutionary change, beginning as early as the eighth century CE, while others claim that it was more rapid, occurring over a vast geographical region in the span of only one or two generations.[2]

Regardless of how quickly it developed, the decades leading up to the eleventh century saw the once-small villages and hamlets of the American Bottom begin to expand and develop more intense horticultural, domestic and social practices. People began adding maize to their diets of seeds, squashes, and gourds, creating cloth and red pottery tempered with shells, and started playing community games. All of this built on top of each other, and by the turn of the century, a greater level of political centralisation in the form of complex chiefdoms and hierarchical societies with a shared belief system and material culture had developed.

The Year 1050: A Big Bang, and North America's First City

Around 1050 CE, a migratory cultural event that has been described as a "Big Bang" occurred in the American Bottom.[3] While much of the Early Mississippian period appeared as a continuation of sites belonging to the Late Woodland period with some evidence of "Mississippianisation" and shifting communities,[4] populations elsewhere were on the move. Evidence from archaeological excavations and surveys indicate that people abandoned many of their villages and hamlets and migrated into and around the floodplain. New settlements of dispersed farmsteads and villages appeared, grouped near larger central settlements with earthen mounds and enlarged plazas. In the centre of this collection of settlements and sprawls, was the site of Cahokia.

Cahokia was the largest pre-Mississippian settlement and in 1050 CE it underwent a rapid expansion, essentially becoming a centralised capital, and the first city in North America. In the decades following 1050 CE, its population increased five to ten times, eventually housing upwards of 10,000 to 15,000 people. In what seems to be an event of careful yet monumental grid planning, massive earthen mounds were built, along with large open plazas. Over a hundred mounds, both rectangular and circular in shape, were built at the site, the largest being Monks Mound, which measured 30.5 metres high and covered an area of 13.8 acres. The mound consisted of four terraces and would have had large wooden buildings sitting on top of its flat surface.

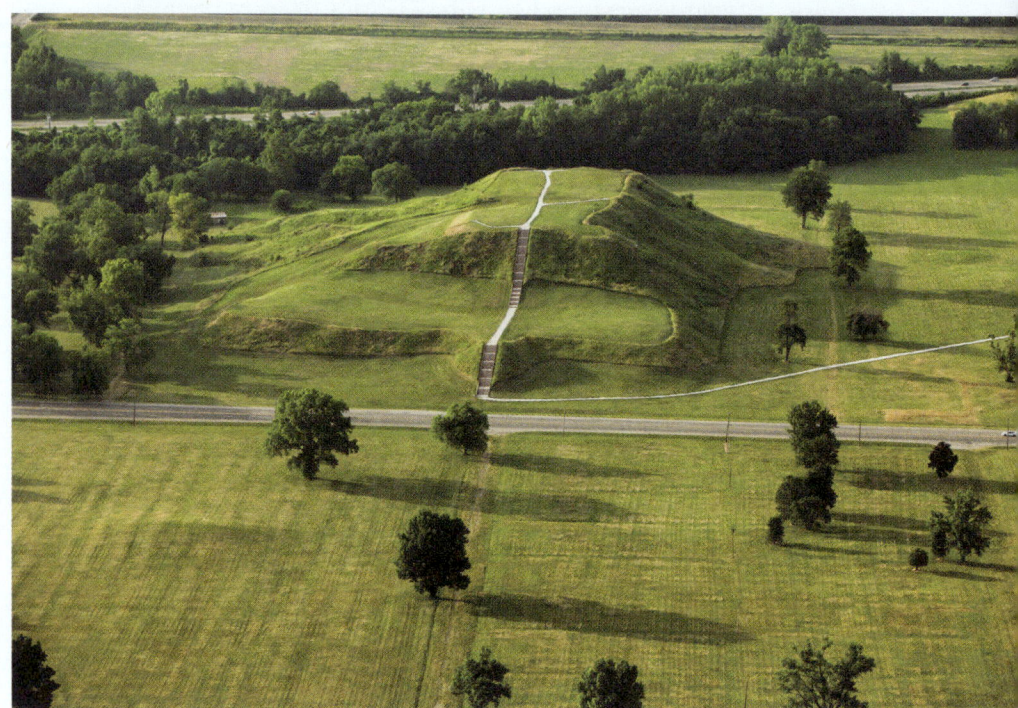

Cahokia

This sprawling city appears to have had sections devoted to specific craft specialisations. Microlithic drill bits alongside broken beads and mollusc shells in one area suggest jewellery manufacturing, whereas other areas with broken pottery, weapons, and the remains of feasting appear to have been more sacred or ritual spaces. Residential areas that would have held hundreds of houses were found along the sides of Cahokia's plazas and mounds, along with other forms of monumental architecture such as large buildings and smaller plazas. Storage huts and granaries were located throughout, and each plaza (including those in outlying towns) had a large, central wooden post installed that was possibly cosmological in nature.

While it is the largest and likely the most important site in the American Bottom, Cahokia was not alone in its position. The city was one of three monumental precincts that made up a "central political-administration complex."[5] To the southwest was the East St. Louis site, the second largest settlement, which contained fifty mounds with temples and walled compounds. These two sites were connected via a trail of small mounds and sites that followed the banks of an ancient channel of the Mississippi River. Immediately across the river from the East St. Louis site was the St. Louis site. This settlement has been dubbed "Mound City" and contained twenty-six pyramids and a singular large plaza. With Cahokia at its political and religious centre, this larger region became a complex chiefdom. While not all Mississippian groups were as complex in their social organisation, by the end of the eleventh century, smaller villages and farmsteads around the American Bottom appear to have been integrated into the Cahokian way of life on the basis that much of the city's architecture and material culture had been adopted.[6]

This level of expansion, influence and growth would have required high levels of coordination and centralisation overseen by a small group of people and adhered to by the thousands of people who lived in Greater Cahokia and participated in its construction. This could only have been accomplished thanks to the addition of maize into the Mississippian diet and improved agricultural practices that created a food surplus, therefore providing the opportunity for craft specialisation and a centralised hierarchical society to be created. While Cahokia's influence most likely did not extend past the region of the American Bottom, objects from the city and artefacts reflecting specific Cahokian styles have been found outside of the floodplain. This suggests that they had contact and possibly an element of long-distance trade with outside Mississippian and Non-Mississippian communities.[7]

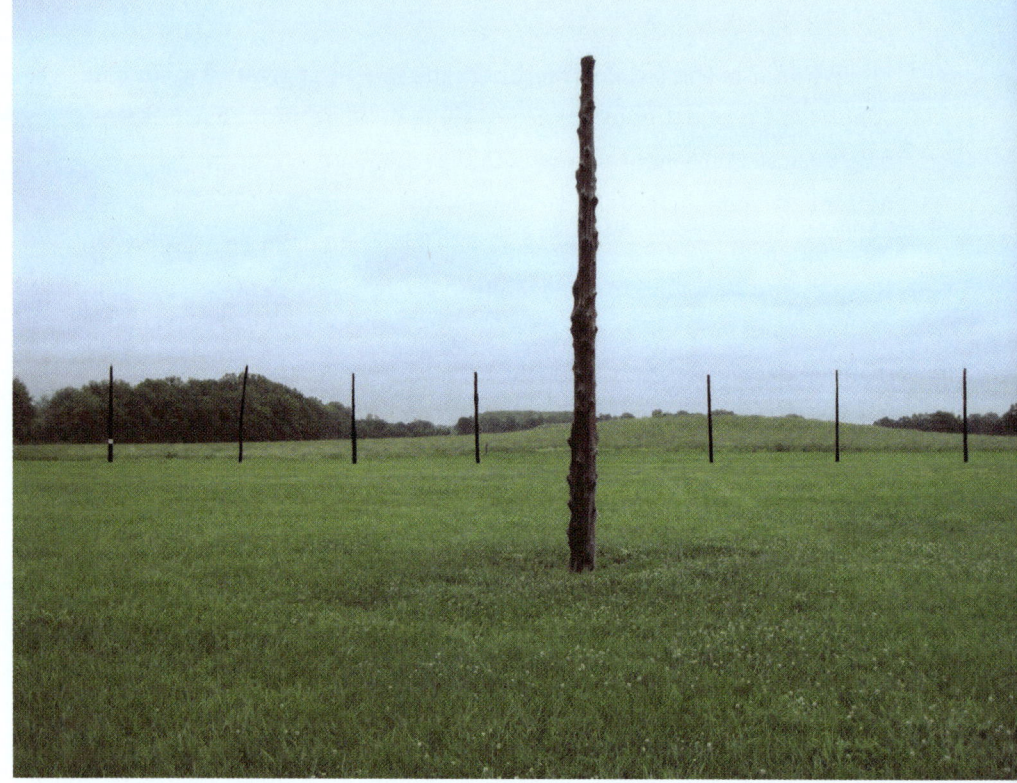

Multiple post-circle or Woodhenge monuments were built at Cahokia and are thought to represent the solar calendar while also possibly marking other celestial and lunar events. This is a reconstruction of Woodhenge III.

The Multiple Manifestations of Mounds

The large earthen structures built by the Mississippians come in many shapes and sizes and have been called both mounds and pyramids. Mississippian polities built mounds throughout their area of influence that were used for numerous purposes and were vital for the establishment of their communities.[8] Mounds were often built to be rectangular with flat tops. These levelled areas possibly served as stages for public ceremonial performances related to agricultural fertility, and regularly supported wooden structures that served as residences for those belonging to the highest ranks, sweat lodges, council houses, temples, or burial structures. Based on the archaeological evidence, it's clear the events that took place on these mounds would have served to bring communities together.

Evidence of such community events can be found not solely on the mounds, but also in the large pits that were created when the earth was taken from the ground to build them. Sometimes called borrow pits, excavations have uncovered several events in which they were backfilled with debris from large-scale gatherings. The borrow pit at Cahokia shows signs of seven separate events that have been interpreted as large-scale public ritual events revolving around the crafting of many new objects and feasting.[9] Each event was probably held for visiting elites and would have had hundreds to thousands of people in attendance. Archaeological evidence suggests that hundreds to thousands of deer were consumed at these events alongside other foods like pumpkins and squashes, and thousands of broken pots and tobacco seeds were left behind. It has also been suggested that these events were opportunities for the redistribution of food and medicinal surpluses that were stored at Cahokia.[10]

Mississippian mounds were also popularly used as burial sites. Burial practices varied greatly throughout the Mississippian cultural region. Structures that are often referred to as temples served as final resting places for prominent ancestors, and important objects such as pottery, shell ornaments, stone figurines, chunkey stones (see below), arrows or arrowheads, beaded necklaces and garments, and copper ear ornaments, were interred alongside them. Only a small portion of the Mississippian population would have been buried at these sites. Mound burials were reserved for high rank individuals, and the visibility of their burials served as public reminders of the legitimacy of the power held by those who could claim ancestry to those interred there.[11] Other burials found in mounds have been of single individuals and sacrificial victims.

Some Mississippian burials were elaborate and grouped affairs. Spiro's Great Mortuary has been dubbed a "King Tut" tomb, with its mass burial and hoard of finely crafted weapons, religious objects, tools, pots, ornaments, and garments.[12] In Mound Seventy-Two at Cahokia, an internment dubbed the "Beaded burial" or "Birdman burial" consisted of two men and a falcon-shaped cape covered in 20,000 mollusc-shell beads. One man was laid atop the cape, while the other was found beneath it. The associated finds with this burial have possible celestial connotations, and it has been suggested that these people represented the Morning Star god-man and possibly his Thunder twin underneath.[13] Other bodies were found in association with these two men, most notably a group of seven people who may represent the seven stars of the Big Dipper or the Pleiades.

The great theatrics and wealth displayed in burial mounds were balanced with other mortuary rituals, like sacrifices. Some mass burials were found to be filled with the bodies of executed women and men who were either shot with arrows or clubbed over the head. Other excavations have uncovered decapitated human remains that were also missing their hands. Chemical analysis of the bone chemistry of one of these people suggests that some sacrificial victims were not from the area and may have been migrants, or captives from a raid.[14]

Nodal Farms and Prefabricated Walls

The numerous Mississippian settlements outside of mound centres and smaller town complexes typically consisted of farmsteads and multi-house communities with populations of a few hundred people. Residential areas within larger settlements were filled with densely packed houses and outdoor storage pits, though by the twelfth century, storage facilities moved inside houses, indicating that Mississippian subsistence shifted from a communal to a household-centric economy.[15]

Large farmsteads located at key locations outside of the mound centres called nodal farms were dotted across the rural landscape of Greater Cahokia. These appear to have been homes for important families and served as places of power, linking rural areas to the Cahokian network. Nodal farms were larger than typical farmsteads, and contained special buildings such as sweat lodges and mortuary shrines that signified their importance. They also possessed more high-value materials that would have been obtained through long-distance trade.[16] These nodal farms only existed during Cahokia's political peak, disappearing once the city began its decline after the year 1200.

Mississippian structures were built out of wood and consisted of a new unique architectural feature: wall trenches. Thanks to the development and widespread use of hoes with large stone blades, wall trenches were used to support constructed frameworks in the central Mississippi River Valley. These narrow trenches allowed walls made of wooden poles sometimes thatched with horizontal branches to be prefabricated on the ground and set into place. The posts were then likely bent over and tied in the centre of the structure to form the roof that was then thatched. House floors were dug into the ground, and the dirt that was removed to create them was then likely heaped up against the exterior walls for further stability and to protect it from weather.

Like a Rolling Stone

Many circular discs, often made of stone with concave sides, have been found while excavating Mississippian burials and midden deposits. These stones would have been used for the popular game of chunkey. Possibly originating at Cahokia as early as 600 CE, chunkey is a popular game that was, and still is, played throughout the eastern woodlands and northern plains of North America. This team sport involves two teams who throw

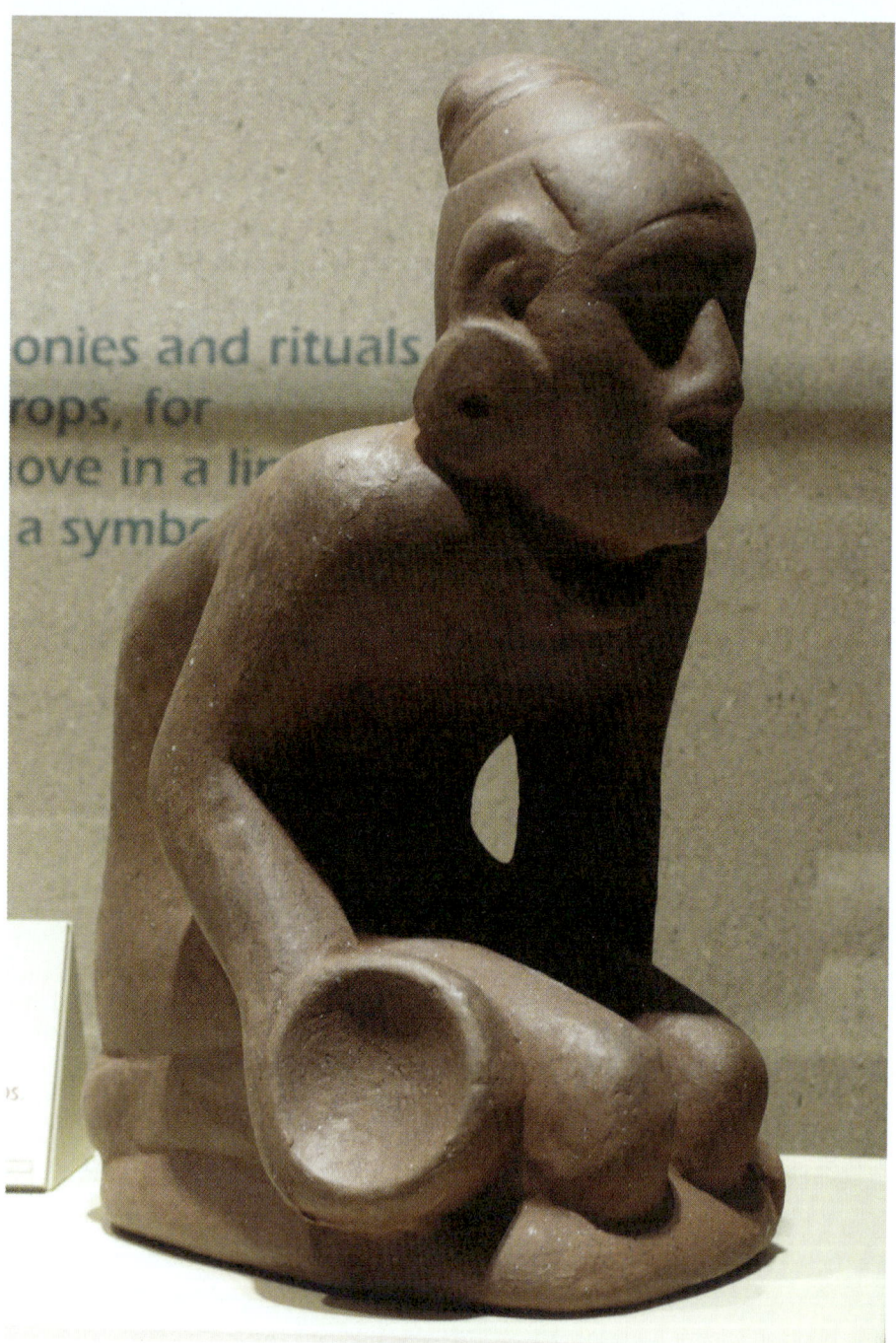

Statue of a Chunkey player

special sticks or spears after one person hurls the chunkey stone down a field. The aim of the game was to get your stick to land as close to the stone once it stops rolling. This required a great deal of skill and precision, as the spear had to be thrown before the stone fell.

Gameplay most likely took place in the levelled plazas, such as the nineteen-hectare Grand Plaza at Cahokia, where thousands of people would have gathered for important events that involved gaming, feasting and other rituals throughout the year. People of every social status would have come from far and wide to participate in chunkey games while the elite watched from atop their great mounds. Gambling often took place during the game, but a gathering such as this would also have aided in the formation and strengthening of communities and longer-distance connections or allegiances. Chunkey possibly also had more cosmological and cultural purposes than just good community fun.[17] The game was possibly associated with Falcon Impersonators who represented a Mississippian deity, and also had ties with Cahokia's central mortuaries. Chunkey may have been used to create societal narratives, and it has been suggested that the rolling stone could have signified the flight of a legendary arrow or the movement of the sun across the sky.

Climate Change and Building Palisades

During the later phases of the Mississippian culture, an increase in competition for land appears to have provoked widespread violence and the construction of palisades around towns and villages. This occurred at different times in different areas, but as early as 1200 CE, fortified settlements appeared in the upper Midwest and Midsouth and showed evidence of frequent incineration. During Cahokia's early phases, there is no evidence of palisade walls or fortifications of any kind around the city or in outlying settlements. It appears that the area was able to maintain a level of peace, both internally and externally.

Yet, only a few decades after the Big Bang, a widening in the social hierarchies appears to have become relevant, as some elite buildings in Cahokia were surrounded by walls. By 1150 CE, many surrounding villages and farmsteads were mysteriously abandoned. At the same time, a palisade wall measuring three kilometres in length and consisting of 20,000 wooden logs and equally spaced bastions was built around Cahokia. By the end of the twelfth century, many Mississippian settlements in the central and upper Mississippi River Valley had followed suit and became well protected to fend off this escalated violence.[18]

An expanding population of more sedentary farmers seems to have increased hostile relationships in the Middle Mississippian region.[19] The appearance of more ritual weaponry and iconographic depictions of violence can be seen as an adoption of a widespread warrior culture, and there is evidence of large-scale (though not long-lasting or frequent) violence at some sites.[20] The self-sufficient nature of these smaller Mississippian settlements made it possible for smaller factions to break away from larger centres such as Cahokia, and rivalries became more frequent.

By 1200 CE, a large migration out of Cahokia and the American Bottom appears to have taken place, and by 1450 CE (if not earlier), much of the area including the central Illinois River Valley and the Ohio River and Mississippi River confluence was abandoned.[21] Whatever the reason for leaving, it is clear that the Mississippian societal structure that was built and expanded after the year 1050 CE was no longer a viable way of life in the area after only a few generations. It is unclear where the thousands of people who called the American Bottom home went, but it is likely that they spread in all directions, with multiple groups dispersing and becoming or assimilating into other ethnic groups.

Climate change may have also influenced the social changes that led to Mississippian decline. Mississippian expansion and rise to prominence occurred during a climatic event that is called the Medieval Warm Period, where warm ideal conditions were prevalent in various parts of the world. The Little Ice Age began around 1300, which would have brought on more unreliable swings in temperature as well as an unpredictability in food supply. A drought in the Ohio River and Mississippi River confluence around the same time would have drastically weakened populations in the area. The uncertainty of subsistence would only have added to any social unrest and violence that was building amongst and between Mississippian societies.

It is also known that some Mississippian peoples encountered the army of Spanish conquistador Hernando de Soto in 1540. As a result of this and further encounters with Europeans, new diseases were introduced to indigenous populations who had no resistance to them. As a result, thousands died, officially bringing the Mississippian culture to an end.

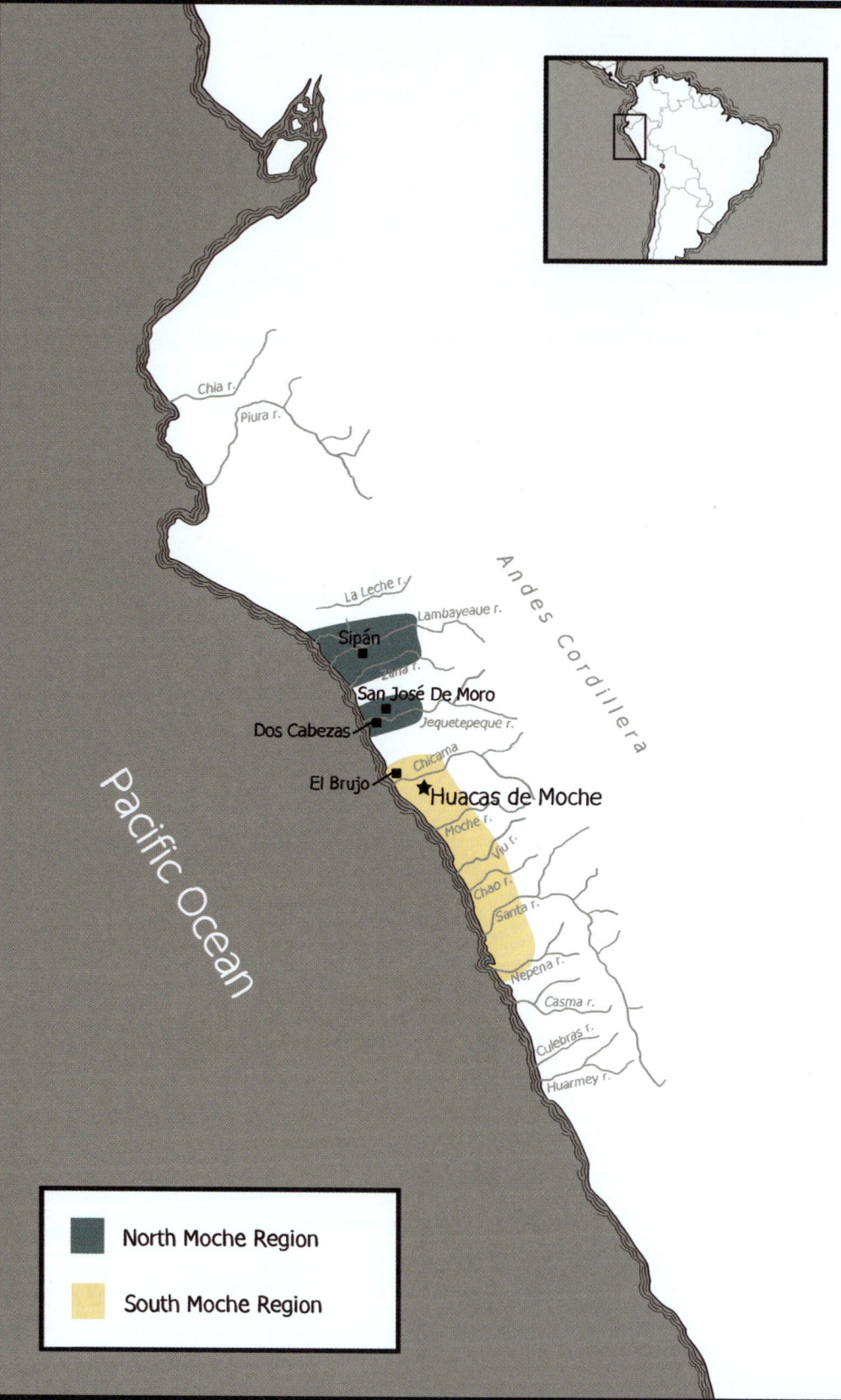

Chapter Twelve

Moche

50 Shades of Sex Pots

The lump of clay the master potter had been relentlessly kneading was finally starting to take shape. Forming it into a rough trapezoidal prism, he grabbed his wooden modelling tools and began to carve away from the lump to free the face he knew was hiding inside.

It had been a few years, but the face emerging from the clay was a familiar one. The potter had carved this figure multiple times before. Each time, the eyes became a bit more knowing, the scar above the lip changing shape as worry and wisdom accrued over the years.

Once the potter was satisfied, he left the portrait to dry, setting it down with the rest of the clay objects in line for the next firing.

Two weeks later, the potter took the now-fired head out of the kiln and inspected his handiwork. The portrait had held up and he was satisfied with the detailing of the figure's signature scar. Bringing it over to his workstation, he sat down and began packing a thick layer of clay around the portrait to create a mould, carefully adding a vertical cut around the head to create two distinct halves.

A few days later, once it was fully dry, the potter removed the two halves of the mould from its matrix and placed them in the kiln. He would make a few more before sending them off to their respective workshops for the pots to be made, their spouts added, and the face finally painted and brought to life by local craftsmen.

The potter thoughtfully held his original mould matrix, running his thumb over the details he had carved a few weeks earlier. In a few years he would make another portrait for more moulds, and he couldn't help but wonder what that face would look like then.

The Desert Between the Ocean and the Andes

The remains of the Moche culture have been found in ten valleys along the narrow strip of arid desert of what is the northern coastline of modern-day Peru. Sandwiched between the Andean Cordillera and the Pacific Ocean, the rivers that cut across these valleys, bringing water from the mountains to the coast, allowed for the construction of a complex irrigation system to support a prosperous agricultural lifestyle along this barren strip of land. Alongside growing a wide variety of crops such as corn, beans, avocados, and guava, the Pacific Ocean and the rivers that fed into it provided the Moche with an abundant supply of fish, molluscs, shrimp, crabs, and crayfish. Llamas, guinea pigs, and ducks were domesticated for additional sources of meat, and other animals, birds, and wild plants served to round out their already rich diet.

Like many archaeological cultures, the Moche were named according to their geography. *Moche* comes from the Moche Valley and the monumental archaeological remains that have been found there, a site known in Spanish as the *Huacas de Moche*. The name of the valley and site of these remains probably comes from the word *Muchik*, the name of a now-extinct language that was spoken on the northern coast of Peru at the time of Spanish contact in 1532. Archaeologists also use the term *Mochica* to refer to the Moche, a term also derived from the name of this language. Muchik survived until the eighteenth century, though we still do not know which language or languages were spoken by the Moche.

The origins of the Moche are still unclear, though it is thought that they derived from the Salinar and Gallinazo cultures. They were also likely influenced by the Chavín culture. In the centuries leading up to the emergence of the Moche, the area was home to these highly stratified societies. These early cultures that inhabited the North Coast were already building monumental structures, weaving textiles, creating pottery, and forging metal objects. Sometime between 200 and 400 CE, a series of transformations took place, allowing the Moche to build on the arts, technology, and social organisation from these previous cultures and create their own distinctive tradition. New settlements and monumental centres were built, and the overall political organisation of the North Coast was forever changed.

The Moche were long considered to be the first stratified state society in South America, though recent archaeological research and our further understanding of the culture have since proved otherwise.[1] Rather than one state ruling over multiple valleys, the Moche appear to have been split in two cultural regions separated by the Pampa de Paiján Desert. The northern region consisted of a collection of smaller independent polities, whereas the south is considered to have been one single state. Rather than a single, homogeneous entity, the Moche were then a collection of small states, connected through complex relationships. Apart from their internal connections, the Moche also traded with other cultures far beyond the confines of the coast. Turquoise from modern-day Chile and Spondylus shells from modern-day Ecuador were fashioned into intricate pieces that would have been worn by the highest echelons of Moche society.

Mountains Made from Bricks

Moche society was heavily reliant on the irrigation canals they constructed to water their crops. While these may seem like simple innovations, the building and maintenance of these canals would have required a great deal of social cohesion and organisation. Little is known about the lives and dwellings of ordinary farmers, labourers, and craftspeople who lived in small villages across the valleys of the North Coast. In general, it is understood that Moche houses were made from adobe bricks or cut stones that formed either the entirety or part of the walls, with the upper part fashioned from vegetable material covered with clay. These rectangular domestic buildings consisted of several rooms, each designated for a purpose such as sleeping, storage, and cooking, and opened to a patio.

For over a hundred years, the majority of archaeological work examining the Moche has been concentrated on the sumptuous royal tombs, and the adobe brick, flat-topped pyramids called *huacas* (loosely translated as temple or shrine) and their surrounding structures. These monumental structures consisted of millions of bricks. It is estimated that Huaca del Sol at the site of Moche consisted of as many as 130 million bricks, and measured up to fifty metres high. Huacas housed large structures with multiple rooms and courts where both public and private rituals would have taken place.

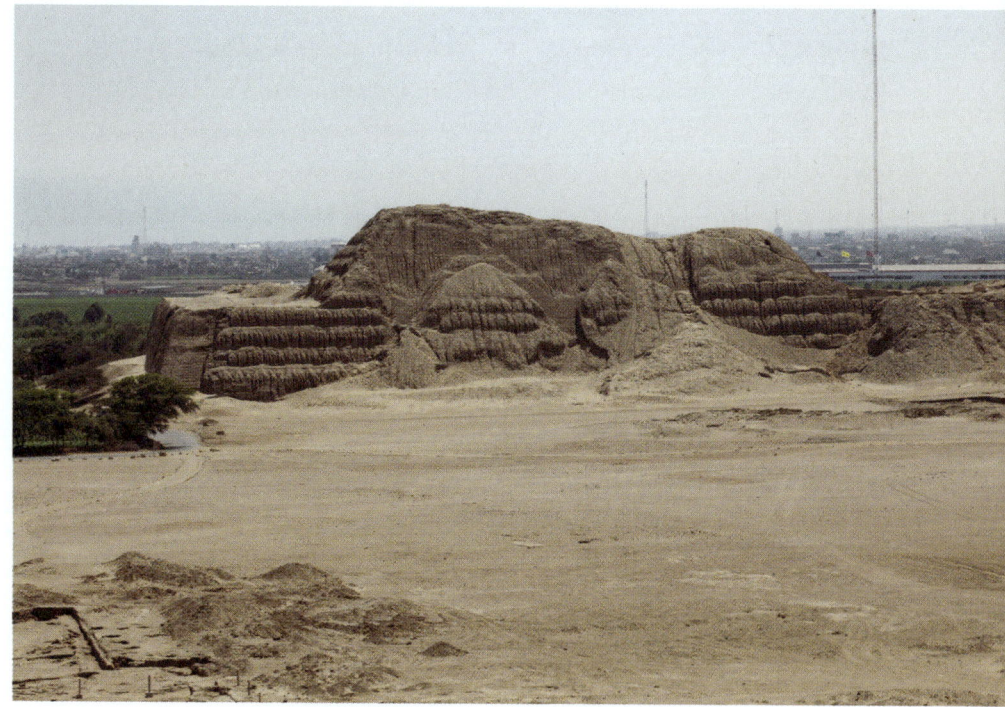

Huaca del Sol at the site of Moche.

Large huacas were brightly painted both inside and out to impress the masses who would congregate in the plazas below as well as to convey religious importance. For example, the polychrome murals at Huaca Cao Viejo at the site of El Brujo depict larger-than-life scenes of captives showing signs of torture being led to the top of the huaca, surrounded by an array of bright dancers and mythical figures. Excavations at Huaca de la Luna have uncovered skeletal remains of tortured and mutilated sacrificial victims, adding a stark reality to these artistic depictions. Burials of high-ranking individuals also took place as a form of ritual performance on huacas. The discoveries of chamber tombs at Huaca Cao Viejo, Sipán, and San José de Moro filled with gold and other precious objects, animals, and people, all speak to the massive amounts of wealth spent on these events.

Public rituals involving human sacrifice and the burials of the upper echelons of society took place on top of huacas and would have been large public displays of both mass political communication and power. Those who controlled the huacas, therefore, could shape the ideology and beliefs of the thousands of people who attended these events.[2] Huacas also had enclosed and restricted spaces that would not have been visible to the public, adding an air of mystery and exclusivity to the happenings on high.

The purpose of the huaca and its role in Moche society has been the subject of much debate. Apart from ritual centres, some researchers believe that some huacas served as neutral locations and mediators for resolving local disputes or reinforcing political alliances.[3] The act of gathering large masses for spectacular ceremonies where the remains of special foods such as llama meat and chicha, an alcoholic beverage made from corn, would have brought together people of all walks of life, from far and wide. The ceremonies and rituals performed at the huacas could have aided in reinforcing a collective identity and community cohesion.[4] Other huacas may have been the seat of oracles, acted as redistribution centres for agriculture, manufactured goods such as ceramics or metal objects, or actively engaged in warfare due to their heavy militaristic imagery.[5] Regardless of their higher level of purpose, the huacas of the Moche appear to have always been centred around control and the maintenance of new beliefs and practices that made up their society, and legitimised the ruler's power and wealth.

The site of Moche is home to two huacas: Huaca de la Luna and Huaca del Sol. Between the five hundred metre gap separating them lies a well-planned city filled with streets, plazas, water canals, houses, and craft production and storage areas that well exceeded the domestic needs of the city's population. A network of streets and plazas was created to connect large and complex buildings that served multiple functions, and that also appeared to have increasingly restricted access over time due to the number of sealed doors found.[6] Residential complexes show areas with grinding stones and sleeping platforms, and craft production areas were possibly organised by specialty such as dedicated ceramics, textile, and metal workshops. These structures appear to have been created to house an urban middle class and perhaps even some of the highest ranks in Moche society.

Sacrifice Ceremonies: Art Imitating Life

A reoccurring scene in Moche art is the sacrifice ceremony. Images of bound, naked men being sacrificed by means of their throats being slit are depicted on temple wall murals and on ceramic vessels. Other characters in this scene then offer the victims' blood in a goblet to what appear to be supernatural beings. Moche art contains numerous depictions of multiple forms of torture. For example, individuals can be seen strapped to wooden structures, on which they would have probably been attacked and mutilated by vultures before their eventual sacrifice and dismemberment.

Human sacrifice appears to have been a major aspect of Moche religion and symbolism, though its impact and associations on social and political aspects of life are still not well understood.[7] Nevertheless, archaeological excavations have confirmed that rituals depicted in these violent artworks did indeed take place. Investigations carried out in elaborate, high-status tombs have uncovered the remains of participants and victims of the sacrifice ceremony. Two main characters of the ritual were found in the tombs at Sipán and one of the female presenters at San José de Moro. These tombs were filled with extraordinary metalwork, weaponry, garments, and ornaments. Individuals were buried in the same attire and regalia as the figures depicted in the sacrifice ceremony. These burials were found throughout the Moche region and spanned several generations, which suggests that this ritual would have occurred on a regular basis.[8]

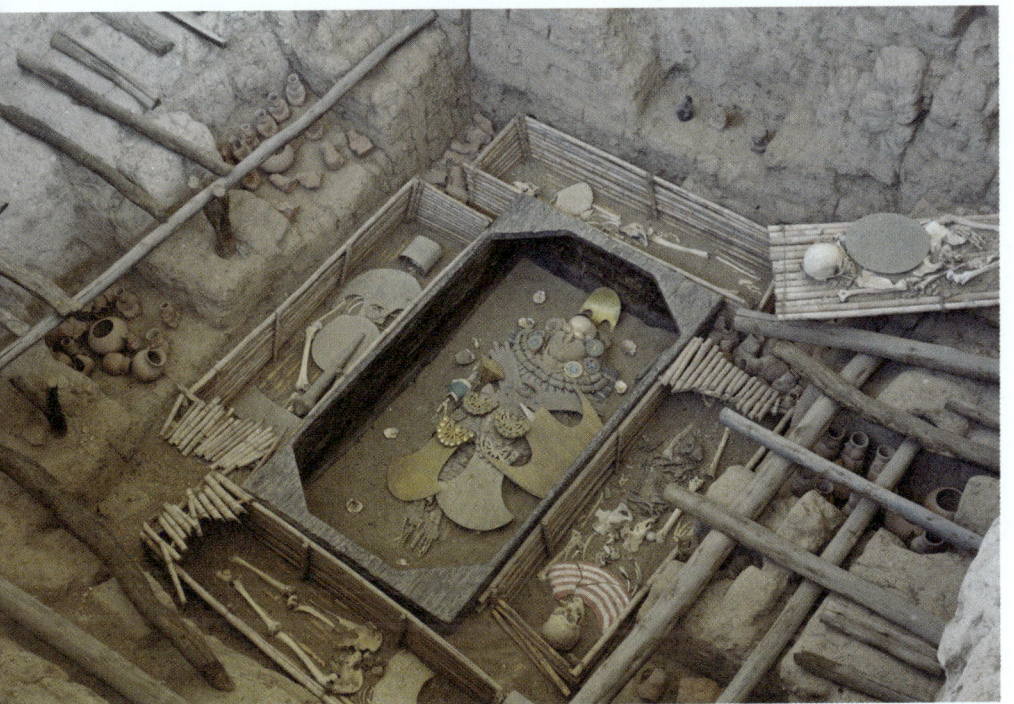

Royal burial at Sipán.

Further discoveries at Huaca de la Luna, Huaca Cao Viejo, and Dos Cabezas provide even more evidence for ritual violence and beg further questions: Who were the people being sacrificed? What was the purpose of these ceremonies—war, or something else? The remains of sacrificial victims uncovered at these sites were all male and of warrior age. The bones show the conditioning typical of those who train for combat, as well as evidence of trauma associated with battle. Other markers on the human remains indicate that they were tortured shortly before death.[9] While these men were warriors, the weapons they were buried with tell another story.[10] Their shields were too small to have served much of a purpose for protection, and the wooden weapons covered in sheet metal were constructed to be relatively fragile and ineffective. By all intents and purposes, the nature of this "battle" and sacrifice appears to have been ritual.

Moche warfare is still a matter of debate among archaeologists. Moche artists chose to represent ritual combat over traditional full-scale warfare. There are no artistic depictions of warriors attacking fortified settlements or slaying enemies. But this lack of artistic evidence does not mean it didn't happen. There is evidence that warfare did take place between various Moche communities, but away from the huacas in smaller settlements fortified with defensive walls and observation platforms.[11]

Warfare could have provided the huacas with the captives required for these ritual sacrifices. Others have suggested that painted representations of battles on ceramics are planned skirmishes with predetermined outcomes that took place with a select group of specially trained individuals under the supervision of the Moche elite.[12] It appears that the main objective of battle for the Moche was not to kill one's opponent. By looking at Moche iconography, blows to the face or legs appear to have been preferred when taking enemy captives for sacrifice.[13]

Sex Acts and Storytelling through Pottery

The agricultural surplus and redistribution of crops that was practised by the Moche allowed some people to become full-time artisans. This group of individuals created masterful pieces that have left a vibrant artistic collection in the archaeological record, providing a window into what Moche life would have looked like. From metal objects of gold, silver, and copper fashioned out of sheet metal or lost wax casting, to brightly patterned textiles, these pieces would have been created for the wealthiest in Moche society and allowed them to materially exhibit their power and wealth.

The Moche are most well-known for their elaborate ceramic tradition. Their pots depict various scenes of daily life, including domestic activities like hunting and fishing, as well as ritualistic combat and ceremonies, and even scenes from mythology. A wide array of animals adorn vessels, ranging from monkeys to molluscs, and people from all walks of life are celebrated, from blind musicians to powerful rulers. These ordinary scenes, though familiar to modern-day onlookers, also appear to have been highly charged in symbolism.

Moche ceramics were produced by extremely talented potters, creating realistic scenes and three-dimensional figures, all painted in bichrome colours ranging from red-to-brown and cream-to-white. Using this medium, the Moche created lifelike portrait vessels either in the form of a human head or of their full figure. These vessels were modelled with individual traits and features that evoke their personalities so well, that they appear to have been modelled after living people, most likely belonging to the social and religious elite.

Created from moulds fashioned by master potters, the figures depicted in these portraits were adorned with various ear and nose ornaments, headdresses, face and neck designs, and jewellery. These portraits are so detailed that researchers today have been able to identify individuals possessing infectious and neurological diseases, mutilation, and congenital disorders.[14] People were masterfully sculpted with various conditions such as Down syndrome, extra toes, and cleft lips. Their jewellery and decorative clothing also indicate that these individuals were highly respected in Moche society.

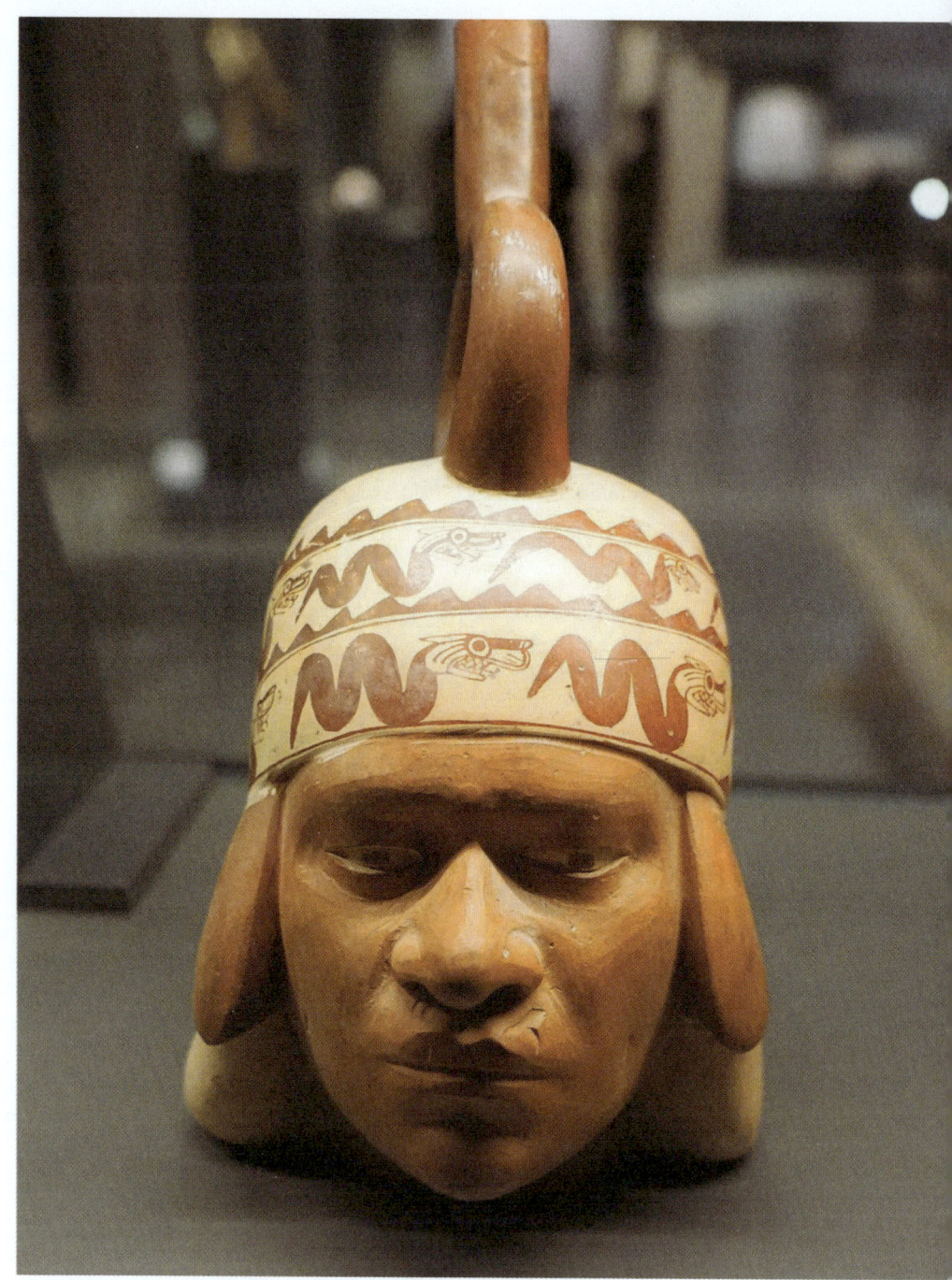

Stirrup vessel depicting the Cut Lip persona.

Many individuals have been identified to have had at least two portraits created, and as many as forty versions of their likeness.[15] While each one differs slightly with variations in painting, colouration, and ornamentation, the detail and realism expressed in their features are easily identifiable. Portraits of the same individual have been found at multiple Moche sites, sometimes long distances apart and across valleys. This could indicate that moulds were made at one site and distributed to other workshops along the North Coast.

Some individuals appear to have had portraits created throughout their lifetimes. One such person, identified as the Cut Lip persona due to a scar located above his lip, seems to have had his first portrait made at the age of ten, with new moulds being made at different times throughout his life until he reached his mid-thirties.[16] Archaeologists have noted this in part due to the cut changing from a wishbone shape, to two slightly converging lines as this individual aged.

The creation of portrait vessels may have served as part of the sacrifice ritual.[17] For many characters that had sequential portraits made, their final portrayal is as a bound sacrificial victim. Broken portrait vessels, each sculpted in the form of a naked, seated prisoner with a rope around their neck, have been found among the remains of over seventy people who had been mutilated, sacrificed, and dismembered. No two faces are the same, meaning they could have resembled those who were taken captive and sacrificed during the ceremony. Other portrait vessels such as the Cut Lip persona have been interpreted as representing quasi-historical or mythical figures. These individuals could have been easily identifiable to the Moche, and their final sacrificial depiction could then possibly be symbolising a hero who met their death after an act of bravery or justice.

Another notably distinctive form of Moche pottery are the renowned sex pots. These vessels contain scenes of couples performing various acts, most frequently sodomy, oral sex, and masturbation. The scenes are mostly heterosexual, but not always human, and are sometimes mixed with animals and skeletons. Often, there is a small baby lying next to

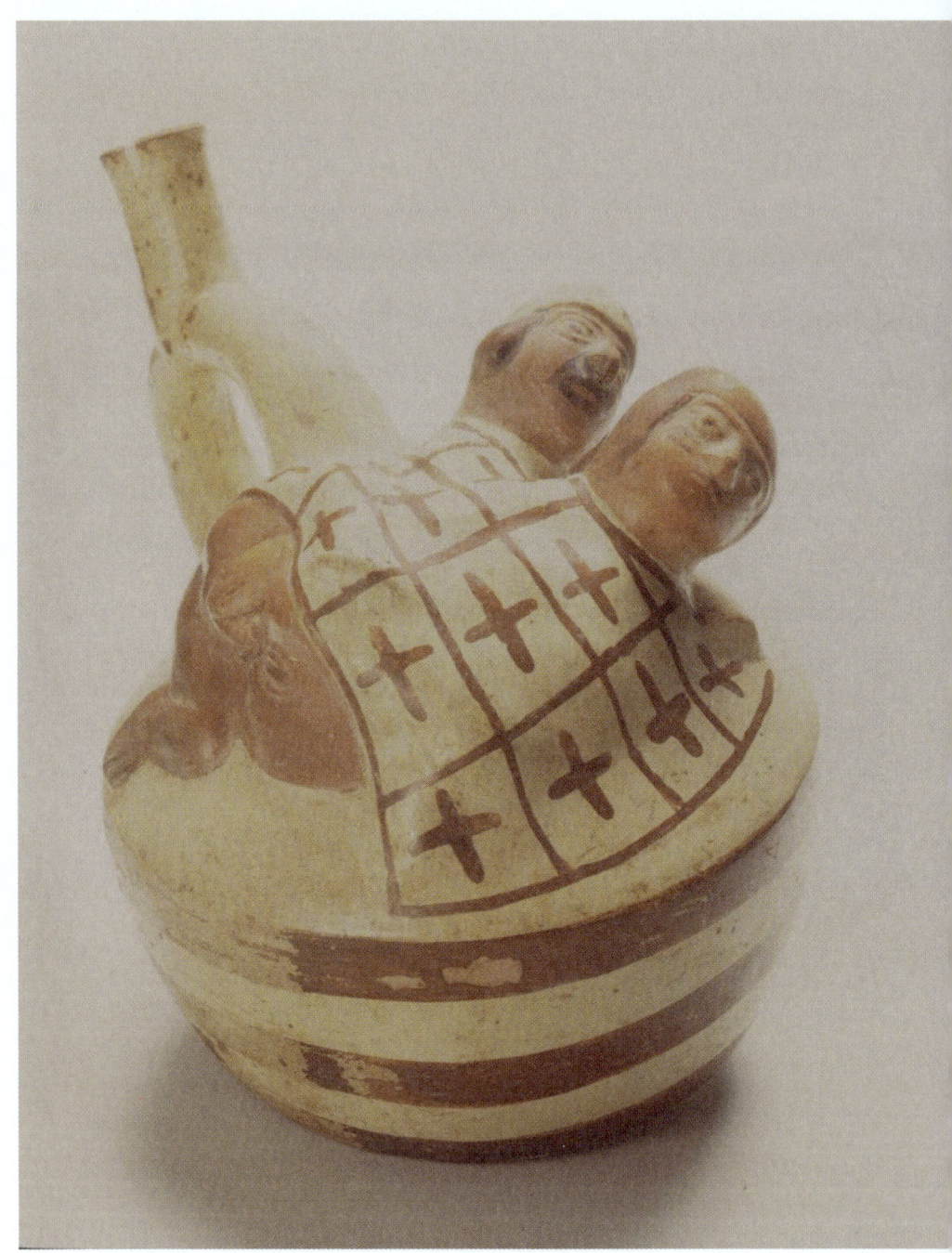
Ceramic vessel depicting anal sex.

the woman, being breastfed while she is having sex. Some pots are even performative in nature, preventing the user from drinking from the vessel unless it is through an opening in the shape of exaggerated genitalia. As with other Moche pottery, the sex pots were charged with symbolism and their own ritual identities.

Sex pots have been found in the graves of almost every kind of person who lived in Moche society, including those belonging to infants. Many archaeologists believe that Moche sex pots have strong ties to fertility, death, and the afterlife, and their associated rituals.[18] It is possible that fertility flowed from the dead and was the source of ancestral power. This fertility could have been tied to farmland and the harvest, which was essential for their survival. Skeletal masturbation scenes (either with or without a living woman) possibly also represent continuity and connection between the living and the dead.

El Niño and Foreign Influences

What caused the decline and the end of the Moche is still unknown. Around 650 CE, dramatic changes start to appear in the archaeological record. The appearance of new ceramic and architectural traditions, the possible abandonment of the huacas at Moche, and the establishment of new cultural centres mark a shift in Moche organisation. It has been proposed that environmental factors also led to a significant change.[19] A series of El Niño events and droughts would have destroyed houses and temples, along with irrigation systems and farmsteads. This environmental instability could have caused or increased the effects of the social and economic changes occurring at this time.

Simultaneously, another culture called the Wari was establishing itself in the southcentral highlands of Peru. The Wari, and other new states, brought about much change to this area of South America. Neither the Wari nor other foreigners attacked or took over the Moche in the traditional sense. Rather, they formed relationships with various polities, and their influence began to show in the ceramics produced at late Moche sites. Some Wari ceramics have even been found in burials and at the site of Moche.[20] The extent of their influence is difficult to determine as it would have varied throughout the valleys, but the arrival of new ideas and cultures from the Central Coast and the highlands, and the possibility of political takeovers enveloped the Moche into events happening on a greater geographical scale than they had previously experienced.

By 800 CE, the Moche culture began to disappear from the archaeological record, having underwent what appears to have been an internal societal collapse. By 900 CE, the end of their political and ideological structures allowed the region to come under the control of the Chimù and Lambayeque (Sicán) cultures. A few centuries later, the Inca Empire would emerge and dominate the landscape well beyond the golden valleys of the Moche.

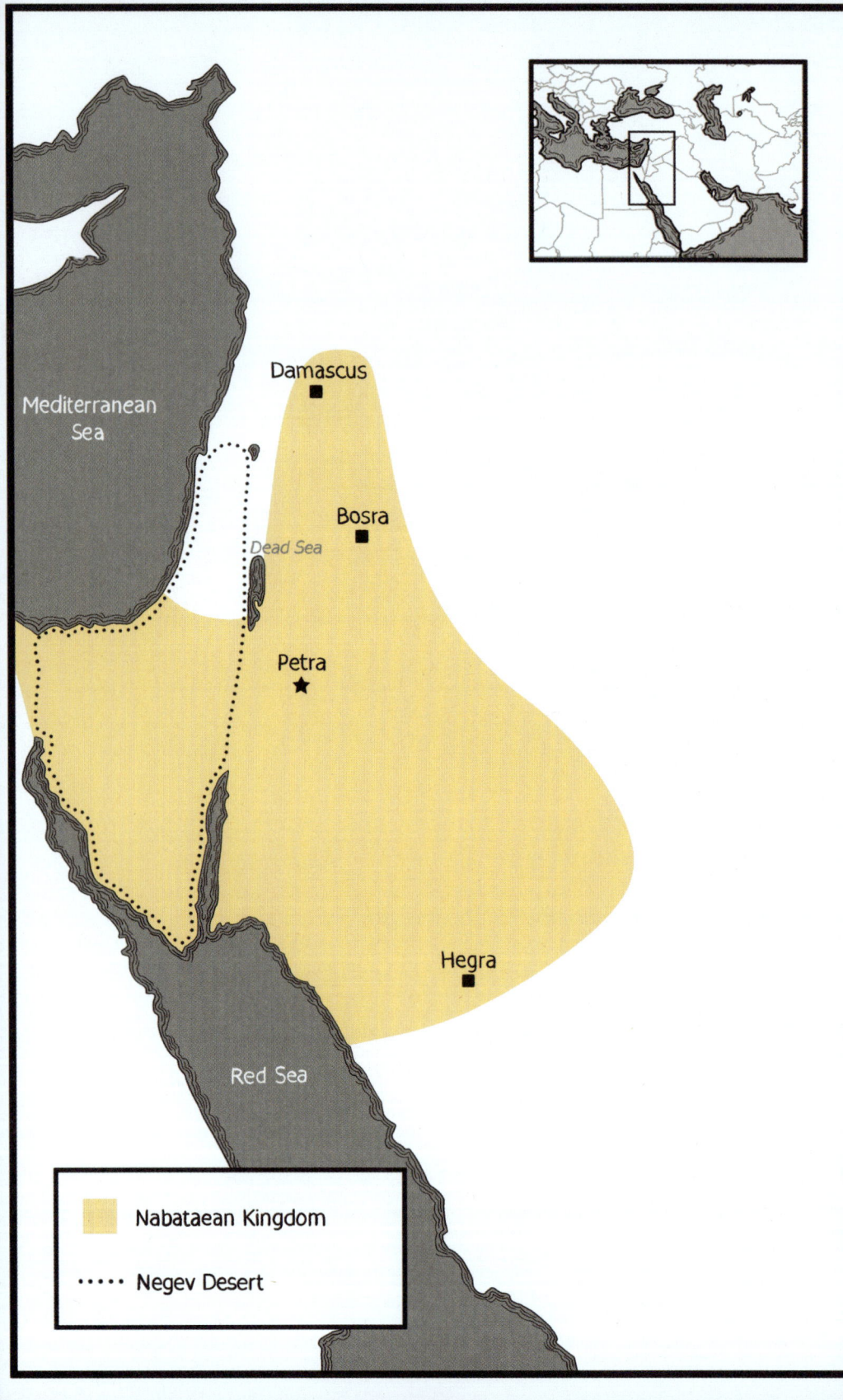

Chapter Thirteen

Nabataeans
The Nomads Who Built a City

The desert air was a cool shock to the man's face as he opened the flaps of his tent and stepped out into the centre of the camp. Hoping his activity would wake the others, he quickly set to packing up his tent and preparing his camel for the final leg of their journey. They were only a short distance from Petra, and while the others had discussed aiming to reach the city before midday last night, the man wanted to arrive earlier. He would never admit it to his fellow merchants camped around him, but reaching the city at sunrise was his favourite sight and he had been waiting months for a glimpse of that view again. Thankfully, the man's efforts were not in vain, and he soon heard the others rustling in their tents.

—

"Why does the last part of any journey always feel the longest?" the man asked himself. The sky was waking up, and he could feel the sun blooming into the horizon behind him. His plan had worked! The caravan had made it to the entrance of Petra and they were about to witness the city in all its rosied glory.

Though he had come and gone from Petra many times, the view that greeted the man differed every time. Cliffs that were bare when he left now had the beginnings of tombs being carved into their facades, their crowsteps and cornices adding dramatic shadows on the rock face thanks to the low angle of the sun. He had heard stories from his elders—they all had—of a *time before their people carved in stone. When tents and caves were all his people knew. The man wondered what his ancestors would think if they saw the power and influence their people had today, the riches they gathered, and the far-off lands they reached.*

An Unknown Origin

The emergence of the Nabataeans onto the world stage is an elusive one. As one of the many nomadic tribes that followed and camped along well-travelled routes across Arabia with their flocks and herds, their story could easily have been lost to the sands for eternity. Instead, the Nabataeans were able to set themselves apart and become one of the most influential peoples in the Hellenistic Near East. The origins of the Nabataeans are still unknown and debated today. While most scholars agree that they were Arabs, the precise location from whence they came remains unconfirmed. Potential locations such as Yemen, Bahrain or Saudi Arabia have been suggested, and it is possible that they may have even come from Mesopotamia and migrated west into Arabia.[1] A tribe called the *Nabatu* was mentioned twice as a rebellious Arab tribe in the annals of Assyrian kings in the eighth century BCE. Regardless of their place of origin, by the end of the fourth century BCE, the Nabataeans were an established culture in Arabia that soon began to garner international attention and influence.

First Encounters

The first historical reference to mention the Nabataeans is by historian Diodorus Siculus, meaning that they once had direct contact with the ancient Greeks.[2] Although he lived during the first century BCE, Diodorus references reports from Hieronymus of Cardia, an officer of Alexander the Great dating to 311/312 BCE when one of Alexander's successors, Antigonus Monophthalmus, attempted a number of unsuccessful raids in an attempt to bring Nabataean territory under his control. Diodorus describes the Nabataeans as pastoral nomads who fiercely protect their freedom, live in the open air, and have strict rules—punishable by death—to refrain from planting any grain or fruit-bearing trees, using wine, or building houses.

The reason for such a restrictive lifestyle was one of safety and longevity for the tribe. Agriculture and cumbersome or immovable possessions such as houses or large stocks of goods would prevent them from disappearing into the desert when threatened by enemies, or else leave many of their goods vulnerable to destruction. The Nabataeans could navigate the desert like no one else, and they dug large underground water reservoirs throughout the desert, lined with stucco and filled with rainwater to sustain them in the arid landscape, before sealing and marking them in a way recognisable only to them. This control over water helped the Nabataeans retain their freedom in the desert and would prove beneficial when establishing their capital city of Petra.

Wandering Merchants of the Sands

The Nabataeans chose to capitalise on their transient way of life by becoming skilled traders. While it is unclear if they were merchants or providers of safe passage and supplies for those traversing through their territory, the Nabataeans played an active and vital role in the process, while also imposing heavy taxes on all goods passing through. By the fourth century BCE, they established themselves as a vital part of the northern segment of the incense route that stretched from Saudi Arabia, up to the Mediterranean coast and in parts of the Red Sea, eventually expanding farther east.

Though they had some of their own products, like bitumen, which was already a sought-after product in places like Egypt in the fourth century BCE, the main source of wealth for the Nabataeans came from frankincense, myrrh, and other valuable spices originating from the

Minaean Kingdom located at the southern part of the Arabian Peninsula. Within the span of a few centuries, the Nabataeans came to dominate the overland caravan routes, and with the collapse of the Minaean Kingdom in the second century BCE, became the principal middlemen between Arabia and the rest of their known world.

By the first century BCE, the Nabataeans were renowned traders and middlemen for some of the most precious objects in the world—some from as far away as India and China—and their power and wealth reflected this. The Romans used incense heavily and with its growth over the centuries, demand for the fragrant method of communicating and sustaining the gods rose, and to the benefit of the Nabataeans, so did the prices. This allowed the Nabataeans to establish a vast kingdom that stretched from parts of southern Syria, the Transjordan, the Negev, the Sinai Peninsula, and northwestern Saudi Arabia. A relief carving found in the Siq, the current main entrance to the city of Petra, of a camel caravan shows just how important trade was to both the people and the wellbeing of the kingdom.

The Nabataeans took great care to protect their trading routes by choosing to traverse along the roads less travelled, down through hidden gullies, and ascending near-vertical cliffs that only they could navigate. They built garrisoned forts with cisterns and caravanserai near permanent water sources. The Nabataeans would also have required a strong military to ensure their protection. We have evidence of the Nabataeans fighting many battles against the Hasmonaeans and Herodians, and they were even mercenaries in Roman armies. At the height of their trading power, the Nabataeans established colonies over a vast area, and archaeologists have found evidence of their presence at no less than a thousand sites across the Near East.[3]

Despite these protective measures, the trading routes and power of the Nabataeans were always at risk of becoming obsolete. The possibility of trade routes between Egypt and the Arabian Peninsula shifting to the Red Sea, and those connecting the Near East to Rome through Palmyra in what is today Syria, were serious threats to Nabataean livelihood. This concern may have been the reason that we have reports of them turning to piracy.[4] During the late third century BCE, the Nabataeans attacked Ptolemaic Egyptian merchant ships on the Red Sea when they began circumventing the overland routes in favour of a naval one—possibly due to the Egyptians gaining an understanding, and taking advantage of, monsoon winds. These rebellions were actively suppressed but are great indicators of how far the Nabataeans would go to protect their way of life. While trade and traversing the desert were the pillars of the Nabataean economy, their power and wealth also gave rise to the building of a metropolitan city that is today regarded as one of the wonders of the world.

Settling Down

By the end of the fourth century BCE, Petra was already established as a political and religious centre, and the seat of the Nabataean royalty and nobility. This began a process of sedentarisation for the tribe, where over the course of three hundred years, they shifted from living predominantly in tents and rock-cut caves, to building houses in the first century BCE (it should be noted that living in tents and caves didn't disappear altogether, nor did it mean they could be any less luxurious in comparison).[5] The shift towards permanent settlements was most likely due to their domination of the caravan routes. The new commercial nature of the Nabataean economy required depots to house goods not currently in transit, caravanserais along trade routes, and other commercial structures, as well as the development of distinctly Nabataean pottery and coins to conduct business and retain control over the area.

The great success the Nabataeans achieved through their extensive trading allowed them to create a royal capital filled with large temples, palaces, and rock-cut tombs that still invoke wonder to this day. When writing about the Nabataeans, the ancient Greeks said they had a special rock (petra) that was virtually impenetrable. This is where we get the name for the city today, even though the Nabataeans referred to their capital city as Reqem.[6] Petra became a cosmopolitan haven in the desert, with many foreigners living amongst the Nabataeans, and was a central hub in Southwest Asia.

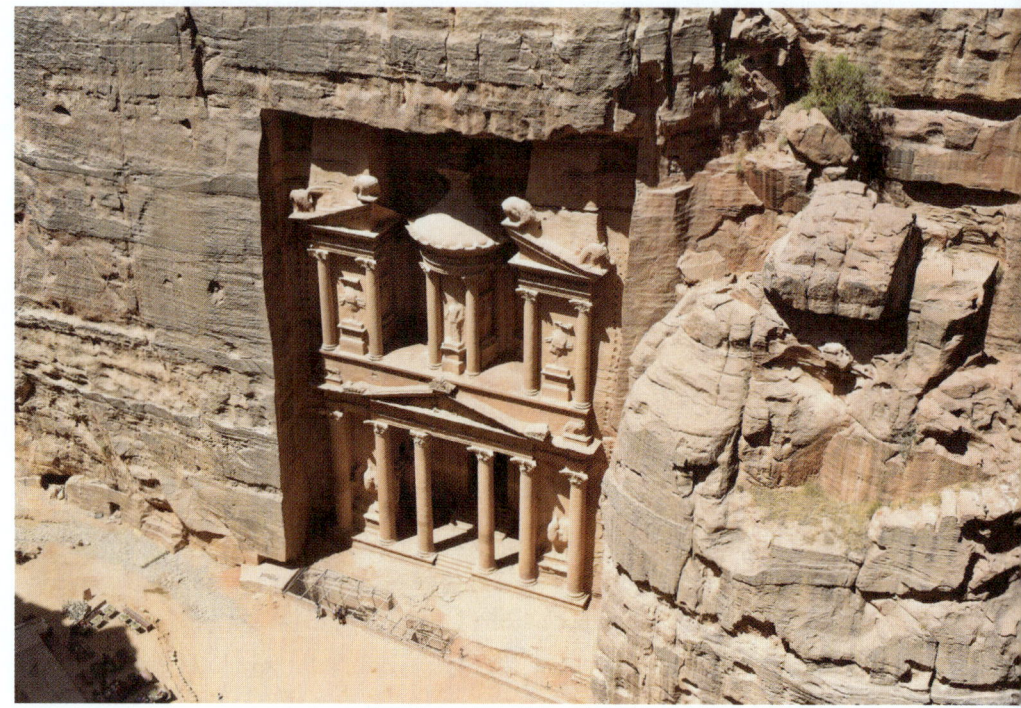

View of the famous Treasury of Petra from above. Its hidden location truly speaks to the "impenetrable" nature of the landscape.

This dramatic shift towards city life also came with a shift in lifestyle and values for the Nabataeans. Whereas previously collecting possessions and partaking in agriculture were rejected, they now honoured anyone who increased their ownership of precious items such as gold, silver, spices, and other trading goods, publicly fining anyone who diminished them.[7] Items once seen as impractical to nomadic life and a threat to their freedom and security were now sought after and celebrated. One aspect that carried over from desert life was their well-governed democratic way of life that extended to even the king, who during feasts would not only serve himself wine, but sometimes even get up to serve the rest of his guests.[8] The Nabataeans strove to keep peace with each other and everyone else they traded with. Petra was an unwalled city due this peace. But as they had already proven to the outside world, they were always ready to protect their commercial interests at all costs.

The Rose City

Petra is often called the Rose City because of the pink hues of the stone it was carved from. The earliest known buildings in the city date to around the third century BCE. These were simple structures made from stones and clay and were possibly built next to tents to store goods that they did not want to take with them after they broke camp and moved on. As their trading influence and wealth grew, so did Petra. The Nabataeans increasingly settled down into agricultural communities, planting crops and raising sheep, cattle, and camels, and they began to build simple residential structures in the first century BCE—a dramatic shift from the days when nomads building houses was forbidden and punishable by death.[9]

Ascetic principles required for life on the move were no longer needed, and Petra quickly grew to house royal residences, public buildings, stone-built houses, temples, and elaborate tombs adorned with such expertly carved and painted decoration that other cities quickly followed in its footsteps. Nabataean public architecture developed into a distinctive grandiose and eclectic blend of ideas and styles from every land and culture they encountered: Mesopotamian, Egyptian, Hellenistic, and, later, Roman. The opulence and grandeur of the city can still be seen today. One can only imagine traders and merchants traversing through these mountains and wadis (low, dry river valleys), witnessing the rapid transformation of the landscape around them.

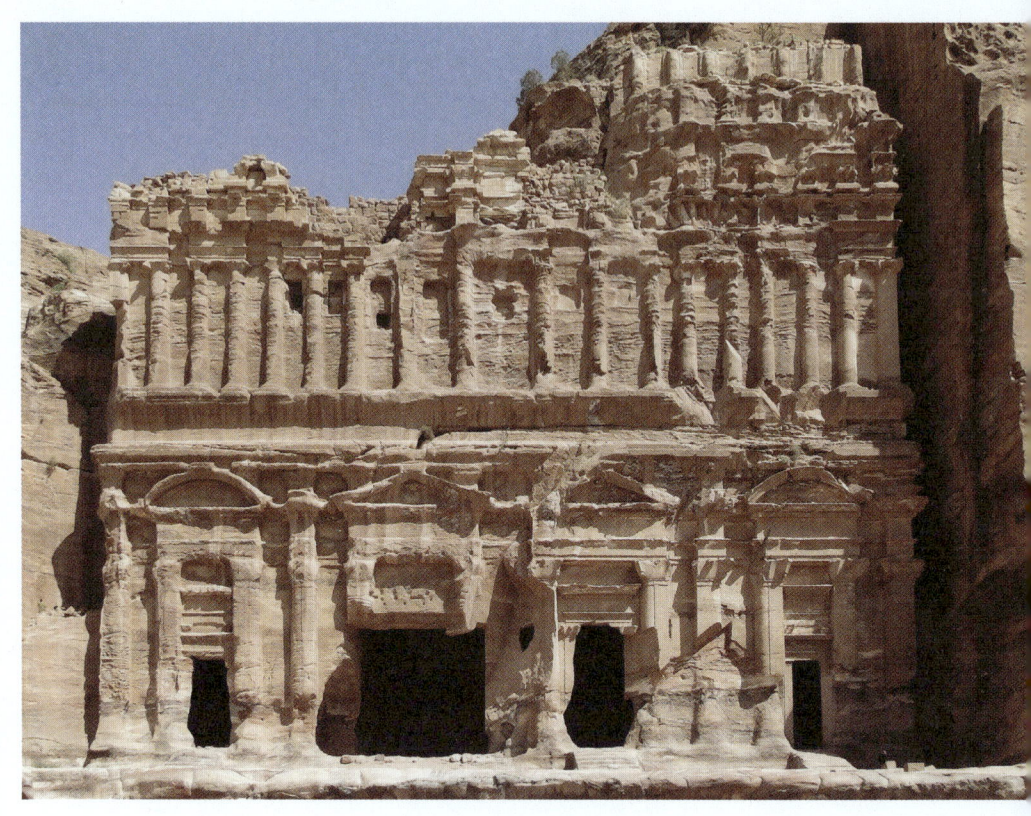

Palace tomb at Petra.

Perhaps the most striking and well-known structures built at Petra and other Nabataean sites are the hundreds of rock-cut tombs that dominate the landscape. These tombs were mostly carved between the first century BCE and the first century CE during the height of the Nabataean kingdom. Carved into the mountain faces and wadis that surrounded the city by working from the top down, the distinctive fusion of architectural traditions created a wide variety of styles that became distinctively Nabataean and is not found anywhere else in the world. Depending on one's socioeconomic standing, these rock-cut tombs ranged from pit graves and shaft tombs, to larger and masterfully carved and decorated monumental facade and block tombs. These block tombs were positioned at the highest parts of the city as a visual representation of the wealth and status of the people who built them.[10]

The extensive looting of these tombs means archaeologists have struggled to learn about Nabataean funerary customs. What we can tell from studying the layouts of these tomb complexes is that the inclusion of courtyards, dining rooms, exterior benches, and cisterns and reservoirs indicates that some form of commemorative gathering or feasting was possibly taking place to honour the dead.[11] The most famous of these rock-cut tombs is the Kazneh, or Treasury of Petra. This was possibly the tomb of a Nabataean king or other royal person, and obtained its name from an Arabic folktale that claimed there was a mythical treasure located in the urn at the top of the facade that was placed there by a magician. No treasure has been detected inside the urn, and decorations on the facade are distinctively funerary. Still, bullet holes can be seen along the facade of the Kazneh from local Bedouin tribes attempting to find said treasure.

A Room of One's Own

The Nabataeans mainly lived in two types of houses: regular stand-alone stone-built structures or those cut out of living rock. Permanent houses seem to have generally been built haphazardly using the original floor space of the tent that once stood in its place. While foundations were dug, little planning was put into the stability of a new structure built out of stone. This resulted in some walls bulging or collapsing. It appears that the Nabataeans kept to their familiar layout of a nomadic camp, which means, unlike Petra's public buildings and temples, there was less emphasis on proper urban planning in domestic areas.[12]

Less attention to planning, though, does not mean the Nabataeans were living in poor conditions. House floors were paved with flagstones, and interiors were decorated with stucco and wall paintings. Domestic buildings were normally two stories high with a central courtyard and a balcony on the top floor overlooking the space. There were no windows on the outside. Instead, living and working areas were open towards the internal courtyard. Due to their nature, rock-cut houses also had to be carefully laid out and conform to the lay of the land. They were often constructed vertically, with spaces staggered over two or three terraces, and rooms were positioned horizontally along each one.[13]

Masters of Hydraulics

The Nabataeans were already masters of water management and control centuries before they became sedentary, but the increase of agriculture in their society meant they required more elaborate irrigation systems and networks for water collection, storage, and distribution throughout their kingdom. In fact, it was these achievements in hydraulic engineering that provided them with the means to support themselves and rely less on overland trade when seafaring trade and other routes that bypassed their camps and towns became more popular in the first century CE.[14]

Petra does not have any continuous water flow apart from a few small springs. With some scholars estimating the urban population of Petra reaching 30,000 at its height,[15] the Nabataeans needed to ensure a constant water supply for their people to thrive. As a result, they built dams and cofferdams to capture rainwater from the torrential downpours that occurred in the winter months, and canals using the gravity system as well as pressurised ceramic pipes would bring in water from sources as far as seven kilometres away.[16] Cisterns and reservoirs have been found all over Nabataean territory to store water and maintain a healthy supply. Some reservoirs even had the capacity to hold up to 2.5 million litres of water.[17] The Nabataeans also used a method of decantation to ensure the water was drinkable by passing it through consecutive basins to reduce the speed of the flowing water, allowing heavy particles to sink to the bottom of the reservoirs. It seems only fitting that these historic desert dwellers would all too well know the importance and fragility of an ample water supply. It then comes as no surprise that they would become some of the most proficient hydraulic engineers of the ancient world.

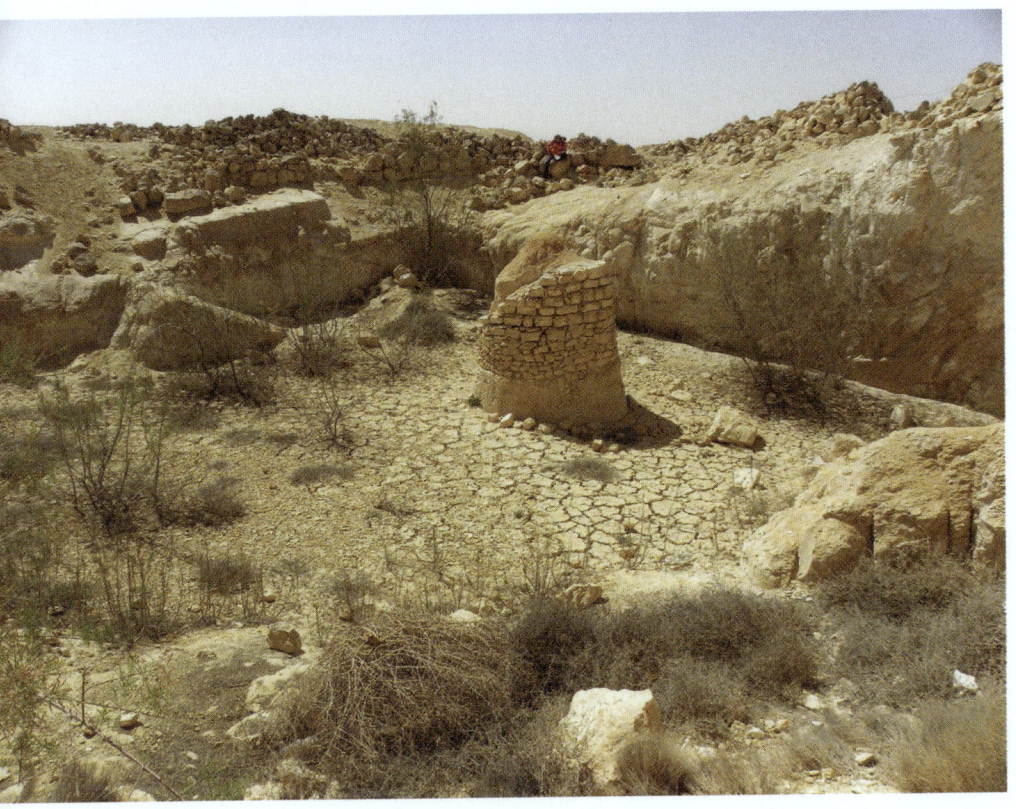

Nabataean cistern.

The Empire Expands

Towards the end of the first century CE, the Nabataeans began to clash with the ever-expanding Romans. After it was conquered by the Romans in 63–64 CE, it remained an independent state but had to pay tribute to the Roman Republic. In 106 CE, during the reign of emperor Trajan, the last Nabataean king, Rabbel II, died. While there is no hard evidence, there are some claims that he had made a deal with the Romans to take control over the city of Bosra and its territory upon his death, leaving the rest of the Nabataean kingdom to his sons who revolted against Rome. Regardless if this truly happened or another event prompted it, the Nabataean kingdom was annexed by Rome and incorporated into its new province: Arabia.

While Bosra became the new administrative centre of the province, Petra remained a largely populated (albeit less important) city in the centuries following the annexation. Once incorporated into the Roman Empire, the Nabataeans fell into obscurity, becoming a faction within a larger province and appearing only occasionally in literary and epigraphic records. Their once prosperous trading empire was absorbed and replaced by the rise of other routes, such as through Palmyra, but Petra's routes were still mentioned, despite their decline after 106 CE. Despite the Nabataeans being absorbed into the Roman province of Arabia, their culture survived well into the late Roman period.

Petra was greatly damaged in an earthquake in 363 CE. Following this devastation, the city was never restored to its former glory, and many of those who could afford to leave, did. Those who were not as well off had no choice but to stay and live among the ruins. These Nabataeans possibly reverted to a semi-nomadic lifestyle in the fashion of their ancestors, while others might have tried to continue as wayfaring traders dealing in new commodities that were not their traditional aromatics.[18] Because Christianity was now the dominant faith in the area, the use of incense in religious rituals was suspended for a time as it was too closely related to pagan worship. When the market for incense bounced back in the late fourth century CE, it was a shadow of what it once was, and much of it was now transported by sea.

Even with its diminished population, Petra remained a stronghold for the Nabataean community well into the Byzantine Empire when it became a seat of a Bishopric. Archaeologists uncovered 150 carbonised papyrus rolls in a Christian church in Petra that contained information about the property and people of the city in the mid-sixth century CE.[19] With their land and culture divided, and their peoples returning to the sands that once brought them immeasurable wealth, the millennium in which the Nabataeans mastered the desert may seem just as transient as their nomadic origins. Regardless, their ingenuity in engineering and architecture has left a legacy of a trailblazing civilisation that capitalised on opportunity without ever forgetting from whence they came.

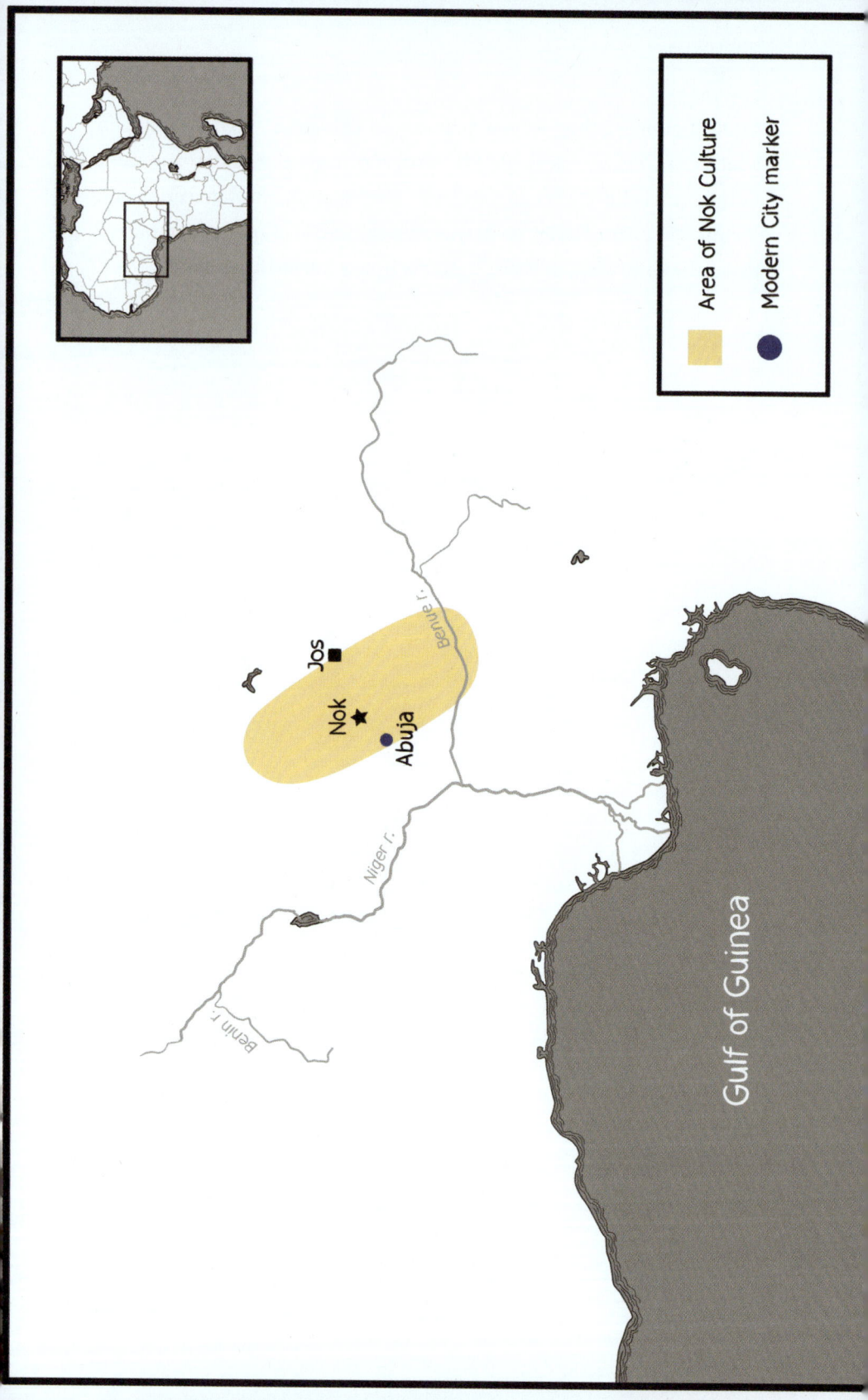

Chapter Fourteen

Nok

The Terracotta Heads in the Tin Mine

The rhythmic beat of the drums being played behind the group was coursing through the man's body, vibrating through his core, down his arms, and into his hands. They had not been back to this area in many years. The soil had washed away, requiring them to move on to another place to grow their crops. Today, they had come back to this place, the home of their ancestors, to pay them tribute. The man stared down at the scattered, broken terracotta pieces surrounding the graves. Not long ago, whole statues stood where these fragments now lie, expertly modelled by the craftspeople of their homestead. Strong, imposing figures with piercing eyes left to stand watch over those who had passed on. Now nature had taken its toll, and these fallen figures needed a new home.

The man straightened and set off with the other members of his tribe, gathering fragments and bringing them to a pit that had been dug not far from where they first stood. He felt the weight of his ancestors with each piece he picked up, their presence when stroking the terracotta strands of hair and the ridges of their necklaces and bracelets, so similar to the ones he currently wore. The drumbeats coursed through his fingers into the ceramic pieces, and he could feel their power returning.

The man and his tribe went about selecting which pieces to give back to the earth. Only a select few would remain here, resting alongside those they were made to protect. The rest would travel back with them to their new home so the memories of the dead would remain with their tribe and bring good fortune to their harvests. The man placed his chosen pieces into the ground, and watched as a fire was lit inside the pit. Once the dancing flames died down, his ancestors were covered with the soil that had once brought them so much life.

The Discovery of Nok

In the 1940s, a new archaeological culture was accidentally discovered in the British colonial tin mines of central Nigeria. Terracotta heads and figurines emerged from the mines, alerting archaeologists to the discovery of something not seen before in this part of the world. Together, with the discovery of beaded necklaces, pottery, stone tools, and debris from the fabrication of iron that all fit into the same timeline and setting, the assemblage of artefacts was given a name: Nok.

The Nok culture is named after the small village of Nok, where the first pieces of these terracotta figurines were found. The village is located around seventy kilometres northeast of the capital city of Abuja in central Nigeria. The Nok culture is one of the earliest known societies of Sub-Saharan Africa and is attributed with creating the earliest sculptural tradition in Africa outside of Egypt.[1] The Nok were also possibly one of the earliest to smelt iron in the area.

Terracotta Wonders

The Nok culture is most famous for its captivating terracotta figurines. The fragments found so far are known for their bold, abstract features and pierced eyes. They usually have large heads, big, almond-shaped eyes, parted lips, and intricate hairstyles. These figures are commonly shown wearing a loincloth, those worn by men lying flat with a tapered band, and those for women having two strips of cloth tucked under the belt on either side of their hips. Other fragments have them wearing a variety of clothing, with braided cords, pleats, and knots in their textiles. They all sport amazingly intricate hairstyles, and can be found with decorated eyelids and eyebrows, beards, scarifications, headdresses, and large necklaces and bracelets. If these figurines were made to depict realistic images of the Nok, we can then imagine a people and culture who loved body ornamentation. The necklaces and bracelets we see on the figures could have even been made from the iron that the Nok culture became experts at extracting.[2]

Some figurines carry tools that would have been used in daily farming life, and other, possibly ritual, objects like axes. Some figurines were also created to display illnesses and sicknesses like elephantiasis, eye disease, ulcers, and facial paralysis. These particular depictions may have been created to protect against illness, but their exact meaning to the Nok is still unknown.

Archaeologists have also found sculptures of the people of the Nok culture partaking in activities, such as a model of a dugout canoe that depicts two figures transporting four piles of goods. This could indicate that they were part of an extensive trading network in the area. A male figurine with a seashell on his head may also prove that they had contact with other peoples as far as the West African Coast. The shell was made in such a detailed way that it was able to be identified as being from the Atlantic Ocean, around seven hundred kilometres away from the site where the figurine was found.[3]

Apart from people, terracotta figurines were made that combined elements of both humans and animals. One head that was found looks mostly human, but it has fangs coming out of its mouth, a wide nose, and a hood that resembles a cobra. Another human head has a bird beak where the mouth should be.

It is unknown where the Nok tradition of terracotta sculpture came from. It appears in the archaeological record as a fully-fledged and independent art form, with no current examples of earlier pieces that may hint at its development.[4] Microscopic analysis of these figures shows that, no matter where they were found, the clay used for all of them came from the same place.[5] This means that there was either a settlement devoted to the crafting of these sculptures where specialists could share ideas and ensure the artistic rules for creating these figurines were followed, or that

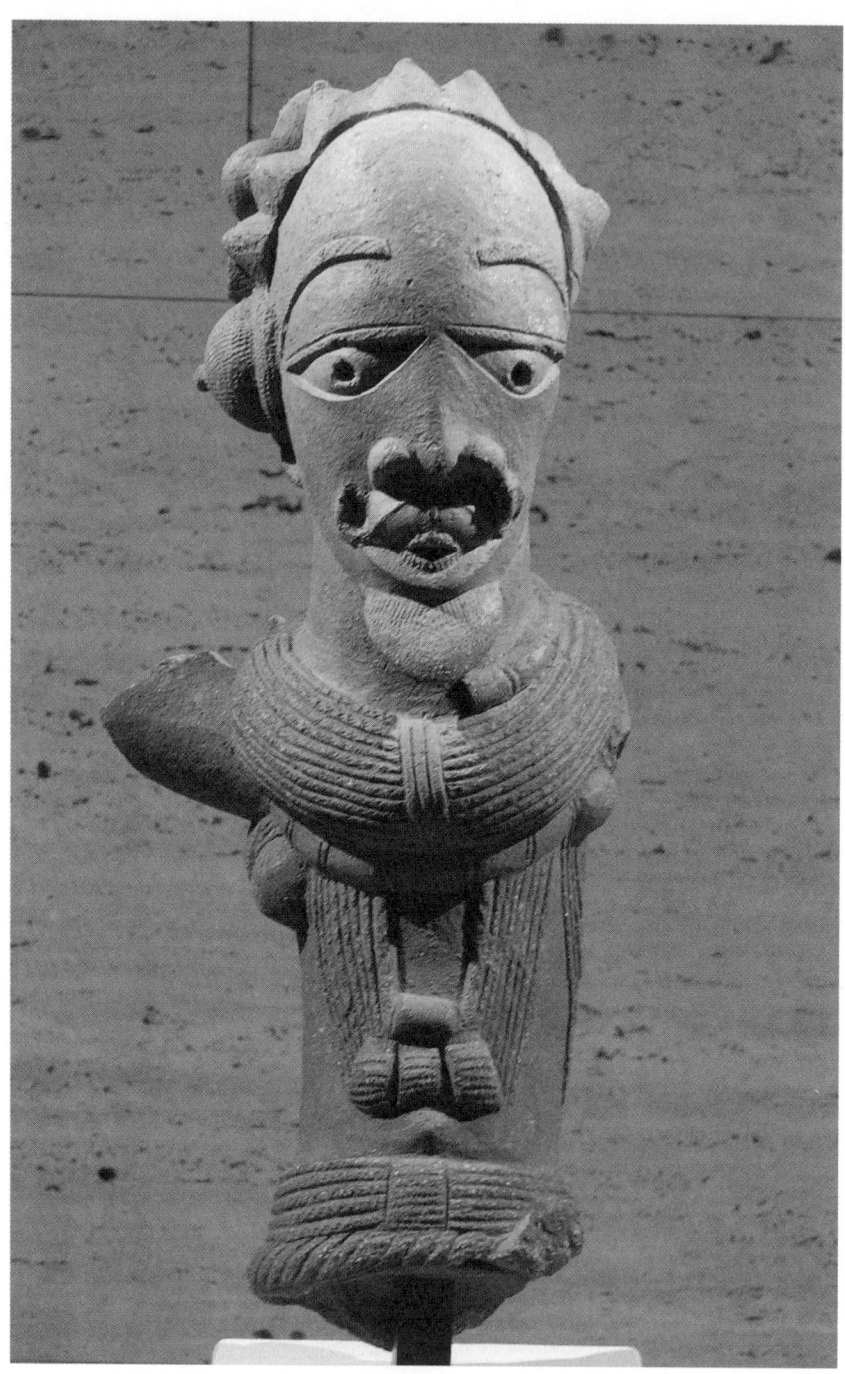

Nok terracotta figure of a male

the (still-highly specialised) potters of local communities knew the cultural standards and where to find the right clay for the job. If this one day proves true, the Nok artistic tradition may represent the earliest evidence of craft specialisation within the Sub-Saharan African cultures.[6]

The figurines themselves were expertly crafted from terracotta clay by hand. Although terracotta sculptures are usually created by a process called hand building, where bits of clay are added and shaped during its construction, some of the Nok sculptures were created using a reduction technique similar to sculpting or wood carving.[7] This method of construction might have been the reason for their unique style and composition. Nok potters were also knowledgeable in their firing of the terracotta. They added ventilation holes to prevent pressure from building while the figurine was in the furnace or kiln to ensure it didn't explode.

Where Did They Come From?

The discovery of these terracotta sculptures immediately sparked the question: Who made these impressive works of art? Most archaeologists followed that up with: How did these people live, and what purpose did these figurines play in their societies?

The Nok culture was originally radiocarbon dated to have existed from somewhere between 500 BCE until 200 CE, but recent new carbon dates have come to light which place them much earlier in the historical timeline.[8] The earliest evidence we have for settlement and farming that correlates to Nok culture now dates to the middle of the second millennium BCE (c. 1500 BCE), with no Nok sites dating after the turn of the Common Era (c. 1 CE).[9]

Investigations into the sites and artefacts have enabled archaeologists to separate the Nok culture into three periods: Early Nok (c. 1500–900 BCE), Middle Nok (c. 900–400 BCE) and Late Nok (c. 400 BCE–1 CE). We see the earliest farming appearing during the Early Nok period, but the appearance of the terracotta figurines dates to the Middle Nok

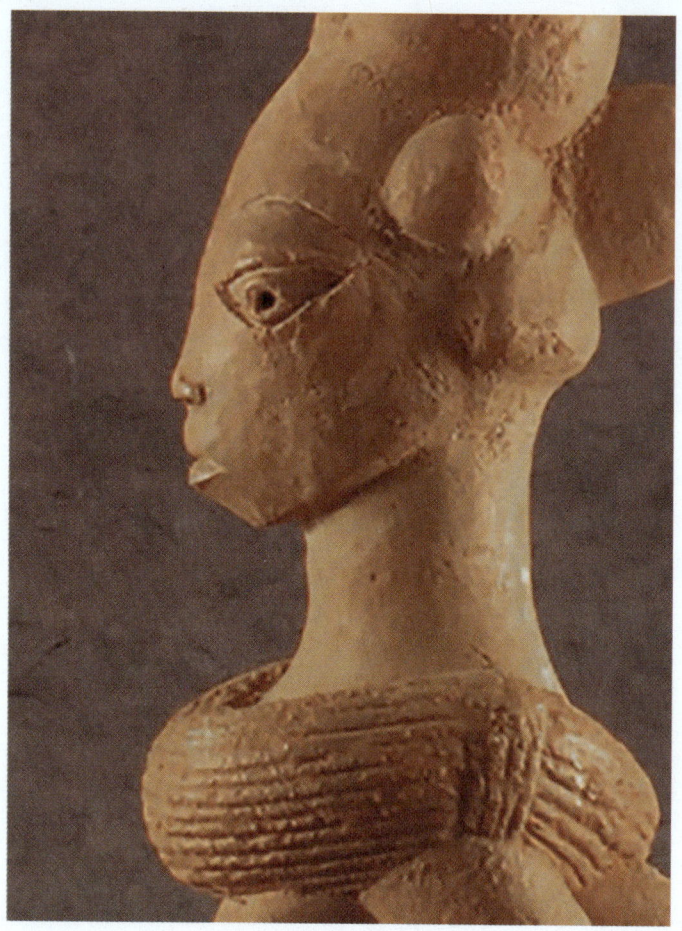
Female Nok sculpture.

period, which is also when we see an increased number of sites, and evidence of iron smelting through the appearance of iron slag, smelting furnaces, and a few iron objects. This period is what archaeologists consider to be the main Nok phase. After 400 BCE, sites containing terracotta figurines decreased, as did the number of sites. We don't yet know what happened to the people of the Nok culture, and the heavy looting of sites over the years since the culture's discovery has destroyed a great deal of information that could have helped in answering this question. The end of Nok could possibly have been due to exhausting the land they lived on, and a heavy reliance on charcoal for iron smelting, which requires lots of trees, potentially causing deforestation.[10]

Life as Nok

Archaeological excavations at Nok sites have shown that the people who were part of this society did not originate in this area. There is no evidence of settlement before the Early Nok period, meaning that people would have migrated to this spot.[11] Archaeologists are still trying to find out where these people came from, and why they moved from their place of origin. It is also likely that the formation of the Nok culture didn't all happen in the same place. People would have spread out across the larger region of central Nigeria and maintained contact through trading and ritual traditions. Given the finds at every Nok site that has currently been excavated all have the same characteristics, there would have been a sense of shared cultural community across the area, even though they didn't settle in larger villages or towns.

The Nok culture defies all norms of what we would expect from a complex society that has specialised craftsmanship and metal production. No permanent structures were found, and there was no centralised workshop for the production of the culturally important terracotta figurines. The people who inhabited this area didn't live in cities; they did not collect materials that would signify any inequality or signs of hierarchy, and, other than the depictions of seashells on a few terracotta figurines, there aren't any indicators of trading or exchange with other peoples at the time. We also see no communal architecture or buildings, and we have yet to find any structures for storing surplus food from farming.

The Nok seem to have been a collection of autonomous small groupings of farm-and-homestead communities of various sizes. Some larger settlements housed populations of over a thousand, while others were much smaller. It is possible that this variation of settlement size denoted various functions for different political, ritual or economic purposes.[12] Some settlements exhibit the remains of potential fortifications, meaning there may have been a risk of war or raiding that would have required the collective to come together and organise to ensure the community's safety. Their social hierarchy (if any) is unknown, so how communal projects were organised remains a mystery.

These groups of sedentary farmers would have lived autonomously in dispersed settlements, with enough contact and shared ritual ideology between each other that they collectively began creating terracotta figurines and smelting iron. Evidence for iron smelting is of great significance at this time in West Africa. Archaeologists have found sites where both stone and iron tools were being used simultaneously.[13] This reinforces a hypothesis long held by many that there was no intermediary copper or bronze ages between the evolution from manufacturing tools from stone to those made of iron like in many other parts of the world. Excavations at the site of Taruga show evidence that Nok terracotta figurines were indeed associated with the smelting of iron.[14] These two unique and seemingly linked crafts appear to then have been of equal importance to the Nok.

From the beginning of the Nok period, farming was the backbone of their livelihood. An abundance of pearl millet seeds has been found, and it seems they were a sedentary agricultural community. It's likely that they ate both plants and meat, but we are unable to determine if they domesticated animals or relied on them at all, because the acidity of the soil deteriorated most of the organic materials that would have provided this evidence. Of course, the absence of evidence does not mean meat wasn't consumed, or farm animals weren't kept, it is simply how the ecosystem of the site affected preservation.

Most Nok settlements were located on hilltops or slopes, though some still existed in the plains. Nok houses would have mostly been made from organic materials such as wood and plant stalks. While we have no traces of the houses themselves, evidence of daub that would have been used in the wattle and daub method of building has been found during excavations. Wattle and daub constructions were made of woven branches or reeds and then coated in a sticky material, most likely a mix of clay, wet soil, animal dung, and straw.

Although we have many settlement sites, there is not a single one where the finds are in the same position that they were left in. Only pits of different shapes and sizes that we don't know the exact purpose of appear to be a constant occurrence at every site. These pits are where the majority of finds from the Nok culture have come from. The best explanation of these pits is that they could have been created when the clay required for creating the daub to build their houses was dug out of the ground.

Nok sites didn't exist for long and were only occupied for a brief period.[15] This could have been due to soil depletion, a shift to farm a different plant, or even social reasons. This is why there are so many dispersed farmsteads across the Nok cultural area. Sites were visited and inhabited several times over an extended period, which suggests that people kept returning to what could have been considered an ancestral area.[16] The reason for this could have had to do with a communal ritualistic or religious practice. Early Nok artefacts are found to be more scattered over the site, whereas Middle Nok finds are mostly in a few pits—filled particularly with terracotta figurines, stones, and charcoal. These may have been rubbish pits, but researchers have also suggested that they might have returned to these abandoned spots to bury fragments of broken terracotta figurines.

Not one of the terracotta figurines uncovered at Nok sites have been found whole or intact. The sculptures were either discovered broken in a way that the pieces could not be joined back together again, or their other halves were never recovered at the same site. As these pits were intentional burials, that means the terracotta sculptures would have to have been broken before they were deposited into the ground. It seems these fragments could have been ritually buried by lighting a fire in the pit due to the amount of charcoal found buried with them. The answer might lie in a feature missing in the Nok archaeological record until recently: graves.

Protecting the Dead

Several metres next to a terracotta deposit at the site of Pangwari, two groups of upright stones, some of which were grinding stones, were found deeper than any other finds. Between the stones were three examples of decorated ceramic pots. At the site of Ido, a necklace of stone beads was uncovered next to its own set of stones and pottery.[17] These intentionally placed objects have been interpreted as graves. The absence of human remains of any kind is again due to the acidity of the soil, which would have dissolved the bones of the people buried there.

Between these stone layers were intentionally dug pits filled with broken terracotta sculptures. This has led archaeologists to believe that the terracotta sculptures were part of a burial ritual. While this doesn't solve every question about the Nok, or speak for every piece of terracotta found at Nok sites, it could aid in filling in one more piece of the archaeological puzzle, bringing us one step closer to understanding the people of the Nok culture.

Apart from a few examples of travelling by boat or beating a drum, the terracotta figurines are mostly portraits with expressionless faces and stiff postures, giving them a lifeless air. These stoic figures may have been created to represent Nok ancestors and were perhaps even placed at graves as a sort of marker for protection. Once they had fallen over or broken, they were collected, and parts of their broken bodies were buried with the dead, while the rest were carried back to the village where living descendants were currently residing. This could also explain why some pits were thought to be trash.[18]

Notes on Nok

The Nok culture of central Nigeria was remarkable for its expert craftsmanship in terracotta and was perhaps the first culture in Sub-Saharan Africa to produce iron. Their mastery of terracotta sculpture while not living in a complex societal structure is a testament to the sharing of ideas and rituals within a larger collective. Nok society was a powerful community, able to continue their preferred way of life, while still being part of something bigger than their close-knit settlements. Little is known about the decline and end of the Nok, though evidence shows that their population declined sometime after 200 CE. Regardless of how they met their end, the Nok left an outstanding legacy in the history of Western Africa.

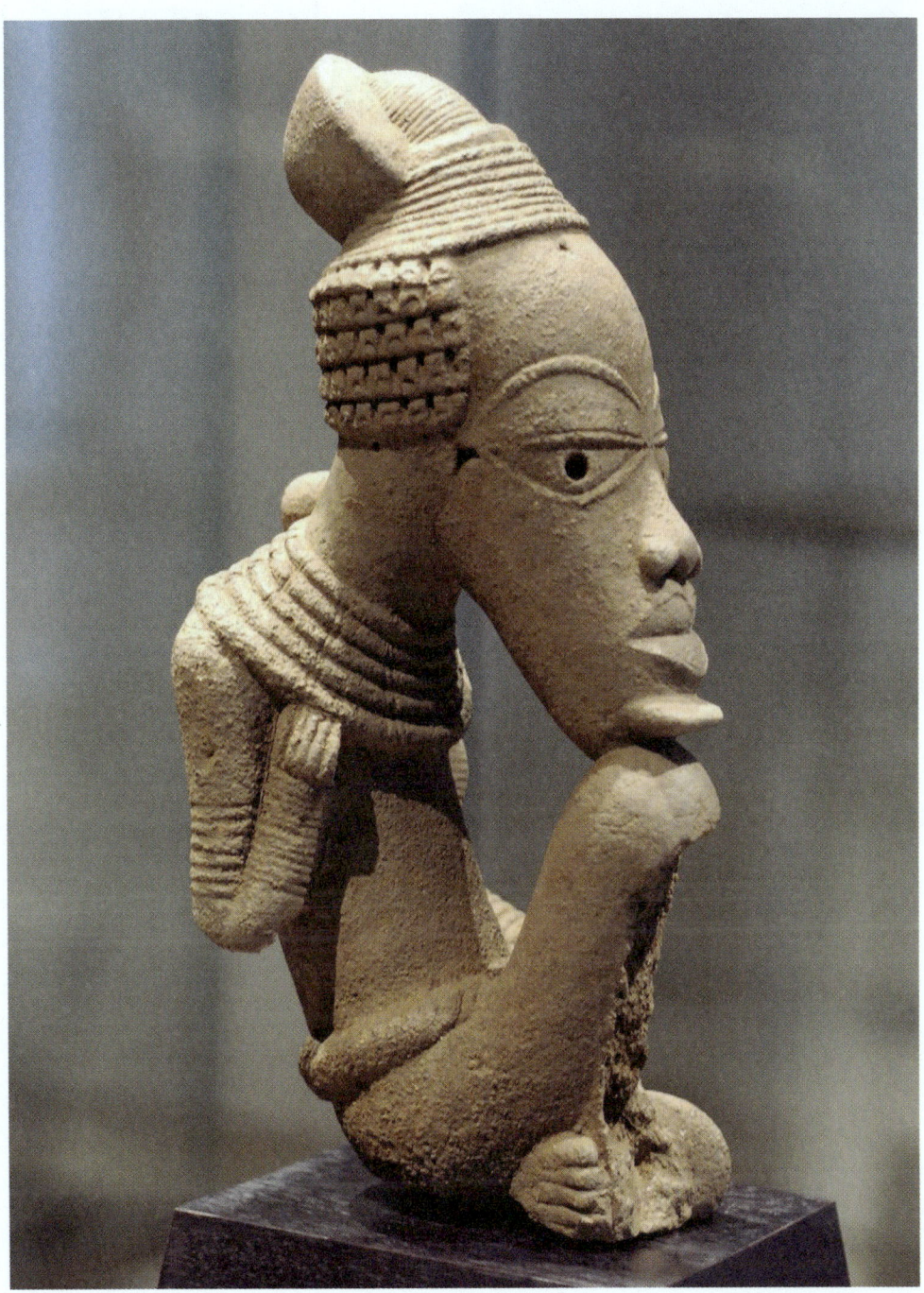

Nok figurines are noted for their large, expressive eyes but overall stoic nature.

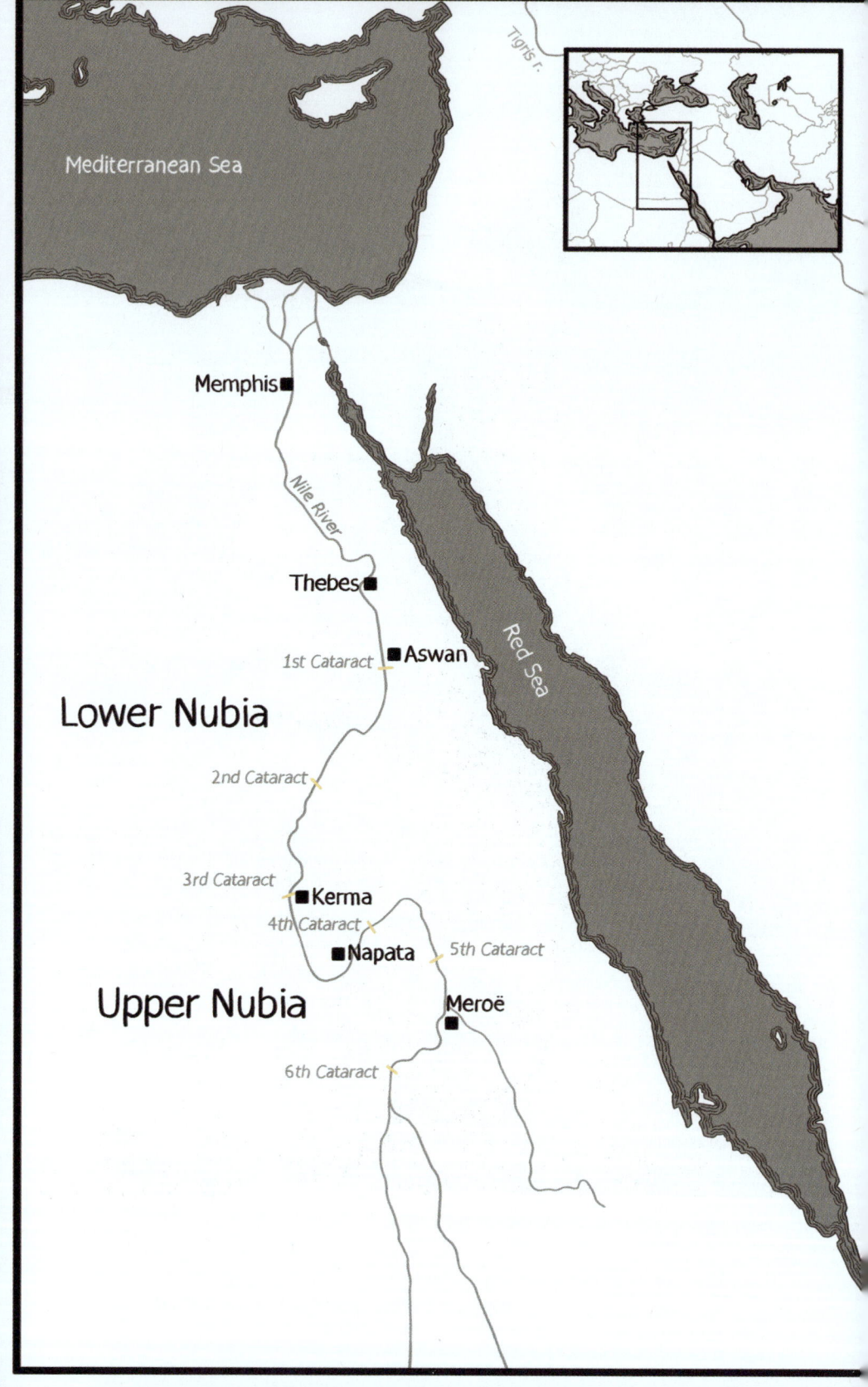

Chapter Fifteen

Nubians (Kingdom of Kush)
More Pyramids Than Egypt & a Tale of Three Cities

The desert sun beat down on Harkhuf as he and his caravan rode along the banks of the Nile. The trek was long, but going by boat would have proven more arduous and dangerous due to the rocky rapids of the river's cataracts. The boats would have to be removed and carried along the coast to the other side. No, his cargo was too precious to risk such a venture. This was Harkhuf's third trading expedition to Yam. The first, years ago, was with his father, Iri, who had shown him the way and introduced him to trading partners south of Egypt. Harkhuf took the family business seriously and was proud of this mission's booty. For the glory of the king, he was bringing back goods beyond comparison. In his company, he had three hundred donkeys loaded to the brim with incense, ebony, henku oil, panther skins, elephant tusks, and so much more.[1] This alone would have brought him fame and fortune in his home of Elephantine, but Harkhuf also had with him a troop of soldiers from Yam and there was no telling what favour that would incur with the king.

Despite the success of his latest mission, Harkhuf couldn't help but notice something changing in this foreign land. The last time he passed through these lands, two territories had united and were governed under one ruler. This time, another had joined the ranks. Their leader had offered Harkhuf oxen and goats upon seeing the might of the party he was travelling with, strengthened by the addition of the troops from Yam. He even became their personal guide, bringing the caravan over the Korosko hills so they could avoid taking the long route around the bend of the Nile.[2] They had been away from home for eight months, with many more ahead of them, so this shortcut was greatly welcomed by all men, eager to get home to their families and farms. The tribes of Nubia were uniting, Harkhuf could feel it. But what this meant for the future of his homeland of Egypt, he could only imagine. That would have to wait for his next expedition.

What's in a Name?

When we're told to name a great ancient civilisation in Africa, the first to come to people's minds is Egypt. Egypt is often thought of as a lone wolf, an outlier on the continent. In reality, it was one of many thriving ancient cultures that developed in northeast Africa prior to the seventh century CE, before the spread of Islam introduced Arabization into the area. Just to the south of the ever-popular ancient Egypt, was an all too often forgotten society that built the earliest cities, states, and empires of inner Africa. A society that was a long-time trading partner, and even an enemy, to their neighbours to the north and one that left us more pyramids than Egypt: ancient Nubia.[3]

The Nubians sprang to life along the Middle Nile, roughly from the city of Aswan and the first cataract of the Nile, down to Sudan's current capital, Khartoum. Archaeological work in Nubia began in 1821 when Turco-Egyptian forces invaded the Middle Nile Valley and turned it into a province, though this early work (continuing even up until recent decades) was carried out through the guise of Egyptology. Until recently, Nubia was seen as a neighbour, a trading partner, and an enemy to the ancient Egyptians, and it was studied in the context of another ancient civilisation instead of as its own main character.

Nubia has a rich cultural history spanning from prehistory to present day, but the story of the Kingdom of Kush starts at the city of Kerma, around 2500 BCE.

The name "Nubia" or "Nubians" might have come from the ancient Egyptian word for gold: *neb* or *nebu*. Nubia had rich gold mines that were greatly desired by the Egyptians, who tried relentlessly to keep them under their control. Another theory is that the term could also have come from the names of the tribes that settled in the region called the "Nuba" or the "Noba." Even though the term "Nubia" may have come from the ancient Egyptian language, ancient Nubians never used the term, and it was never used to refer to this part of the world. Instead, the ancient Egyptians referred to this southern region as *Ta-sety*, which means "Land of the Bow," because the Nubians were skilled archers.

By the ancient Egyptian Middle Kingdom (c. 2030–1650 BCE), Nubia was being referred to as "Kush." The Kushite peoples or kingdom is now used to refer to the Napatan (c. 800–300 BCE) and Meroitic (c. 300 BCE–350 CE) periods of Nubia, when they grew into their own and ruled far beyond their borders into Egypt.

Kerma

Kerma was the first major capital of Nubia, and the culture that emerged there in the middle of the third millennium BCE quickly grew and spread south from the second cataract of the Nile to the fourth. The success of the Kushite power that established itself at Kerma led to the expansion and establishment of a multi-ethnic empire sometime after 1750 BCE.[4] The city of Kerma was a large urban settlement that developed around the city's main temple, the Western Deffufa, a monumental mudbrick building that served as the religious centre for the city. Surrounding this three-story structure was a city filled with activity. Secondary chapels, workshops, storerooms, bakeries, bronze workshops, and residences dedicated to priests or rulers made of unfired mudbrick were built, along with a fortification wall.

An Eastern Deffufa was also built, but this area was dedicated to the cemetery of Kerma. While only the mudbrick survives, these structures would have been decorated with glazed tiles in ancient times. The people of Kerma were buried in the foetal position between leather covers, and instead of being placed in a coffin, they were laid on beds decorated with animals and mythical creatures.⁵ Those who could afford it were buried with jewellery, pottery, and fans made from ostrich feathers. The all too famous Nubian archers were even found with their archer's rings still around their thumbs.

Kerma kings were buried in vaulted chambers underneath huge man-made hills called tumuli. The pathways to the burial chambers of royal and elite tombs were also filled with the skeletons of human sacrifices meant to serve the deceased in the afterlife. Though these burials may seem gruesome today, Kerma funerals appeared to be quite social events. Archaeologists have found evidence of vessels placed purposefully upside down, which could be the living sharing food with the dead. Communal beer filter straws were also found, suggesting that these feasts were times for society to come together.⁶

Throughout the Old Kingdom of ancient Egypt, Lower Nubia was, at times, viewed as both a threat and a trading partner. An Egyptian settlement at Buhen in Lower Nubia was built to solidify trade networks with the rest of Nubia and to access the natural resources of the area. The effects of this trade can be seen in the cultural influences both kingdoms had on each other. For example, the treasure of the founding mother of the New Kingdom in Egypt, Queen Ahhotep, contained a Kerma-type dagger, and an ornament showing strong Kushite influence that became a military decoration in the eighteenth dynasty. On the other side, Egyptian influence can be seen in Kushite architecture such as the winged sun-disc found carved into a stone that was once above a chapel in Kushite territory.⁷

Though tensions between both parties sometimes became fraught, efforts were made to maintain trading connections due to their mutual reliance on a continual exchange of goods. As Kerma grew into a powerful monarchy by the Middle Kingdom (c. 2055–1650 BCE), fifteen forts were constructed and renovated between the Second and Third Cataracts of the Nile in an attempt to annex the region and regain control of these resources. These were also made to protect the Egyptians from any attacks after the decentralisation of the Egyptian government during the First Intermediate Period (c. 2181–2055 BCE).

These forts failed to completely prevent attacks however, as Nubia continued to conduct raids into southern Egypt, resulting in the capture of many spoils of war. Furthermore, the forts did nothing to quell the power of Kerma. By the Second Intermediate Period (c. 1700–1550 BCE), with ancient Egypt weakened once more, the Nubians expanded to their greatest extent, creating an alliance with the Hyksos, who had invaded and were ruling over Lower Egypt, to try and crush what was remaining of Egypt from both sides. This was never to be, as the pharaoh Kamose attacked the south and captured territories up to the second cataract of the Nile.

Once King Ahmose, the founder of the New Kingdom (c. 1550–1070 BCE), rose to power and defeated the Hyksos, he set his sights on Lower Nubia, attacking south of the second cataract. His grandson Thutmose I (r. 1520–1492 BCE) continued Ahmose's campaigns when he ascended the throne, pushing Egyptian power south to the fifth cataract. Thutmose I established forts at the third cataract at the site of Tombos to control all trading traffic on land and sea, and gold mining operations. The end of the Kerma period is usually attributed to an attack on the capital city by Thutmose I in c. 1500 BCE. And thus began five hundred years of Egyptian domination and colonisation, with a new city as its capital.

Napata

Though it may have been settled long before the Egyptians arrived, King Thutmose III (r.1479–1425 BCE) began construction works at Napata, located at the fourth cataract of the Nile. The city became an important location for both the Nubians and the Egyptians as a great political and religious centre. It's clear by the archaeological remains at the site that the ancient Egyptians had quite the influence on Nubian culture—most notably with the resurgence of a well-known mortuary structure.

Return of the Pyramids

During Napata's reign as the capital city of the Kushite Kingdom, we see pyramids being constructed for the Nubian elites and the Egyptians living in the area. First appearing at the royal cemetery of El-Kurru in 751 BCE,[8] these pyramids differed from those constructed during the Old Kingdom in Egypt, such as the pyramids of Giza. These new pyramids to the south were made from smaller blocks of local Nubian sandstone and were a fraction of the size of their predecessors. Though smaller, Nubian pyramids are taller in proportion to their bases, with a steep slope of sixty to seventy degrees. For context, those in Egypt were sloped at fifty degrees. The pyramids also had chapels attached to the east face and enclosure walls. Beneath these pyramids were a series of two or three small chambers carved out of solid rock. People were no longer buried in a foetal position on a bed, but laid to rest straight, sometimes in a coffin.[9]

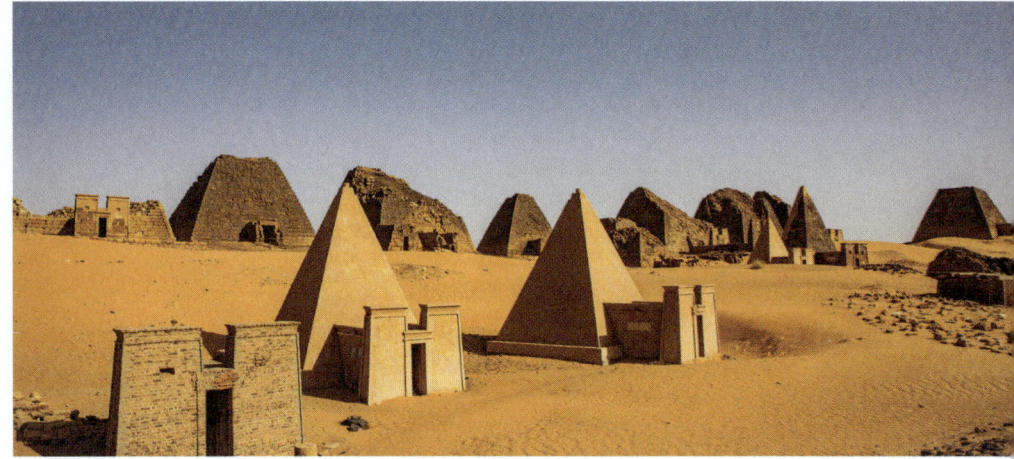

Pyramids of Meroë.

Napata was also home to the Temple of Amun, built during the rule of Thutmose III below the mountain of Jebel Barkal. This became the most important religious site in Nubia for much of its history.

Following New Kingdom colonisation, we see a lack of written texts and archaeological remains for this period until the beginning of the twenty-fifth dynasty in Egypt (c. 760–656 BCE). What we do know from this informationally sparse era is that the Nubians adopted Egyptian hieroglyphs as a writing system for their own language and took heavy inspiration from ancient Egyptian architecture and kingship. They even went as far as integrating Egyptian mythology into their own indigenous traditions. While the Egyptianisation of Nubia could appear complete on paper or from the Egyptian perspective, the degree to which this influence and change extended onto the indigenous population differed according to their social status.[10] Elite families adhered to Egyptian education, were buried in the Egyptian style, and often adopted Egyptian names. Conversely, there is archaeological evidence that indigenous mortuary rites were still practised amongst the lower levels of society throughout the span of Egyptian rule.

As ancient Egyptian power began to decline once more after five hundred years of domination (two hundred of which were filled with rebellions against Egyptian rule), they abandoned Nubia at the beginning of the Third Intermediate Period (c. 1070 BCE). This retreat allowed the Nubians to come into their full power and become a force to be reckoned with. The Kingdom of Kush had emerged.

The Nubians Take Over: The Kushite Dynasty

The collapse of Egypt's colonial power in Nubia left a power vacuum that allowed the earliest Kushite rulers to gather and command troops and bring the Kingdom of Kush into significance.[11] Napata was chosen as the capital for the newly independent Kushite Kingdom under a king named Alara, who unified the area. While they still traded with Egypt, their newfound independence allowed the Nubians to expand their networks to other nations.

Kashta (c. 760–747 BCE) succeeded Alara, and seeing the opportunity in front of him, set his sights on Egypt. His march northward was the first attempted expansion into Egypt since the Kerma period, over six hundred years before, and it's possible he may have gotten as far as Thebes. There, he installed his daughter Amendiris I as God's Wife of Amun, a powerful position that allowed her to ingratiate herself into the elite of Thebes, allowing Kashta's successor, Piye, to travel safely during his military campaigns. This position was also passed down through adoption, which meant that the power of this important temple was now in the hands of the Kingdom of Kush.[12]

Piankhy, also known as Piye (c. 747–716 BCE) continued campaigns into Egypt once he came to rule, attacking more rebellious cities, and possibly solidifying Nubian power at Thebes. But it was Piye's successor and brother, Shabaqo (c. 716–702 BCE), who conquered Memphis and marked the official beginning of the twenty-fifth dynasty in Egypt.

Nubians in Egypt: A Double Kingdom

The people of Nubia and Egypt had commingled for millennia, with both peoples living and thriving on either side of the border. With such a high level of exchange, cultures inevitably mixed and is most prominently seen in an artistic innovation that came to a peak in the twenty-fifth dynasty. As ancient Egypt's new rulers, the Nubian kings used this hybridised art style to their advantage.

Shabaqo restored existing Egyptian temples at Thebes and created a stone monument inscribed with an ancient Egyptian text that has been described as "the oldest written record of human thought."[13] The monument describes the Memphite Creation Story, where the god Ptah created the world through his mind and his words. It is known today as the Shabaqo stone and was reused at some point in history as a grinding stone, resulting in some of the story eroding away. In the text, Shabaqo claims to have found the story written on a worm-eaten papyrus, and in order to preserve it, carved it on this stone for eternity.[14]

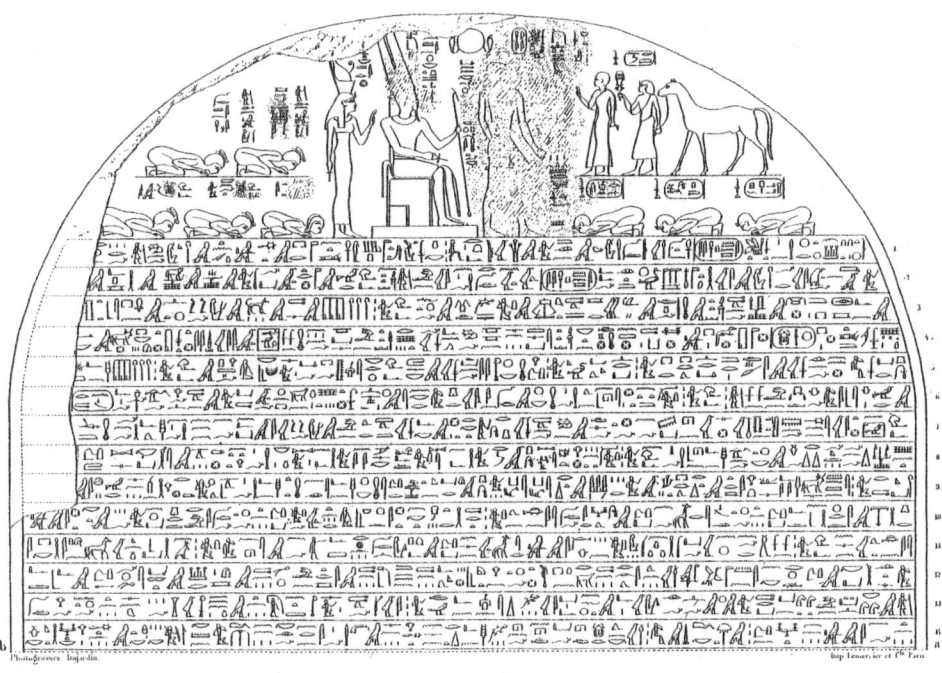

Victory stela of Piye.

Integrating traditional ancient Egyptian religion, iconography, and traditions is something we see the Napatan rulers using to legitimise their control. This act was known as archaism, and with ancient Egypt possessing a culture that was already deeply entrenched in its historical complexity, the past was used as a source of authority and familiarity. Nubian kings adopted the five Egyptian royal names, created statues that showed them wearing Egyptian regalia and in familiar poses, and began building projects using traditional architecture. Archaism was a smart move for Nubian rulers, as the use of Egyptian imagery would have made the transition over to their rule easier as they were expressing their kingship not as foreigners, but as legitimate Egyptian kings.

As time went on and they became more comfortable in their position, Napatan rulers then began to incorporate some of their traditional iconography into their statues, mixing the two artistic styles together. One of the most recognisable symbols is the royal crown and headdress.[15] The traditional double crown of Egypt was swapped out for the Nubian skullcap that fit over the head and had a diadem overtop with one or two uraeus serpents coming out at the front and streamers hanging down the back. The Egyptian-looking snakes were eventually replaced by a lion head, which probably represented their lion-headed god Apedemak.

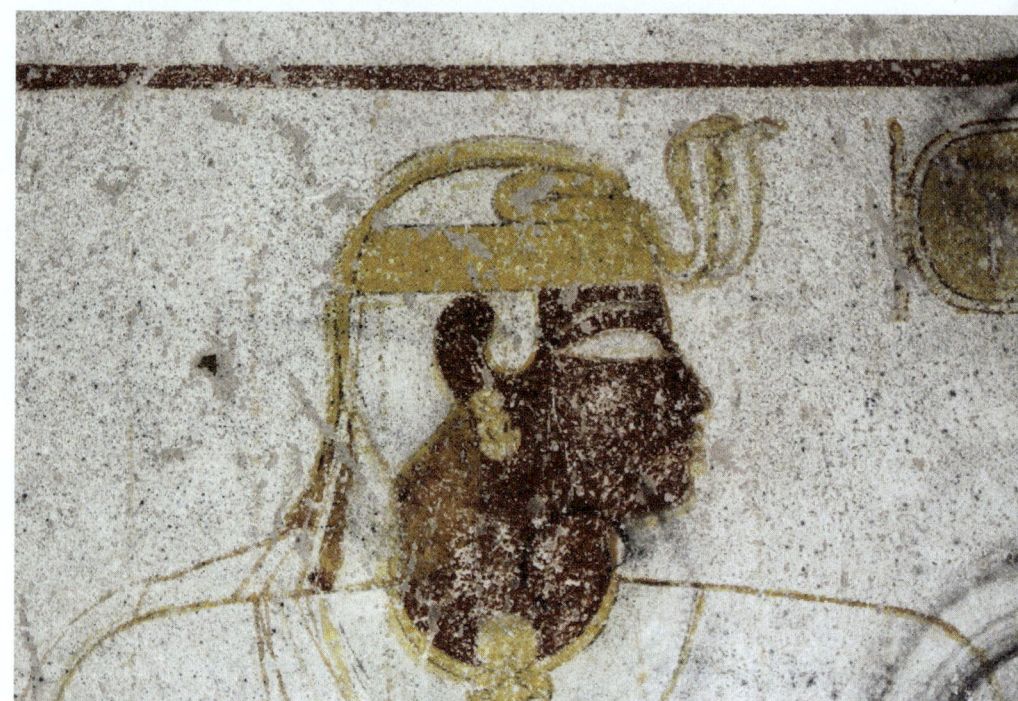

Portrait of Pharaoh Tantamani, the last king of the twenty-fifth dynasty of Egypt, wearing the Nubian skullcap diadem.

A Return Back Home

Nubian presence in Egypt lasted from around 747 to 656 BCE. During this time, they conducted trade with the Assyrians to the east, but they soon became a threat. The kingdoms in Palestine were rebelling against Assyrian domination, and Nubian rulers assisted in the defence of Jerusalem. During the reign of King Taharqo (c. 690–664 BCE),

Assyrian king Esarhaddon had enough and marched west to reclaim Palestine. Two years later, Esarhaddon set his sights on Egypt, capturing Memphis. His successor, Assurbanipal, captured Egypt as far south as Aswan.[16] Taharqo was forced to retreat to Napata. Nubia would never again control Egypt.

Meroë

After the Nubians retreated from Egypt, they continued to rule at Napata, but in the third century BCE, moved their capital to Meroë. This move was possibly due to increasing pressure from Egypt and Assyria,[17] a new dynastic line originating from this city, or simply due to a want to separate themselves from the ever-powerful priesthood at the Temple of Amun. Meroitic rulers controlled Nubia for six hundred years. The area was rich in minerals and forests, and it was located at an intersection of five main trading routes around Africa. This allowed the Nubians to prosper, undertaking great building projects, and quickly abandoning Egyptian hieroglyphs for their own, still-undeciphered Meroitic script.[18] After Alexander the Great's conquest of Egypt in 332 BCE, the Mediterranean opened again for the Nubians, and Greeks even travelled to and lived in Nubia, bringing their culture and ideas with them and adding to the mix of an already rich culture. Contact continued into Roman times, as archaeologists have found Roman jewellery and ceramics in Nubia.

Apart from the Mediterranean world, Meroë was in contact with other African kingdoms, such as Aksum to the east, and remained relatively peaceful. Rulers continued to emulate Egyptian traditions for a time, until they shifted back to Kushite iconography, assimilating the Egyptian gods they had worshipped for hundreds of years into their pantheon. Kings were now shown with the traditional Nubian cloak knotted at the shoulders over a leather loincloth, and linen tunic with a tasselled rope.

In Meroë we see the establishment of powerful female monarchs called Kandakes (also known as Candaces and Kentakes).[19] While not the first instances of women playing a significant role in Nubia, they certainly left their legendary mark on foreign civilisations. The title of Kandakes first appears between the first century BCE and the first century CE, with the title being reserved for the king's sister and the mother of the future king. The importance of the female line in royal Nubian society is evident from this title, but queens who held it appeared as monarchs undefined by their relationship with men. Three of these queens even had the title of *qore*, which was typically reserved for the king,[20] meaning they could very well have been sole rulers of Nubia. Kandakes are even depicted alongside their royal husbands smiting their enemies on monumental temple gates.

While queens from Napata were depicted wearing a long, fringed cloak over a shorter dress with an animal tail hanging down their back, Meroitic Kandakes and *qores* were depicted with accentuated thighs, hips, and large breasts—possibly to exaggerate their fertility and importance in continuing the royal line. They wore clothing similar to their husbands, with a pleated and fringed cloak over a long undergarment with a tasselled cord hanging from their shoulders.

One of these famous powerful queens was Amanirenas, who ruled from c. 40–10 BCE. She held both royal titles, and despite being blind in one eye, led raids on the Roman-controlled towns of Philae, Aswan, and Elephantine in 25 BCE. She is also thought to have been the queen who fought against C. Petronius in the war between Meroë and Rome that was mentioned by the writer Strabo, and who negotiated peace treaty terms with the emperor Augustus.[21] One of the most famous pieces she and her army took when they raided the Roman cities was a bronze head of Augustus, which she buried upside down beneath the stairs leading into a temple at Meroë. Anyone entering this holy place from then on, would trample over the head of the Roman emperor.

Thanks to its prosperous iron industry, Meroë was so successful, it was said that even the poorest who lived there were still better off than anyone else in the known world. The elite built large houses and palaces on broad streets, while the lower classes lived in mudbrick homes and huts. But reliance on natural resources cannot last forever. Iron ore extraction from mines requires massive amounts of wood to create charcoal for the smelting furnaces. Eventually, this caused mass deforestation and Meroë depleted its local wood supply. This, combined with overuse of their fields, led to the complete exhaustion of their environment. By the time the Aksumite Empire invaded and sacked Meroë c. 330 CE, claiming victory over the Kingdom of Kush, the people of Meroë had essentially already destroyed themselves. The city of Meroë fell into disuse and was finally abandoned c. 350 CE.

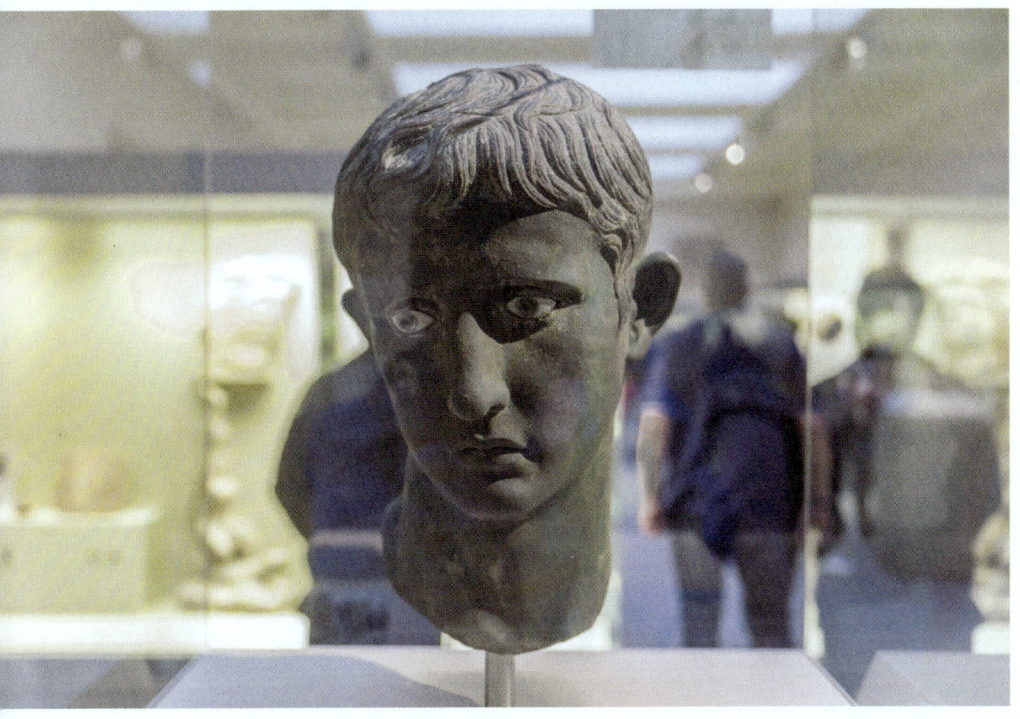

Bronze head of Augustus found underneath a temple at Meroë.

The Kingdom of Kush lasted for over a thousand years and influenced one of the longest-lasting and most powerful civilisations of the ancient world. Yet, for over a century they were seen only as an extension of Egypt. Even though they shared similarities with their Egyptian neighbours to the north, the Nubians remained a distinct African culture with its own rich history of highs, lows, and an everlasting legacy.

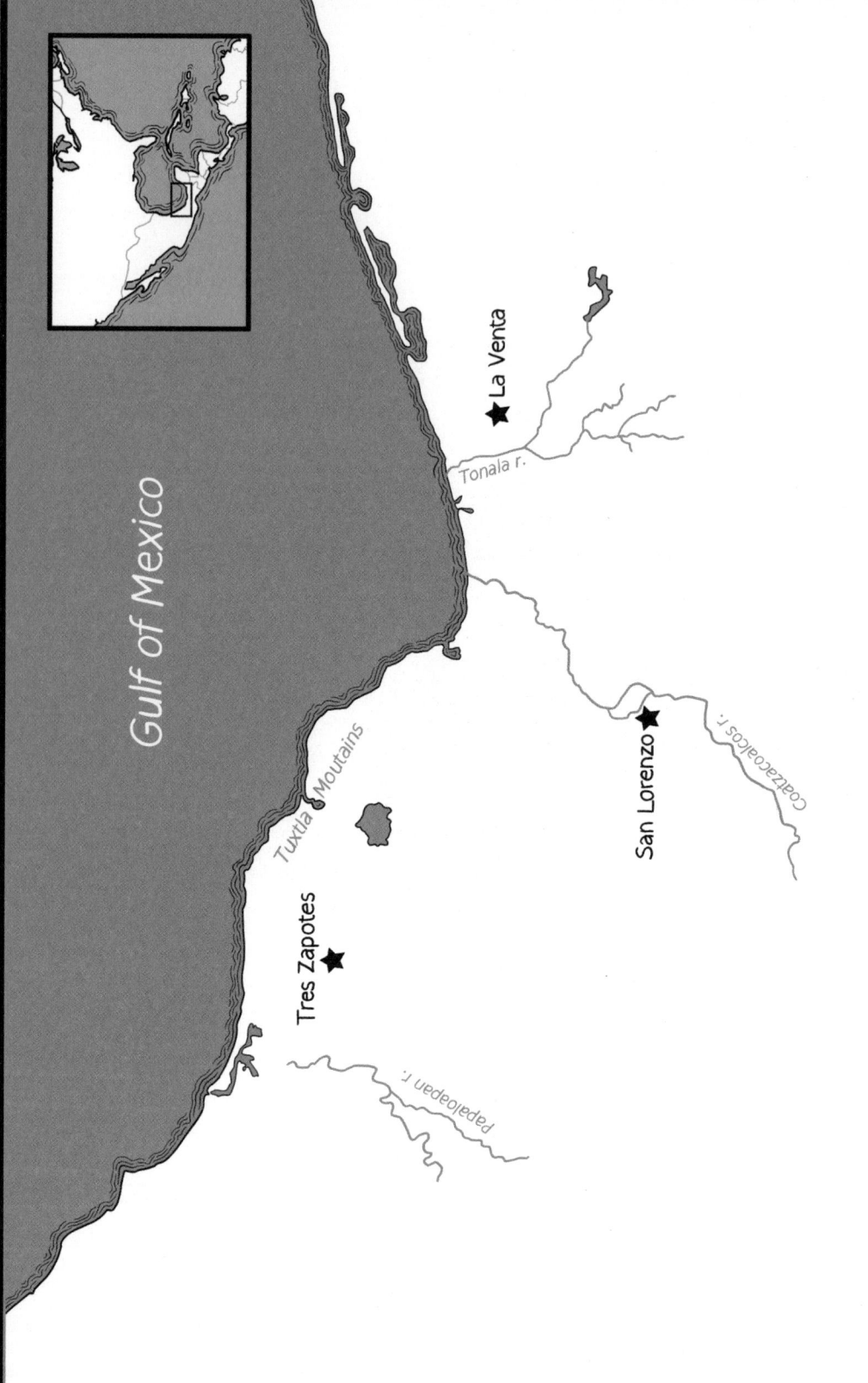

Chapter Sixteen

Olmec

Land of Rubber and Colossal Stone Heads

"Careful...watch it!" A loud snap of breaking cords echoed in the forest as the man jumped out of the way of the falling boulder just in time and watched it splash into the river.

"I told you the ropes weren't secure," he panted, trying to regain his composure. The remainder of his team looked down at their feet trying to hide their embarrassment. Looking down the hill into the river, the man locked eyes with those peering up from the basalt block that was now half-submerged in the riverbed. While the lips weren't necessarily carved into a snarl, the man couldn't help but see it as one after this blunder. The face of his ruler, sneering in discontent at the treatment of his new stone monument.

The men worked quickly to free the colossal head from the riverbed before it sank too far into the mud. They hauled it back onto the shore and then onto the wooden raft they had fashioned out of logs the day before.

Ensuring it was properly secured this time, the man signalled to the rest of the team to gather around him at the back end of the raft; this was the moment of truth.

"Three, two, one!" he shouted, and with that the men groaned in unison as they pushed the boulder into the river. The colossal head glided into the water and floated, causing the men to cheer and the man to breathe a sigh of relief. After the earlier mishap, this moment of triumph was what everyone needed to sustain them on their long journey home.

The men made quick work securing the raft to multiple canoes and loading up the rest of their traded wares into the sterns. And with that, they were off. The man was happy to finally be on the water but knew that this was only the beginning. The real challenge lay at the other end, when they would have to carry this boulder over land.

The First Mesoamerican Civilisation

The remains of Mesoamerica's first identified civilisation are marked by the stone monuments that have survived in the hot and humid tropical rainforests, swamps, and savannahs of the crescent-shaped regions of southern Veracruz and western Tabasco that hug the Gulf of Mexico. This is the Olmec heartland. The Aztecs later dubbed this area Olman (or Ulman), which means "Land of Rubber" in their Nahuatl language, and referred to the people who inhabited the region as the Olmeca (Ulmeca).[1] This is the name modern scholars have given to the archaeological culture that consisted of the closely interacting societies in the area, as well as the art style that was popular across Mesoamerica between around 1200 BCE to 400 BCE.

Not much is known about the people who created Olmec art. We don't know by which name they called themselves, if they all identified as one unified people, or where they came from. Some scholars proposed that they were migrants from the Pacific coast of Chiapas to the south, who brought with them early social stratification and upgraded strains of maize, while others believe that it evolved from local indigenous populations.[2] Recently, archaeological fieldwork in Olman shows the beginning of what can be identified as distinctive Olmec social and ritual traditions as early as 1700 BCE, proving that the development of this culture was a local one rather than an invasion from neighbouring territories.[3]

Urban Centres and Royal Compounds

Most of what we know about the Olmec comes from the major cities that rose to prominence throughout their history. The first to emerge was San Lorenzo, a hilltop settlement located near the flat bottomlands of the Coatzacoalcos River. First settled around 1800 BCE, it became a full-blown urban city by 1200 BCE. Being Mesoamerica's first city, and perhaps the oldest centre anywhere in the Americas, San Lorenzo served as the capital for its region, though not much is known about the communities that surrounded it or how it rose to prominence.

San Lorenzo was home to what archaeologists describe as a "Royal Compound" located on a summit that included houses with painted floors of red hematite and a large residence dubbed the "Red Palace." The Red Palace was a large structure with red gravel floors and mud walls plastered with red sand. Attached to it was a workshop where artisans would have carved monumental basalt and greenstone sculptures and stone tools. Many of the sculptures found in and around the Royal Compound appear to have been in the process of being recarved or stored for other sculpture recycling projects. Sculptors likely used this workshop as a sculptural junkyard where they could store monuments that were no longer needed and carve new ones, both from older pieces as well as from "virgin" stone, as well as manufacture grinding implements for maize. The palace also included basalt columns and a curved drain system that wound its way beneath the building. This probably had a mostly utilitarian purpose, but likely also possessed a ritual function.

The inhabitants of San Lorenzo were engineers far beyond the confines and skill of the Red Palace. They built a drain system out of U-shaped basalt troughs with covers that would have required a considerable knowledge of engineering. These drains were connected to stone-lined ponds across the plateau that were made out of expensive, imported materials.[4] Potable water would have been an important commodity on a hilltop settlement, and drains most likely served the dual purposes of sustaining daily life and being used for rituals. Evidence for similar drains has been found at other Olmec sites, suggesting that they were a main feature in Olmec daily and ritual life.[5]

By 1000 BCE, San Lorenzo's time as a regional power had come to an end. The exact reason for its decline is unknown. One possible explanation is that the river courses around the city had shifted around this time. This would have severely impacted San Lorenzo's ability to control the local transportation network, diminishing their interactions with surrounding communities and their ability to trade for both luxury goods and the staples required to sustain a thriving community.[6] Regardless of the reason, the decline of San Lorenzo opened the door for a new regional power to the northeast to come into its own: La Venta.

Ceremonial Mounds and a Great Pyramid

Located on an island in a coastal swamp, La Venta was first occupied around 1200 BCE, and developed into the major city in Olman by 1000 BCE. Between then and 400 BCE, it became the largest of all known Olmec sites, and its inhabitants constructed a carefully planned monumental and ceremonial centre with over thirty large earthen mounds upon the salt dome plateau on which it was founded.

The layout of these mounds was deliberately thought out, oriented eight degrees west of north. This has been thought to be a three-dimensional cosmic model that served as a ritual location for ceremonies that represented the renewal of the world, as well as a space for reenacting creation myths. This architectural design is also thought to have been built to coincide with the orientation of the Milky Way, or even be a model of the Isthmus River.[7] The mounds themselves were most likely used as substructures for houses or important ritual buildings. Some may also have functioned as open-air stages for rulers and religious figures to carry out ritual events for the public to watch from below, or vice versa.

Perhaps the most notable mound at La Venta is the Great Pyramid, located at the centre of the city. The pyramid itself was square with stepped sides and inset corners, and it had an elevated platform built around three sides that may have functioned as a stage for public rituals. Some scholars think that it could an imitation of a volcano, while others have put forward the idea that the Olmec pyramid at La Venta was a large-scale attempt at creating what is called a "mountain of sustenance."[8] This mountain is described as a place of bountiful gifts from nature that would be given to the people by the Olmec rain god. The pyramid itself would have been the focal point for all the other (no less impressive) mounds and plazas that appear to have been constructed out of different coloured clays and were painted red, yellow, and purple.

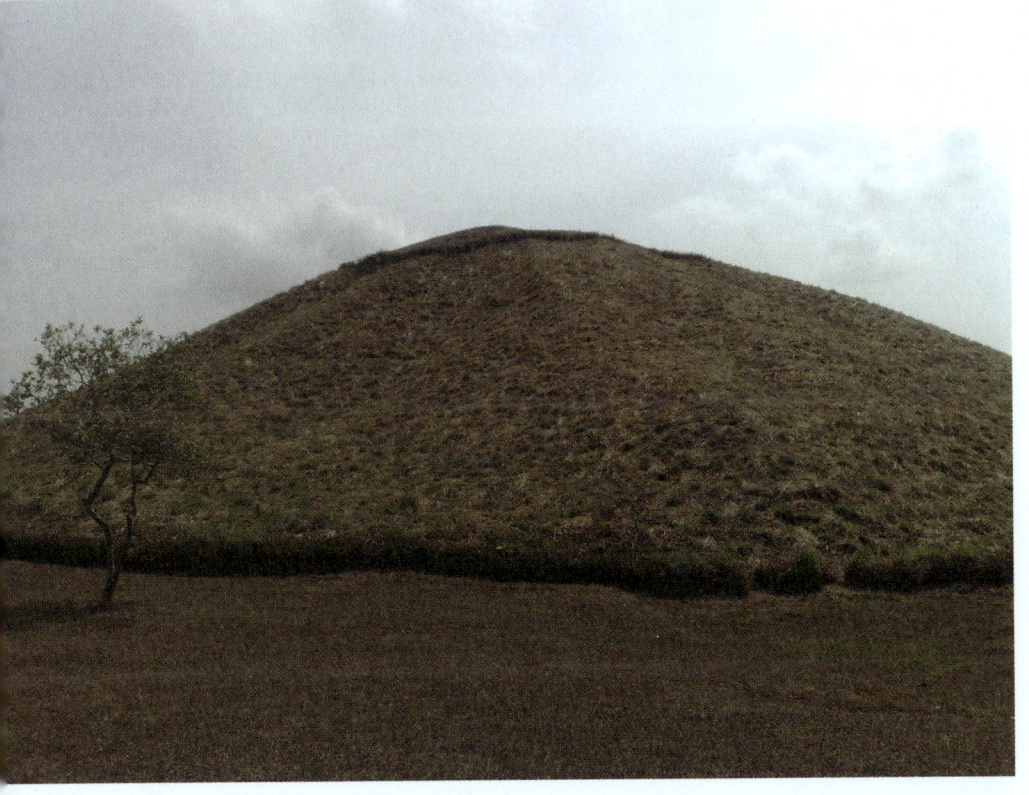

Great Pyramid mound of La Venta.

La Venta is best known for its grand and numerous buried offerings, as well as being home to some of the most well-known Olmec objects ever found. The rulers of La Venta imported thousands of tonnes of serpentine which were buried intentionally along with other prestige objects and hundreds of jade ornaments. A great number of basalt sculptures have been found scattered in front of every monumental building project at La Venta, and archaeologists have found buried offerings of stone tools similar to an axe or hoe, called celts, and even a large mosaic made out of greenstones such as jadeite and serpentine.

For all its splendour, the city of La Venta was eventually abandoned around 400–300 BCE. Even though it no longer functioned as a city or ritual centre, the importance of the site appears to have never been lost to the people who inhabited the area. The ruins of La Venta still received pottery offerings a few hundred years after its abandonment, and a purposefully buried olive jar from the early colonial period of Mesoamerica has also been found.[9]

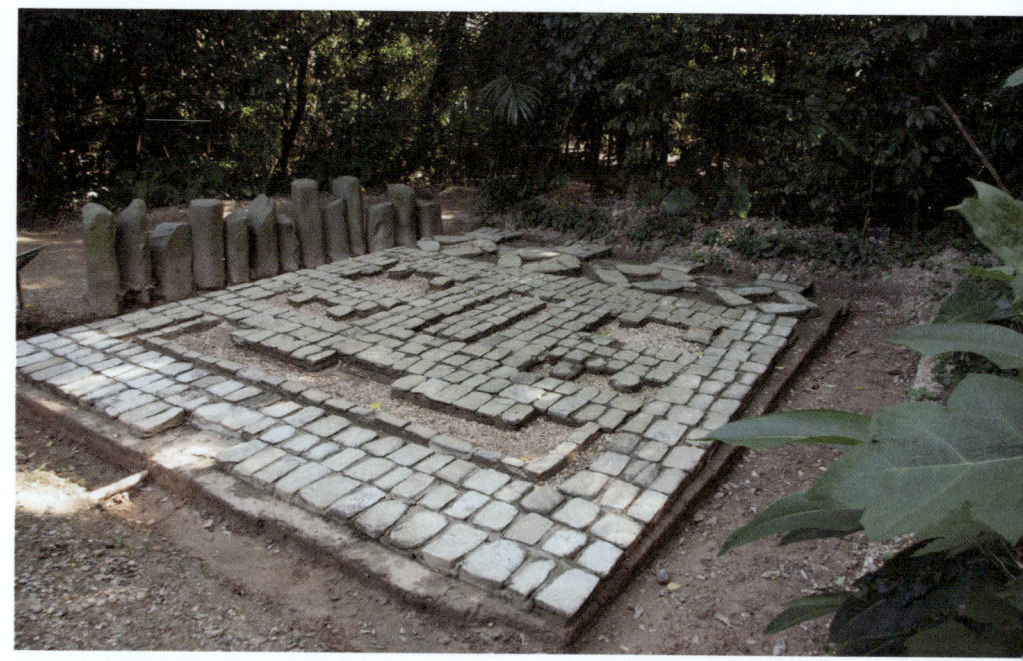

Large greenstone mosaic at La Venta.

Life Beyond the Mounds

Due to the acidity of the soil in Olman, our already limited understanding of the Olmecs is even further hindered because they constructed buildings in less-resilient materials. It is still unclear how the Olmecs organised their societies, but elaborate graves, restricted access to specific land and control over trading routes, and evidence of a strong religious institution hint at a hierarchical state with a hereditary elite class. Apart from the major centres of San Lorenzo and La Venta, smaller villages and hamlets, including some larger mound settlements, are where the majority of the Olmecs lived and thrived. Special-purpose settlements such as shrines and seasonal camps for fishing were also built to serve the needs of Olmec society.

Regular people made their homes in villages or hamlets on the terraces, rivers, streams, swamps, and oxbow lakes below the plateaus for their fertile land and trade connections. They congregated in closely packed houses made of wooden poles, clay daub, thatched roofs, and earthen or gravel floors. Housing complexes probably consisted of a main building, lean-to shelters, a courtyard, and a small garden encircled by a fence. Inside, houses might have had benches and sleeping platforms, as well as storage areas and a shrine or altar dedicated to their ancestors.

The Olmecs ate a mix of foods, from fish and other marine life such as molluscs and turtles to fruits, plants, beans, and an array of animals such as deer, crocodiles, and domesticated dogs. By 1500 BCE, maize had become such a vital crop that they created a maize god, bestowing some of the most important symbols of the Olmec world onto it.[10] The Olmecs also appear to have been avid chocolate drinkers.[11] Scientific analysis on the interior of pottery sherds has shown that it was the Olmec of San Lorenzo and other contemporary Mesoamerican cultures that first discovered the process of turning cacao seeds into both edible and drinkable chocolate.

The Olmec civilisation is best seen as a collection of closely interacting, autonomous societies that shared cultural and religious similarities with one another.[12] The many branches of the Coatzacoalcos River allowed for them to maintain a high level of connectivity between communities, which contributed to a widespread adoption and cohesive collection of artefacts found by archaeologists. Olmec works were not just restricted to Olman, though, as artefacts in their distinctive style have been found in other parts of Mexico and Central America as far as Pacific Guatemala, El-Salvador, Honduras, Guerrero, and Costa Rica.

Olmec sites were filled with prestigious objects, often made from materials that were unobtainable in Olman such as iron ore, obsidian, jade, and serpentine. The Olmecs therefore had trade networks spanning much of modern-day Mexico as far as two hundred kilometres away in order to acquire them. Olmec sites at the edges of Olman could have been established as trading stations, and there is evidence of an Olmec colony at the site of Cantón Corralito around four hundred kilometres southeast of San Lorenzo.

Hybrid Beings and Colossal Heads

Olmec art is the defining and most recognisable aspect of their civilisation. This bold, symbolic, and metaphorical yet realistic art style and iconographic system appeared suddenly in the archaeological record with no identifiable or known predecessors. One defining feature was the combination of human and animal attributes, particularly wild felines such as jaguars, pumas, and ocelots, the most famous of which being were-jaguar figurines and carvings. In these composite objects, the human is usually shown as a young child or infant, with puffy facial and body features, snarling mouths, toothless gums, or long fangs. Some of them even have claws and there is a cleft at the top of the head to symbolise where corn emerges from the earth.

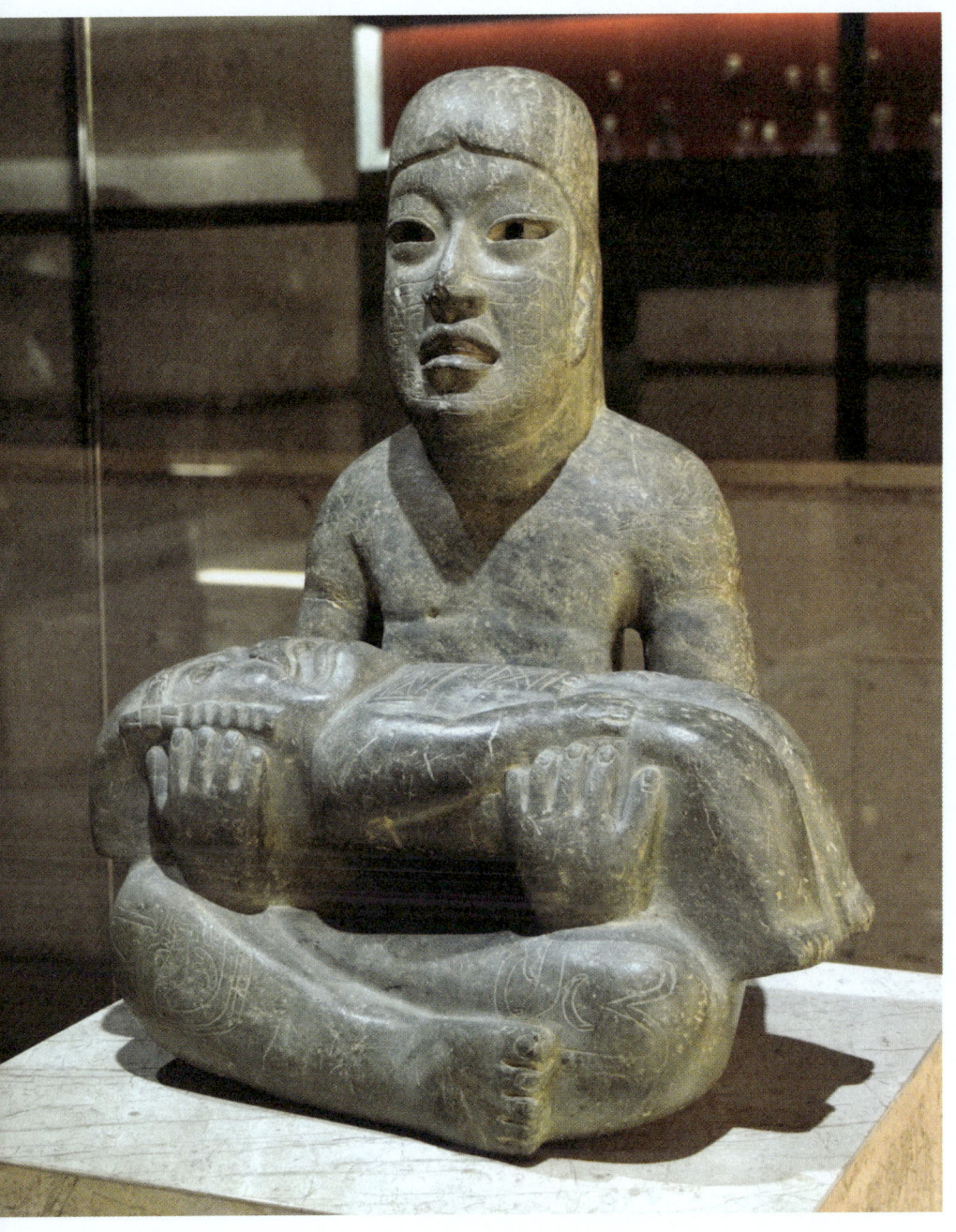

Lord of Limas sculpture depicting a young man in a seated position holding a were-jaguar infant.

While Olmec style art can be seen on various materials like ceramic and wood, Olmec artisans were first and foremost carvers and sculptors of stone. Finely carved figurines, ear spools, pendants and celts were created from greenstone, while larger monumental sculptures were hewn from basalt; all of which can be traced back to the Cerro Cintepec volcano in the Tuxtla Mountains. All carving was performed with finely manufactured stone tools able to create sharp and precise lines as well as soft curves that provided their art with unprecedented naturalism. Some sculptures appear to have even been arranged as tableau scenes that may have changed throughout a multi-day ritual.[13] One particular sculpture of a kneeling man was created to have movable wooden arms.

The most iconic of all Olmec sculptures were the colossal heads. Seventeen have been found in total; the majority at San Lorenzo (ten), while the rest were spread over the sites of La Venta (four), Tres Zapotes (two), and La Cobata (one). Measuring up to 2.85 metres high and weighing up to twenty-five tonnes, each colossal head represents an adult man with distinct features such as jowly cheeks and flat noses. Carved out of large spherical boulders and from larger existing sculpted basalt thrones, the heads were originally thought to represent ball players. Today, most scholars agree that the persons represented in these carvings were prominent individuals, most likely Olmec rulers or chiefs.

The colossal heads are adorned with distinctive helmet-like headdresses, interpreted as protective gear, that would have been worn both in war and during ceremonial rubber ball games that were popular throughout Mesoamerica. These headdresses were most likely made from cloth or animal skin, and similarities on some have led some scholars to suggest that they identify specific dynasties or individual rulers.[14] Each face is unique in its expression, ranging from gentle smiles to stern stares. The heads can be identified as distinct individuals through symbols such as ropes, jaguar paws, and eagle claws carved onto their headgear. Remnants of stucco and purplish paint were found on one head at La Venta, suggesting that some would have been painted in bold colours.

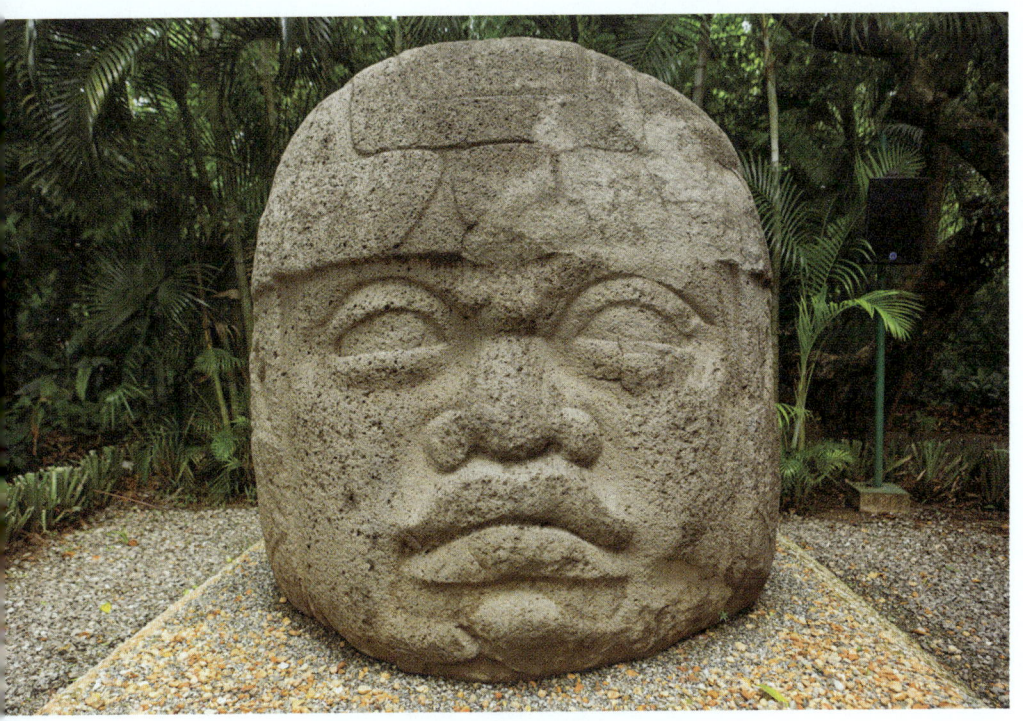

Colossal stone head found at La Venta.

Due to their archaeological context and the acidic soils of Olman, archaeologists are unable to determine where the tradition of carving colossal stone heads came from, or how long it lasted, as they are impossible to date. It's entirely possible that precursor heads made of wood could have been produced but not have survived.[15] How the colossal heads were displayed is also unknown. Only the head of the current ruler may have been allowed to be on display, with older ones being buried after the ruler they represented died. Alternatively, the heads may have been collected and arranged as a permanent ancestral record.

Most of the colossal heads were mutilated with deep, circular pockmarks and V-shaped gouges. These markings were at first thought to be from rivals in the community or invaders to the region. The latest evidence now suggests that instead, they were made to possibly extract the power that the stone held during the previous ruler's lifetime and neutralise the influence they

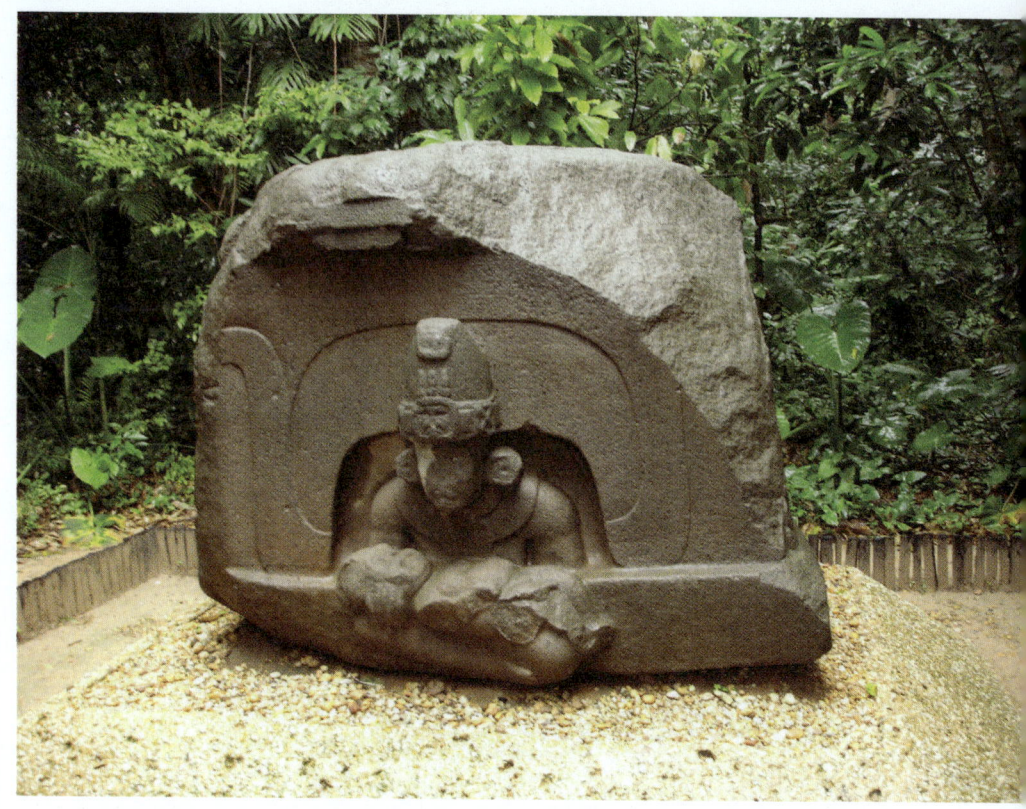

Olmec altar at the site of La Venta. The central figure can be seen holding a were-jaguar baby, possibly hinting at child sacrifice. The current agreement is that these "altars" were thrones upon which rulers would sit during important rituals or ceremonies.

accrued, mark the change from one ruler to the next, or even dispelling the legitimacy of a previous dynasty.

How the Olmec transported such large blocks of basalt to create these colossal heads and other large objects like their thrones and aqueducts remains a mystery. Basalt was found in the Tuxtla Mountains, some eighty kilometres away from San Lorenzo in a straight line. The only archaeological clues we have are two sculptures depicting rectangular basalt blocks bound with ropes and a human figure mounted on top. One hypothesis is that the stones were placed on large balsa rafts, possibly towed by canoes down the coast of the Gulf of Mexico and up the Coatzacoalcos River during the dry season when the waters were easier to navigate.[16] Once arriving at their destination, the stones would then have to be carried overland and uphill, probably by hundreds of men, onto the plateau, possibly with rollers or wooden sledges as the wheel had not yet been invented in this area. Another hypothesis is that the boulders were dragged overland the entire way from source to workshop. Regardless of how the stones reached their destination, the operation was no small feat. Some of the basalt monuments weighed over twenty tonnes, and it has been estimated that transporting a single colossal head would have required the work of over 1,500 people and have taken three to four months.[17]

The Origins of Writing in Mesoamerica?

There has been much debate as to which language the Olmecs spoke. While some argue they spoke a Mayan language, later inscriptions and studies looking into loan words of other Mesoamerican languages now point to them speaking an ancestral form of Mixe-Zoquean, a family of languages that are still spoken in the area of Olman today—one of which is still spoken in the Tuxtla Mountains where they obtained their highly valued basalt.[18] While we'll never have the chance to speak to an Olmec person and determine how or what they spoke, there is evidence that they may have developed the first writing system in the Americas.

Multiple Olmec-style jade and serpentine objects incised with currently undecipherable hieroglyphs have been found over the past century. For example, local villagers uncovered a serpentine block with hieroglyphs representing sixty-two signs at the site of El Cascajal near San Lorenzo. The signs bore much resemblance to Olmec iconography, but none to any later Mesoamerican script. The most compelling find came from the site of San Andrés, Tabasco, located around five kilometres from the centre of La Venta. A cylinder seal and a carved greenstone plaque were found bearing hieroglyphs and even identifiable speech bubbles on them. Dating to around 650 BCE, these items predate other Olmec examples that contain some form of writing, and show that the key aspects of other Mesoamerican writing systems were included in Olmec writing.[19] The use of the 260-day calendar, and the combination of pictographic and glyphic elements to represent speech are related to later Isthmian and Mayan systems, which suggests that this type of writing system originated in the La Venta region.

A Change in Course

By 400 BCE, the Olmec civilisation had come to an end. La Venta's ritual centre and the surrounding villages around both there and San Lorenzo were deserted around the beginning of the fourth century BCE. Olmec style sculptures in basalt and jade, and pottery were no longer being made, and the vast trade networks that connected Olman with most of Mesoamerica declined. The reason for such a drastic decline and for farming communities completely abandoning an entire region are not known, but environmental factors may have been a leading cause.

Geomorphic studies show that the rivers around La Venta and San Lorenzo changed course quite a bit over the past four thousand years.[20] Shifts in the Coatzacoalcos River coincided with the decline of San Lorenzo, and the same occurred at La Venta five hundred years later. Human activity of clearing forests for agriculture could have also caused erosion and silting of the river. Whatever the reason for environmental changes, the cultural shifts that occurred as a result could have led to the development of civil unrest, the rise of rivals wanting to control the region, or the loss of political power or control over trade routes. Whatever the reason, it must have been something quite serious to cause the complete depopulation of eastern Olman.

Even though one area was abandoned, people continued to live and thrive in other parts of Olman, and a new culture soon arose at the site of Tres Zapotes at the northwestern edge of the Tuxtla Mountains from around 300 BCE to 200/250 CE. Sometimes called the Epi-Olmec, the culture that emerged at Tres Zapotes bridged the gap between the Olmec and the later Veracruz culture. Tres Zapotes consisted of about fifty earthen mounds that ran along the bank of a stream for 3.2 kilometres but was still smaller than previous Olmec centres, lacking in large public monuments, elite burials or exotic goods acquired from long-distance trade. Stone monuments remained an important aspect of Epi-Olmec art, and they also made strides in astronomy, writing, and the development of the Mesoamerican calendar.

Olmec culture did not simply disappear with the rise of the Epi-Olmec. Much of it evolved with the changing of the tides, and their descendants drew upon their symbols and iconographies, adapting them into new sculptural and political traditions. The Olmecs also left a legacy on future cultures that would arise in Mesoamerica in the following centuries. They are credited with being the first peoples in Mesoamerica to carve stone sculptures on a monumental scale, create extensive trade networks, and assign value to exotic materials such as greenstone and iron ore.[21] Furthermore, the Olmec invented the Long Count calendar used by the Maya, the ball game and the ritual use of rubber. They were the first to create sacred sites and cosmological town plans, and an elaborate system of symbols in their art. Such a long-lasting impact in southern Mesoamerica has led some to state that all later civilisations that arose in this area, such as the Maya, had their roots planted in the Olmec world.[22]

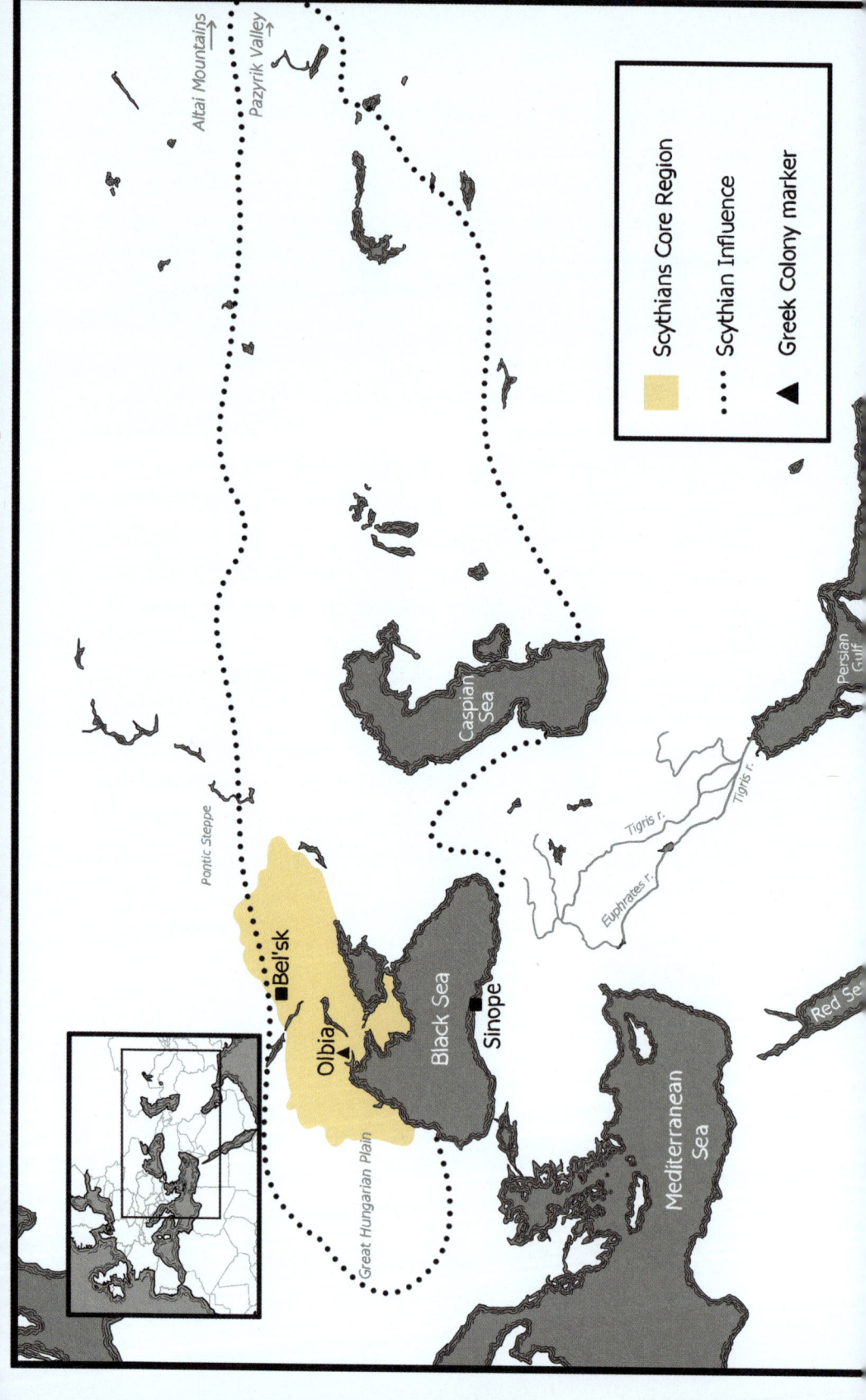

Chapter Seventeen

Scythians

Mounted Warriors of the Steppes

The young man winced as the blade sliced through his palm, but the pain dulled as warm blood quickly spilled into his hand. Clenching his fist so as not to drip too much onto the soft floor of the tent, the man tilted his arm and poured the blood into the drinking horn filled with wine being held by his soon-to-be blood brother. He had done the same for him just moments before. The blood of the two warriors swirled into the wine, adding an even richer colour to the dark liquid they had imported from Greece for the occasion.

Next came the incantations. The noble crowd surrounding the pair began to chant holy blessings over the wine as they took turns dipping their weapons into the mixture. First their beloved arrows, then their spears, swords, daggers, and lances. With each new dip into the wine, the chanting became louder, filling more and more of the room before being swallowed up by the heavy tapestries hanging on the walls of the tent.

While the young man had taken part in blood oath ceremonies before, it had only been to serve as a witness for the creation of this sacred bond. Now that he was in the thick of it, he could feel the immensity of this moment. The young man locked eyes with his soon-to-be brother. His dear friend from childhood, they had fought many battles at each other's side over the years. And today they were committing to always defend one another and fight to the death for the other's honour. They were each entrusting the other with their lives, and the young man knew there was no one else to whom he would give this honour.

When the chanting finally subsided, the young man and his friend drew closer together, their sides touching and ready for the final step. In front of the nobility of the surrounding tribes, they lifted the horn to their mouths and drank the now-blessed mixture of wine and blood. Their bond was sealed and they were connected forever, both in this life and the next.

They Came from the East

The history of the flat, grassy plains of the Eurasian Steppe that extends from modern-day China to the Great Hungarian Plain is one of successive waves of migrants and raiders from the east who brought much change to the indigenous groups already settled in the west. This giant carpet of grassland sweeping across the Eurasian continent acted as an easy passageway for people to spread, share cultures, and trade goods from far-off lands. Climatically, it differed greatly from east to west, with areas in what is modern-day Mongolia being quite cool and dry, but the farther west one travelled, a much milder, damper climate appeared due to the air streams flowing over Europe from the Atlantic. This made the grasses greener, literally, on one side, resulting in a constant flow of nomadic pastoral groups looking for greener pastures for their animals.

One group of these invading peoples was the Scythians. Archaeological evidence suggests that the Scythians were of Iranian descent and migrated west from Central Asia, eventually settling in the Pontic Steppe that stretched from eastern Bulgaria and Romania, through Ukraine, over the north Caucasus mountains and along southern Russia around 750 BCE. The Scythians were the first historically well-known nomadic group that came to the western steppe and became a major power.[1] Upon their arrival, they quickly garnered the attention of Greek colonies that had been established along the coast of the Black Sea, the Assyrians, and even distant empires like Persia.

"Scythians" is a collective name for multiple nomadic tribes that moved west but were so similar in their art, culture, economy, and beliefs that they can all be included in the Scythian world.[2] The name comes from the ancient Greeks, who used this term to refer to the pastoral nomads that settled on the Pontic Steppe. The Scythians who lived north of the Black Sea called themselves *Skolti* after their first king, Colaxais. The Persians referred to both the European and Asian nomads as *Sakā,* though now this term is reserved for nomads who lived on the eastern Eurasian Steppe.

Cultural similarities between those living across the entire Eurasian Steppe from the Black Sea to the Altai Mountains in Mongolia have caused much debate and confusion around where the Scythians end, and other tribes begin. Archaeologists have noted the similarities Scythians share with groups to the east, such as elite mound burials and the so-called Scythian Triad of animal-style art, weapons, and horse gear.[3] These similar traits have been used to bundle together groups of people who lived thousands of miles apart, even though at their core they may have been quite different. For simplicity, we will touch only lightly on nomadic evidence from the eastern steppe when it serves to add context to the focus of this chapter: the Scythians proper, who inhabited the Pontic Steppe and became fierce warriors, avid traders, and lovers of luxurious goods.

Life on the Steppe

The earliest evidence for nomadism in the steppes dates back to the third millennium BCE. Because the environment of the steppe cannot be tamed and used for intensive agriculture, a horse-centric, pastoral nomadic lifestyle became the norm in the early first millennium BCE. This mobile lifestyle of moving from pasture to pasture with their livestock dictated every aspect of Scythian life from what they ate, how they cooked and dressed, and the structures in which they lived.

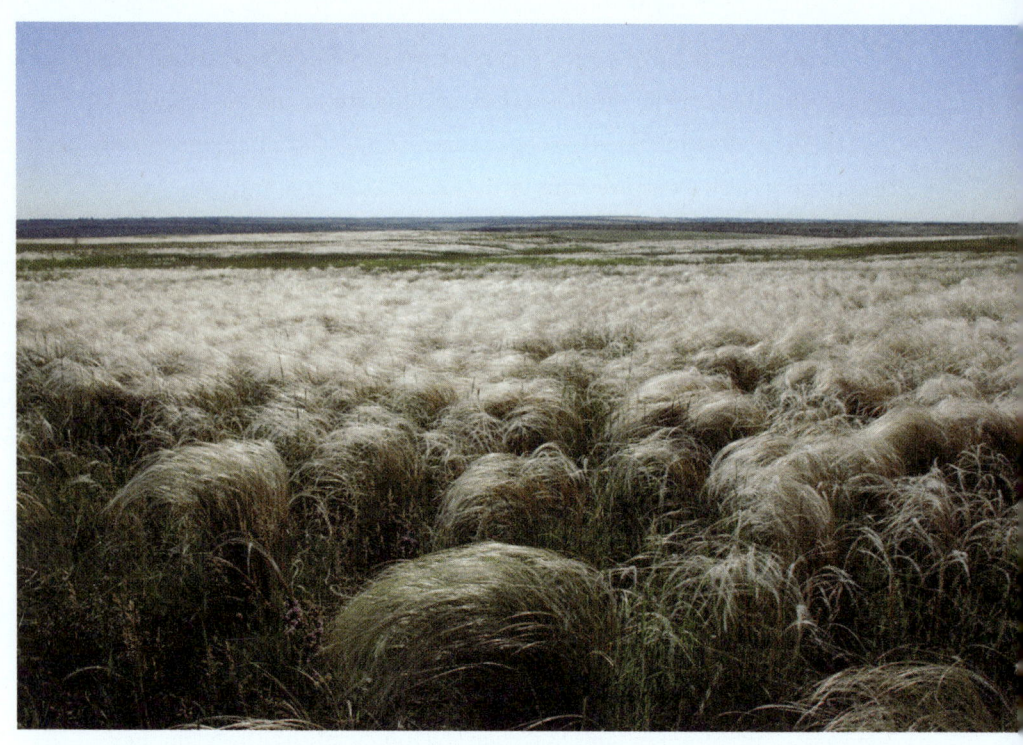

View of the Streltsovskaya Steppe in Ukraine.

According to written sources, Scythia consisted of a vast array of people, from those working fields in the forest steppe, to husbandmen and nomads, all ruled by the Royal Scythians. From what historians have gathered, the area was always ruled by three kings at the same time, with one given the title and rank of "King in Chief," entitling them to the largest kingdom.[4] Scythian dependence on their livestock meant that they required large areas of green pasture for their animals to roam freely in order to avoid overgrazing or destroying the land they relied so heavily upon.

With such a mobile life, permanent settlements were impractical and would have taken up valuable grazing land. As a result, the Scythians preferred to travel in wagons and set up temporary camps with tents or yurts. Wagons were pulled by oxen or workhorses and would have carried household goods as well as women, children, and the elderly, while men rode on horseback, forming a caravan. From small clay models found in burials, wagons had four to six wheels and were divided into two or three compartments inside. The upper parts were built using hoops of flexible wood and roofed with felt.

One family would have required several wagons to fit and transport their worldly possessions. With so many wagons, domestic animals, and mounted warriors, these caravans traipsing through the steppes would have been quite the sight. There were probably multiple types of covered wagons. Some of them would have served as permanent mobile homes that the Scythians would return to every night, while others might have been convertible, with removable superstructures that could be taken off the wagon and set up as a tent or yurt. They may also have carried larger tents with them to set up and tear down every few days that would have been stored in their wagons.

Not many full-size examples of wagons have been found in Scythian tombs, so it is difficult to determine the extent of their design other than that they were made to carry heavy loads on long journeys. What we can tell is that the Scythians enjoyed living lavishly and didn't let their temporary accommodation get in the way of luxury. Scythian tombs were designed to reflect and contain everything that was needed in daily life. Floors would have been covered in layers of soft felt for sitting, eating, and sleeping, and richly embroidered and colourful fabrics or carpets were hung on walls.

Furniture found in tombs that would have been used day-to-day also adds to this interpretation of a colourful and comfortable life for the Scythians. Mattresses, cushions, and pillows would have provided extra comfort on top of the felt flooring, and furniture like the popular low, collapsible four-legged tables with raised rims for dining,[5] would have created a warm, inviting atmosphere, acting as a sharp contrast to the monotonous plains that surrounded them.

Other items found in tombs that would have been of everyday use were wooden and clay plates, bronze cauldrons for cooking stews, and ceramic pots for holding koumiss, fermented and mildly alcoholic mare's milk.

Koumiss is a popular nomadic drink that strengthens the nervous system, stimulates blood formation and regulates gastric acid, and is packed full of vitamins. It acted as a nutritional supplement to the meat-heavy Scythian diet.[6] The Scythians were also avid wine drinkers and became well-known for enjoying undiluted wine, which, according to the ancient Greeks, was only done by barbarians. Seals on amphorae found in Scythian tombs tell archaeologists that they held expensive wine from the Greek Islands.

When the Scythians arrived at the Pontic Steppe, they found themselves in an ideal location between the farming communities of the forest steppe to the north who produced grain, iron, furs, and slaves, and the Greek colonies along the Black Sea coast to the south who were in need of these commodities. This allowed the Scythians to establish a trade network that linked not only the forest steppe, but Persia and areas farther to the east, making them extremely wealthy. By trading commodities from the forest steppe, the Scythians were able to obtain Greek luxury goods to show off their status. By the seventh century BCE, the Scythians started to become more sedentary. While this might have been due to climate change, their growing trade with the Greek world could have also been a strong influence on this societal shift.

Around 650 BCE, large, fortified settlements were established and acted as entrepots for shipping goods and trading with larger Greek colonies such as Olbia. One of these settlements stands out in particular due to its sheer size. Bel'sk, located in the Poltava region in east central Ukraine, was the largest complex in Iron Age Eurasia[7] with three separate settlements encompassed by a fortification wall that measured thirty-three kilometres around. The settlements within Bel'sk probably housed a diverse population with various craftspeople and acted as a major stop along the Scythian trade route. While some Scythian groups remained true nomads, the establishment of these fortified settlements is a clear indicator that the Scythians were enjoying their life on the Pontic steppe and taking full advantage of the trading opportunity in which they found themselves.

Horseback Warriors

The Scythians had a strong warrior culture and apart from trading, warfare was one of the main male occupations. Scythian clans were ruled by warlords, and a warrior's status came from the number of kills and the booty they brought back from raids or missionary assignments. Moving to the more stable environment of the Pontic Steppe brought about an easier life for the pastoral nomads. Without having to expend all their energy on the survival of their herds or families, the Scythians began to extend their boundaries, raiding neighbouring lands like the forest steppe, travelling south of the Caucasus mountains, and making contact with states in Asia Minor and the Near East.

Long-distance raids and acting as warriors for hire greatly benefitted the Scythians, who often returned with plunder or diplomatic gifts that elevated their status in society.[8] The extent of how far they would go to obtain riches can be seen by their distinctive trefoil arrowheads found in defensive walls in Mesopotamia, Egypt, and Syria dating from the sixth and seventh centuries BCE. Along with the Medes and the Babylonians, the Scythians also took part in the defeat of the Assyrian Empire, with the sacking of Nineveh in 621 BCE.

To these raids and battles, the Scythians brought with them a sophisticated collection of weapons and hit-and-run tactics that would have intimidated any enemy they encountered. Their weapon of choice was the double curved composite bow fashioned out of horn and strung with sinew. The Scythian bow and arrow were so distinctive of their culture that they have been found in even the simplest graves, explaining why ancient writers referred to them as mounted archers. Reports have stated that Scythians were ambidextrous when handling the bow, and they seem to have invented a special case called a *gorytus* that held both bow and arrows and hung from their left hips, ensuring they were always ready to shoot from horseback. Apart from the bow, Scythians fought with lances, spears, swords, daggers, whips, flails, and axes for hand-to-

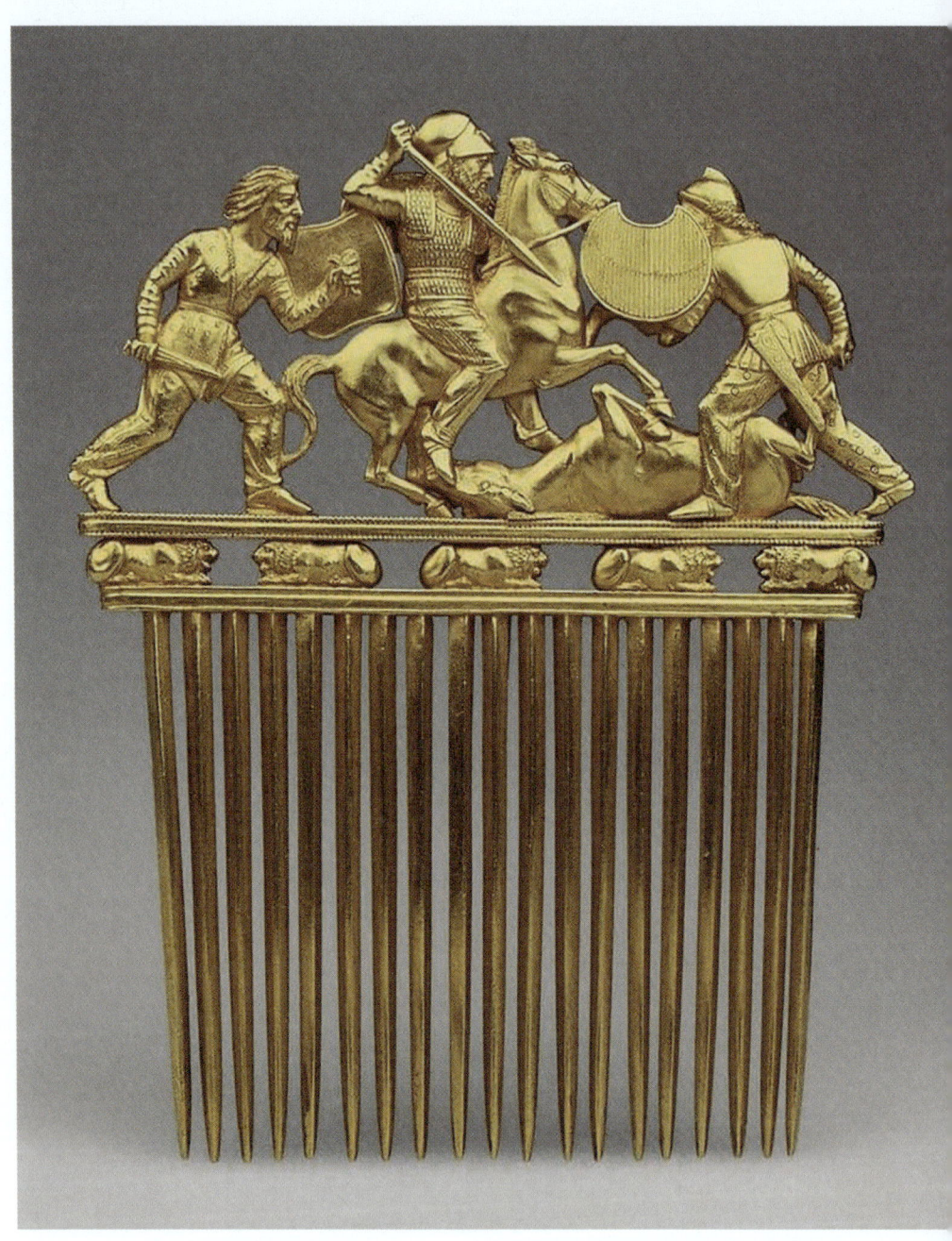

Gold comb depicting a battle scene on horseback.

hand combat. For protection during battle, they wore armour made of overlapping bronze or iron scales sewn onto leather.

Garnering this reputation and skill, however, would have been impossible without their beloved horses. The open grassland of the steppe was the ideal environment in which to become horse masters. The exact date and place where horse riding originated is still unknown, but it appears that the Pontic Steppe might have been where it all began. The earliest evidence found suggests horse domestication originated in the middle Volga region of Russia around 4800 BCE. Scythian warriors understood the importance of the animals they relied on in battle. Examination of horse hooves found in burials has shown that horses kept for riding and warfare were well cared for in comparison to work horses or those reared for food.[9]

The Scythians are also credited with the invention of the saddle in the seventh century BCE. Early saddles were made of two felt cushions stuffed with animal hair mounted on felt sweatbands with an attached tail strap and breast band to keep it in place. A reconstruction of a saddle found in a burial in the Altai Mountains belonging to the Central Asian Scythian Pazyryk culture showed that saddles were quite sophisticated and were comfortable for both horse and rider.[10] The design also made it easier to handle the horse without stirrups (they wouldn't be invented until centuries later) than with a hard saddle. Like most things crafted by the Scythians, saddles were colourful and highly decorated with wool, felt and leather appliqué, and wooden carvings covered in gold foil of highly stylised geometric and animal shapes. As can be seen today, the saddle became highly popular, and by the end of the fifth century BCE, Scythian saddles were adopted by every sedentary culture that came in contact with the pastoralists, from Greece all the way to China.[11]

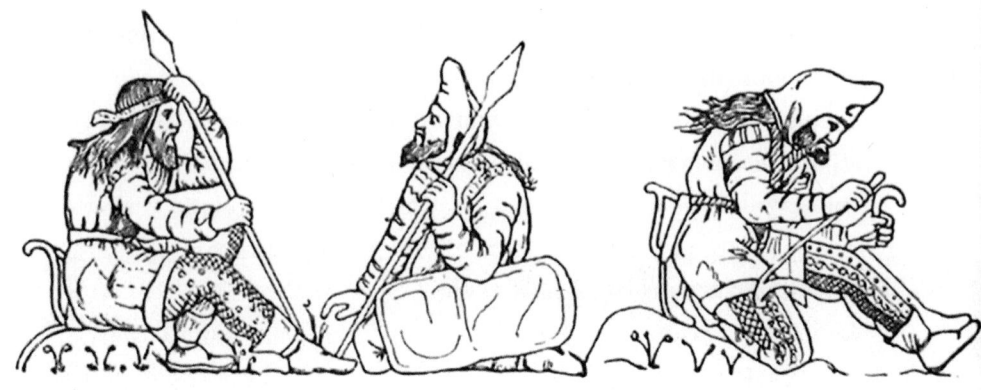

Drawing of Scythian warriors taken from an electrum cup found at the Kul'Oba kurgan burial.

A Thirst for Blood

With such a strong warrior culture, the Scythians developed practices that strengthened their bond with one another on the battlefield, as well as those that reinforced their raiding lifestyle that linked directly to their status within the community. Much of this warrior culture revolved around one theme in particular: blood.

Numerous artefacts depicting two warriors drinking from a single vessel or horn represent a special ritual in which they became blood brothers. We know from ancient literature the close bonds these blood brothers shared and the dedication they showed to one another. The two men would create a mixture of wine and their own blood, in which their arrows, spears, swords, and other weapons were dipped, to swear allegiance to each other until death and possibly even afterwards. The mixture had long incantations murmured over it, and then the two men would lean in close to drink the mixture simultaneously to seal the bond. The ceremony was attended by noble warriors from surrounding areas, marking the importance of the event.

Other ancient sources discuss how Scythians used blood in other ways within the context of their warrior culture. They created their own poison by finding snakes that had just given birth and leaving them to rot for several days. Once this was complete, they mixed the juice of that snake with the floating parts that result from decomposing human blood in a jar. Arrows would then be dipped into this concoction, making them doubly deadly and striking even more fear into their opponent.

Blood was quite symbolic for the Scythians. On the battlefield, it was customary for them to drink the blood of the first man they killed, and the amount of loot they were given after a battle was often related to how many heads they collected and brought before the king.[12] Not killing any enemies in battle was seen as the ultimate disgrace in Scythian society. They also believed the spirits of their enemies could be controlled, and their powers absorbed by turning their skulls into drinking cups.

A Flurry of Animals

For all this bloodlust and fighting, the Scythians still had a taste for the finer things in life. For archaeologists, it's often difficult to understand the daily life of nomadic, unsettled societies due to their lack of permanent settlements. Fortunately, the permafrost of the Eurasian Steppe has preserved many burial mounds called *kurgans* that provide us with valuable glimpses into how the Scythians lived. These mounds are filled with organic objects that would have otherwise decomposed. A moment frozen in time, it seems that Scythians expected death to mirror life and were buried with everything they would need to continue what they did on earth.[13]

Within these tombs, including those across the entire Eurasian Steppe, countless decorated objects have been found made with expert craftsmanship and in numbers far surpassing anything produced by any other ancient people of a similar size.[14] From clothing and everyday household items, to carpets, jewellery, and even their weapons, bridles, and saddles, everything was richly coloured and ornamented. Scythian art was full of expression and featured many aspects that reflected their beliefs, important events, and daily life.

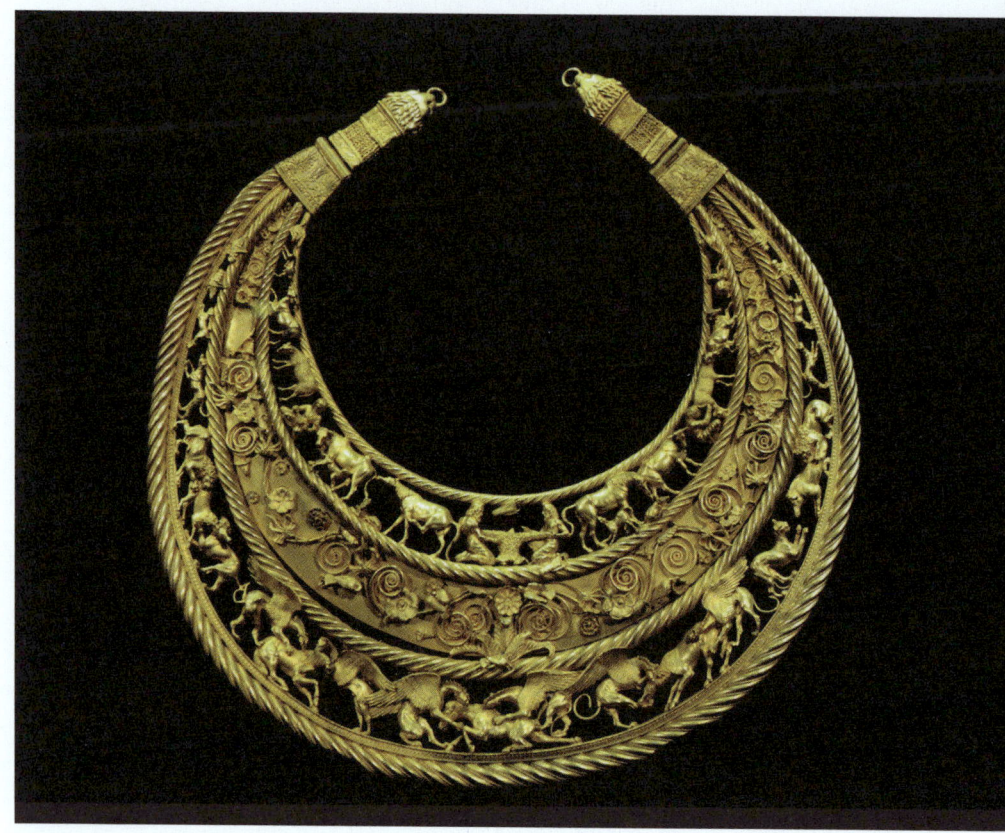

Gold pectoral depicting various stylised animals.

Although many of their neighbours regarded them as warriors, the Scythians were first and foremost pastoralists. This means their worldview was closely tied to the animals they relied upon for sustenance and survival. Such proximity and interaction with these beasts allowed the Scythians to obtain a profound understanding and appreciation of them, which translated into the development of their distinctive "animal-style" art that celebrated these creatures in fantastic ways. This type of art was based on three main motifs: feline predators, birds of prey, and herbivores with hooves and antlers, particularly the stag. These animals are often highly stylised and depicted in conflict with one another, the predator hunting its prey. Other times, animals are fantastical in nature, combining elements of multiple creatures such as griffons with antlers, a beak, and a tail. Though animal-style may have been popular, Scythian art was not solely restricted to this artform. Many objects have been found depicting the struggles of daily life such as horse training, or were solely comprised of geometric patterns.

It is clear by looking at their art that the Scythians were influenced by the other cultures they encountered through trade and warfare. They borrowed designs and iconography from places like Greece and China, and incorporated them into their own mythology and aesthetic.[15] Scythian art was a unifying feature across much of the Eurasian Steppe and has been found on everything they used. Mummified human remains found in Pazyryk burials in the Altai Mountains show that they even boasted these animated animals on their skin through the act of tattooing.

Burial and Cleansing

Scythian funerals (the royal ones in particular) seem to have been elaborate affairs. The deceased would have been buried in structures sometimes built to resemble the tents they spent their lives in, covered in mounds that sealed them off for eternity. These tombs were not only filled with domestic items needed for daily life and weapons in anticipation of battles and raids in the next life, but also bodies that were lavishly adorned with riches beyond comparison.

People were buried forty days after their death, as they believed the spirit remained close to the body after passing away.[16] Due to the climate of the steppe, burials could only take place during warmer months when the ground had thawed. This meant that bodies of those who died in colder seasons had to be preserved by cleaning out their internal organs and filling the empty cavities with strong herbs to mask the smell of decay. Bodies were also covered in wax to prevent insect infestation. Archaeologists have found evidence of funeral processions and feasts, making funerals a community event. On top of this, a number of human and horse sacrifices were performed to accompany the deceased into the afterlife, with the volume of sacrifices indicating their status.

After the funeral, the ancient writer Herodotus claimed the Scythians never washed with water and took vapour baths to purify themselves. They would crawl into a small felt tent that had a brazier with hot stones and hemp seeds in it to inhale the smoke. Herodotus even claims the Scythians would howl with pleasure after inhaling. This interpretation may have been him comparing this activity to a Greek vapour bath, as it's possible they went into the tent naked and made it steamy by throwing water on the hot rocks.[17] In reality, it appears this ritual served other purposes than physically cleansing oneself.

Archaeological evidence has since proven this hemp-inhaling practice was indeed a reality for the Scythians. Whole sets of hemp-inhaling equipment including tent poles, felt fabric, braziers, and charred hemp seeds have been found at twenty-three Scythian sites, including Pazyryk burials of both men and women.[18] These tents were quite small and were seemingly built to only allow for one person to put their head under the coverings to inhale at a time. The use of braziers for smoking hemp could have caused a phenomenon called "bronze fever" that would have heightened the effect of the hemp while also causing an accumulation of copper in the body.[19] Scythians would have inherited this hemp tradition from earlier Bronze and Iron Age cultures in southeastern Europe, and they were likely the ones to introduce hemp cultivation to the Celtic, Slavic, and Finno-Ugric cultures, spreading the practice across Europe.[20]

Another Wave Always Follows

After reaching their peak in the fourth century BCE, the power of the Scythians began to decline as they saw increasing conflict with Macedonia and other encroaching tribes from all sides. Additionally, they became the victims of the same actions that brought them new land and power centuries before. Towards the end of the first millennium BCE, new waves of nomads were making the same westward journey along the Eurasian Steppe, and the Scythians were gradually defeated and displaced from the Pontic Steppe they called home.

In the fourth and third centuries BCE, Sarmatians from the Volga River moved westwards into Scythian territory. This influx of new people didn't change the culture of the Pontic Steppe very much, as the Sarmatians have been described as similar to the Scythians, but there is evidence of the destruction of multiple Scythian settlements and their retreat from the Pontic region. In the same manner as the Scythians had arrived, a new wave had washed over the steppe, beginning their own story on the plains.

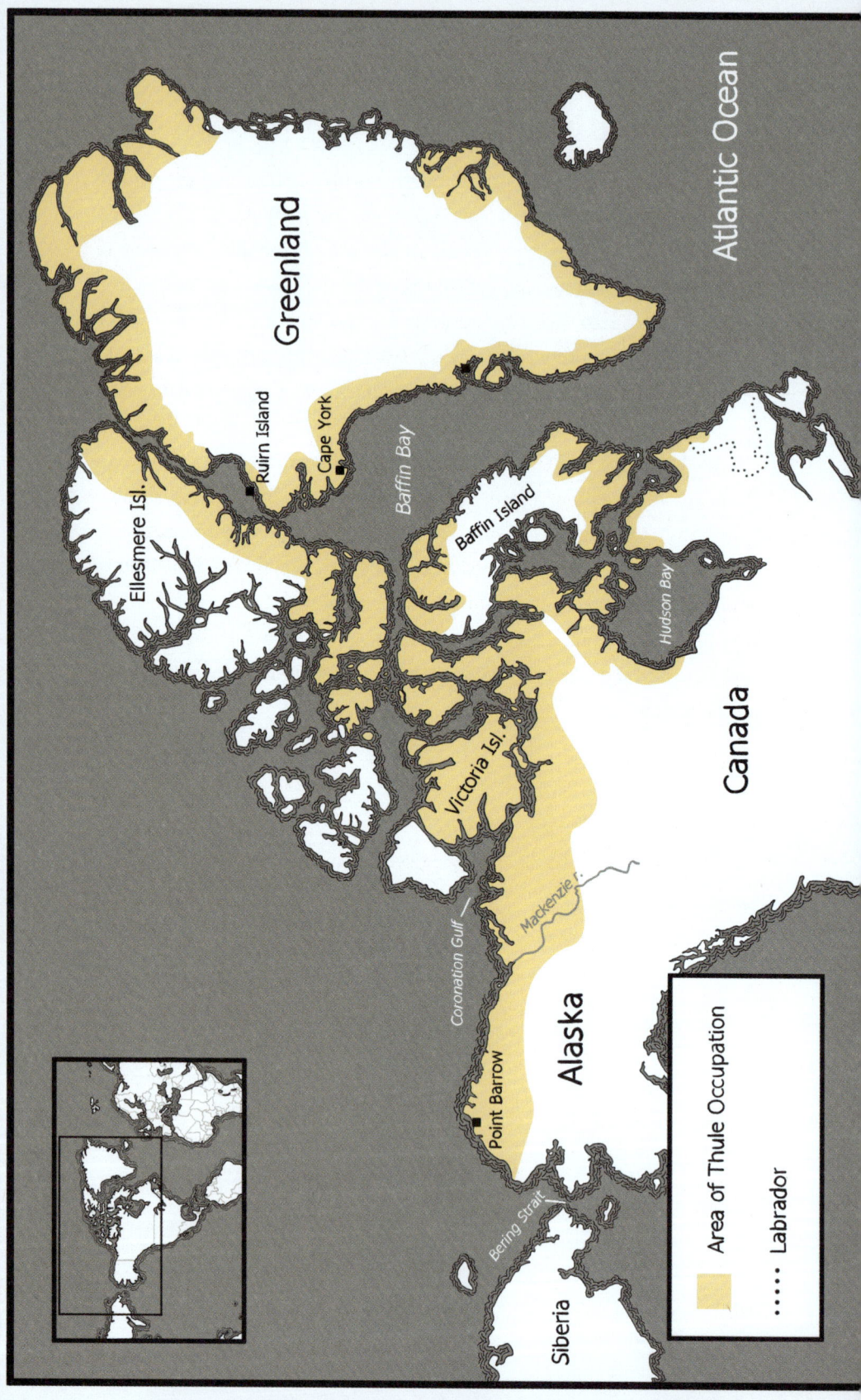

Chapter Eighteen

Thule (Early Inuit)

Whaling Ancestors of the Inuit

The snow stung the woman's face as gusts of wind blew up the fresh powder that had fallen the night before. Even with her parka done all the way up and her hood strapped on tightly, the Arctic wind still found the weak points in her defences.

The woman scanned the horizon through the thin slats of her snow goggles. She had already checked her surroundings when she left the house a few minutes ago to gather the blubber and meat needed for this evening's meal from a nearby storage pit, but the recent sightings of a polar bear by men returning from the hunt last night had her on edge.

Once she felt the coast was clear, the woman held her gathered supplies close to her chest, and on her hands and knees began to crawl through the small tunnel back into the house. She was immediately grateful to be out of the wind. The light of the central lamp grew brighter as she reached the end of the tunnel, and as she climbed up the step that kept the cold air out of their sanctuary, she was met with a wall of warmth that made her immediately forget about the looming threats outside.

Careful not to wake her elderly mother resting on the raised sleeping platform opposite the entrance, the woman quickly removed her outdoor gear and placed it on the rack over the fire to dry. She then added more blubber to the fire to keep her mother comfortable, and got to work preparing the food she had brought in. As a special treat, and to remind her family of the warmer *weather that was soon to come, the woman had taken out some muskox meat that was stored away before the cold came. This would be a welcome change from the seal they had been surviving on these past few dark months. Placing the meat in the cooking pot warming over the kitchen fire, the woman breathed in the gamey scent that only comes from lean summer animals. As the smell filled the house, she sat back and dreamed of warmer days.*

A Name of Many Meanings

The Thule Inuit were the first Neo-Inuit culture in the North American Arctic and are the direct ancestors to the present Iñupiat and Inuit communities in Canada and Greenland. These ancestors were given the name Thule by Danish archaeologist Therkel Mathaissen, the term coming from the settlement of Uummannaq (Thule) in Polar Greenland.[1] The name itself comes from Greek geographers who used it to describe the northernmost place in the world, which has been interpreted to be various places ranging from the Shetland Islands in northern Scotland, to northern Scandinavia.

In twentieth-century Germany, this mythical version of Thule became a fascination to a particular group of occultists and nationalists. A group called the "Thule Society" was founded in the 1910s, and their members formed the foundation for what became the National Socialist (Nazi) Party. While this society was in no way related to the Arctic culture, it is important to maintain a distinction. To help ensure this, the following chapter will refer to this culture and peoples as both the Thule Inuit and the Early Inuit in keeping with contemporary publications. The term Early Inuit generally refers to the "Classic Thule" or "Classic Inuit" periods, dating around 1200 to 1500 CE. Some Inuit Elders and Knowledge Keepers also refer to the earliest Inuit peoples as Taissumanialungmiut, "the people of a very long time ago."[2]

They Came from the West

The Thule Inuit most likely developed from the Birnirk culture, a group of people that descended from the marine mammal hunting Old Bering Sea cultures that originated around the Bering Strait coasts of Siberia and North America around 200 BCE. Becoming recognisable as a distinct technologically and socially complex culture in northwest Alaska by around 1000 CE, the Thule Inuit began to expand and move eastward throughout the North American Arctic, reaching Greenland by the thirteenth century and rounding its southern tip to reach the east coast by the fifteenth century.[3] The Thule Inuit even reached areas of South Greenland that were occupied by the Norse. It's unclear when the two populations met, but both archaeological and oral tradition point to the two coexisting for some time.

The migration of the Thule Inuit eastwards from Alaska and possibly Siberia has been described as one of the most dramatic episodes of history in the North American Arctic.[4] It is widely agreed that it involved several linked movements of people from differing regions around the Bering Strait. Many of the early Thule Inuit sites are small, and it has been suggested that these migrations were undertaken by "compound families," or one or more related extended families.[5] This migration has been studied by archaeologists for a hundred years, yet even with all this research it is not as well understood as many would believe. Based on early radiocarbon dates, it was originally thought the Thule Inuit migration took place around 1000 CE. This would have placed the event in the middle of the Medieval Warm Period, which would have allowed for easier exploration around the Eastern Arctic. Recent reinterpretation of those dates now points towards a thirteenth-century migration, meaning the Warm Period would not have been an initial trigger for the expansion, and that the migration was more rapid and widespread than initially believed.[6]

Across every site in the east, the uniformity of the Thule Inuit culture and the similar dates determined at early sites across the Arctic has been interpreted as a rapid migration from Alaska to Greenland. If the migration didn't take place until the thirteenth century and occurred at such a pace, it suggests that sites were briefly occupied before moving on farther east, and the "Classic" Thule Inuit period as a whole only lasted around two hundred years before evolving into other diverse Inuit societies. Given the dates, the Thule Inuit would have arrived in the Eastern Arctic within a century and established a network of communities that would have begun to unravel a short few hundred years later.

Did the Thule Inuit move faster than expected, or was there a sense of urgency that motivated the move? Some scholars have called this new theory into question.[7] If the Thule Inuit migration began in the thirteenth century, vast distances would have had to be traversed each year without much scouting or knowledge of what lay ahead, and with limited population increase to maintain a presence at the sites settled along the way. A slower migration that spanned multiple centuries would have allowed local populations to grow and scout new regions before expanding throughout the Canadian Arctic and into Greenland. The motivation for subsequent migrations east would then have evolved with the newer generations partaking in this northern exploration.

The reason for this expansive Thule Inuit migration is still unknown. While there may have been some climatic instability or changes that could have created some economic stress, by the thirteenth century, Alaska was already densely settled with diverse cultures interacting and trading with each other. Archaeological evidence points to an increase in warfare-related artefacts such as armour and human remains with wounds from combat, indicating that there seems to have been territorial conflicts between groups.[8] Those who decided to leave may have been involved with this interregional conflict or blood feuds, or have been subject to economic pressures.[9] Excavations in funerary contexts have also uncovered evidence of social inequality, leading to one scholar suggesting that those who migrated east were most likely from the lower classes looking to escape or change their social circumstances.[10]

Other potential reasons are centred on the draw of the east. An important source of food, fuel and shelter for the Thule Inuit was the bowhead whale. It has been suggested that wanting to follow the movements of this animal may have been a major motivator for some to expand eastward, especially as the development of technology needed for open water whaling (large wooden framed boats covered with animal skin called *umaiks*) is what most likely made the expansion possible.[11] This may have sparked the initial migration and formed the path that was taken from Alaska and Siberia, but the Thule Inuit quickly moved past the best whaling locations and continued east. It's possible the route taken by the Thule Inuit would have been influenced by their expanding knowledge of the area, their need for subsistence and other important materials such as metal, wood, and soapstone, as well as by interactions with other Arctic cultures such as the Dorset.

Another driving factor that could have been one of the main reasons for the Thule Inuit migration was their desire to acquire metal.[12] In Alaska, the Thule Inuit used Eurasian smelted metal that was traded in the Bering Strait. Iron and copper were highly desired, especially as they had not yet developed a way of smelting it themselves. Objects made from these materials were then considered to be prestigious and would have been a great motivating factor for expanding east. In the Eastern Arctic, the Coronation Gulf was a source for copper, and northwest Greenland had the Cape York Meteorite, the largest known iron meteorite on the planet, and some of the earliest eastern Thule Inuit sites discovered have been located relatively close by. Furthermore, Greenland had the potential for iron and bronze trade with the Norse. In fact, many houses near Ruin Island contain Norse metal objects, though there is debate as to whether these were from trade or from salvaging a Norse shipwreck.[13]

Desire for metal as the main motivation for Thule Inuit migration is difficult to confirm and is likely improbable. How they would have learned of such far away resources is not known. It is possibly only through interaction with the Dorset culture after their migration had already started, and when they were already almost halfway from Alaska to Cape York in Greenland, that they could have gleaned any knowledge of metal sources.[14] Furthermore, no iron from Greenland or of Norse origin has yet been found in the Western Arctic.[15] If the motivation for migrating was to access these commodities for trade back in Alaska, this never came to fruition. The reason for the Thule Inuit migration may not have been due to one motivating factor. Motivations may also have shifted and evolved to match a changing environment with each step east. Nevertheless, some sites have proven to retain their ties with their western homeland, such as sites in the western Coronation Gulf area that continued to use Western Arctic pottery vessels instead of using soapstone, which had become the popular material in the east.[16]

Semi-Subterranean Kind of Life

The Thule Inuit adapted their lifestyle to the changing seasons. During the warmer spring and summer months, from May to October, some families and communities moved farther inland to hunt caribou and fish, while others remained on beaches near the coast. They set up circular tents of animal skins weighed down with large stones on flat, dry ground that had access to fresh water but was also near the sea for hunting large game such as walruses.

During colder months, the Thule Inuit moved into permanent winter villages to hunt seals and bowhead whales where they were plentiful. Stone supports for kayaks and umaiks have been found in close proximity to these sites, indicating the importance of the hunting of sea mammals for sustenance during this time of year. These settlements were filled with clusters of houses that probably consisted of extended families.[17] Winter houses are the most common archaeological evidence for the Thule Inuit culture and much of our knowledge of their way of life comes from these remains. Overall, winter houses would have provided a safe, comfortable, and warm living space with a large amount of storage to provide solace from the harsh and dark winter months.

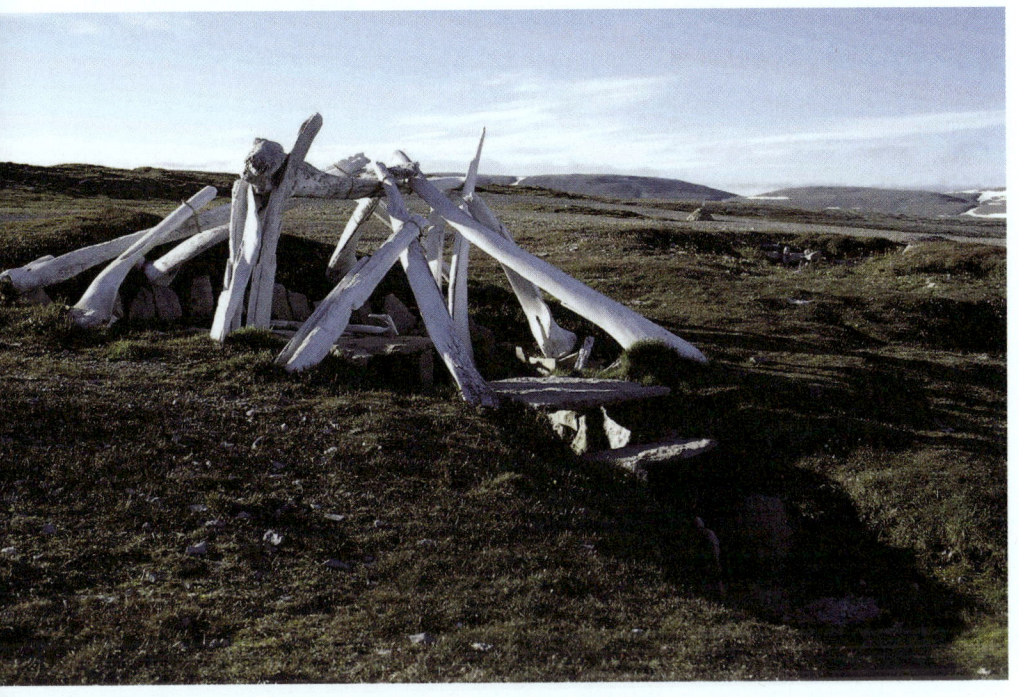

Reconstructed whale bone structure of a Thule Inuit dwelling.

Thule Inuit winter houses varied in construction, both in tools and materials, based on the geographic location of the site. Nevertheless, a general pattern emerged that makes these houses distinctly Thule Inuit. Winter houses were large, ranging in shape from oval to more rectangular depending on the area and time period. They were semi-subterranean, built partly into the ground, and were accessed by a long, narrow tunnel that had to be crawled through. These entryways were built around forty centimetres below the floor level of the house, forming an air trap that helped keep the colder, heavier air outside. Entrance passages were lined with flat stone slabs and may have even been extended with snow to act as a windscreen. Evidence of refurbishment and maintenance indicates houses were occupied for multiple winters, possibly even multiple generations.[18]

Winter houses were enclosed by stones, animal skins, and blocks of sod built over a framework made from driftwood or whale bones. Post holes have been found inside some examples, meaning wooden posts would have provided additional support to the roof. Inside the main room of winter houses, floors were generally made of gravel, but were sometimes paved with flagstones. Raised sleeping platforms, made of earth, sand, or gravel, provided a warmer place to rest than on the frozen ground. In some houses, archaeologists have found vertical stone slabs where a stone oil lamp would have been kept. The main room often had storage areas such as pits or even upright stone lockers just outside the kitchen area that held meat and blubber.

In earlier examples of Thule Inuit winter houses, it was common for kitchen extensions to be connected to the main room through a short tunnel. In the back of these rooms were multiple raised cooking platforms sectioned off with upright stones set on top of grease-covered floors. These would be used as open fires, maintained with blubber, bone, and wood, with clay or soapstone cooking vessels supported on the upright stones. Kitchens in later houses of the Eastern Arctic evolved into small alcoves attached to the main room,[19] and were eventually replaced with a central large stone or ceramic oil lamp that provided both heat and light for the inhabitants.[20] This later period of the Thule Inuit culture also saw the use of another type of house called a *qarmaq*. These were used in autumn and spring, and were a mix between summer and winter houses, with foundations dug into the ground but only having a skin covering similar to a tent. The Thule Inuit also had the ability to construct snow houses in winter, though there is little archaeological evidence to support this, and they would have been less comfortable than the well-built winter houses.[21]

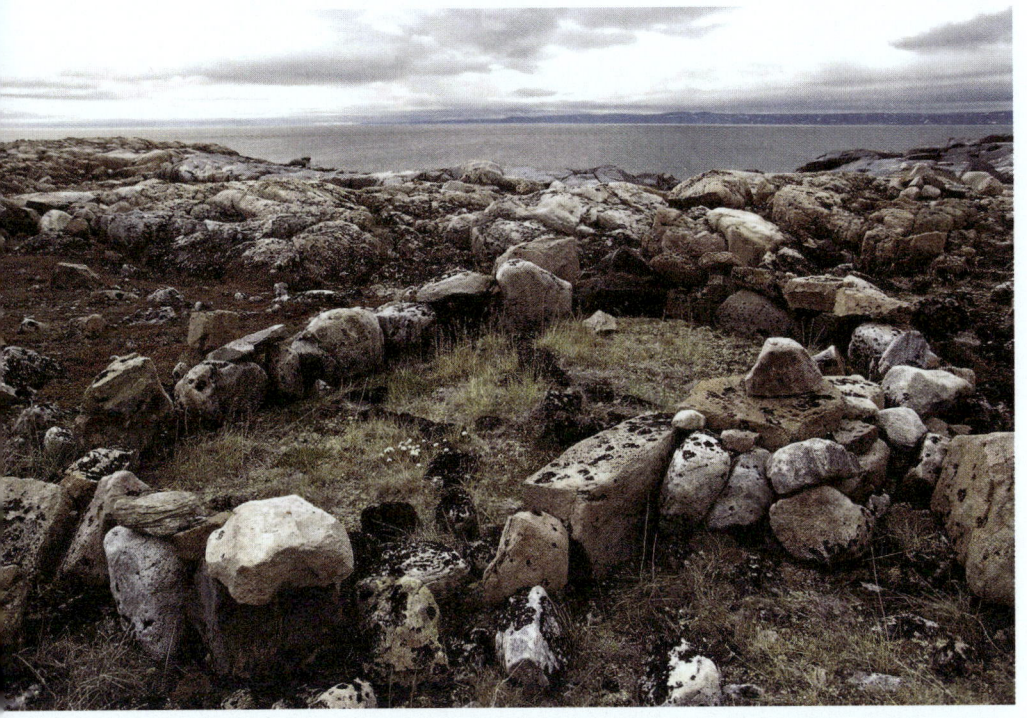

Foundations of a Thule Inuit qarmaq.

Apart from family dwellings, there is evidence for the use of community structures called *qagsse*. These buildings, such as those found on Ruin Island in Greenland, were square or rectangular in shape with flagstone floors, a central pole for structural support, and stone seating lining the walls. Debris such as wood shavings, broken tools, and pieces of baleen hint that these buildings were workshops where hunting tools would have been crafted and animal skins would have been prepared. *Qagsse* have been compared to Alaskan Karigis, men's working or clubhouses, that are the focus of village and religious life.[22]

Changing with the Seasons

Like their houses, Thule Inuit subsistence and economy were highly dependent and adapted to the seasons and climate in which they lived. Archaeological evidence is not abundant enough to construct the movements and practices of Thule Inuit societies, but collaboration with Inuit Elders and Knowledge Keepers has aided in understanding what life in the Arctic looked like a thousand years ago. The winter months were much less active in terms of hunting. Subsistence was dependent on caches of meat obtained from hunts in the summer and fall, and supplemented with hunting seals and walruses by waiting near their breathing holes, or at the ice edge. When a change from a predominantly sea mammal diet was desired, the Thule Inuit would have dipped into their stores of muskox, birds, and eggs. With the arrival of early spring, hunting for small mammals such as muskox and hare resumed, with bear hunting season following shortly after, and the return of migratory birds to add to Thule Inuit sources of food and skins. Spring and summer were the primary seasons for seal hunting. Late summer and early autumn saw Thule Inuit groups moving farther inland to take advantage of hunting caribou and fishing during the major char runs. This was a vital part of the Thule Inuit economy, as caribou skins (along with sealskin) were the best for creating warm and light winter clothing.[23]

Thule Inuit technology was highly sophisticated and diverse, and they have been called the most gadget-oriented people in prehistory.[24] Transportation technology was one of the key aspects of Thule Inuit culture, as it allowed them to migrate large distances and sustain their communities through hunting. The Thule Inuit had two kinds of watercraft: kayaks, which held one person and were predominantly used for hunting small seals, and umiaks that could hold over a dozen. Umiaks were essential to Thule Inuit migration due to their large capacity for both people and technology, but they were also important for hunting bowhead whales, as they allowed for multiple paddlers to steer and maintain the boat's position while the harpooner stood ready for action. When the ground was covered in snow, dog sleds were used. Evidence of sled shoes, thin slats of antler bone or ivory that would have attached to the bottom of wooden sled runners, as well as buckles made from walrus teeth or ivory to hitch dogs to sleds are commonly found at Thule Inuit sites. Snow goggles were also used to protect one's eyes from the sun's glare off of the snow and ice.

Hunting was the backbone of the Thule Inuit subsistence economy. Because it was so central in their life, they created an extensive and diverse collection of complex weapons to take down the large animals they relied on, both on land and in the sea. In comparison to earlier Arctic cultures such as the Dorset, the Thule Inuit had a wider range of types of harpoon heads, and created floats made from seal skins with bone or ivory mouthpieces plugged with a wooden peg to attach to harpoon lines for more success in hunting marine mammals in open water. Some harpoons were found to have ice picks made of bone or ivory attached at the end.[25] These picks were jammed into the ice and helped secure the harpoon line by bracing the harpoon shaft against the weight of the seal or walrus that had been speared, preventing it from sinking into the sea. Once on land, flensing knives made of bone, stone, and ivory were used to remove the outer layer of blubber.

While the hunting of bowhead whales was thought to have been a major source of meat and blubber for the Thule Inuit economy, recent research indicates that it wasn't as significant as previously thought. Instead, the ringed seal was the most widely hunted sea mammal.[26] Nevertheless, the Thule Inuit were still proficient at hunting bowhead whales, and this skill and reliance on large baleen whales is unique to the Thule Inuit in relation to other hunter-gatherer communities throughout history and around the world. Bowhead whale hunting was a highly complex ordeal and would have required the cooperation of multiple families, whether if done on an umiak, or simply from the ice edge. The Thule Inuit also hunted other large sea creatures such as bearded seals, narwhals, walruses, and beluga whales. It was this ability, along with their careful planning and storing of food during the warm season, that allowed them to settle into permanent winter communities.

Thule Inuit technology allowed them to successfully hunt almost every major species they came in contact with across the vast regions they inhabited.[27] They used a wide range of hooks and spears for fishing and relied heavily on bows and arrows for hunting land mammals such as caribou, muskox, foxes and hares. Bows were made from wood or baleen, and arrowheads from walrus ivory or narwhal tusk. Evidence for the use of bolas, throwing weapons made up of a number of weighted balls attached to strings of braided sinew or baleen lashed together at the ends, has also been found.[28] These were used to snare migratory birds, as when thrown, the balls would have spread wide before the strings wrapped around the bird as the bola hit its target, inhibiting it from further flight.

A Break from the Hunt

Thule Inuit sites provide a plethora of objects that hint at daily life. *Ulus,* multipurpose knives made specifically for women, and sewing kits including needles and thimbles made from animal skins, bring attention to another side of Thule Inuit society. Tools for living in large quantities of snow such as snow shovels and knives made from whale bone, baleen snow beaters possibly used to clean snow off parkas, and circular drying racks made to suspend over fires to dry clothing, show how they adapted to survive in harsh Arctic conditions.

Trade between Thule Inuit communities was widespread, with metals, soapstone, and ivory found distributed widely across their vast area of habitation.[29] Most likely, organic materials such as animal skins, blubber, food, and wood would also have been included in these traded items. What's interesting is that many of the ceramics found at Thule Inuit sites in the Eastern Arctic are made from raw materials that originated in Alaska. Despite being hundreds of kilometres away, certain Thule Inuit communities seemed to want to keep a close cultural connection

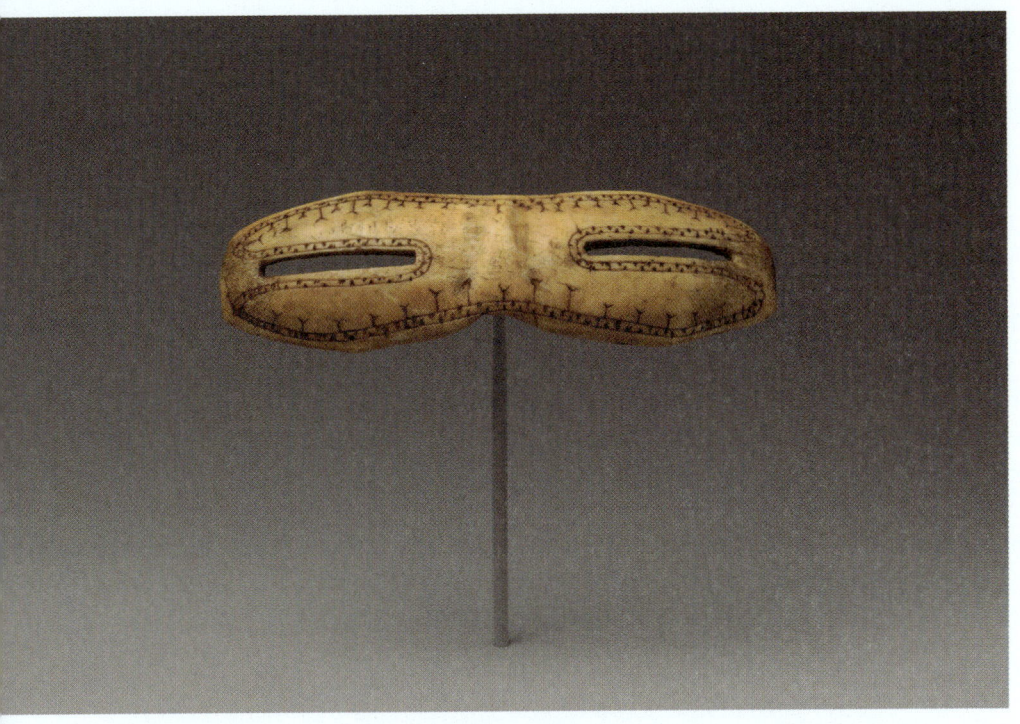

Thule snow goggles. These goggles were used to shield one's eyes from the glare of the sun on snow and from windblown ice.

with their western counterparts. Over time, soapstone vessels became more popular due to its local availability, and in rare cases, it even became a medium for artistic carving.[30]

Not-so-utilitarian artefacts have been found at multiple sites, hinting at a more playful and ritual side of Thule Inuit life. Toys such as small harpoon heads, mini bows and arrows, harpoon throwing boards, boats, and knives provide glimpses of what children would have occupied their time with in preparation for becoming fully-fledged members of their communities. A seal humerus tied to a wooden pin with baleen found on Ruin Island has been described as a traditional game called Ajagaq.[31] It is similar to the cup and ball game and is played by throwing the attached bone into the air while trying to get one of the holes drilled into the bone onto the pin. Animal and human figurines are also fairly common, and drum frames have been found which could hint to a form of ritual dancing and singing.[32]

Contact and Climate Change Cultures

By the fifteenth century, Thule Inuit sites began to change and decline, but it was not an end to the people who were part of this culture. Rather, it became a transition into a new way of life. There are multiple theories for the cause of Thule Inuit decline. The onset of the Little Ice Age, which began around the fourteenth century and lasted until the end of the nineteenth century,[33] resulted in cooling climates and an increase of sea ice in both its duration and size. The Thule Inuit way of life in some parts of the Arctic would have become difficult—if not impossible—as colder temperatures would have had a significant impact on the diversity of animals they relied upon for sustenance.

More ice resulted in declining whale populations in the Central Arctic and accessibility of caribou, but a more stable population of ringed seals and walruses. This led to more ice-edge and breathing-hole hunting, which is the foundation for modern Inuit cultures. Such a dramatic shift in hunting may have also led to the shift in population movements and habitats. Permanent winter house settlements dependent on food storage were abandoned in favour of spending the winter months in snow houses built on sea ice in the Central Arctic.[34] There was also a southward shift in migration, and a new preference towards large multifamily structures to combat this new uncertainty of food supply.

Another important factor in the cultural shift of the Thule Inuit is European contact. The sixteenth century saw a great deal of change in the Arctic due to a shift in interactions with European populations. The abandonment of Thule Inuit occupations in the High Arctic at this time coincides approximately with the disappearance of the Norse Greenland colonies.[35] These colonies would have been excellent trading contacts for metal. With their disappearance, accompanied with the arrival of

European traders, explorers, and whalers around Baffin Island, Labrador, and Hudson Bay around the same time, the Thule Inuit would have been drawn farther south and encouraged to be more mobile in order to take advantage of new opportunities. The final centuries of the Thule Inuit from 1650 until 1900 saw them interacting with Russian, Danish, English, and eventually American and Canadian populations. Each new cultural exchange would have influenced the Thule Inuit way of life, eventually evolving into the Inuit cultures that are present throughout the Arctic today.

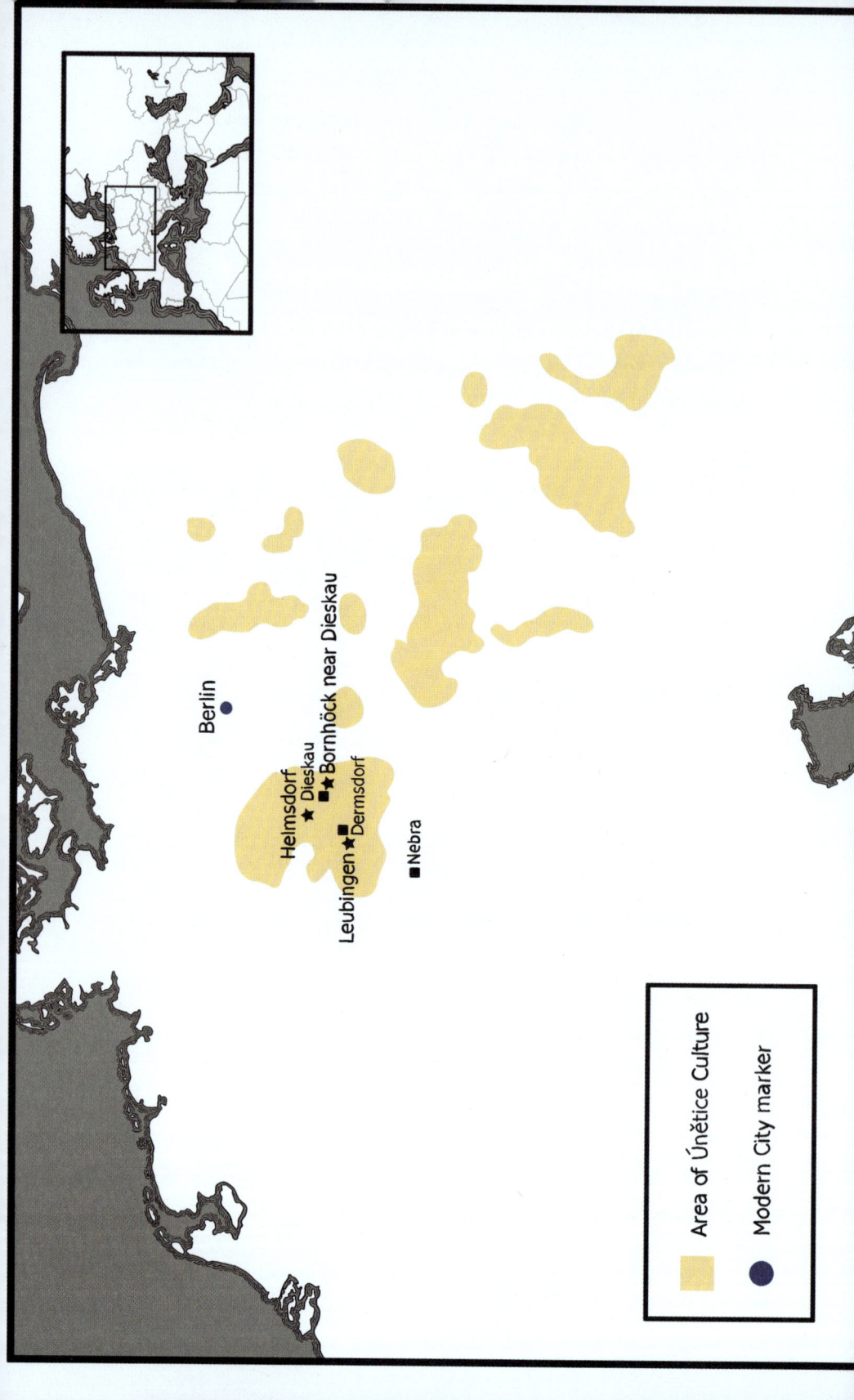

Chapter Nineteen

Únětice

Astronomical Bronzemasters of Central Europe

The warriors filed out of the longhouse and gathered tightly around the freshly dug pit that lay at the entrance. They were careful not to get too close to the edge, as the heavy rain that had been falling for the past two days had made the soil soft. While the pit wasn't deep, they didn't want to risk falling in or cause any disruption to the solemn ceremony they were about to perform.

Grasping at their cloaks to try and shield themselves from the storm, the highest-ranked warriors began chanting, the rest of them soon following. Had the weather been clear, the low harmonic rumbles of a hundred voices would have echoed throughout the soft hills and have been heard in the neighbouring hamlets. Instead, the rain and the wind prevented all but those present from hearing their lament for their fallen ruler.

As the chanting reached its zenith, one man picked up the large ceramic vessel sat next to the longhouse door and placed it into the pit. One by one, the warriors walked up to the cavity, took out their beloved, precious axe heads, and tossed them into the container. Their prince had given them these weapons, a symbol of their unity and loyalty to their ruler. While they would get new ones from the new prince, it was still a sorrowful goodbye to the axes that brought them so much glory on the battlefield.

Once the final weapon was deposited, the warriors had to act quickly to finish this ceremony so as to not let too much water accumulate in the vessel. The same man who had dug the pit now stepped forward, placed a lid over the sacrificed weapons, and proceeded to fill it back in. When the earth was packed and whole again, the warriors filed back into the longhouse, where the promise of shelter from the rain and a warm fire awaited.

Two Become One

The Únětice culture, also known as the Aunjetitz Culture, is an archaeological culture that takes its name from a cemetery of sixty culturally identifiable graves found in the village of Únětice, located north of Prague in Czechia (also known as the Czech Republic). Current research points to the Únětice developing from two earlier archaeological cultures dating back to the late Neolithic period in Central Europe: the Corded Ware and Bell Beaker cultures. These cultures originated from the east and the west respectively, and converged in Central Germany around 2600 BCE, where they coexisted for a period of time.[1] From these Neolithic cultures came the Únětice, emerging around 2200 BCE and replacing its predecessors in Czechia, western Slovakia, Austria, southern Poland, and much of Central Germany.

Genetic evidence on human remains indicates that while the material culture of the area changed, the people living in Central Europe did not.[2] Únětice burials contain genetic markers linking them to both the Corded Ware and Bell Beaker cultures.[3] This evidence suggests that the Únětice culture was therefore created from the merging of two separate population groups over a period of existence in the third millennium BCE. While this is a remarkable event, two cultures within close proximity and influencing each other is not a phenomenon unique to Central Europe.

"Princely" Barrows Mixing, Erasing, and Creating a Unified Hierarchical Society

The blending of Corded Ware and Bell Beaker cultures is particularly evident in the lavish, so-called "princely" tombs of the Únětice. The Leubingen tumulus (a mound of earth and stone raised over one or multiple graves) in Central Germany is the earliest proven "princely" burial attributed to the Únětice and is a prime example of the convergence of these two Neolithic cultures. The burial mound, the wooden tent-like burial chamber, and the vast amount of weaponry on display with the deceased are reminiscent of the Corded Ware culture. The weapons themselves—two axes, three daggers, a halberd (a scythe-shaped bronze blade attached to a wooden pole), and arrowheads—the forging tools, the ceramic cups found in the burial, and the orientation of the body to face east are all characteristic of the Bell Beaker culture.

From this evidence, the "prince," or those burying him, had a clear intention of incorporating elements from the "princely" burials of the Corded Ware and Bell Beaker cultures into a new burial tradition unique to the Únětice. In contrast to this mixing of cultures in one context, Únětice pottery is for the most part undecorated and largely standardised in design.[4] As a result, some researchers speculate that this was a deliberate act to aid in the unification of a new culture under one stratified society, making the previously distinguishable cultures indistinguishable.[5]

Únětice "princes" were deliberate in their creation of new traditions and cultural norms. Ancient artefacts, such as a shafted stone axe from the middle Neolithic (c. 4500–3100 BCE)[6] found in the "princely" grave at Helmsdorf dating to around 1800 BCE, are thought to have been used to add historical legitimacy to their status.[7] This fabricated image and status can also be seen in the manufacture of an identical set of gold ornaments that were found in both "princely" burials at Leubingen and

Helmsdorf and made from the same specific gold sources.[8] The presence of "princely" burials that stand out amongst

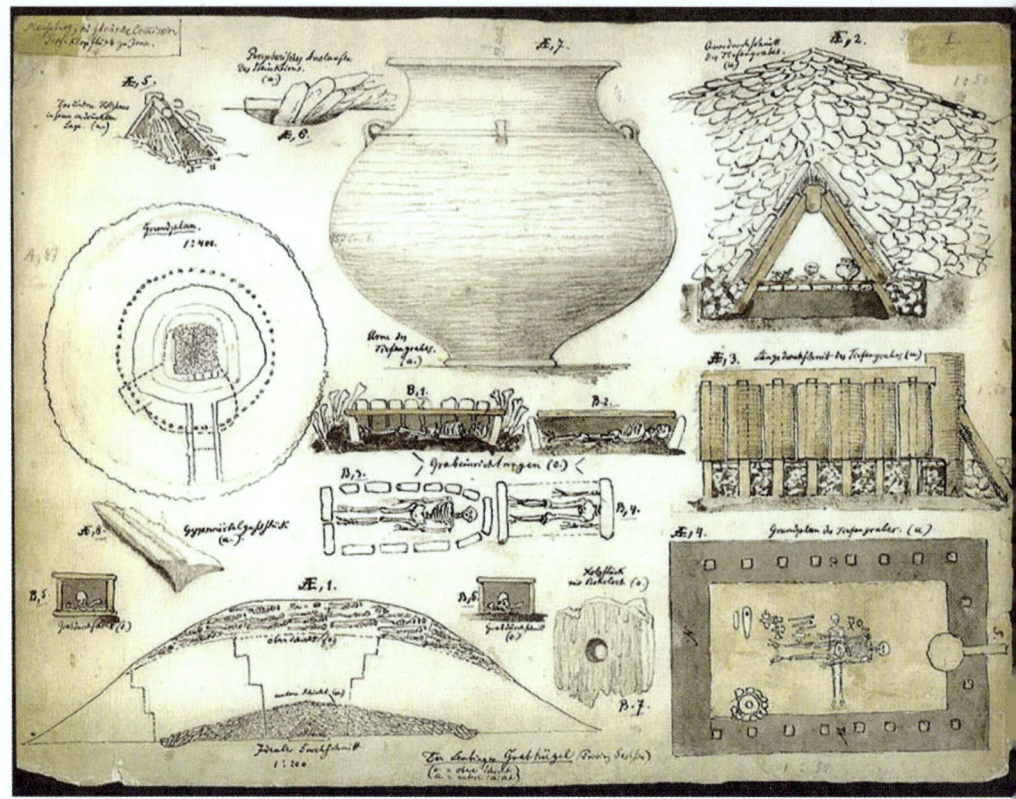

Drawings of the Leubingen barrow excavations.

other, less lavish, interments indicates that the Únětice culture was highly stratified. The building of these burial monuments alone would have required a large amount of materials, massive investments of labour, and a particular level of social cohesion and organisation. But it is their contents that shed even further light on what this society may have looked like.

The Bornhöck "princely" burial is the largest known of these elaborate mounds, with its diameter measuring sixty-five metres and reaching over twenty metres in height. The grandeur and size of this burial has led researchers to believe that the individual buried inside was on a higher political and social level than the other two "princely" burials mentioned above, and that this area was a centre of power from around 1900 BCE to 1600/1550 BCE.

Alongside its hoard of weapons, the Bornhöck burial has allowed researchers to gather more insight into the economic organisation of the Únětice culture.[9] Inside the tomb were multiple well-made grinding stone slabs designed for processing large amounts of grain and are markedly different from others that have been found in regular domestic contexts. The presence of such large stones in a burial of this stature is a telling indication of centralised agricultural production, where food surplus was controlled by an upper class. The processing of such large amounts of food also hints at an army that would be dependent on this surplus, meaning that power in Únětice society was possibly held by force.

The type of stratified power structure exhibited by the Únětice culture was incomparable in Central Europe at this time, both in size and longevity.[10] Weapons are rarely found in common Únětician burials, so it seems they were strictly reserved for "princely" tombs. The individuals buried within them could therefore have been seen as commanders and warriors. From evidence found in excavated burials alone, archaeologists have been able to identify as many as seven distinct social hierarchies within Únětician society.[11] These burials ranged from the elite Bornhöck mound, to the "princely" graves of Leubingen and Helmsdorf with their elaborate weapons and standardised gold jewellery, then progressively lower to modestly furnished flat graves without a mound containing minimal bronze items (sometimes axes and daggers), and simple graves containing ceramic vessels or nothing at all.

The reason for the formation of such a unique social hierarchy is still not known. Certainly, their location between the Elbe and Oder rivers placed them in a position to control trade between societies to the north and south of them, allowing the Únětice to gather power, wealth and prestige. Areas in which the Únětice existed have been found near copper deposits, for example those found in the Harz foothills, as well as other highly sought-after materials such as tin and salt. What's certain is that this power structure appeared extremely stable, as there is a distinct lack of fortified settlements in Central Germany, and there is evidence of a constant supply of raw materials from the same sources dating from the eighteenth century BCE onwards.

The distinct lack of weaponry in common burials and fortified hilltop settlements, however, does not necessarily mean that peace was the norm in Únětice society. Indeed, for the Únětician rulers to maintain their position of power, they would have required the force of an organised, professional army that could keep the peace both internally and externally. Burials containing human remains with trauma from arrows and axe wounds show evidence of violence within Únětice communities. Instead of being found in burials to portray individuals as warriors, most weapons have been found in metal hoards. Although early hoards mainly contained jewellery and other accessories, weapons such as axes were added later.

Hoards have been interpreted as possible sacrificial offerings or gifts to the gods. But, with the gradual change of adding more weapons, with some only containing militaristic equipment, the purpose of these hoards has been brought into question.[12] For example, excavations at the site of Dermsdorf revealed a hoard containing ninety-eight metal axe blades with traces of use, and two blanks of the scythe-shaped halberd blades inside a vessel in front of a large longhouse that possibly belonged to a person of high rank. The deposit has been interpreted to belong to a group of soldiers or warriors who were garrisoned at this longhouse, which was in sight of the Leubingen "princely" grave. A possible timeline for the weapons is that they were issued to these warriors by the "prince," and were then sacrificed in front of a ritual building when he died. The new "prince" that rose to power would then have issued new weapons to the soldiers in order to secure their loyalty. Whatever the case is for these buried axes, what's clear is that if an army did exist to serve the Únětice "princes," their presence served the intended purpose as there appears to be no evidence for internal wars over the vast area of Únětice occupation for several centuries.[13]

Bronze Masters of Central Europe

The efficiency of Únětice farming allowed them to amass an agricultural surplus. This ability then enabled them to become the first producers of bronze in Central Europe.[14] While copper was widely found in the area, the only source of tin in Central Europe was within Únětice-controlled territory: the Erzgebirge (Ore Mountains) located today along the border between Czechia and Germany. Control over both copper and tin mines allowed the Únětice not only to create a unique culture centred on metalwork and the trade of these precious raw materials and finished products, but to also amass great wealth. From metal daggers, halberds, pins, axes, and jewellery such as their signature spiral arm bands, Únětice metalwork caught the attention of peoples far from the confines of their surrounding neighbours.

Because copper and tin are unevenly distributed, the metals trade around Europe was a major economy during the Bronze Age. The Únětice therefore developed a trade network, spreading bronze, gold, and amber across the continent, reaching as far as the Baltic shores, the British Isles, and even Mycenaean Greece. The Únětice seem to have made quite a name for themselves as bronze masters. Eyelet pins made of bone and flint daggers with fake "casting seams" to make them look more like metal ones have been found in Scandinavia, proving just how valued Únětice-made bronze items were to surrounding cultures and beyond.[15] This period has been called a "Bronze Boom" by some, stating that, although it brought massive success and stability to Únětice communities, it could also have led to their eventual collapse.[16]

The Únětice mainly traded their bronze for other luxury products such as gold and amber. Most of the amber dating to the Early Bronze Age can be attributed to the Únětice, with Bohemia in Czechia being the main concentration where resinous small beads and circular pendants have been found.[17] This amber originated from the Baltic and was most likely exchanged for bronze tools, ornaments, and weapons. Large quantities of it were transported into Únětice territories between around 2000–1775 BCE and was subsequently traded farther south into surrounding cultures and societies, with some evidence of it even reaching Greece. While other high-value items such as people, animal hides, honey, and wool would have also been traded, the inorganic nature of amber makes it the best archaeological material to study the vast exchange network that made the Únětice a household name throughout Europe.

Life in Longhouses

Not much is known regarding daily life for Únětice communities, as it has not been as extensively studied as the cemeteries that first enamoured archaeologists in the 1800s. Nevertheless, settlements comprising farmsteads, hamlets, and villages have been found and have started to reveal a much broader picture of the Únětice culture. Many settlements were established along rivers and other waterways which would have provided fertile soils for agriculture. Such practices allowed the Únětice to create a food surplus that boosted their economic status while providing them free time to hone their metalworking skills. What is interesting about these Únětice settlements, is that in most cases they were surrounded by other societies and cultures that had not yet adopted metal tools and were continuing a late Neolithic way of life.

The Únětice relied on several grains and legumes to sustain themselves, particularly barley, spelt, einkorn, lentils and beans. They had a number of "snack foods" such as nuts, and even seasonal treats or delicacies like freshwater mussels. The number of cavities found in teeth from studies on human remains also hint at the Únětice having a bit of a sweet tooth.[18] It appears their diet consisted of fruit, porridge, milk, beer, or other alcoholic beverages like apple cider or fruit wines, and honey.

Longhouses appear to have been the shelter of choice for the Únětice. Early houses were semi-subterranean structures with wicker walls covered in clay, but in later periods, above-ground houses with gabled roofs became the dominant architecture of Únětice settlements. These houses were characteristically long. Some, such as the one found at the site of Břenzo in Bohemia, measured thirty-two metres in length. While Únětice settlements appear to have been densely populated, the average settlement consisted of only five long buildings. Four buildings have been uncovered in Únětice sites that are enormous in size, measuring up to five hundred metres squared. Construction at this scale would have required an extremely well-coordinated labour force as well as considerable amounts of raw materials. The function of these buildings has not yet been confirmed, but like the longhouse at Dermsdorf, it is believed that they would have been related to the ruling class in some way, either for ritual purposes or to house their standing army.[19]

Astronomical Anomalies

Not much is known regarding the Únětician religion or belief system, though a few impressive archaeological finds have opened a window into a world closely linked to fertility, life, death, rebirth, and the cosmos. Like many other cultures in the Bronze Age, celestial bodies and the deities that were created to associate with or emulate them were key elements of religion at this time. The most widely known artefact belonging to the Únětice culture is the Nebra Sky Disc. It was discovered as part of a hoard containing a chisel, two swords, two flanged axes, and two spiral bracelets by treasure-hunting metal detectorists in 1999 on the Mittelburg hill near the village of Nebra in Germany. With the hoard dating to around 1600 BCE, the Nebra Sky Disc was probably made one to two hundred years before. So far, it is the only narrative scene that can be attributed to the Únětice culture.

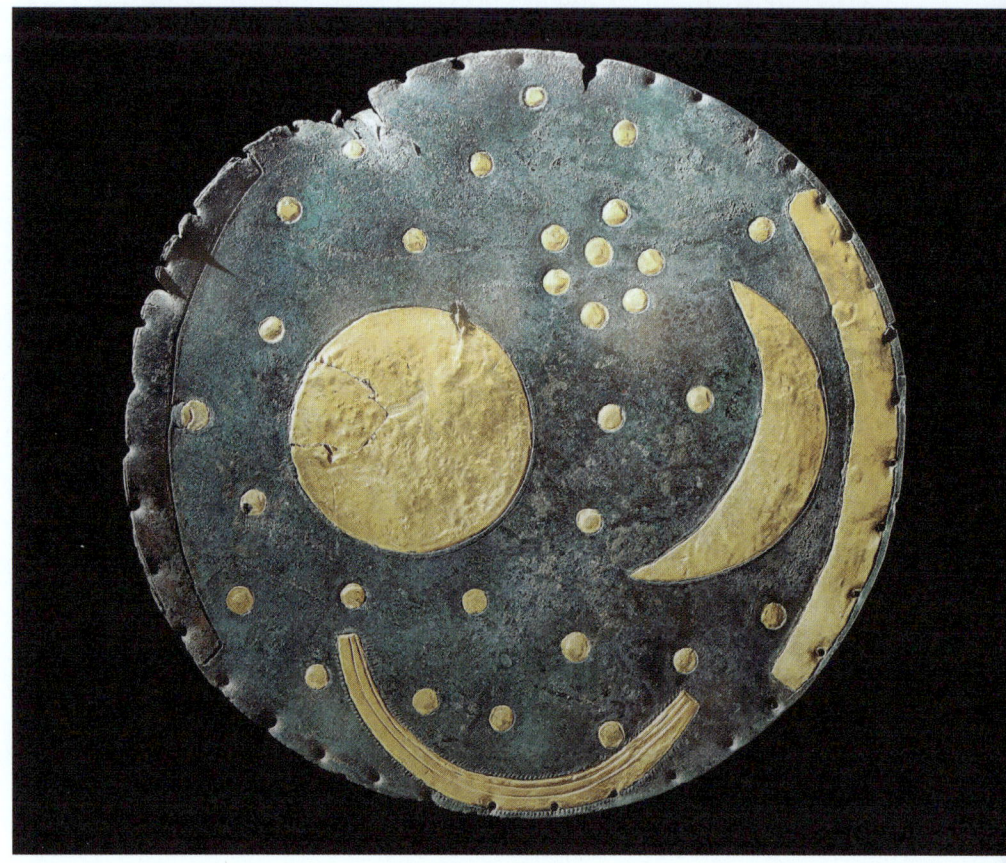

Nebra Sky Disc.

The Nebra Sky Disc is an amazing representation of advanced knowledge and understanding of the cosmos. The bronze and gold disc, originally consisting of thirty-two stars, a crescent moon, and either a full moon or a sun, would have been used to synchronise the solar and lunar years, as the lunar year is eleven days shorter. A cluster of seven stars has been identified as the Pleiades, a constellation that disappears on March 10 every year and returns on October 17. This could have aided in calculating the solar year, but was also accurate in predicting lunar eclipses. The simplicity and utilitarian design of the Disc suggests that the astronomical knowledge needed to accurately use the Nebra Sky Disc would have been restricted to only a few people.[20] It could also have been used by the Únětice "princes" to help legitimise their rule by regulating annual festivals.

Studies on the Nebra Sky Disc show that it underwent multiple iterations. In the second phase of its life, two gold horizon arcs were added to each side of the disc to mark where the sun would rise and set between the summer and winter solstices. Next, a sky ship was added to the bottom. This imagery of the sun being transported by a boat is reminiscent of ancient Egyptian symbolism and mythology. The addition of such a religious symbol suggests that the original meaning and purpose of the Nebra Sky Disc changed over time from something functional, to a more mythological or religious object.[21] Evidence of this can be seen in the subsequent phase of the disc's use, as the entire rim was perforated, most likely to mount it onto an organic textile or wooden backing for parading in public. Some of the motifs would have been hidden by this mount, meaning it was now simply another representation of a solar disc.

The story of the Únětice that can be told by studying the Nebra Sky Disc is one of a society that were once astute observers of the sky, the movements of the heavens an important part of their culture. Indeed, the Únětice had a strong understanding of astronomy, developed a cyclical and linear concept of time, and comprehended hemispheres centuries before the ancient Greeks. In the following centuries, this knowledge seems to have been gradually lost, eventually being intertwined with mythology and symbolism. In its final stage, the Nebra Sky Disc was buried with the other artefacts found in the hoard, an assemblage reminiscent of the "princely" tombs so characteristic of the Únětice. The left horizon arc was removed from the disc before burial, making it no longer usable, but its presence in such a hoard has led researchers to speculate that the disc was a representation of the body of its last princely owner.[22]

The Únětice didn't solely constrain their astronomical beliefs to metal objects. Two sites have been uncovered in Central Germany containing circular enclosures of monumental architecture and evidence of burials and potential sacrifices. The site of Pömmelte is characterised by a monumental enclosure consisting of several concentric circles of posts, pits, and ditches that appear to have been the site of complex ritual performances, with the largest circular enclosure measuring 115 metres wide. Dating from around 2300–2050 BCE, Pömmelte is often described as continental Europe's Stonehenge as parts of it resemble Woodhenge and the bluestone oval of Stonehenge, both located in the United Kingdom. Recent excavations of the enclosure have led researchers to suggest that the henge-like enclosures were monumental sanctuaries used for communal gatherings and ritual performances.[23]

The two main entrances of the Pömmelte enclosure were oriented to align with sunset during the winter solstice, and sunrise at the summer solstice. This seasonality suggests that any feasting or rites performed at the site followed a seasonal cycle that was most likely intended for the participants to communicate or become closer to the cosmos.[24] Burial pits have been found containing ceramic vessels, stone axes, animal bones, grinding stones, drinking cups, and the skeletal remains of women and children, all of which speak to the ritual nature of the site. Four of the human burials had suffered severe trauma to the skull as well as other injuries before death, though it isn't yet clear if these were ritual sacrifices or if they were victims of some form of conflict.[25] Other interments found on the site belonged to individuals of higher status and were buried carefully facing east, another indication of the importance of the sun in Únětice mythology.

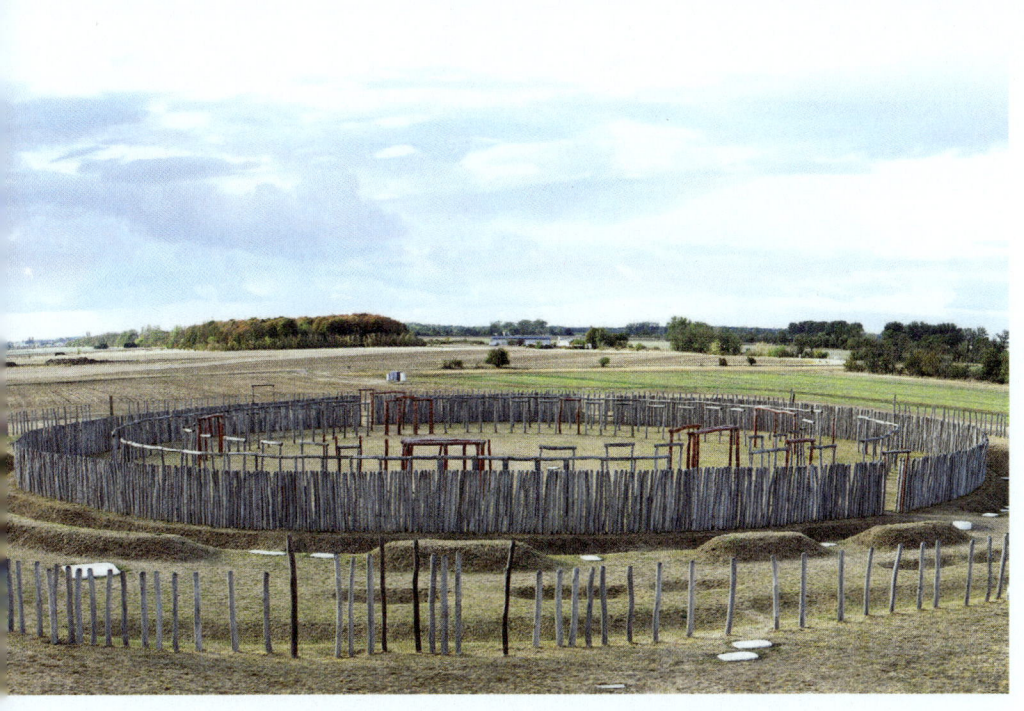
Reconstruction of the Pömmelte circular enclosure.

From Boom to Bust

Around 1600 BCE, at the pivotal transition between the Early Bronze Age and the Middle Bronze Age, the Únětice culture collapsed. Afterwards, much of their former territory remained abandoned for around two hundred years. The reason for their rapid disappearance is not yet clear, but shifting trade routes, environmental or social collapse, and resource shortages for making bronze or the discovery of new metal ore deposits outside of their territory have all been suggested. As with many other ancient cultures and civilisations, collapse is often a mixture of multiple possibilities.

What can be seen archaeologically is the discontinuation of settlements in the northern regions of Únětice occupation, and an increase in fortifications in the southwest and southern regions that continued until the onset of the Middle Bronze Age. Sites, such as the fortified settlement of Bruszczewo in Poland, exhibited signs of excessive overuse of natural resources and was subsequently abandoned around 1650 BCE.[26] Bronze was still a rare commodity in the Early Bronze Age. Therefore, the Únětice were in a unique position to hold a monopoly over this resource in Central Europe.[27] When this "Bronze Boom" occurred, Únětician society expanded at a rapid pace. Agriculture, building, and the use of firewood for metallurgy all increased. This would have put a strain on the environment in which the Únětice once thrived and drastically altered their ecosystems. Such changes would have eventually taken their toll on Únětice agriculture, reducing their standard of living and in the end, resulted in the necessary abandonment of settlements, forcing a significant proportion of the population to find a new home. Depleted areas would then have required an immense amount of time to recover before they were suitable for habitation again.

The consequences of a large increase in income for the majority of the Únětice culture most likely led to an increase in wealth, spending, and demand for luxury goods. Pursuit of such wealth would have shifted the focus of the Únětice from agriculture and creating a surplus to sustain their communities, to metallurgy in order to sustain the demand both for their trading network as well as their desire for finery. This decline in agriculture and increased demand for food would have resulted in inflated prices, a reduction in their purchasing power, and eventually societal collapse from multiple contributing factors. It appears the excitement of new technology and an eager market allowed the Únětice to thrive and prosper for a few centuries, providing them the opportunity to create masterful works of metallurgy in a condensed period of time. Unfortunately, they lost sight of their agricultural foundation, and as with all "booms" that have occurred throughout history, the bust was waiting around the corner.

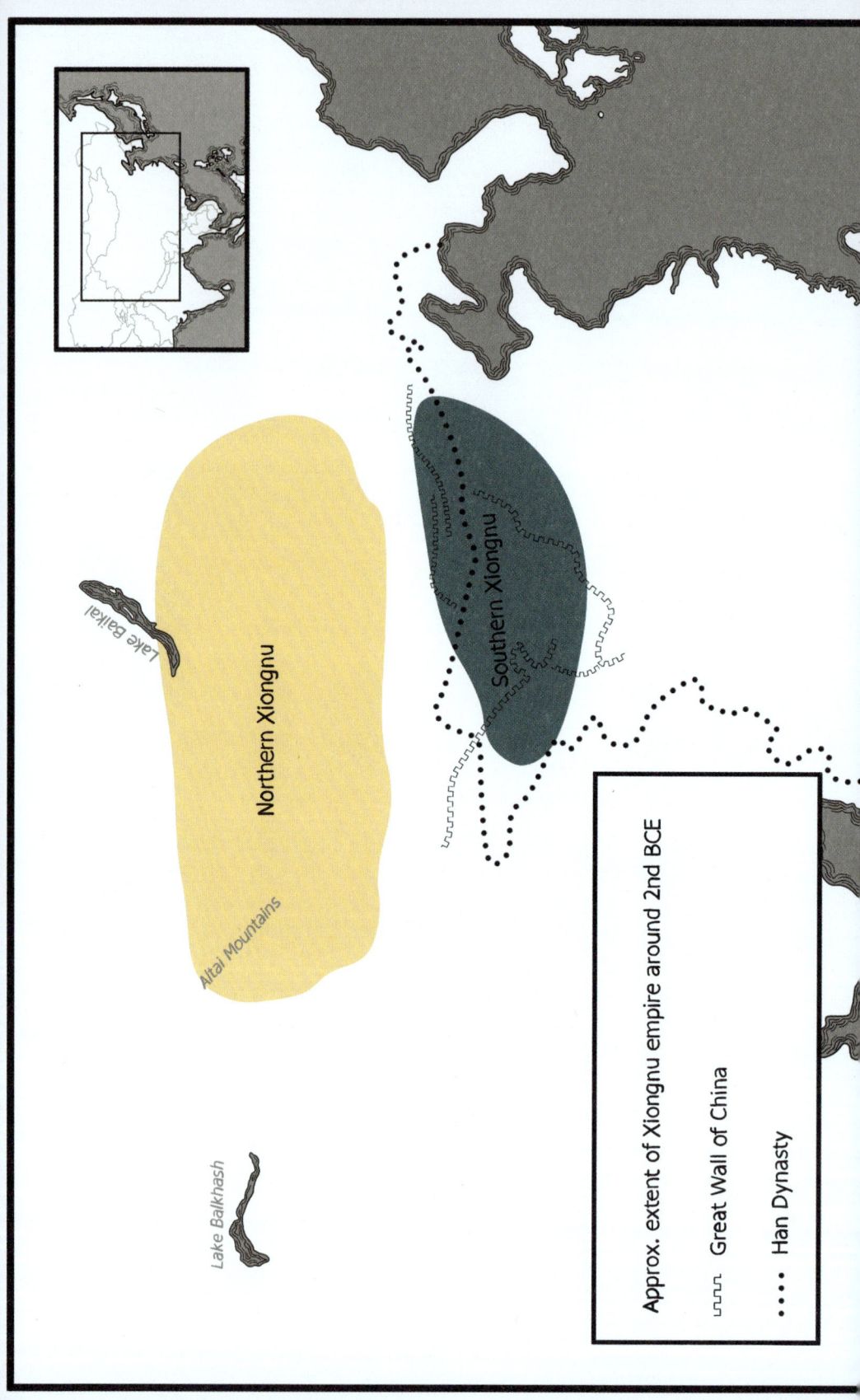

Chapter Twenty

Xiongnu
Nomadic Enemies of China

"Hyah!"

The boy dug his heels into the sheep and clenched its wool tight as it trotted through the grasses of the steppe. Remembering what his father told him, he tried to sit deep in the pillow that had been strapped onto the sheep's back. It was no use; the sheep's gait was too bumpy, and it was all he could do to stay upright as he bounced up and down.

The older kids raced past him, cheering and waving their bows in the air. They made it look so easy. The boy couldn't wait for the day when he'd be steady enough on his steed to hunt rabbits and foxes with the others. He could see it now, leaning back into his sheep's canter, bow in hand and becoming one with the animal, his father's face when he came back to their wagon with a rabbit for dinner, his mother's tears seeing her son all grown up.

All this daydreaming distracted the boy and gave his sheep the chance it needed to jolt him off. With one hard bounce, the boy flew off the animal, scuffing his knees as he hit the ground.

The boy's mother, never too far from him, rode over on her horse and effortlessly scooped him into her arms.

"Don't worry," she whispered in the boy's ear, "Your father would never tell you this, but he was even worse on a sheep than you are when he was your age. And look at him now, one of the greatest warriors in the empire."

Giggling, the boy wiped the tears that had welled up in his eyes and hugged his mother. She placed him back onto the ground and he ran to catch up with his sheep and get back on the saddle.

Of Empires and Great Walls

The Xiongnu culture was the first and longest-lasting civilisation and nomadic empire of the eastern Eurasian Steppe. While its heartland was in Mongolia, at its height its influence and reach extended from the Ordos Plateau in northern China up to Lake Baikal, and from Manchuria to eastern Kazakhstan. "Xiongnu" was not what this group of people called themselves. Rather, it was the term used by Chinese court historians when chronicling diplomatic and military transactions with leaders of the northern steppe. They were described as a group of people, not adherent to a single language or ethnic affiliation. In reality, the Xiongnu culture refers to the numerous groups, peoples, and tribes from diverse regions, cultures, and societal structures that made up a confederation with a formalised integrative imperial system.[1]

Due to this diversity, the origins of the Xiongnu culture are difficult to determine. Excavations in Inner Mongolia and surrounding areas show a sudden appearance of the Xiongnu culture around the third century BCE. Analysis of skeletal remains also hints at the possibility that (at least some) of the people who made up the Xiongnu might have immigrated from northern Taiga, the boreal forests in present-day Russia.[2] From current knowledge, a great number of people from North Asia appeared and were culturally integrated in the Northern Zone of China from the middle and late Spring and Autumn period (c. 770–481 BCE). This was possibly due to the southern migration of the Slab Grave Culture, whom recent genetic research indicates were the primary ancestors of the Xiongnu.[3]

The Xiongnu left no written records of their own. Therefore, much of what we know about them comes from the limited archaeological excavations and surveys conducted in the area, and the chronicles from Chinese historians between the second century BCE and the third century CE that provide accounts for the Xiongnu Empire's role in relation to China's Qin and Han Dynasties. When first mentioned in these written records, the Xiongnu were described as an already established group alongside three other Chinese states who had joined together to attack the state of Qin in 318 BCE. A century later in 221 BCE, after the Qin dynasty unified China, the Xiongnu were driven beyond the Yellow River and the Great Wall was built to keep them, and other potential threats, out.

The Great Wall created much more than a physical divide. Those who did not agree with the agricultural lifestyle of China retreated beyond the Great Wall. As a result, the Xiongnu formed alliances with these groups and others, gradually uniting in 209 BCE under a powerful ruler (*shanyu*) by the name of Maodun. An outstanding commander, Maodun invented a signalling arrow that made a whistling sound in flight, directing his men to shoot towards the sound without hesitation. This level of influence allowed him to create a confederacy that gave the Xiongnu control of Inner Asia.

From the outset of Maodun's reign, the Xiongnu grew to rival the Chinese dynasties, launching multiple destructive raids along the Yellow River and repeated invasions over the Great Wall—even successfully annexing the northern part of it at one point. Efforts from the Han, though sometimes effective in pushing the Xiongnu north of the desert, allowing them to strengthen their ties with the Eurasian Steppe and therefore aiding in their unique cultural development, often proved futile. In 198 BCE, a treaty was signed declaring peace between the two polities. The Han Emperor was made to hand over one of his daughters to the Xiongnu as a princess bride, as well as make regular deliveries of grain, silk, and alcohol. The Han even recognised the Xiongnu Shanyu as an equal to the emperor, which completely went against the precedent that the Chinese ruler was the universal sovereign of all domains.[4] This original treaty

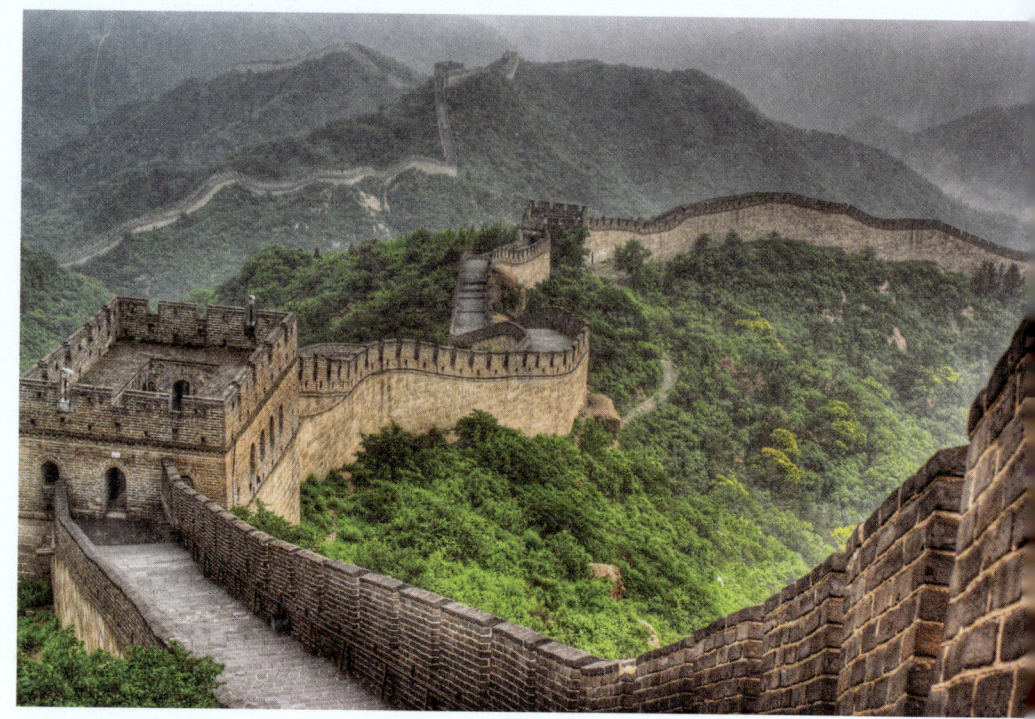

Great Wall of China.

only brought a temporary halt to the attacks, and a pattern of raiding both people and property, followed by generous appeasement in favour of the Xiongnu from the Han, continued for over sixty years until 133 BCE when Emperor Wudi decided to take action.

Emperor Wudi launched an aggressive campaign against the Xiongnu. Pursuing the nomads deep into their territory, he successfully forced them farther north, sending armies to occupy their lands, and setting up Chinese colonies to create a buffer zone of protection. As a result, the northern route of the Silk Road became defined, and communication and trade between China and the rest of the world began. Wudi's grandson Emperor Han Xuan finally defeated the Xiongnu. Those not brought under control of the Han were eventually driven west and migrated across the Eurasian Steppe. This loss of land and power led to internal conflicts among Xiongnu leaders, and civil war ensued from 57–47 BCE. By the end of the war, Shanyu Hu-han-yeh restored sovereignty and ushered in a century of prosperity for the Xiongnu after turning to the Han for assistance and acknowledging subordination to China. Despite this agreement, he was fortunately able to preserve Xiongnu statehood and all of its symbols of sovereignty.

In the middle of the first century CE, internal conflicts regarding rulership ended in the Xiongnu Confederation separating into two factions. Southern tribes migrated to the northern Chinese frontier, eventually surrendering to the Han and creating the "Southern" Xiongnu that survived until the fifth century CE. The "Northern" Xiongnu, on the other hand, maintained their independence until they were attacked at the end of the first century CE by the allied forces of the "Southern" Xiongnu and the Chinese. The "Northern" Xiongnu ended up migrating westwards and disappeared from Chinese records after the second century CE.[5]

A Nomadic Empire

The Xiongnu were an empire in the sense that it was a political entity that extended well beyond its core territory of Inner Mongolia and brought multiple regions and peoples under its control.[6] They themselves were made up of multiple groups of people, divided into twenty-four major tribes that each consisted of kinship groups, clans, and familial heritage. At the height of their empire, they had conquered regions stretching from Korea to the Altai Mountains, and from the Chinese border to the southern regions of Lake Baikal. The Xiongnu became influential in Central Inner and East Asia and established lucrative trading networks across Eurasia, exchanging exotic items from Greece, Rome, China, Egypt, and Persia.

How a pastoral society on the move came to form an empire in the Inner Asian Steppes has been speculated by many scholars. Climate change, economic pressure and a naturally adopted militaristic lifestyle have all been suggested.[7] Other more in-depth theories involving the relations between them and China have also been put forward. For example, the Xiongnu Empire being the result of a long-lasting coevolutionary process in which China and the Xiongnu were dependent on each other while each side formed into imperial polities.[8] The way in which the Xiongnu expanded differed in each region. With other nomadic groups around northern China, local kings were defeated and they were absorbed into the empire while maintaining relative autonomy. Other areas farther north and west required a more violent approach.

The Xiongnu were heavily reliant on Chinese agriculture. Therefore, during times of conflict, other sources of grain and sustenance would have been required to sustain their communities. This resulted in the Xiongnu attempting to subjugate semi-nomadic and sedentary agrarian communities, as well as other nomadic groups, into "frontier" or "buffer" zones to maintain a stable food supply.[9] These sedentary peoples produced surpluses of animals, grain, and other pastoral products that became the primary trading items for their economy. Being assimilated into the Xiongnu Empire did not mean mandatory assimilation into the culture, though. Unlike the Han, the Xiongnu did not gain their political power through cultural domination. Rather, the various groups that made up the empire were able to maintain their cultures and way of life, only under new jurisdiction.

The success of the Xiongnu Empire was largely due to their military prowess. When Maodun became Shanyu, he reorganised the army and replaced heavily armed soldiers on horseback with a more agile light cavalry highly skilled in the long composite bow. It has been hypothesised that in Xiongnu society, a male's status and role were determined by their success in war.[10] This desire for military success could therefore have heavily influenced the expansion of the empire. Men weren't the only warriors either; historical sources state that Xiongnu women were equally impressive on horseback and with a bow, often assisting in defending children and the elderly from enemy attacks.[11] Children were also encouraged to develop these skills from an early age by riding sheep and shooting arrows at small animals such as birds, rats, rabbits, and foxes.

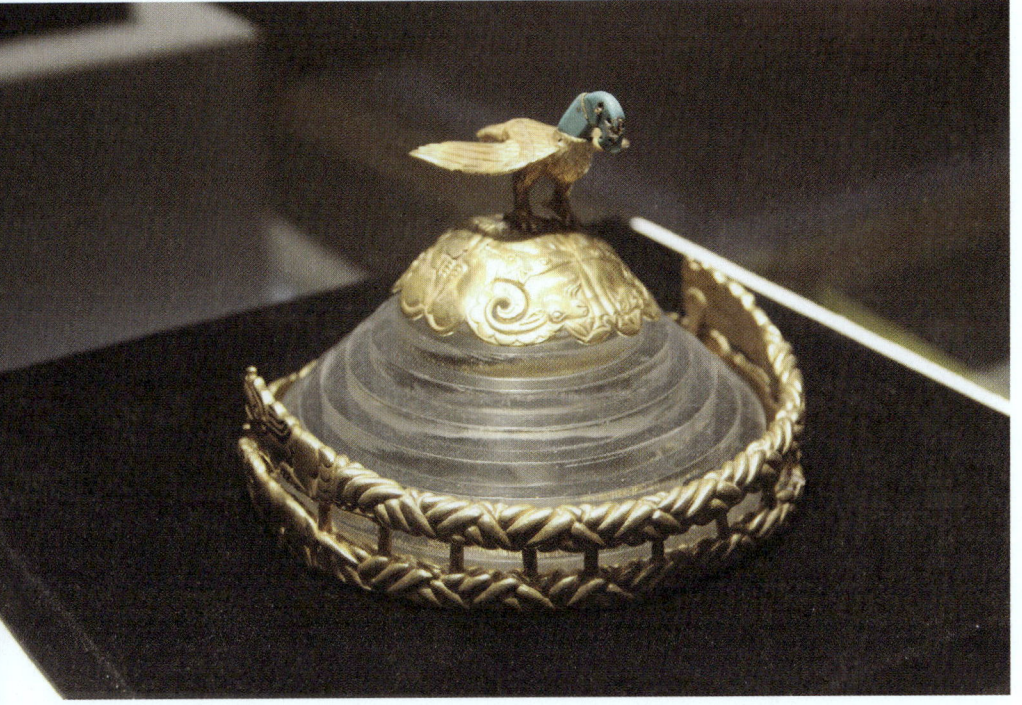

Xiongnu gold crown.

Written vs. Archaeological Evidence: How the Xiongnu Lived

Chinese historical sources describe the Xiongnu as constantly moving in search of water and grazing lands for their horses and oxen. They did not build permanent settlements or cities, nor did they themselves practise agriculture. The traditional view of the Xiongnu is that they introduced the covered wagon on high wheels as their mobile home of choice.[12] Not only did these wagons provide ample protection from the elements, they also offered the freedom and security of being able to relocate with all of one's possessions if any danger encroached the camp. The historical sources go a step further to state that the Xiongnu had no permanent settlements, although they did have (what are likely to have been permanent) places where chieftains would meet at various times of the year to carry out sacrifices and other administrative and ceremonial activities.

Written sources, especially those written by a rival territory, don't always tell an accurate or full story. Not every person in the Xiongnu Empire lived on the road, nor were they forced to adopt this way of life. The Xiongnu Empire was a radically new kind of political entity that consisted of both nomadic and sedentary groups across its region of influence. When looking at the archaeological evidence, the existence of, and need for, semi-permanent and permanent settlements becomes quite clear. Pastoral campsites, which could have been used as semi-permanent establishments and were most likely used for seasonal pasturelands, have been identified from small collections of debris. Archaeologists have also discovered several walled sites with platforms that probably held some sort of central or monumental position. The same can be said for cemeteries that specific Xiongnu groups returned to regularly in order to bury their dead.

The existence of cast bronze and iron art pieces and everyday tools belonging to the Xiongnu culture also added to the necessity of permanent sites because their production required complex procedures and foundries manned by skilled artists and craftsmen. We also have evidence of Xiongnu fortresses, such as Ivolga, where an iron plough alongside wheat, barley, and millet were found, pointing to them practising their own agriculture. Recently, permanent settlements such as Boroo Gol in Mongolia have been identified and excavated, and they can tell us a great deal about how people who chose a more settled existence lived.

Some dwellings at Boroo Gol were rectangular in shape, with rounded corners and constructed partly buried in the ground, their floors dug down to around one metre below the surface. Each of these dwellings had a fireplace in the northern corner made from slabs of stone and large fragments of pottery. Attached to these fireplaces were smoke pipes made of ceramic slabs that ran along the western walls and functioned as heating tubes. The presence of a heating system like this implies that the Xiongnu were living there during the winter. Remnants of post holes in these dwellings indicate that domestic buildings were repaired multiple times and probably lived in by several generations.[13]

Excavations on the floors of these dwellings have uncovered the remains of everyday life. Animal bones, personal ornaments, objects made out of bone, hammerstones, pottery, and tools have all been found. The amount of pottery recovered proves that Boroo Gol was occupied during the summer as well, as this craft was carried out during the warmer dry season.[14] Boroo Gol is just one example of the current work being done to change the singular view of Chinese historical documents. The Xiongnu had sedentary groups of farmers and craftspeople living within their empire. This diversification of settlement type has been thought by some to be an attempt for the Xiongnu to expand their economy past nomadic pastoralism and incorporate agriculture and handicraft.[15] Furthermore, all known Xiongnu sites appear to have been strategically located. They are all situated along a line oriented north-south, and follow a road that connects Irkutsk in Russia to the Chinese border, and could even be extended to Xianyang (Xi'an), the capital of the Han Empire.

A Culture Influenced

Because of the sheer extent of the Xiongnu Empire, it was able to collect influences from many different places and become the unique culture it is deemed today. While variety can be seen from site to site due to their regional distances, the Xiongnu culture still forms a whole that is distinct from the rest, with its homogeneous weaponry and pottery. One key item in which we can see these cultural influences, is their metal belt plaques used to decorate the waist. These plaques portrayed various scenes depicting both mythical and social scenes filled with fantastical creatures, everyday animals either in combat or preying, and humans in scenes of wrestling, or warfare.

When looking at foreign influences on the Xiongnu culture, it is most similar in form, décor, and iconography to the Pazyryk culture from the Altai Mountains. For example, the Tree of Life is a common symbol used in the European steppe and something similar is represented on Xiongnu belt plaques with animals standing under it, its branches entwining around the animal's horns or antlers. Plaques with dragons on the other hand show both Altaian and Chinese influence.

Encircled Tombs

Most of the archaeological evidence for the Xiongnu currently comes from their burial sites, particularly in eastern Mongolia and the Transbaikal region. The majority of burials that have been found were rectangular shaft graves with wooden coffins or other wooden chambers. Elite graves were marked by rings of thick stones on the surface, while everyday people were likely buried under less meticulous stone formations or without any markings at all.[16] These differences, and more, indicate that there was a form of social or political hierarchy within the Xiongnu Empire.

Burials typically included the bones of sacrificed animals, particularly their skulls and legs, that were placed above the head of the deceased. They also sometimes contained weapons, horse gear, and jewellery or ornaments. Elites and nobles were often buried with horse

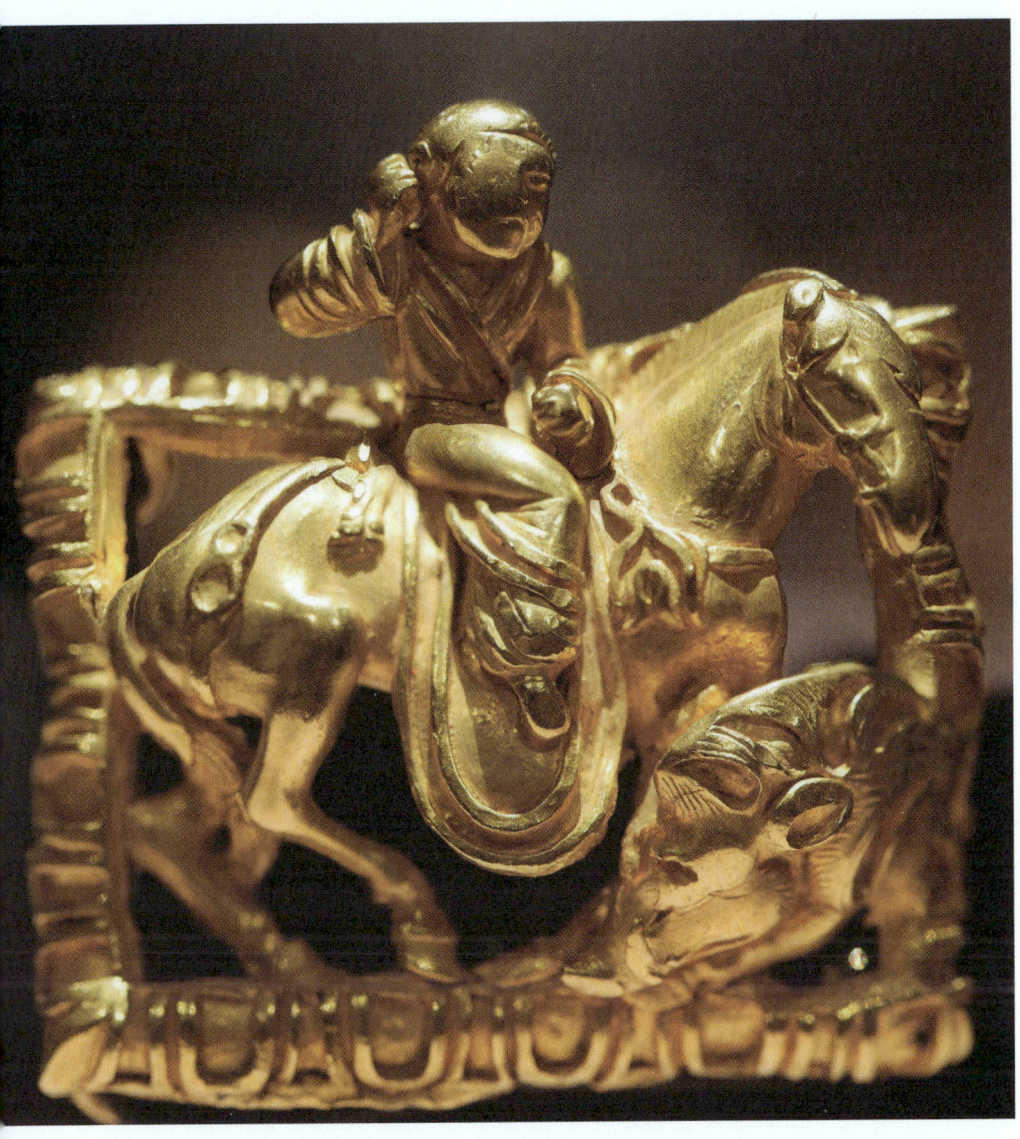

This decorative belt plaque may have been made specifically for a Xiongnu patron. The rider is dressed in characteristically steppe clothing and his hair is fashioned in an East Asian steppe fashion. The horse is also wearing characteristically Xiongnu accessories.

sacrifices and luxury goods, including coins and other imported objects from China, and rugs and textiles from Bactria and Parthia.

The most opulent burials were the terrace tombs flanked by satellite burials, interpreted as being for the highest echelons of the Xiongnu Empire. Constructed out of rectangular or trapezoidal earthen platforms, these tombs were elevated about one metre above the ground and could measure as large as forty-six metres squared. Raised terraces were enclosed with stone, and the surface was divided into different sections. Each tomb has a descending ramp varying in length from eight to eighteen metres, and taking the shape of an inverse pyramid. The ramp ends at a steep drop before the bottom of the tomb chamber, meaning that it is less likely to have been used to bring the deceased's body into the burial and probably served a ritual function.[17]

Most of the terrace tombs had wooden burial chambers built inside that housed multi-layer coffins, some of which had diamond-shaped gold foil patterns with flowers in the centre. These chambers had a layer of stone constructed on top of them, and one showed significant signs of ritual burning on top of it.[18] Covered with various kinds of greenery, pinecones, and wood, an enormous fire was lit over the burial chamber and the pit was filled in while the flames were still dying down.

Terrace tombs were filled with elite luxury items such as Han-style lacquer ware, sets of horse gear in gold and silver, and even Han-style carriages. What's interesting to note is that some of the richest, high-status tomb complexes in the frontier regions of the Xiongnu Empire appear to have belonged to women.[19] While more research is needed, this could indicate the powerful role that women played within the upper echelons of Xiongnu society.

Related to the Huns?

There has been some speculation over the years as to whether the Huns, who appeared in the west almost 250 years after the Xiongnu, were in some way related to this Empire. Archaeologists have looked at the material culture of the Huns in comparison to the Xiongnu, and while some items can be traced from the east, none originate as far into Inner Asian regions where the Xiongnu lived. While the Xiongnu could have made it farther west than is currently known, it is unlikely that the Huns originated from them. Instead, some scholars have linked the Mongols to the same ethnic group as the Xiongnu.[20] Regardless of how the Xiongnu culture ended or what it transformed into, it is certain that they were influential enough to leave a profound influence on later steppe cultures and civilisations, and the nomads that roamed those lands.

Acknowledgements

This book would not exist without Hugo Villabona from Mango reaching out to me to ask if I wanted to write about my passion. I had just come out of a long hiatus from sharing stories of the ancient world, and needless to say, this project allowed me to dive back into the world I thought I no longer had a place in. Thank you for your patience as I waded through the waters of being a first-time author and my outdated method of research and note taking.

To my London crew, thank you for your patience and for always extending an invite even though you knew I would be chained to my desk. Daniel Nuth was always there with a supportive message to keep going after every chapter; Harry Cumming reminded me to always go at my own pace. Eva Otlewski and Eric Leon are planners extraordinaire and have always shown up when it mattered throughout the year—without exception. Dr. Jay Sullivan made the British Library feel a little bit more like home. Countless others always maintained their enthusiasm and asked for progress reports whenever I resurfaced. If I tried to name you all I'd no doubt forget some, so I will extend my undying gratitude to you in person. I promise that you will be seeing a lot more of me from now on.

Across the pond back home, my mother, Sheila, and grandparents Gilbert and Irene are the reason I have had the bravery to accomplish all that I have in this life. Danielle, Melissa, and Tasha, thank you for being my core. The decades we have known each other speak louder than any words ever could. A good teacher can be one of the most important influences on your life; I was extremely privileged to have four. To Mr. Scallen, Symeonides, Bennett, and Kerr (not forgetting his two-headed llama), thank you for continuing to inspire this self-proclaimed history nerd through some very tumultuous years.

Call it a twist of fate, or just a coincidence, but I am so privileged to call Dr. Judyta Olszewski a friend. Her voice echoes through most of these chapters, whether through physical edits or between the lines in the countless voice notes filled with my rambles while trying to sort everything out. Jude, you have helped me through more than just my academic career and have become a true pillar in my life.

Thank you to all those who read chapters, provided feedback, and pointed me in the right direction with my research, especially Teresa Wight, Alexandra Slucky, and Dr. Matthew Piscitelli. And to Rose Woollett for coming on in the final months to make the most extraordinary book cover and maps, thank you for learning geography for me.

It is amazing who you might cross paths with once you start sharing your life on the internet. Over the past two years, two such women have reminded me just how powerful female friendships are. Erica Stevenson has been my number one fan from the start, and I am now hers. From putting in countless hours to help this book reach as many people as possible, to being an ear when things got hard, she has been a rock on which many of my waves have crashed. From Venus de Milo earrings sent to the other side of the world during the pandemic, to finally connecting in London with a series of (sometimes) unorthodox shenanigans, Cosima Carnegie is a tour de force to have in your corner. I only hope I can return the unconditional love, support, and friendship that you both have given me in kind.

Most importantly, Luke. Thank you for everything. Words cannot begin to describe how much you have meant to me over the past year. This book could not have been written without your unwavering support, your knowing when I needed to take a break and your pep talks when I was ready to walk away from it all and needed the motivation to go on. Thank you for the meal prep, the countless teas, and for staying up late for nights on end while I worked away at the desk of our Murphy bed. I love you, *ya ruhi.*

Finally, to my amazing community on YouTube, Instagram, and all other social platforms. Thank you for sticking with me all these years. Through the countless ups and downs, I would not be here if it wasn't for your unwavering support. Little did I know that deciding one day to rant about archaeology on my phone in an Airbnb after I had just moved to Germany with no friends or hope of learning the language, would have turned into what it is today. I owe all of this to you, and I will dedicate the rest of my archaeological career to sharing as much wonder about the ancient world as humanly possible. Stay dirty, my friends. ;)

Bibliography

Adams, E. (2017) *Cultural Identity in Minoan Crete Social Dynamics in the Neopalatial Period*. New York: Cambridge University Press.

Adams, W.Y. (1977) *Nubia: Corridor to Africa*. Princeton: Princeton University Press.

Al Halwachi, H. (2020) 'The Copper Bull's Head at Barbar Temple: Chemical Composition and Casting Alloy,' *Journal of Archaeological Science: Reports*, 32, p. 102390. doi:10.1016/j.jasrep.2020.102390.

Al Thani, Haya. (2005) *Making Dilmun seals speak : stylistic elements of Dilmun glyptics and their implication for social and economic life in early Dilmun c. 2000–1800 BCE/ Haya Al-Thani*. Thesis (PhD Archaeology)—University of London, 2005.

Alberti, B. (2002) 'Gender and Figurative Art of Late Bronze Age Knossos,' in Y. Hamilakis (ed.) *Labyrinth Revisited: Rethinking 'Minoan' Archaeology*. Oxford: Oxbow Books, pp. 98–117.

Alexeyev, A.Y. (2017) 'The Scythians in Eurasia,' in S.J. Simpson and S. Pankova (eds.) *Scythians Warriors of Ancient Siberia*. London: Thames and Hudson, pp. 20–26.

Alt, S. (2008) 'Unwilling Immigrants: Culture Change and the "Other" in Mississippian Societies,' in C.M. Catherine (ed.) *Invisible Citizens: Slavery in Ancient Pre-state Societies*. Salt Lake City: University of Utah Press, pp. 205–222.

Ambrose, S.H. and Krigbaum, J. (2003) 'Bone Chemistry and Bioarchaeology,' *Journal of Anthropological Archaeology*, 22(3), pp. 191–192. doi:10.1016/s0278-4165(03)00032-1.

Ambrose, W. (2019) 'Plaited Textile Expression in Lapita Ceramic Ornamentation,' in S. Bedford and M. Spriggs (eds.) *Debating Lapita: Distribution, Chronology, Society and Subsistence*. Acton ACT: Australian National University Press, pp. 241–256.

Andersen, H. (2003) *The Barbar Temples*. Højbjerg: Jutland Archaeological Society.

Anthony, D.W. (1990) 'Migration in Archeology: The Baby and the Bathwater,' *American Anthropologist*, 92(4), pp. 895–914. doi:10.1525/aa.1990.92.4.02a00030.

Atwood, R. (2011) 'The Nok of Nigeria,' *Archaeology*.

Bagnall, R. *et al.* (2013) 'Akkad (Agade),' in *The Encyclopedia of Ancient History*. Malden, MA: Wiley-Blackwell, pp. 266–267.

Bartoloni, G. (2014) 'Gli atigiani metallurghi e il processo formativo nelle « Origini » degli Etruschi,' *Mélanges de l'École française de Rome. Antiquité* [Preprint], (126–2). doi:10.4000/mefra.2314.

Bawden, G. (1996) *The Moche*. Cambridge, MA: Blackwell.

Beckman, G.M., Bryce, T. and Cline, E.H. (2012) *The Ahhiyawa Texts*. Atlanta: Society of Biblical Literature.

Beckwith, C.I. (2009) *Empires of the Silk Road: A History of Central Eurasia from the Bronze Age to the Present*. Princeton, NJ: Princeton University Press.

Bedford, S. and Spriggs, M. (2007) 'Birds on the Rim: A Unique Lapita Carinated Vessel in its Wider Context,' *Archaeology in Oceania*, 42(1), pp. 12–21. doi:10.1002/j.1834-4453.2007.tb00010.x.

Best, S. (2004) *Lapita: A View from the East*. Auckland: New Zealand Archaeological Association (Monograph 24).

Beyer Williams, B. (2021) 'Kush in the Wider World During the Kerma Period,' in G. Emberling and B. Beyer Williams (eds.) *The Oxford Handbook of Ancient Nubia*. Oxford: Oxford Academic, pp. 178–200.

Beyer Williams, B. and Emberling, G. (2021) 'Nubia, a Brief Introduction,' in G. Emberling and B. Beyer Williams (eds.) *The Oxford Handbook of Ancient Nubia*. Oxford: Oxford Academic, pp. 1–4.

Billman, B.R. (2010) 'How Moche Rulers Came to Power: Investigating the Emergence of the Moche Political Economy,' in J. Quilter and L.J. Castillo (eds.) *New Perspectives on Moche Political Organization*. Washington, DC: Dumbarton Oaks Research Library and Collection, pp. 181–200.

Binford, L.R. (2001) *Constructing Frames of Reference: An Analytical Method for Archaeological Theory Building Using Hunter-Gatherer and Environmental Data Sets*. Berkeley: University of California Press.

Bodine, J.J. (2009) 'The Shabaka Stone: An Introduction,' *Studia Antiqua*, 7(1).

Boëthius, A. (1978) Etruscan and Early Roman Architecture, revised by Rasmussen, T. and Ling, R. Harmondsworth: Penguin Books.

Bourget, S. (2005) 'Rituals of Sacrifice: Its Practice at Huaca de la Luna and its Representation in Moche Iconography,' in J. Pillsbury (ed.) *Moche Art and Archaeology in Ancient Peru*. Washington: National Gallery of Art, pp. 89–109.

Boutin, A.T. et al. (2012) 'Face to Face with the Past: Reconstructing a Teenage Boy from Early Dilmun,' *Near Eastern Archaeology*, 75(2), pp. 68–79. doi:10.5615/neareastarch.75.2.0068.

Bowersock, G.W. (2008) 'The Nabataeans in Historical Context,' in G. Markoe (ed.) *Petra Rediscovered: Lost City of the Nabataeans*. London: Thames & Hudson, pp. 19–26.

Brandt, G. (2017) *Beständig ist nur der Wandel! Die Rekonstruktion der Besiedelungsgeschichte Europas während des Neolithikums mittels paläo—und populationsgenetischer Verfahren*. Forschungsberichte des Landesmuseums für Vorgeschichte Halle 9. Halle (Saale): Landesamt für Denkmalpflege und Archäologie Sachsen-Anhalt.

Braudel, F. (1994) *A History of Civilizations*. Translated by R. Mayne. New York: Penguin Books.

Breunig, P. (2017) *Exploring the Nok Culture* Peter Dahm Robertson. Translated by P.D. Robertson. Frankfurt: Goethe University, Institute for Archaeological Sciences.

Breunig, P. and Rupp, N. (2016) 'An Outline of Recent Studies on the Nigerian Nok Culture,' *Journal of African Archaeology*, 14(3), pp. 237–255.

Briquel, D. (2013) 'Etruscan Origins and the Ancient Authors,' in J.M. Turfa (ed.) *The Etruscan World*. London and New York: Routledge, pp. 36–55.

Brosseder, U. (2009) 'Xiongnu Terrace Tombs and their Interpretation as Elite Burials,' in H.P. Jan Bemmann, E. Pohl, and D. Tseveendorzh (eds.) *Current Archaeological Research in Mongolia* (Bonn Contributions to Asian Archaeology, Bonn Univ. Press), pp. 247–280.

Brosseder, U. (2016) 'Xiongnu Empire,' in J. Mackenzie (ed.) *The Encyclopedia of Empire*. 1st ed. Wiley Online Library. doi.org/10.1002/9781118455074.wbeoe149.

Brosseder, U. and Miller, B.K. (2011) "State of Research and Future Direction of Xiongnu Studies." In U. Brosseder and B. K. Miller (Eds.), *Xiongnu Archaeology: Multidisciplinary Perspectives of the First Steppe Empire in Inner Asia*. Bonn Contributions to Asian Archaeology 5. Bonn: vfgarch.press uni-bonn, pp. 19–33

Brown, J.A. (1996) *The Spiro Ceremonial Center: The Archaeology of Arkansas Valley Caddoan Culture in Eastern Oklahoma*. Museum of Anthropology, Memoirs 29. Ann Arbor: University of Michigan.

Bryce, T. (1998) *The Kingdom of the Hittites*. Oxford: Oxford University Press.

Bryce, T. (2005) *The Trojans and Their Neighbours*. London: Routledge.

Bryce, T. (2019) *Warriors of Anatolia: A Concise History of the Hittites*. London: I. B. Tauris & Company, Limited.

Bryce, T. and Birkett-Rees, J. (2016) *Atlas of the Ancient Near East: from Prehistoric Times to the Roman Imperial Period*. New York: Routledge.

Burch, E.S. (2006) *Social life in Northwest Alaska: The Structure of Iñupiaq Eskimo Nations*. Fairbanks: University of Alaska Press.

Burley, D.V., Freeland, T. and Balenaivalu, J. (2019) 'Small Islands, Strategic Locales and the Configuration of First Lapita Settlement of Vanua Levu, Northern Fiji,' in S. Bedford and M. Spriggs (eds.) *Debating Lapita: Distribution, Chronology, Society and Subsistence*. Acton ACT: Australian National University Press, pp. 155–167.

Castleden, R. (2016) *Minoans: Life in Bronze Age Crete*. London: Routledge.

Castillo Butters, L.J. (2010) 'Moche Politics in the Jequetepeque Valley: A Case for Political Opportunism,' in J. Quilter and L.J. Castillo Butters (eds.) *New Perspectives on Moche Political Organization*. Washington, DC: Dumbarton Oaks Research Library and Collection, pp. 83–109.

Castillo Butters, L.J. and Uceda Castillo, S. (2008) 'The Mochicas,' in H. Silverman and W.H. Isbell (eds.) *Handbook of South American Archaeology*. New York: Springer, pp. 707–730.

Ceccarelli, L. (2016) 'The Romanization of Etruria' in S. Bell and A.A. Carpino (eds.) *A Companion to the Etruscans*. West Sussex: John Wiley & Sons, Inc, pp. 28–40.

Chang, C. (2012) 'Lines of Power: Equality or Hierarchy Among the Iron Age Agro-Pastoralists of Southeastern Kazakhstan,' in C.W. Hartley, Y.G. Bike, and A.T. Smith (eds.) *The Archaeology of Power and Politics in Eurasia: Regimes and Revolutions*. Cambridge: Cambridge University Press, pp. 122–142.

Chakrabarti, D.K. (ed.) (2004) *Indus Civilization sites in India: New Discoveries*. Mumbai: Marg Publications on behalf of the National Centre for the Performing Arts.

Chapdelaine, C. (2005) 'The Growing Power of a Moche Urban Class,' in J. Pillsbury (ed.) *Moche Art and Archaeology in Ancient Peru*. Washington: National Gallery of Art, pp. 69–87.

Chirikure, S. (2020) *Great Zimbabwe: Reclaiming A 'Confiscated' Past*. Abingdon: Routledge.

Chirikure, S. and Pikirayi, I. (2008) 'Inside and Outside the Dry Stone Walls: Revisiting the Material Culture of Great Zimbabwe,' *Antiquity*, 82(318), pp. 976–993. doi:10.1017/s0003598x00097726.

Chirikure, S. *et al.* (2016) 'What was the population of Great Zimbabwe (CE 1000–1800)?' *PLOS ONE*, 12(6). doi:10.1371/journal.pone.0178335.

Chugunov, K.V., Rjabkova, T.V. and Simpson, S.J. (2017) 'Mounted Warriors,' in St John Simpson and S. Pankova (eds.) *Scythians Warriors of Ancient Siberia*. London: Thames and Hudson, pp. 194–201.

Cimadomo, P. (2018) 'The Controversial Annexation of the Nabataean Kingdom,' *Levant*, 50(2), pp. 258–266. doi:10.1080/00758914.2019.1614769.

Clark, J.E. (1994) 'El Sistema Economico de Los "Primeros Plmecas,"' in J.E. Clark (ed.) *Los Olmecas en Mesoamerica*. Mexico City: Citibank, pp. 189–201.

Cobb, C.R. and Butler, B.M. (2002) 'The Vacant Quarter Revisited: Late Mississippian Abandonment of the Lower Ohio Valley,' *American Antiquity*, 67(4), pp. 625–641. doi:10.2307/1593795.

Coe, M.D., Urcid, J. and Koontz, R. (2019) *Mexico: From the Olmecs to the Aztecs*. London: Thames & Hudson.

Collins, B.J. (2007) *The Hittites and Their World*. Leiden: Brill.

Coltrain, J.B., Tackney, J. and O'Rourke, D.H. (2016) 'Thule Whaling at Point Barrow, Alaska: The Nuvuk Cemetery Stable Isotope and Radiocarbon Record,' *Journal of Archaeological Science: Reports*, 9, pp. 681–694. doi:10.1016/j.jasrep.2016.08.011.

Conklin, E. (1998) *Getting Back into the Garden of Eden*. Lanham, MD: University Press of America.

Cork, E. (2005) 'Peaceful Harappans? Reviewing the Evidence for the Absence of Warfare in the Indus Civilisation of North-west India and Pakistan (c. 2500–1900 BC),' *Antiquity*, 79(304), pp. 411–423. doi:10.1017/s0003598x0011419x.

Crawford, H. (1996) 'Dilmun, victim of world recession,' Proceedings of the Seminar for Arabian Studies, 1996, Vol. 26, Papers from the twenty-ninth meeting of the Seminar for Arabian Studies held in Cambridge, 20–22 July 1995, pp. 13–22.

Crawford, H. (1998) *Dilmun and its Gulf Neighbours*. Cambridge: Cambridge University Press.

Cunliffe, B.W. (2019) *The Scythians: Nomad Warriors of the Steppe*. Oxford: Oxford University Press.

David, B., Alpin, K. and Peck, H. (2019) 'Moiapu 3: Settlement on Moiapu Hill at the Very End of Lapita, Caution Bay Hinterland,' in S. Bedford and M. Spriggs (eds.) *Debating Lapita: Distribution, Chronology, Society and Subsistence*. Acton ACT: Australian National University Press, pp. 61–88.

Dawson, P. (2016) 'The Thule-Inuit Succession in the Central Arctic,' in T.M. Friesen and O.K. Mason (eds.) *The Oxford Handbook of the Prehistoric Arctic*. New York: Oxford University Press, pp. 915–936.

Dawson, P. *et al.* (2007) 'Simulating the Behaviour of Light Inside Arctic Dwellings: Implications for Assessing the Role of Vision in Task Performance,' *World Archaeology*, 39(1), pp. 17–35. doi:10.1080/00438240601136397.

Di Cosmo, N. 2011. "Ethnogenesis, Coevolution and Political Morphology of the Earliest Steppe Empire: The Xiongnu Question Revisited." In U. Brosseder and B. K. Miller (Eds.), *Xiongnu Archaeology: Multidisciplinary Perspectives of the First Steppe Empire in Inner Asia*. Bonn Contributions to Asian Archaeology 5. Bonn: vfgarch. press uni-bonn, pp. 35–48.

Diehl, R.A. (2004) *The Olmecs: America's First Civilization*. London: Thames & Hudson.

Diehl, R.A. and Coe, M.D.(1995) 'Olmec Archaeology,' in E.P. Benson and J. Guthrie (eds.) *The Olmec World Ritual and Rulership*. Princeton: The Art Museum, Princeton University, pp. 11–25.

Driessen, J. (2021) 'Revisiting the Minoan Palaces: Ritual Commensality at Sissi,' *Antiquity*, 95(381), pp. 686–704. doi:10.15184/aqy.2021.30.

Donnan, C.B. (2004) *Moche Portraits from Ancient Peru*. Austin: University of Texas Press.

During Caspers, E.C.L. (1971) 'The Bull's Head from Barbar Temple II, A Contact with Early Dynastic Sumer,' *East and West* 21: 217–233.

Durusu-Tanrıöver, M. (2023) 'Signs of Ancient Climate Crisis as the Hittite Empire Unravelled,' *Nature*, 614(7949), pp. 625–626. doi:10.1038/d41586-023-00271-2.

Dye, D.H. (2004) 'Art, Ritual, and Chiefly Warfare in the Mississippian World,' in R.V. Sharp (ed.) *Hero, Hawk and Open Hand: American Indian Art of the Ancient Midwest and South*. New Haven: Yale University Press, pp. 191–206.

Eidem, J. and Højlund, F. (1993) 'Trade or diplomacy? Assyria and Dilmun in the Eighteenth Century BC,' *World Archaeology*, 24(3), pp. 441–448. doi:10.1080/00438243.1993.9980218.

Emerson, T. E.(1989). Water, serpents, and the underworld: An exploration into Cahokian symbolism. In *The southern ceremonial complex: Artifacts and analysis: The Cottonlandia Conference*, ed. P. Galloway. Lincoln: University of Nebraska Press. 45–92.

Emerson, T.E. (1997) *Cahokia and the Archaeology of Power*. Tuscaloosa: University of Alabama Press.

Emerson, T.E. (2007) 'Cahokia and the Evidence for Late Pre-Columbian War in the North American Midcontinent,' in R.J. Chacon and R.G. Mendoza (eds.) *North American Indigenous Warfare and Ritual Violence*. Tucson: University of Arizona Press, pp. 129–148.

Emerson, T.E. and Lewis, R.B. (1991) *Cahokia and the Hinterlands: Middle Mississippian Cultures of the Midwest*. Urbana and Chicago: University of Illinois Press.

Erickson CL (2008) Amazonia: The historical ecology of a domesticated landscape. In: Silverman H, Isbell WH (eds) *The Handbook of South American Archaeology*. New York: Springer, pp. 157–183.

Ernée, M. (2012) 'Amber in Czech Únětice (Aunjetitz) Culture—On the Origin of the Amber Route,' *Památky archeologické*, 103, pp. 71–172.

Evans, S.T. (2013) *Ancient Mexico & Central America: Archaeology and Culture History*. 3rd ed. New York: Thames & Hudson.

Fagg, A. (1994) 'Thoughts on Nok,' *African Arts*, 27(3), pp. 79–83 + 103. doi:10.2307/3337204.

Farmer, S., Sproat, R. and Witzel, M. (2004) 'The Collapse of the Indus-Script Thesis: The Myth of a Literate Harappan Civilization,' *Electronic Journal of Vedic Studies*, 11(2), pp. 19–57.

Feinman, G.M. and Carballo, D.M. (2022) 'Communication, Computation, and Governance: A Multiscalar Vantage on the Prehispanic Mesoamerican World,' *Journal of Social Computing*, 3(1), pp. 91–118. doi:10.23919/jsc.2021.0015.

Finkelstein, S.A., Ross, J.M. and Adams, J.K. (2009) 'Spatiotemporal Variability in Arctic Climates of the Past Millennium: Implications for the Study of Thule Culture on Melville Peninsula, Nunavut,' *Arctic, Antarctic, and Alpine Research*, 41(4), pp. 442–454. doi:10.1657/1938-4246-41.4.442.

Fitton, J.L. (2002) *Peoples of the Past: Minoans*. London: British Museum Press.

Forrer, E. (1924) 'Die Griechen in den Boghazköi-Texten,' *Orientalistische Literaturzeitung*, 27(1–6). doi:10.1524/olzg.1924.27.16.57.

Foster, B. R. (2013) 'Akkad (Agade),' in Roger S. Bagnall, Kai Brodersen, Craige B. Champion, Andrew Eskine, and Sabine R. Huebner (eds.) *The Encyclopedia of Ancient History*. Malden, MA: Wiley-Blackwell, pp. 266–267.

Franke, G. (2016) 'A Chronology of the Central Nigerian Nok Culture—1500 BC to the Beginning of the Common Era,' *Journal of African Archaeology*, 14(3), pp. 257–289.

Freidel, D.A., Schele, L. and Parker, J. (1993) *Maya Cosmos*. New York: William Morrow.

Friesen, T.M. (2016) 'Pan-Arctic Population Movements: The Early Paleo-Inuit Migrations,' in T.M. Friesen and O.K. Mason (eds.) *The Oxford Handbook of the Prehistoric Arctic*. New York: Oxford University Press, pp. 673–692.

Friesen, T.M. and Arnold, C.D. (2008) 'The Timing of the Thule Migration: New Dates from the Western Canadian Arctic,' *American Antiquity*, 73(3), pp. 527–538. doi:10.1017/s0002731600046850.

Galipaud, J.C. (2006) 'The First Millennium B.C. in Remote Oceania: An Alternative Perspective on Lapita,' in I. Lilley (ed.) *Archaeology of Oceania Australia and the Pacific Islands*. Malden: Blackwell, pp. 228–239.

Garlake, P.S. (1973) *Great Zimbabwe: New Aspects of Archaeology*. London: Thames & Hudson.

Gentelle, P. (2009) 'Aménagement du Territoire Agricole de la Ville de Pétra: La Terre et l'eau,' *Stratégies d'acquisition de l'eau et société au Moyen-Orient depuis l'Antiquité*, pp. 133–148. doi:10.4000/books.ifpo.1315.

Gibbons, A. (1993) 'How the Akkadian Empire was Hung out to Dry,' *Science*, 261(5124), pp. 985. doi:10.1126/science.261.5124.985.

Gijseghem, H.V. (2001) 'Household and Family at Moche, Peru: An Analysis of Building and Residence Patterns in a Prehispanic Urban Center,' *Latin American Antiquity*, 12(3), pp. 257–273. doi:10.2307/971632.

Gimbutas, M. (1965) *Bronze Age Culture in Central and Eastern Europe*. Paris: Mouton.

Graf, D.F. (2007) 'The Nabataeans Under Roman Rule (After AD 106),' in K.D. Politis (ed.) *The World of the Nabataeans: Volume 2 of the International Conference 'The World of the Herods and the Nabataeans' Held at the British Museum, 17–19 April 2001*. Stuttgart: Franz Steiner, pp. 173–186.

Graf, D.F. and Sidebotham, S.E. (2008) 'Nabataean Trade,' in G. Markoe (ed.) *Petra Rediscovered: Lost City of the Nabataeans*. London: Thames & Hudson, pp. 65–74.

Gralak, T. (2021) 'The Nature of Artistic Expression of the Únětice Culture's People,' *Studia Hercynia*, 24(1), pp. 66–77.

Green, A.S. (2020) 'Killing the Priest-King: Addressing Egalitarianism in the Indus Civilization,' *Journal of Archaeological Research*, 29(2), pp. 153–202. doi:10.1007/s10814-020-09147-9.

Gross, M. (2021) 'Saving Scythians from Oblivion,' *Current Biology*, 31(8), pp. R359–R361. doi:10.1016/j.cub.2021.04.004.

Grove, D.C. (1981) 'Olmec monuments: mutilation as a clue to meaning,' in E.P. Benson (ed.) *The Olmec and Their Neighbors: Essays in Memory of Matthew W. Stirling*. Washington, DC: Dumbarton Oaks Research Library and Collections, pp. 48–68.

Gulløv, H.C. (1997) *From Middle Ages to Colonial Times: Archeological and Ethnohistorical Studies of the Thule Culture in South West Greenland 1300–1800 AD*. Copenhagen: Dansk Polar Center.

Gulløv, H. C., & McGhee, R. (2006) 'Did Bering Strait people initiate the Thule migration?' *Alaska Journal of Anthropology*, 4(1–2), pp. 54–63.

Guzzo, M.G.A. and Schneider, E.E. (2002) *Petra*. Chicago: University of Chicago Press.

Habu, J. (2004) *Ancient Jomon of Japan*. Cambridge: Cambridge University Press.

Hammond, P.C. (1973) *The Nabataeans: Their History, Culture and Archaeology (Studies in Mediterranean Archaeology, V. 37)*. Gothenburg: Paul Astroms Forlag.

Healey, J.F. (2001) *The Religion of the Nabataeans: A Conspectus*. Leiden, etc.: Brill.

Heurgon, J. and Linderski, J. (2012). 'Religion, Etruscan,' *The Oxford Classical History*. 4th ed. Oxford: Oxford University Press.

Higgins, R.A. (1981) *Minoan and Mycenaen Art*. Oxford: Oxford University Press.

Hoffner, H.A. (2003) 'Daily Life Among the Hittites,' in R.E. Averbeck and D.B. Weisberg (eds.) *Life and Culture in the Ancient Near East*. Bethesda: CDL Press, pp. 95–118.

Houmard, C. and Grønnow, B. (2017) 'A Technological Study of a Canadian Thule Type-Site: Naujan (ca. AD 1300–1900),' *Bulletin de la Société Préhistorique Française*, 114(3), pp. 445–468. doi:10.3406/bspf.2017.14802.

Huffman, T.N. (1987) *Symbols in Stone: Unravelling the Mystery of Great Zimbabwe*. Johannesburg: Witwatersrand University Press.

Ibrahim, M. (1982) *Excavations of the Arab Expedition at Sar El-Jisr, Bahrain*. Manamah: State of Bahrain, Ministry of Information.

Ishjamts, N. (1994) 'Nomads in Eastern Central Asia,' in J. Harmatta, B.N. Puri, and G.F. Etemad (eds.) *History of Civilizations of Central Asia Volume II: The Development of Sedentary and Nomadic Civilizations: 700 BC to AD 250*. Paris: Unesco Publishing, pp. 151–170.

Jansen, M. (1989) 'Water Supply and Sewage Disposal at Mohenjo Daro,' *World Archaeology*, 21(2), pp. 177–192. doi:10.1080/00438243.1989.9980100.

Jimenez Salas, O. H. (1990). Geomorfologia de la region de La Venta, Tabasco: un sistema fluvio-lagunar costero del cuatemario. Arqueologia (Segunda Epoca) 3: 5–16, Direction de Arqueologia del INAH, Mexico.

Johnson, J.A. (2020) 'Trade, Community and Labour in the Pontic Iron Age Forest-Steppe Region, c. 700–200 BC,' *Masters of the Steppe: The Impact of the Scythians and Later Nomad Societies of Eurasia*, pp. 198–209. doi:10.2307/j.ctv1fcf8hh.20.

Jolicoeur, P. (2006) *Early Inuit (Thule Culture), The Canadian Encyclopedia*. Available at: www.thecanadianencyclopedia.ca/en/article/thule-culture (Accessed: 16 January 2024).

Kansa, S.W. and MacKinnon, M. (2014) 'Etruscan Economics: Forty-Five Years of Faunal Remains from Poggio Civitate,' *Etruscan Studies*, 17(1), pp. 63–87. doi:10.1515/etst-2014-0001.

Kenoyer, J.M. (1998) *Ancient Cities of the Indus Valley Civilization*. Oxford: Oxford University Press.

Kenrick, D.M. (1995) *Jomon of Japan: The World's Oldest Pottery*. London: Kegan Paul International.

Kerr, R.A. (1998) 'Sea-Floor Dust Shows Drought Felled Akkadian Empire,' *Science*, 279(5349), pp. 325–326. doi:10.1126/science.279.5349.325.

Kirch, P.V. (1988) 'Long Distance Exchange and Island Colonization: The Lapita Case,' *Norwegian Archaeological Review*, 21(2), pp. 103–117. doi:10.1080/00293652.1988.9965475.

Kirch, P.V. (1996) 'Lapita and its Aftermath: The Austronesian Settlement of Oceania,' *Transactions of the American Philosophical Society*, 86(5), pp. 57–70. doi:10.2307/1006621.

Kirch, P.V. (1997) *The Lapita Peoples: Ancestors of the Oceanic World*. Cambridge: Blackwell Publishers.

Kneisel, J. (2012) 'The Problem of the Middle Bronze Age Inception in Northeast Europe—or: Did the Únětice Society Collapse?' in J. Kneisel et al. (eds.) *Collapse of Continuity?: Environment and Development of Bronze Age Human Landscapes. Proceedings of the International Workshop 'Socio-Environmental Dynamics Over the Last 12,000 Years: The Creation of Landscapes' (14th–18th March 2011) In Kiel*. Bonn: Habelt, pp. 209–233.

Knoll, F. & Meller, H. (2016) 'Die Ösenkopfnadel—Ein »Klassen«-verbindendes Trachtelement der Aunjetitzer Kultur. Ein Beitrag zu Kontext, Interpretation und Typochronologie der mitteldeutschen Exemplare In Meller H., Hahn, H.P., Jung, R. & Risch, R. (eds) 2016, *Rich and Poor—Competing for Resources In Prehistoric Societies [Arm und Reich—Zur Ressourcenverteilung in prähistorischen Gesellschaften]*, 283–370. Halle (Saale): Tagungen des Landesmuseums für Vorgeschichte Halle 14.

Kobayashi, T. and Nakamura, O. (2004) *Jomon Reflections: Forager Life and Culture in the Prehistoric Japanese Archipelago*. Oxford: Oxbow.

Kolb, B. (2007) 'Nabataean Private Architecture,' in K.D. Politis (ed.) *The World of the Nabataeans: Volume 2 of the International Conference 'The World of the Herods and the Nabataeans' Held at the British Museum, 17–19 April 2001*. Stuttgart: Franz Steiner, pp. 145–172.

Kolb, B. (2008) 'Petra—From Tent to Mansion: Living on the Terraces of Ez-Zantur,' in G. Markoe (ed.) *Petra Rediscovered: Lost City of the Nabataeans*. London: Thames & Hudson, pp. 230–238.

Koons, M.L. (2015) 'Moche Sociopolitical Dynamics and the Role of Licapa II, Chicama Valley, Peru,' *Latin American Antiquity*, 26(4), pp. 473–492. doi:10.7183/1045-6635.26.4.473.

Koons, M.L. and Alex, B.A. (2014) 'Revised Moche Chronology Based on Bayesian Models of Reliable Radiocarbon Dates,' *Radiocarbon*, 56(3), pp. 1039–1055. doi:10.2458/56.16919.

Korolkova, E. (2020) ' "Animal Style" Art: Influences and Traditions in the Nomadic World,' *Masters of the Steppe: The Impact of the Scythians and Later Nomad Societies of Eurasia*, pp. 216–226. doi:10.2307/j.ctv1fcf8hh.22.

Kramer, S.N. (1981) *History Begins at Sumer: 39 Firsts in Man's Recorded History*. Philadelphia: University of Pennsylvania Press.

Larsen, C.E. (1983) *Life and land use on the Bahrain Islands: The Geoarchaeology of an Ancient Society*. Chicago: University of Chicago Press.

Laursen, S.T. (2008) 'Early Dilmun and its Rulers: New Evidence of the Burial Mounds of the Elite and the Development of Social Complexity, c. 2200–1750 BC,' *Arabian Archaeology and Epigraphy*, 19(2), pp. 156–167. doi:10.1111/j.1600-0471.2008.00298.x.

Laursen, S.T. (2017) *Royal Mounds of A'ali in Bahrain: The Emergence of Kingship in Early Dilmun*. Vol. 100. Aarhus: Aarhus University Press.

Lee, H. et al. (2019) 'Traumatic Injury in a Cranium Found at Rakhigarhi Cemetery of Harappan Civilization as Anthropological Evidence of Interpersonal Violence,' *Journal of Archaeological Science: Reports*, 23, pp. 362–367. doi:10.1016/j.jasrep.2018.11.001.

Lee, J. et al. (2023) 'Genetic Population Structure of the Xiongnu Empire at Imperial and Local Scales,' *Science Advances*, 9 eadf3904 (15). doi:10.1126/sciadv.adf3904.

Lilley, I. (2019) 'Lapita: The Australian Connection,' in S. Bedford and M. Spriggs (eds.) *Debating Lapita: Distribution, Chronology, Society and Subsistence*. Acton ACT: Australian National University Press, pp. 105–114.

Linduff, K.M. (2008) 'The Gender of Luxury and Power Among the Xiongnu in Eastern Eurasia,' in K.M. Linduff and K.S. Rubinson (eds.) *Are All Warriors Male? Gender Roles on the Ancient Eurasian Steppe*. Lanham: AltaMira Press, pp. 175–194.

Liverani, M. (2014) *The Ancient Near East: History, Society and Economy* Soraia Tabatabai. Translated by S. Tabatabai. London: Routledge.

Lockho, N. and E. Pernicka (2014) 'Archaeometallurgical investigations of Early Bronze Age gold artefacts from central Germany including gold from the Nebra hoard,' in: H. Meller, R. Risch, E. Pernicka (eds.), *Metalle der Macht—Frühes Gold und Silber*. Halle (Saale): Tagungen des Landesmuseums für Vorgeschichte Halle 11, pp. 223–235.

Lorenz, J. and Schrakamp, I. (2011) 'Hittite Military and Warfare,' in H. Genz and D.P. Mielke (eds.) *Insights into Hittite History and Archaeology*. Leuven: Peeters, pp. 125–152.

Luckenbill, D.D. (1927) *The Annals of Sennacherib, Chicago*. Chicago: University of Chicago Press.

MacGillivray, J.A. (1994) 'The Early History of the Palace at Knossos (MMI–II),' in D. Evely, H. Hughes-Brock, and N. Momigliano (eds.) *Knossos, a Labyrinth of History: Papers Presented in Honour of Sinclair Hood: The British School at Athens*. Oxford: British School at Athens, pp. 45–55.

Macqueen, J.G. (1986) *The Hittites and Their Contemporaries in Asia*. London: Thames and Hudson.

Männel, T. M., and Breunig, P. (2016). The Nok Terracotta Sculptures of Pangwari. *Journal of African Archaeology* 14, 3, 313–329. doi.org/10.3213/2191-5784-10300.

Marinatos, N. (1989). The bull as an adversary: Some observations on bull-hunting and bullleaping. Ariadne 5, 23–32.

Mason, O.K. (2009) 'Flight from the Bering Strait: Did Siberian Punuk/Thule Military Cadres Conquer Northwest Alaska?' in H. Maschner, O.K. Mason, and R. McGhee (eds.) *The Northern World, AD 900–1400*. Salt Lake City: University of Utah Press, pp. 76–128.

Mason, O.K. (2020) 'The Thule Migrations as an Analog for the Early Peopling of the Americas: Evaluating Scenarios of Overkill, Trade, Climate Forcing, and Scalar Stress,' *PaleoAmerica*, 6(4), pp. 308–356. doi:10.1080/20555563.2020.1783969.

Mason, O.K. and Friesen, T.M. (2017) *Out of the Cold: Archaeology on the Arctic Rim of North America*. Washington, DC: The Society of American Archaeology Press.

Mathiassen, T. (1927) *The Thule Culture and its Position within the Eskimo Culture: Archaeology of the Central Eskimos Vol II*. Copenhagen: Gyldenda.

Maxwell, M.A. (1985) *Prehistory of the Eastern Arctic*. Orlando: Academic Press.

McCartney, A. P. (1991) 'Canadian Arctic Trade Metal: Reflections of Prehistoric to Historic Social Networks,' in R. M. Eherenreich (ed.) *Metals in Society: Theory Beyond Analysis*. Masca Research Papers in Archaeology Vol. 8. Philadelphia: Masca, The University Museum, University of Pennsylvania, pp. 27–43.

McCullough, K.M. (1989) *The Ruin Islanders: Early Thule Culture Pioneers in the Eastern High Arctic*. Hull: Canadian Museum of Civilization (Archaeological Survey of Canada. Mercury Series Paper 141).

McEnroe, J. (2010) Architecture of Minoan Crete: constructing identity in the Aegean Bronze Age. Austin: University of Texas Press.

McGhee, R. (2005) *The Last Imaginary Place: A Human History of the Arctic World*. Oxford: Oxford University Press.

McGhee, R. (2009a) 'When and Why did the Inuit Move to the Eastern Arctic?' in H.D. Maschner, O.K. Mason, and R. McGhee (eds.) *The Northern World, AD 900–1400*. Salt Lake City: University of Utah Press, pp. 155–163.

McGhee, R. (2009b) 'Thule population size and temporal duration of Thule culture in Arctic Canada,' in B. Grønnow (Ed.), *On the track of the Thule culture from Bering Strait to East Greenland. Papers in honour of Hans Christian Gulløv*. Copenhagen: National Museum of Denmark, pp. 75–89.

McIntosh, J.R. (2001) *A Peaceful Realm: The Rise and Fall of the Indus Civilization*. Boulder: Westview Press.

McIntosh, J.R. (2008) *The Ancient Indus Valley: New Perspectives*. Santa Barbara: ABC-CLIO.

McNairn, B. (1980) *The Method and Theory of V. Gordon Childe: Economic, Social, and Cultural Interpretations of Prehistory*. Edinburgh: Edinburgh University Press.

McPartland, J.M. and Hegman, W. (2017) 'Cannabis Utilization and Diffusion Patterns in Prehistoric Europe: A Critical Analysis of Archaeological Evidence,' *Vegetation History and Archaeobotany*, 27(4), pp. 627–634. doi:10.1007/s00334-017-0646-7.

Meggers, Betty J. and Evans, Clifford. (1957). 'Archeological investigations at the mouth of the Amazon,' *Bureau of American Ethnology Bulletin*. 167:1–664.

Mehrer, M. (2000) 'Heterarchy and Hierarchy: The Community Plan as Institution in Cahokia's Polity,' in M.A. Canuto and J. Yaeger (eds.) *Archaeology of Communities: A New World Perspective*. Abingdon, Oxon: Taylor and Francis, pp. 44–57.

Meller, H. (2013) 'Der Hortfund von Nebra im Spiegel frühbronzezeitlicher Deponierungssitten,' in H.-R. Bork et al. (eds.) *1600—Kultureller Umbruch im Schatten des Thera—AUSBRUCHS?* (Tagungen des Landesmuseums für Vorgeschichte Halle 9). Halle (Saale): Landesamt für Denkmalpflege und Archäologie Sachsen-Anhalt, pp. 493–526.

Meller, H. (2014) 'Die neolithischen und bronzezeitlichen Goldfunde Mitteldeutschlands—Eine Übersicht,' in H. Meller, R. Risch, and E. Pernicka (eds.) *Metalle der Macht—Frühes Gold und Silber. 6. Mitteldeutscher Archäologentag vom 17. bis 19. Oktober 2013 in Halle (Saale) (Tagungen des Landesmuseums für Vorgeschichte Halle 11)*. Halle (Saale): Landesamt f. Denkmalpflege u. Archäologie Sachsen-Anhalt, pp. 611–716.

Meller, H. (2017) 'Armies in the Early Bronze Age? An Alternative Interpretation of Únětice Culture Axe Hoards,' *Antiquity*, 91(360), pp. 1529–1545. doi:10.15184/aqy.2017.180.

Meller, H. (2019) 'Princes, Armies, Sanctuaries: The Emergence of Complex Authority in the Central German Únětice Culture,' *Acta Archaeologica*, 90(1), pp. 39–79. doi:10.1163/16000390-09001004.

Meller, H. (2021) 'Die Himmelsscheibe von Nebra—Astronomie und Zeitbestimmung als Quelle von Macht,' in H. Meller, A. Reichenberger, and R. Risch (eds.) *Zeit ist Macht. Wer macht Zeit? 13. Mitteldeutscher Archäologentag*. Halle [Saale]: Tagungen Landesmus. Vorgesch. Halle 24, pp. 149–163.

Messerschmidt, L. (1903) *The Hittites. The Ancient East, No. VI*. London: David Nutt.

Metropolitan Museum of Art (2000) *Nok Terracottas (500 B.C.–200 A.D.): Essay: The Metropolitan Museum of Art, The Met's Heilbrunn Timeline of Art History*. Available at: www.metmuseum.org/toah/hd/nok/hd_nok.htm#:~:text=Although%20terracottas%20are%20usually%20formed,tradition%20may%20have%20influenced%20them (Accessed: 20 April 2023).

Middleton, G.D. (2017) 'The Hittites and the Eastern Mediterranean,' in *Understanding Collapse: Ancient History and Modern Myths*. Cambridge: Cambridge University Press, pp. 155–181.

Milner, G.R. (1998) *The Cahokia Chiefdom: The Archaeology of a Mississippian Society*. Washington, DC: Smithsonian Institution Press.

Milner, G.R. (2007) 'Warfare, Population, and Food Production in Prehistoric Eastern North America,' in R.J. Chacon and R.G. Mendoza (eds.) *North American Indigenous Warfare and Ritual Violence*. Tucson: University of Arizona Press, pp. 181–201.

Milner, G.R. (2021) *The Moundbuilders: Ancient Societies of Eastern North America*. London: Thames & Hudson Ltd.

Mizoguchi, K. (2020) 'Making Sense of Material Culture Transformation: A Critical Long-Term Perspective from Jomon- and Yayoi-Period Japan,' *Journal of World Prehistory*, 33(1), pp. 1–23. doi:10.1007/s10963-020-09138-0.

Moorey, C. (2019) *A History of Crete*. Chicago: Haus Publishing.

Morrison, D. (1982) 'Thule Culture in Western Coronation Gulf, N.W.T.' *Archaeological Survey of Canada*, no. 116. doi:10.1353/book65349.

Nayeem, M.A. (1990) *Saudi Arabia; Volume One: Prehistory and protohistory of the Arabian Peninsula*. Hyderabad: Hyderabad Publishers.

Neil, S. (2016) 'Materializing the Etruscans: The Expression and Negotiation of Identity During the Orientalizing, Archaic, and Classical Periods,' in S. Bell and A.A. Carpino (eds.) *A Companion to the Etruscans*. West Sussex: John Wiley & Sons, Inc, pp. 15–27.

Neves, E.G. (2008) 'Ecology, Ceramic Chronology and Distribution, Long-term History, and Political Change in the Amazonian Floodplain,' in H. Silverman and W.H. Isbell (eds.) *Handbook of South American Archaeology*. New York: Springer, pp. 359–379.

Nikolaev, N.N. and Pankova, S.V. (2017) 'After the Scythians,' in S.J. Simpson and S. Pankova (eds.) *Scythians Warriors of Ancient Siberia*. London: Thames and Hudson, pp. 324–328.

Nissen, H.J., Damerow, P. and Englund, R.K. (1993) *Archaic Bookkeeping: Early Writing and Techniques of Economic Administration in the Ancient Near East*. Chicago: The University of Chicago Press.

Ndoro, W. (1997) 'Great Zimbabwe,' *Scientific American*, 277(5), pp. 94–99. doi:10.1038/scientificamerican1197-94.

Norman, L. and Friesen, T.M. (2010) 'Thule Fishing Revisited: The Economic Importance of Fish at the Pembroke and Bell Sites, Victoria Island, Nunavut,' *Geografisk Tidsskrift-Danish Journal of Geography*, 110(2), pp. 261–278. doi:10.1080/00167223.2010.10669511.

Noshiro, S., Kudo, Y. and Sasaski, Y. (2016) 'Emergence of Prehistoric Management of Plant Resources During the Incipient to Initial Jomon Periods in Japan,' *Quaternary International*, 426, pp. 175–186. doi:10.1016/j.quaint.2016.04.004.

Obata, H., Sano, T. and Nishizono, K. (2022) 'The Jomon People Cohabitated with Cockroaches—The Prehistoric Pottery Impressions Reveal the Existence of Sanitary Pests,' *Journal of Archaeological Science: Reports*, 45, p. 103599. doi:10.1016/j.jasrep.2022.103599.

Ortiz Pérez, M.A., Cyphers, A. (1997). La geomorfología y las evidencias arqueológicas en la région de San Lorenzo Tenochtitlán, Veracruz. In: Cyphers, A. (Coord.), Población, Subsistencia y Medio Ambiente en San Lorenzo Tenochtitlán. Instituto de Investigaciones Antropológicas, Universidad Nacional Autónoma de Mexico, México, DF, pp. 31–53.

Ortloff, C.R. (2005) 'The Water Supply and Distribution System of the Nabataean City of Petra (Jordan), 300 BC–AD 300,' *Cambridge Archaeological Journal*, 15(1), pp. 93–109. doi:10.1017/s0959774305000053.

Pachajoa, H. et al. (2021) 'Genetic and Congenital Disorders in Pre Hispanic Moche Pottery,' *American Journal of Medical Genetics Part C: Seminars in Medical Genetics*, 187(2), pp. 269–277. doi:10.1002/ajmg.c.31904.

Park, R.W. (2023) 'The Thule Migration: A Culture in a Hurry?' *Open Archaeology*, 9(1). doi:10.1515/opar-2022-0326.

Parpola, A. (1994) *Deciphering the Indus Script*. Cambridge: Cambridge University Press.

Parr, P.J. (2007) 'The Urban Development of Petra,' in K.D. Politis (ed.) *The World of the Nabataeans: Volume 2 of the International Conference 'The World of the Herods and the Nabataeans' Held at the British Museum, 17–19 April 2001*. Stuttgart: Franz Steiner, pp. 273–300.

Parr, P.J. (2008) 'The Origins and Emergence of the Nabataeans,' in G. Markoe (ed.) *Petra Rediscovered: Lost City of the Nabataeans*. New York: Harry N. Abrams in association with the Cincinnati Art Museum, pp. 27–36.

Pauketat, T.R. (2000) 'Politicization and Community in the Pre-Columbian Mississippi Valley,' in M.-A. Canuto and J. Yaeger (eds.) *Archaeology of Communities a New World Perspective*. Abingdon, Oxon: Taylor & Francis Group, pp. 16–43.

Pauketat, T.R. (2004) *Ancient Cahokia and the Mississippians*. Cambridge: Cambridge University Press.

Pauketat, T.R. (2005) 'The Forgotten History of the Mississippians,' in T.R. Pauketat and D.D. Loren (eds.) *North American Archaeology*. Malden, MA: Blackwell Publishing Ltd, pp. 187–211.

Pauketat, T.R. (2010) 'The Missing Persons in Mississippian Mortuaries,' in L.P. Sullivan and R.C. Mainfort (eds.) *Mississippian Mortuary Practices: Beyond Hierarchy and the Representationist Perspective*. Gainesville: University Press of Florida, pp. 14–29.

Pauketat, T.R. and Emerson, T.E. (1997) 'Introduction: Domination and Ideology in the Mississippian World,' in T.R. Pauketat and T.E. Emerson (eds.) *Cahokia: Domination and Ideology in the Mississippian World*. Lincoln and London: University of Nebraska Press, pp. 1–29.

Pearson, R. (2006) 'Jomon Hot Spot: Increasing Sedentism in South-Western Japan in the Incipient Jomon (14,000–9250 cal. BC) and Earliest Jōmon (9250–5300 cal. BC) Periods,' *World Archaeology*, 38(2), pp. 239–258. doi:10.1080/00438240600693976.

Pearson, R. (2007) 'Debating Jomon Social Complexity,' *Asian Perspectives*, 46(2), pp. 361–388. doi:10.1353/asi.2007.0015.

Pikirayi, I. (2001) *The Zimbabwe Culture: Origins and Decline of Southern Zambezian States*. Walnut Creek: AltaMira Press.

Pokutta, D.A. (2014) 'Food and Cooking in the Únětice Culture,' *AP Ulum*, 51, pp. 135–159.

Pool, C. (2007) *Olmec Archaeology and Early Mesoamerica*. Cambridge: Cambridge University Press.

Possehl, G.L. (2002) *The Indus Civilization: A Contemporary Perspective*. Walnut Creek: AltaMira.

Prentiss, A.M., Walsh, M.J. and Foor, T.A. (2017) 'Evolution of Early Thule Material Culture: Cultural Transmission and Terrestrial Ecology,' *Human Ecology*, 46(5), pp. 633–650. doi:10.1007/s10745-017-9963-9.

Psarras, S.-K. (2003) 'Han and Xiongnu a Reexamination of Cultural and Political Relations (I),' *Monumenta Serica*, 51(1), pp. 55–236. doi:10.1080/02549948.2003.11731391.

Quilter, J. (2010) *The Moche of Ancient Peru: Media and Messages*. Cambridge: Peabody Museum Press.

Quilter, J. (2014) *The Ancient Central Andes*. New York: Routledge.

Quilter, J. and Koons, M.L. (2012) 'The Fall of the Moche: A Critique of Claims for South America's First State,' *Latin American Antiquity*, 23(2), pp. 127–143. doi:10.7183/1045-6635.23.2.127.

Raghavan, M. et al. (2014) 'The Genetic Prehistory of the New World Arctic,' *Science*, 345(6200), pp. 1255832–1255832.

Ralby, A. (2013) 'Battle of Kadesh, c. 1274 BCE: Clash of Empires,' in *Atlas of World Military History: From Antiquity to the Present Day*. Bath, BA: Parragon Books, pp. 54–55.

Ramseyer, Denis, Nicole Pousaz, and Tsagaan Törbat. (2009) "The Xiongnu Settlement of Boroo Gol, Selenge Aimag, Mongolia" in J. Bremmann, H. Parzinger, E. Pohl and D. Tseveendorzh (Eds.), *Current archaeological research in Mongolia: Papers from the First International 370 conference on "Archaeological Research in Mongolia"* held in Ulaanbaatar, August 19th–23rd, 2007. Bonn: Vor- und Frühgeschichtliche Archäologie, Rheinische FriedrichWilhelms-Universität, pp. 231–240.

Rausch, R. et al. (2014) 'The Riddle of the Springs of Dilmun—Does the Gilgamesh Epic Tell the Truth?' *Groundwater*, 52(4), pp. 640–644. doi:10.1111/gwat.12214.

Raulwing, P. (2005) 'The Kikkuli text: Hittite training instructions for chariot horses in the second half of the 2nd millennium B.C. and their interdisciplinary context,' in A. Gardeisen (Ed.), *Les équidés dans le monde méditerranéen antique: Actes du colloque organisé References 1029 par l'École française d'Athènes, le Centre Camille Jullian, et l'UMR 5140 du CNRS, Athènes, 26–28 Novembre 2003*. Lattes: Association pour le développement de l'archéologie en Languedoc-Rousillon, pp. 61–75.

Rice, M., and Crawford, H. (2000) 'Traces of Paradise: The Archaeology of Bahrain, 2500 BC–300 AD': an exhibition at the Brunei Gallery, Thornhaugh Street, London WC, 12 July–15 September 2000, London: UCL.

Rice, T.T. (1958) *The Scythians*. London: Thames & Hudson.

Risch, R. et al. (2022) 'Architecture and Settlement Dynamics in Central Germany from the Late Neolithic to the Early Bronze Age,' *Proceedings of the Prehistoric Society*, 88, pp. 123–154. doi:10.1017/ppr.2022.10.

Riva, C. (2021) *A Short History of the Etruscans*. London: Bloomsbury Academic.

Rix, H. (2012). 'Etruscan Language,' *The Oxford Classical History*. 4th ed. Oxford University Press: Oxford.

Robbins Schug, G. et al. (2012) 'A Peaceful Realm? Trauma and Social Differentiation at Harappa,' *International Journal of Paleopathology*, 2(2–3), pp. 136–147. doi:10.1016/j.ijpp.2012.09.012.

Roberts, B.W., Thornton, C.P. and Pigott, V.C. (2009) 'Development of Metallurgy in Eurasia,' *Antiquity*, 83(322), pp. 1012–1022. doi:10.1017/s0003598x00099312.

Robinson, A. (2015) *The Indus*. London: Reaktion Books.

Rogers, L.L. and Kaestle, F.A. (2022) 'Analysis of Mitochondrial DNA Haplogroup Frequencies in the Population of the Slab Burial Mortuary Culture of Mongolia (ca. 1100–300 BCE),' *American Journal of Biological Anthropology*, 177(4), pp. 644–657. doi:10.1002/ajpa.24478.

Rolle, R. (1989) *The World of the Scythians*. Translated by F.G. Wells. Berkeley: University of California Press.

Roosevelt, A.C. (1991) *Moundbuilders of the Amazon: Geophysical Archaeology on Marajó Island, Brazil*. San Diego: Academic Press.

Roosevelt, A.C. (1993) 'The Rise and Fall of the Amazon Chiefdoms,' *L'Homme*, 33(126), pp. 255–283. doi:10.3406/hom.1993.369640.

Roosevelt, A.C. et al. (1996) 'Paleoindian Cave Dwellers in the Amazon: The Peopling of the Americas,' *Science*, 272(5260), pp. 373–384. doi:10.1126/science.272.5260.373.

Rowan, K. (2009) 'Revising the Sound Value of Meroitic D: A Phonological Approach,' *Beitrage zur Sudanforschung*, 10.

Rupp, N., Ameje, J. and Breunig, P. (2005) 'New Studies on the Nok Culture of Central Nigeria,' *Journal of African Archaeology*, 3(2), pp. 283–290. doi:10.3213/1612-1651-10056.

Rutherford, I. (2020) *Hittite Texts and Greek Religion: Contact, Interaction, and Comparison*. Oxford: Oxford University Press.

Sanyal, S. (2013) *Land of the Seven Rivers: A Brief History of India's Geography*. New Delhi: Penguin Books.

Savelle, J.M. (1984) 'Cultural and Natural Formation Processes of a Historic Inuit Snow Dwelling Site, Somerset Island, Arctic Canada,' *American Antiquity*, 49(3), pp. 508–524. doi:10.2307/280357.

Savelle, J. M. (1987) 'Natural formation processes and snow-based sites: Examples from Arctic Canada,' in D. T. Nash & M. D. Petraglia (Eds.), *Natural formation processes in the archaeological record* (Vol. 352). Oxford: British Archaeological Reports, pp. 30–50.

Schaan, D. (1997) 'Marajoara Iconography a Structural Approach,' *Naya—Notícias de Arqueología y Antropología*.

Schaan, D.P. (2000) 'Recent Investigations on Marajoara Culture, Marajó Island, Brazil,' *Antiquity*, 74(285), pp. 469–470. doi:10.1017/s0003598x0005969x.

Schaan, D. (2010) 'Long-Term Human Induced Impacts on Marajó Island Landscapes, Amazon Estuary,' *Diversity*, 2(2), pp. 182–206. doi:10.3390/d2020182.

Schellinger, S. (2022) *Nubia: Lost Civilizations*. London: Reaktion Books.

Schledermann, P. (1996) *Voices in Stone: A Personal Journey into the Arctic Past*. Komatik Series No. 5. Calgary: Arctic Institute of North America.

Schrakamp, I. (2020) 'The Kingdom of Akkad: A View from Within,' in Karen Radner, Nadine Moeller, and D. T. Potts (eds), *The Oxford History of the Ancient Near East:*

Volume I: From the Beginnings to Old Kingdom Egypt and the Dynasty of Akkad, New York, 2020; online ed., Oxford Academic, 17 Sept. 2020, doi.org/10.1093/oso/9780190687854.003.0010, accessed 25 April 2024.

Schwarz, R. (2014) 'Goldene Schläfen- und Lockenringe—Herrschaftsinsignien in bronzezeitlichen Ranggesellschaften Mitteldeutschlands. Überlegungen zur Gesellschaft der Aunjetitzer Kultur,' in H. Meller, R. Risch, and E. Pernicka (eds.) *Metalle der Macht—Frühes Gold und Silber. 6. Mitteldeutscher Archäologentag vom 17. bis 19. Oktober 2013 in Halle (Saale) (Tagungen des Landesmuseums für Vorgeschichte Halle 11)*. Halle (Saale): Landesamt f. Denkmalpflege u. Archäologie Sachsen-Anhalt, pp. 714–742.

Schwarz, R. (2015) 'Kultureller Bruch oder Kontinuität?—Mitteldeutschland im 23. Jh. v. Chr,' in H. Meller et al. (eds.) *2200 BC—Ein Klimasturz als ursache für den Zerfall der alten Welt 7. Mitteldeutscher Archäologentag vom 23. Bis 26. Oktober 2014 in Halle (Saale)*. Halle (Saale): Landesamt f. Denkmalpflege u. Archäologie Sachsen-Anhalt, pp. 671–713.

Shapland, A. (2013) 'Jumping to Conclusions: Bull-Leaping in Minoan Crete,' *Society & Animals*, 21(2), pp. 194–207. doi:10.1163/15685306-12341302.

Shennan, S. (1978) 'Archaeological "cultures": an empirical investigation,' in I. Hodder (ed.) *The Spatial Organisation of Culture*. London: Duckworth, pp. 113–139.

Shipley, L. (2017) *The Etruscans*. London: Reaktion Books.

Siculus, D. (1963) *The Library of History* C. H. Oldfather. Translated by C.H. Oldfather. Cambridge, MA: Harvard University Press.

Simpson, S.J. and Stepanova, E.V. (2017) 'Eating, Drinking and Everyday Life,' in S.J. Simpson and S. Pankova (eds.) *Scythians Warriors of Ancient Siberia*. London: Thames and Hudson, pp. 154–185.

Smith, C.J. (2014) *The Etruscans: A Very Short Introduction*. Oxford: Oxford University Press.

Smith, H.W. (1952) *Man and His Gods*. New York: Grosset & Dunlap.

Spatzier, A. (2017) *Das Endneolithisch-frühbronzezeitliche Rondell von Pömmelte-Zackmünde, Salzlandkreis, und das Rondell-Phänomen des 4.-1. Jt. v. Chr. in Mitteleuropa*. Forschungsberichte des Landesmuseums für Vorgeschichte Halle 10. Halle (Saale): Landesamt für Denkmalpflege und Archäologie Sachsen-Anhalt.

Spatzier, A. and Bertemes, F. (2018) 'The Ring Sanctuary of Pömmelte, Germany: A Monumental, Multi-Layered Metaphor of the Late Third Millennium BC,' *Antiquity*, 92(363), pp. 655–673. doi:10.15184/aqy.2018.92.

Spriggs, M. (1995) 'The Lapita Culture and Austronesian Prehistory in Oceania,' in P.S. Bellwood, J.J. Fox, and D.T. Tryon (eds.) *The Austronesians: Historical and Comparative Perspectives*. Canberra, Australia: ANU E Press, pp. 112–133.

Spriggs, M. (2019) 'The Hat Makes the Man: Masks, Headdresses, and Skullcaps in Lapita Iconography,' in S. Bedford and M. Spriggs (eds.) *Debating Lapita: Distribution, Chronology, Society and Subsistence*. Acton ACT: Australian National University Press, pp. 257–273.

Steinkeller, Piotr. (2017) 'The Divine Rulers of Akkade and Ur: Toward a Definition of the Deification of Kings in Babylonia,' in *History, Texts and Art in Early Babylonia: Three Essays, Berlin*, Boston: De Gruyter, pp. 107–157.

Stepanova, E.V. (2016) 'Reconstruction of a Scythian Saddle from Barrow No. 3,' *The Silk Road*, 14, pp. 1–18.

Stone, D. (2023) *The Hittites: Lost Civilizations*. London: Reaktion Books.

Stone, R. (2006) 'Graves of the Pacific's First Seafarers Revealed,' *Science*, 312(5772), pp. 360. doi:10.1126/science.312.5772.360a.

Strabo *LacusCurtius • Strabo's Geography—Book XVII Chapter 1 (§§ 25–54)*, University of Chicago: Penelope. Available at: penelope.uchicago.edu/Thayer/E/Roman/Texts/Strabo/17A3*.html (Accessed: 18 May 2024).

Summerhayes, G.R. et al. (2019)a 'Kamgot at the Lagoon's Edge: Site Position and Resource Use of an Early Lapita Site in Near Oceania,' in S. Bedford and M. Spriggs (eds.) *Debating Lapita: Distribution, Chronology, Society and Subsistence*. Acton: Australian National University Press, pp. 89–103.

Summerhayes, G.R., Szabó, Katherine, et al. (2019)b 'Early Lapita Subsistence: The Evidence from Kamgot, Anir Islands, New Ireland Province, Papua New Guinea,' in S. Bedford and M. Spriggs (eds.) *Debating Lapita: Distribution, Chronology, Society and Subsistence*. Acton: Australian National University Press, pp. 379–402.

Svensson, M.J.O. et al. (2021) 'Methods for Determination of the Source of Iron in Precontact Inuit and Dorset Culture Artifacts from the Canadian Arctic,' *Journal of Archaeological Science: Reports*, 36, p. 102814. doi:10.1016/j.jasrep.2021.102814.

Svizzero, S. (2015) 'The Collapse of the Únětice Culture: Economic Explanation Based on the "Dutch Disease,"' *Czech Journal of Social Sciences, Business and Economics*, 4(3), pp. 6–19. doi:10.24984/cjssbe.2015.4.3.1.

Symonds, S. and Lunagomez, R. (1997) 'El sistema de asentamientos y el desarrollo de poblaciones en San Lorenzo Tenochtitlan, "Veracruz,"' in A.C. Guillén (ed.) *Población, Subsistencia y Medio Ambiente en San Lorenzo Tenochtitlán*. Mexico City: Universidad Nacional Autonoma de México, pp. 119–152.

Swenson, E.R. (2018) 'Assembling the Moche: The Power of Temporary Gatherings on the North Coast of Peru,' *World Archaeology*, 50(1), pp. 62–85. doi:10.1080/00438 243.2018.1474132.

Taylor, J. (2001) *Petra and the Lost Kingdom of the Nabataeans*. London: I.B. Tauris.

Tisdell, C. and Svizzero, S. (2018) 'The Economic Rise and Fall of the Silesian Únětice Cultural Population: A Case of Ecologically Unsustainable Development?' *Anthropologie*, 56(1), pp. 21–38. doi:10.26720/anthro.17.05.10.1.

Török, L. (1997) *The Kingdom of Kush: Handbook of the Napatan-Meroitic Civilization*. Leiden: Brill.

Torrence, R. et al. (2017) 'Tattooing Tools and the Lapita Cultural Complex,' *Archaeology in Oceania*, 53(1), pp. 58–73. doi:10.1002/arco.5139.

Tuck, A.S. (2014) 'Manufacturing at Poggio Civitate: Elite Consumption and Social Organization in the Etruscan Seventh Century,' *Etruscan Studies*, 17(2), pp. 121–139. doi:10.1515/etst-2014-0016.

Turchin, P. 2009. "A Theory for Formation of Large Empires." *Journal of Global History*, 4, pp. 191–21.

University College London (2002) *Meroitic script, Digital Egypt for Universities*. Available at: www.ucl.ac.uk/museums-static/digitalegypt//nubia/mwriting.html (Accessed: 18 May 2024).

Valentin, F. et al. (2015) 'Three-thousand-year-old jar-burials at the Teouma cemetery (Vanuatu): A Southeast Asian-Lapita connection?' in C. Sand, S. Chiu, and N. Hogg (eds.) *The Lapita Cultural Complex in Time and Space: Expansion Routes, Chronologies and Typologies*. Nouméa, Nouvelle-Calédonie: Institut d'archéologie de la Nouvelle-Calédonie et du Pacifique (Archeologia Pasifika 4), pp. 81–101.

Van De Mieroop, M. (2015) *A History of the Ancient Near East, ca. 3000–323 BC*. Hoboken, NJ: John Wiley & Sons.

Velson, J.S., and Clark, T.C. (1975). Transport of stone monuments to the La Venta and San Lorenzo sites. Contributions of the University of California Archaeological Research Facility 24: 1–39.

Verano, J. (2005) 'War and Death in the Moche World: Osteological Evidence and Visual Discourse,' in J. Pillsbury (ed.) *Moche Art and Archaeology in Ancient Peru*. Washington: National Gallery of Art, pp. 111–125.

Wadeson, L. (2012) 'The Funerary Landscape of Petra: Results from a New Study,' *Proceedings of the Seminar for Arabian Studies*, 42 (Supplement: The Nabataeans in Focus: Current Archaeological Research at Petra. Papers from the Special Session of the Seminar for Arabian Studies held on 29 July 2011), pp. 99–125.

Wallech, S. (2016) *China and the West to 1600: Empire, Philosophy and the Paradox of Culture*. Malden: Wiley Blackwell.

Watson, B. (1961) *Records of the Grand Historian of China Translated from the Shih Chi of Ssu-Ma Ch'ien*. New York: Columbia University Press.

Weismantel, M. (2004) 'Moche Sex Pots: Reproduction and Temporality in Ancient South America,' *American Anthropologist*, 106(3), pp. 495–505. doi:10.1525/aa.2004.106.3.495.

Weismantel, M.J. (2021) *Playing with Things: Engaging the Moche Sex Pots*. Austin: University of Texas Press.

Wenning, R. (2007) 'The Nabataeans in History,' in K.D. Politis (ed.) *The World of the Nabataeans: Volume 2 of the International Conference 'The World of the Herods and the Nabataeans' Held at the British Museum, 17–19 April 2001*. Stuttgart: Franz Steiner Verlag, pp. 25–44.

West, S. (2002) 'Scythians,' in E.J. Baker, I.J.F. deJong, and H. van Wees (eds.) *Brill's Companion to Herodotus*. Leiden: Brill, pp. 437–456.

Whitridge, P. (1999) *The Construction of Social Difference in a Prehistoric Inuit Whaling Community*. PhD Thesis. Department of Anthropology, Arizona State University. Available at: www.proquest.com/openview/630ba76d2798ce84ac0eeb68413ac4ff/1?pq-origsite=gscholar&cbl=18750&diss=y (Accessed 15 January 2024).

Whitridge, P. (2002) 'Social and Ritual Determinants of Whale Bone Transport at a Classic Thule Winter Site in the Canadian Arctic,' *International Journal of Osteoarchaeology*, 12(1), pp. 65–75. doi:10.1002/oa.613.

William, D.W.R. (2012). 'Etruscans,' *The Oxford Classical History*. 4th ed. Oxford: Oxford University Press.

Wright, R.P. (2010) *The Ancient Indus: Urbanism, Economy, and Society*. Cambridge: Cambridge University Press.

Yang, J., Shao, H. and Pan, L. (2020) *Metal Road of the Eastern Eurasian Steppe: The Formation of the Xiongnu Confederation and the Silk Road*. Singapore: Springer.

Young-Sánchez, M. and Schaan, D.P. (2011) *Marajó: Ancient Ceramics from the Mouth of the Amazon*. Denver: Mayer Center for Pre-Columbian & Spanish Colonial Art at the Denver Art Museum.

Zgoll (2021) 'Innana and En- edu-ana: Mutual Empowerment and the myth INNANA CONQUERS UR,' in K. Droß-Krüpe, K./Fink, S. (eds.) *Perception and (Self-) Presentation of Powerful Women in the Ancient World, Proceedings of the 8th Melammu Workshop, Kassel 31 January—1 February 2019*, Münster: Zaphon.

Zich, B. (1996) *Studien zur regionalen und chronologischen Gliederung der nördlichen Aunjetitzer Kultur*. Vorgeschichtliche Forschungen 20. Berlin, New York: De Gruyter.

End Notes

Introduction
1. Bawden (1999), 81.
2. Shipley (2017), 13.
3. Braudel (1994), 3.
4. Ibid, 6–7.
5. Shennan (1978).
6. McNairn (1980), 48. The original idea for an archaeological culture and the culture-history movement in archaeology can be attributed to Gordon V. Childe in his 1929 publication, *The Danube Prehistory*.
7. Pool (2007), 280.

Chapter 1: Akkadians
1. Bryce and Birkett-Rees (2016), 73.
2. Foster (2013), 266.
3. Van De Mieroop (2015), 68.
4. Liverani (2014), 137.
5. Van De Mieroop, 68.
6. Schrakamp (2020), 626.
7. Liverani, 139.
8. Van De Mieroop, 69.
9. Liverani, 137.
10. Piotr (2017).
11. Liverani 137; Schrakamp, 623.
12. Liverani, 138.
13. Bryce and Birkett-Rees, 73.
14. Kerr (1998).
15. Gibbons (1993).
16. Ibid.
17. Bryce and Birkett-Rees, 73.

Chapter 2: Dilmun
1. Rausch et al. (2014), 640.
2. Al-Thani (2005), 16–18.
3. Luckenbill (1927), 26.
4. Ibid, 21.
5. Crawford (1998), 1–2.
6. Nayeem (1990), 160.
7. Crawford (1998), 3;
 Boutin et al. (2012), 70.
8. Rausch et al., 641.
9. Conklin (1998), 10.
10. Højlund (2010), 446.
11. Laursen (2008), 136.
12. Højlund (2010); Eidem and Højlund (1993).
13. Feinman and Carballo (2022).
14. Crawford (1998), 94.
15. Laursen (2008).
16. Crawford (1998), 84.
17. Crawford (1998), 102.
18. Andersen (2003); al Halwachi (2020); During Caspers (1971).
19. Al Hawachi (2020), 2.
20. Laursen (2021), 9.
21. Crawford (1996).

Chapter 3: Etruscans
1. Ridgway (2012).
2. Bartoloni (2014).
3. Shipley (2017), 45.
4. Riva (2021), 94.
5. Smith, C.J. (2014), 113.
6. Tuck (2014), 121–39; Kansa and MacKinnon (2014).
7. Smith, C.J. (2014), 60.
8. Rix (2012).
9. Smith, C.J. (2014), 203.
10. Seutonius (*Lives of Caesar* 81–9); Cicero (*On Divination*, 1.1119).
11. Heurgon and Linderski (2012).
12. Smith, C.J. (2014), 197.
13. Boethius et al. (1978).
14. Riva, 80.
15. Ceccarelli, (2016), 30.

Chapter 4: Great Zimbabwe
1. Pikirayi (2001), 79–80; Huffman (1986).
2. Piriyaki (2001).
3. Pikirayi, 123–124.
4. Ndoro (1997), 96.
5. Pikirayi (2001), 125.
6. Garlake (1973), 13; Pikirayi (2001), 128.
7. Chirikine (2020), 349.
8. Ibid, 461.
9. Garlake, 124, 132–133.
10. Chirikine et al. (2016).
11. Ndoro (2001), 96.
12. Huffman (1987), 11.
13. Chirikire and Pikiray (2008).
14. Chirikire (2020), 357.
15. Bent (1893), 125.
16. Huffman (1987).
17. Chirikire (2020).
18. Garlake (1973); Pikirayi (2001).

Chapter 5: Hittites
1. Stone, D. (2023), 29; Bryce (2019), 24.
2. Bryce (2019), 9–10.
3. Bryce (1998), 49–51.
4. Raulwing (2005).
5. Rutherford (2020), 21.
6. Collins (2007), 111–112.
7. MacQueen (1986), 80.
8. Hoffner (2003), 103–105.
9. Collins, 124.
10. Stone, D. (2023), 115.
11. Ralby (2013), 54–55.
12. Bryce (2019), 259.
13. Dursu-Tranriöver (2023), 625.
14. Middleton (2017), 164.
15. Ibid.
16. Dursu-Tranriöver, 626; Middleton, 157–157.
17. Forrer (1924).
18. Beckman, Bryce and Cline (2012), 119–120.
19. Bryce (1998), 397.

Chapter 6: Indus Valley
1. Sanyal (2013).
2. Wright (2010), 4.
3. Robinson (2015), 79.

343

4 Ibid., 84.
5 Possehl (2002), 103.
6 McIntosh (2008), 232.
7 Robinson, 89.
8 Kenoyer (1998), 57.
9 Ibid., 98–99.
10 McIntosh (2001), 94–95.
11 Wright, 122–127.
12 Jansen (1989), 189.
13 Kenoyer, 60.
14 Ibid., 59.
15 Hemphill et al. (1991).
16 Robinson, 165.
17 Robinson, 187, 191.
18 McIntosh (2008), 86.
19 Farmer, Sproat, and Witzel (2004).
20 Kenoyer, 77.
21 Robinson, 198.
22 Green (2020).
23 McIntosh (2008), 392; Kenoyer, 81.
24 McIntosh (2008), 262.
25 Schug et al. (2012), Lee et al. (2019).
26 McIntosh (2008), 253.

Chapter 7: Jōmon
1 Kobayashi and Nakamura (2004), 1.
2 Pearson (2007), 316.
3 Pearson (2006), 239.
4 Habu (2004), 63.
5 Kobayashi and Nakamura, 75–77.
6 Habu, 66–67.
7 Ibid., 68–69.
8 Noshiro et al. (2016), 9.
9 Pearson (2007), 363.
10 Kobayashi and Nakamura, 89.
11 Pearson (2007), 365.
12 Kobayashi and Nakamura, 19–20.
13 Ibid., 23.
14 Obata et al. (2022).
15 Kenrick (1995), xiv.
16 Kobayashi and Nakamura, 110.
17 Ibid., 104–105.
18 Miziguchi (2020), 8.
19 Pearson (2007), 364.
20 Binford (2001), 463.

Chapter 8: Lapita
1 Kirch (1988), 103.
2 Best (2004), 74–75.
3 Kirch (1997), 64.
4 Kirch (1996), 68.
5 Lilley (2019), 106.
6 Kirch (1996), 63.
7 Kirch (1997), 64.
8 Ibid., 65.
9 Kirch (1996), 67.
10 Kirch (1988), 114.
11 Summerhayes et al. (2019a), 91, 98.
12 See Torrence et al. (2017), 1. Obsidian flakes from seven sites in Papua New Guinea, Solomon Islands, and Vanuatu confirms tattooing among the Lapita. Nineteen additional skin-piercing tools were also found. The existence of shared innovations together with variation in the selection of pigments and the shape of the obsidian artefacts used for puncturing skin highlight a complex pattern of similarities and differences within Lapita communities.
13 Summerhayes et al. (2019b), 398.
14 Spriggs (1995), 118.
15 Kirch (1996), 59.
16 Ambrose (2019), 241.
17 Kirch (1997), 145–146. It is possible that the designs on the pots were not faces—but heads! (Spriggs (2019), 265.). Some graves contained cone shell rings placed in lieu of skulls, indicating that they were reopened after burial and heads were ceremonially removed and reburied (Stone 2006, 360a.).
18 Best, 98.
19 Kirch (1996), 63.

Chapter 9: Marajoara
1 Neves (2008); Erickson (2008).
2 Schaan (2000), 470.
3 Roosevelt (1991), 31; Schaan (2008).
4 Roosevelt (1991), 33.
5 Schaan (2011), 68.
6 Young-Sanchez and Schaan (2011), 16.
7 Roosevelt (1993), 273.
8 Young-Sanchez and Schaan, 17.
9 Ibid., 27.
10 Young-Sanchez and Schaan (2011).
11 Ibid., 79.
12 Ibid., 69.
13 Roosevelt (1991), 81–82.
14 Schaan (2023), 2.
15 Young-Sánchez and Schaan, 53.
16 Ibid., 19.
17 Roosevelt (1991), 62; Young-Sánchez and Schaan, 48.
18 Young-Sánchez and Schaan, 56–57.
19 Schaan (2010), 193.

Chapter 10: Minoans
1 Lazaridis et al. (2017).
2 Moorey (2019).
3 Ibid.
4 Adams, E. (2017), 40–41.
5 Ibid., 42.
6 Driessen (2021), 1.
7 Adams, E. (2017), 46.
8 Fitton (2002), 144.
9 Adams, E. (2017), 158.
10 Moorey (2019).
11 Adams, E. (2017), 162.
12 Moorey (2019).
13 Castleden (1991), 135; Adams, 67.
14 Adams, E. (2017), 67.
15 Ibid., 143.
16 Moorey (2019).
17 Adams, E. (2017), 158.
18 Marinatos (1989), 32.
19 Adams, E. (2017), 214.
20 Moorey (2019).
21 Higgins (1981), 74.

Chapter 11: Mississippian
1. Wilson and Sullivan (2017), 4.
2. See Milner (1998), 175, and Emerson and Lewis (1990).
3. Pauketat (2004).
4. Ibid., 11.
5. Pauketat (2004).
6. Pauketat and Emerson (1997), 8; Pauketat (2004), 145.
7. Pauketat and Emerson, 18, 27.
8. Milner (2021), 110.
9. Pauketat (2004), 84.
10. Emerson (1989).
11. Milner (2021), 117.
12. Brown (1996), 43.
13. Pauketat (2010), 24.
14. Alt (2008); Ambrose and Krigbaum (2003).
15. Pauketat and Emerson (1997); Mehrer (2000), 47.
16. Emerson (1997).
17. Pauketat (2005), 192, 106.
18. Emerson (2007), 135–137.
19. Milner (2007), 196.
20. Dye (2004).
21. Cobb and Butler (2002).

Chapter 12: Moche
1. Koons and Alex (2014); Castillo and Uceda (2008).
2. Billman (2010), 186.
3. Castillo Butters (2010); Swenson (2018).
4. Swenson (2018).
5. Quilter and Koons (2012), 137.
6. Chapdelaine (2005), 69–70.
7. Bourget (2005), 106.
8. Ibid., 89.
9. Quilter (2010), 73.
10. Bourget, 94.
11. Quilter (2014), 180.
12. Bourget, 93.
13. Verano (2005), 113.
14. Pachajoa et al. (2021).
15. Donnan (2004).
16. Ibid.
17. Donnan, 135–136.
18. Weismantel (2004).
19. Koons and Alex, 1051.
20. Koons (2015), 488.

Chapter 13: Nabataeans
1. Taylor (2001), 15.
2. *Diodorus Siculus, Library of History, 19.94.2–95.2.*
3. Hammond (1973), 57; Healy (2001), 33.
4. Graf and Sideotham (2008), 68; Taylor, 38.
5. Wenning (2001), 29.
6. Parr (2008), 27.
7. Healy, 28.
8. Taylor, 65.
9. Kolb (2001), 164.
10. Wadeson (2012), 105.
11. Ibid., 107.
12. Taylor, 113
13. Kolb, 149.
14. Taylor, 70.
15. Guzzo and Schneider (2002).
16. Ortloff (2005).
17. Gentelle (2009), 6.
18. Taylor, 211, 214.
19. Bowersock (2008), 25.

Chapter 14: Nok
1. Atwood (2011).
2. Breunig (2017), 13.
3. Männel and Breinig (2016), 324.
4. Fagg (1994), 83.
5. Atwood (2011).
6. Rupp et al. (2005), 284.
7. The Metropolitan Museum of Art, 'Nok Terracottas (500 B.B.–200 A.D.),' (2000).
8. Rupp et al., 284.
9. Franke (2016).
10. Atwood (2011).
11. Breunig (2017), 24.
12. Breunig and Rupp (2016), 238.
13. Atwood (2011).
14. Fagg (1994), 81.
15. Breunig, 42–43.
16. Breunig and Rupp, 249.
17. Breunig, 47.
18. Ibid., 52–53.

Chapter 15: Nubians
1. Strudwick (2005), 331.
2. Goedicke (1981), 16–17.
3. Beyer Williams and Emberling (2021), 1.
4. Beyer Williams (2021), 178.
5. Schellinger (2022), 47.
6. Ibid., 51.
7. Beyer Williams, 188–190.
8. Mitchell (2009).
9. Adams, W.E. (1977), 278.
10. Török (1997), 97.
11. Adams, W.E. (1977), 292.
12. Török (1997), 144–146
13. H.W. Smith (1952), 45.
14. Bodine (2009), 17.
15. Schellinger (2022), 86–87.
16. Ibid, 80.
17. Török, László (1998), 132–133, 153–184.
18. University College London (2002).
19. Rowan (2009).
20. *Török,* 213–214.
21. Strabo, *Geography—*"LacusCurtius," Book XVII Chapter 1 (§§ 25–54).

Chapter 16: Olmec
1. Pool (2007), 5.
2. Diehl (2004), 25.
3. Pool, 18.
4. Evans (2013), 142–143.
5. Coe et al. (2019), 70.
6. Ibid., 72.
7. Friedel et al. (1993).
8. Coe et al. (2019), 73–74.
9. Ibid., 79.
10. Deihl, 87.
11. Coe et al., 72–74. In classic and post-classic Mesoamerica, this stimulating drink was a prerogative of the elite, and was consumed during banquets attended by the king, his court, and other high-ranking officials. This may have also been the case among elite of San Lorenzo.
12. Pool, 134.
13. Deihl, 41.

14 Ibid., 112.
15 Ibid.
16 Velson and Clark (1975); Coe et al., 67.
17 Clark (1994), 191–192.
18 Coe et al., 59–60.
19 Pohl et al. (2002).
20 Jiménez Salas (1990); Pérez and Cyphers (1997).
21 Diehl and Coe (1995), 23.
22 Coe et al., 60.

Chapter 17: Scythians
1 Beckwith (2009), 38.
2 Alexeyev (2017), 20.
3 Gross (2021), R360.
4 Rolle (1980), 123.
5 Cunliffe (2019), 214.
6 Rolle, 93.
7 Johnson (2020), 207.
8 Cunliffe, 114.
9 Rjabkova and Simpson (2017), 199.
10 Stepanova (2016), 14.
11 Rjabkova and Simpson (2017), 200.
12 Rolle, 82.
13 Beckwith (2009), 76–77.
14 Talbot Rice (1958), 174.
15 Karolkova (2020), 218.
16 Cunliffe, 293.
17 Ibid., 210.
18 Rolle, 94.
19 Simpson and Stepanova (2017), 164.
20 Portland and Hegman (2018).

Chapter 18: Thule Inuit
1 Mathaussen (1927).
2 Jolicoeur (2006).
3 Mason and Friesen (2017), 271; Gulløv (1997); Park 2023.
4 Friesen (2016); Gulløv and McGhee (2006).
5 Burch (2006).
6 Friesen and Arnold (2008).
7 Park (2023).
8 Mason (2009).
9 Friesen, 684.
10 Mason (2020), 344.
11 McCullough (1989), 7; Whitridge (2002).
12 Gulløv and McGhee.
13 McCullough (1989); Shledermann (1996).
14 McGhee (2009a); Mason and Friesen (2017), 274.
15 Mason (2020), 330; Svensson et al. (2021).
16 Morrison (1982), 271.
17 Whitridge (1999).
18 McGhee (2009b), 85–86 states that Thule Inuit winter houses were occupied between five and ten winters. According to Houmard & Grønnow (2017), 455, this occupation may have been even longer.
19 Prentiss et al. (2017).
20 Dawson et al. (2007).
21 Savelle (1984, 1987).
22 McCullough (1989), 245.
23 Park (2023).
24 Maxwell (1985), 262.
25 McCullough (1989), 107.
26 Coltrain et al. (2016).
27 Norman and Friesen (2010).
28 McCullough (1989), 124.
29 McCartney (1991).
30 Morrison (1982), 167.
31 McCullough (1989), 21.
32 Mason and Friesen, 285.
33 Finkelstein et al. (2009).
34 Savelle (1987); Dawson (2016).
35 McGhee (2005), 126.

Chapter 19: Únětice
1 Schwarz (2015).
2 Meller (2019), 42.
3 Brandt (2017), 189f.
4 Zich (1996), 43.
5 Meller (2019), 45.
6 Milisauskas and Kruk (1989).
7 Meller (2019), 46.
8 Meller (2014), 628–649; Lockoff and Pernicka (2014), 230–232.
9 Risch et al., (2021).
10 Meller (2013), 520–523.
11 Schwarz (2014), 719–25.
12 Meller (2017).
13 Meller (2017), 1542.
14 Roberts et al. (2009).
15 Knoll and Meller (2016), 85.
16 Svizzero (2015).
17 Ernée (2012).
18 Pokutta (2014).
19 Risch et al. (2022), 134.
20 Meller (2021), 153.
21 Meller (2021).
22 Meller (2013).
23 Spatzier and Bertemes (2018), 655.
24 Spatzier (2017), 242–243; Spatzier and Bertemes (2018), 669.
25 Spatzier (2017), 663.
26 Kneisel (2012), 215.
27 Svizzero (2015), 14.

Chapter 20: Xiongnu
1 Brosseder and Miller (2011), 31.
2 Psarras (2003), 69.
3 Yang et al. (2020), 438; Rogers & Kaestle (2022).
4 Wallech (2016), 106.
5 Brosseder (2016).
6 DiCosmo (2011).
7 Brosseder (2016).
8 Turchin (2009).
9 Chang (2012), 126.
10 Anthony (1990), 898.
11 Watson (1961), 155–156; Ishjamts (1994), 164.
12 Ishjamts (1994), 156.
13 Ramseyer et al. (2017), 234.
14 Ramseyer (2016), 62.
15 Ramseyer et al. (2017), 239.
16 Lee et al. (2023), 1.
17 Yang et al. (2020), 482–483.
18 Ibid., 483.
19 Lee et al. (2023).
20 Wallech (2016), 213.

Photo Credits

"Mask of Sargon," after restoration, in 1936 (*Public Domain*). Page 23.

Victory stele of Naram-Sin (*Shonagon, own work, CC0, Wikimedia*). Page 25.

Disc of Enheduanna (*Mefman00, CC BY 4.0 Wikimedia*). Page 29.

Site of Qal'at al-Bahrain (*Preju, Adobe Stock*). Page 39.

Excavated royal burial mound at Aali (*Dr. Ajay Kumar Singh, Adobe Stock*). Page 41.

Copper bull's head (*Ciacho5, own work, CC BY-SA 3.0, Wikimedia*). Page 43.

Etruscan tomb painting in the Tomb of the Lioness, Tarquinia (*Paolo Gallo, Adobe Stock*). Page 50.

Terracotta vase in the shape of a cockerel (*Metropolitan Museum of Art, New York. Fletcher Fund, 1924. 24.97.21a, b*). Page 52.

Haruspex (*Lokilech, CC BY-SA 3.0, Wikimedia*). Page 54.

Aerial view of the Great Enclosure of Great Zimbabwe (*evenfh, Adobe Stock*). Page 62.

The Great Zimbabwe Hill Complex (*Andrew Moore, CC BY-SA 2.0, Wikimedia*). Page 67.

Conical tower in the Great Enclosure, Great Zimbabwe (*Jan Van Der Voort, Adobe Stock*). Page 68.

Soapstone birds on pedestals, Great Zimbabwe (*Photo by James Theodore Bent, Public Domain*). Page 70.

Relief carving of a Hittite chariot (*muratart, Adobe Stock*). Page 76.

Seated goddess with a child (*Metropolitan Museum of Art, New York. Gift of Norbert Schimmel Trust, 1989. 1989.281.12*). Page 79.

Depiction of Ramesses II in a chariot at the battle of Kadesh in the Great Temple of Abu Simbel (*Vermeulen-Perdaen, Adobe Stock*). Page 81.

Egyptian-Hittite peace treaty after the Battle of Kadesh in Akkadian, Museum of the Ancient Orient, Istanbul Türkiye (*Iocanus, own work, CC BY 3.0, Wikimedia*). Page 83.

Lion's Gate at Hattusa (*Konstantin, Adobe Stock*). Page 84.

Line drawing of the Luwian Seal (*Public Domain, Wikimedia*). Page 87.

Mohenjo-Daro (*robnaw, Adobe Stock*). Page 92.

Indus uniform weights and balance (*Gary Todd, CC0, Wikimedia*). Page 94.

Remains of a washroom and its drainage system at the site of Lothal (*Abhilashdvbk, own work, CC BY-SA 3.0, Wikimedia*). Page 97.

Great Bath at Mohenjo-Daro (*Syed Jawwad Ali, Adobe Stock*). Page 98.

Indus unicorn seal (*Matsyameena, own work, CC BY-SA 4.0, Wikimedia*). Page 101.

"Priest-King" from different angles (*Archaeological Survey of India. Photo by Marshall, John; Mohenjo-daro and the Indus Civilisation, volume III, plate XCVII, Public Domain*). Page 104.

"Flame-rimmed" cooking vessel (Kaen doki), (*Metropolitan Museum of Art, New York. Mary Griggs Burke Collection, Gift of the Mary and Jackson Burke Foundation, 2015. 2015.300.258*). Page 116.

Dogū (clay figurine), (*Metropolitan Museum of Art, New York. The Harry G. C. Packard Collection of Asian Art, Gift of Harry G. C. Packard, and Purchase, Fletcher, Rogers, Harris Brisbane Dick, and Louis V. Bell Funds, Joseph Pulitzer Bequest, and The Annenberg Fund Inc. Gift, 1975. 1975.268.191*). Page 118.

Sannai-Maruyama site in Aomori, Aomori Prefecture, Japan (*beibaoke, Adobe Stock*). Page 120.

Shell jewellery from the Lapita site of Bourewa, Fiji (*Patrick Nunn CC BY-SA 4.0, Wikimedia*). Page 128.

Decorated piece of Lapita pottery from the Bourewa site in Fiji (*Patrick Nunn, CC BY-SA 4.0, Wikimedia*). Page 133.

Burial urn, AD 1000-1250, Marajoara culture, American Museum of Natural History (*Daderot, CC0, Wikimedia*). Page 143.

Phallic figurine of a female (*Dornicke, CC BY-SA 4.0, Wikimedia*). Page 147.

Decorated Tanga (*Dornicke, CC BY-SA 4.0, Wikimedia*). Page 148.

The North Entrance of the Palace with charging bull fresco in Knossos at Crete, Greece (*annaartday, Adobe Stock*). Page 155.

One of the halls with a throne in the Palace of Knossos, Crete (*Anna Pakutina, Adobe Stock*). Page 157.

Horns of Consecration in the Palace of Knossos on Crete (*Linda J Photography*, Adobe Stock). Page 161.

"Snake Goddess" from the Knossos Temple Repositories (*Pecold*, Adobe Stock). Page 162.

Fresco of the Prince of the Lilies (also known as the Priest King fresco) (*xiaoma*, Adobe Stock). Page 164.

Bull-leaping fresco found at Knossos (*xiaoma*, Adobe Stock). Page 166.

Aerial view of Cahokia mounds (*Kent*, Adobe Stock). Page 172.

View of the reconstructed Woodhenge III and its alignment with the equinox pole at Monks Mound, Cakohia (*QuartierLatin1968*, own work, CC BY-SA 3.0, Wikimedia). Page 174.

Statuette of a Chunkey player (*TimVickers*, own work, Public Domain, Wikimedia). Page 178.

Huaca del Sol, Moche (*ecuadorquerido*, Adobe Stock). Page 186.

Royal burial of the Lord of Sipán (*Mark*, Adobe Stock). Page 189.

Stirrup portrait vessel of the Cut Lip persona (*1rhb*, own work, CC BY-SA 4.0, Wikimedia). Page 192.

Moche sex-pot depicting anal sex (*CC BY-SA 3.0*, Wikimedia). Page 194.

The treasury of Petra (Kazneh) (*Photo courtesy of Judyta Olszewski*). Page 204.

Facade of the palace tomb, Petra (*Bernard Gagnon*, own work, CC BY-SA 3.0, Wikimedia). Page 206.

Nabatean cistern north of Makhtesh Ramon, southern Israel. (*Wilson44691*, own work, CC BY-SA 3.0, Wikimedia). Page 209.

Nok male figure (*FA2010*, own work, Public Domain, Wikimedia). Page 216.

Nok terracotta figurine (*Siyajkak*, CC BY-SA 3.0, Wikimedia). Page 218.

Nok sculpture (*Marie-Lan Nguyen*, own work, Public Domain, Wikimedia). Page 223.

Pyramids of Meroë (*evenfh*, Adobe Stock). Page 230.

Victory stele of Piye (*Auguste Mariette*, Public Domain, Wikimedia). Page 233.

Portrait of Tantamani in his tomb in El-Kurru (*Retlaw Snellac*, Public Domain, Wikimedia). Page 234.

Bronze head of Augustus from Meroë (*Takashi Images*, Adobe Stock). Page 237.

Great Pyramid at La Venta (*Alfonsobouchot*, own work, Public Domain, Wikimedia). Page 243.

Jaguar mosaic at La Venta (*Alexander Sánchez*, Adobe Stock). Page 244.

Lord of Limas sculpture (*De Mag2017*, own work, CC BY-SA 4.0, Wikimedia). Page 247.

Olmec colossal head (*Barba Tanko*, Adobe Stock). Page 249.

Altar 5 from La Venta (*Ruben Charles*, CC BY 2.0, Wikimedia). Page 250.

Streltsovskaya Steppe, part of the Pontic-Caspian Steppe (*GalinaGouz*, own work, CC BY-SA 4.0, Wikimedia). Page 258.

Gold Scythian comb, Soloha Kurgan, Hermitage Museum St. Petersburg (*Public Domain*, Wikimedia). Page 262.

Drawing of Scythian warriors from the electrum cup found in the Kul'Oba kurgan burial (*Public Domain*, Wikimedia). Page 264.

Scythian gold pectoral (*Yurii Zushchyk*, Adobe Stock). Page 266.

Thule Inuit house with whale bone roof reconstruction (*Ansgar Walk*, CC BY-SA 2.5, Wikimedia). Page 277.

Thule Inuit Qarmaq (*Ansgar Walk*, CC BY-SA 2.5, Wikimedia). Page 279.

Snow goggles (*Metropolitan Museum of Art, New York. The Charles and Valerie Diker Collection of Native American Art, Gift of Charles and Valerie Diker, 2019. 2019.456.13*). Page 283.

Leubingen barrow excavation drawings (*Friedrich Klopfleisch*, CC BY 3.0, Wikimedia). Page 290.

Nebra Sky Disc (*Frank Vincentz*, CC BY-SA 4.0, Wikimedia). Page 296.

Pömmelte circular enclosure (*Bautsch*, CC0, Wikimedia). Page 299.

The Great Wall of China (*yuri_yavnik*, Adobe Stock). Page 306.

Warring States Xiongnu gold crown (*Gary Todd*, CC0, Wikimedia). Page 309.

Gold belt buckle depicting boar hunting (*Marie-Lan Nguyen*, Public Domain, Wikimedia Commons). Page 313.

About the Author

Raven Todd DaSilva is an award-winning scholar, archaeologist, and art conservator. She has worked on archaeological projects in Greece, Italy, North Macedonia, Oman, and Türkiye, and specialises in the Neolithic period of Southwest Asia. Holding multiple degrees in Classical and Near and Middle Eastern civilisations, heritage, and art conservation and restoration, she has dedicated her life to the study and dissemination of the ancient world.

In 2017, Raven built an online platform entitled *Dig It with Raven*, dedicated to making the ancient past accessible to everyone. As a result of growing this community, she has had the privilege of being featured on and working with notable institutions such as English Heritage and National Geographic. Raven has also been an expert presenter at universities, and has appeared on television, multiple podcasts, and science communication platforms. She currently resides in London.

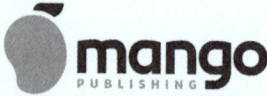

Mango Publishing, established in 2014, publishes an eclectic list of books by diverse authors—both new and established voices—on topics ranging from business, personal growth, women's empowerment, LGBTQ studies, health, and spirituality to history, popular culture, time management, decluttering, lifestyle, mental wellness, aging, and sustainable living. We were named 2019 *and* 2020's #1 fastest growing independent publisher by *Publishers Weekly*. Our success is driven by our main goal, which is to publish high-quality books that will entertain readers as well as make a positive difference in their lives.

Our readers are our most important resource; we value your input, suggestions, and ideas. We'd love to hear from you—after all, we are publishing books for you!

Please stay in touch with us and follow us at:

Facebook: Mango Publishing

Twitter: @MangoPublishing

Instagram: @MangoPublishing

LinkedIn: Mango Publishing

Pinterest: Mango Publishing

Newsletter: mangopublishinggroup.com/newsletter

Join us on Mango's journey to reinvent publishing, one book at a time